The Gender Politics of ICT

Edited by

Jacqueline Archibald

Judy Emms

Frances Grundy

Janet Payne

Eva Turner

The Gender Politics of ICT

First published in 2005 by Middlesex University Press

ISBN 1 904750 46 X

A CIP catalogue record for this book is available from The British Library

Cover design by Soheyla Tavakol

Book design by Helen Taylor

Printed in the UK by Ashford Colour Press Ltd.

Middlesex University Press, Queensway, Enfield, Middlesex EN4 3SF

Tel: +44 (0)20 8411 5734: +44 (0)20 8880 4262 Fax: +44 (0)20 8411 5736
www.mupress.co.uk

Contents

Communications: Exploiting Technology

Education: Context and Content

Employment

Introduction

This book presents a selection of papers from the 6th International Conference of Women into Computing (WiC). The conference took place between 14th and 16th July 2005 at the University of Greenwich, London, UK, under the title *The Gender Politics of ICT* (Information and Communication Technology).

WiC was formed in November 1987 as a pressure group to investigate and publicise the inequalities of women's positions in the computing and ICT industries. WiC has organised conferences since its inception to investigate the status and participation of women in computing and in order to share personal experiences. Efforts to persuade industry, commerce and even higher education to change culture and practice and to encourage and support women have made no significant input. Those of us who started in computing in the 60s and 70s, when the gender ratio was fairly evenly balanced, find it hard to appreciate why the introduction of the PC and the dependence now on ICT has not resulted in women taking their rightful place with this technology. Many of us have worked long and hard to change perceptions, but it feels as if the masculine world is still all-powerful and determined to prevent our full participation. The papers in this book reflect concerns and attitudes that have been with us since the network first convened. This conference has brought together participants from countries in every continent.

Many papers were submitted by academics and researchers working in computing education. The refereeing process consisted of three stages. Each paper was refereed anonymously by two members of the programme committee and their comments were fed back to the authors. Then each new version was refereed again, still anonymously, before final acceptance. A third level of refereeing process was used to select papers for inclusion in this book. The full proceedings of the conference are on the CD that accompanies this book. These proceedings can also be downloaded from www.ablibris.com.

Topics covered in the papers submitted include women's computing education, women's employment in the ICT industries and the way women create and use computing technologies. There were papers on power relations and equality at work and in education, in both the real and the virtual worlds. There were also submissions on on-line communication between men and women and the way women create and use a virtual space, sometimes to their advantage and sometimes not.

It is very apparent from the papers we received that people that care deeply about the way technological development is brought into women's lives without, in most cases, women being allowed or being able to participate in this global development process. Many of them reflect a condemnation of the continuously falling numbers and worsening situation for women in ICT, in the lack of political will to remedy the position of women and in the failure of the computer industry as a whole to perceive the importance of these issues for the role of women in this technological development. Participation in this is an important source of power.

This collection of papers begins with invited contributions from (in order of presentation at the conference) Juliet Webster, Wendy Faulkner, Lesley Ottery and Cecile Crutzen. The papers were grouped into four major themes for the conference and these are reflected in sections two to five of the book. These themes are Gender Politics, Exploiting Technology, Education: Context and Content, and Employment. Several papers covered more than one theme but they have been allocated in the one we felt was most pertinent bearing in mind the other contributions. There was also a panel session to compare and contrast experiences in different cultures and countries.

The papers chosen for inclusion are highly relevant to today's technological debates. The papers address topics such as feminist approaches to using, teaching and creating ICT; women's experiences in on-line and classroom based computing education; women's experiences with large scale software applications and with computer mediated communication; gendered software agents; regional and cultural differences in women's uses of ICT; some consequences for gender arising from the use of Ambient Intelligence; concepts of 'gendered occupational cultures'; the persistent under-representation of women in the IT professions across the European Union and the rest of the world. Most papers draw on experiences of women in their places of work and education.

Contemporary progressive political thinking is reflected in this book, and the papers challenge stereotypical and deterministic approaches to the development and use of ICT. They leave many questions still to be answered and issues still to be resolved.

Books of previous conference proceedings

Lander, Rachel and Adam, Alison (eds) 1997, *Women in Computing*, Intellect Books, Exeter.

Lovegrove, Gillian & Segal, Barbara (eds) 1991, *Women into Computing: Selected Papers 1988-1990,* Springer-Verlag, Oxford.

Acknowledgements

We would like to express our gratitude and thanks to the following organisations and people:

Ab-Libris Ltd

Dr Liz Bacon,
Head of School of Computing and Mathematical Sciences, University of Greenwich

BCS Women

The Council of Professors and Heads of Computing (CPHC)

The Daphne Jackson Trust

The UK Resource Centre for Women in Science, Engineering and Technology (UKRC)

The University of East London and, in particular, **Dr Gavin Poynter**, Head of School of Social Sciences, Media and Cultural Studies, and **Angela Lambert**, conference administrator

The University of Greenwich

ThoughtWorks Ltd

Members of the Conference Programme Committee

Greg Michaelson, Head of Computer Science, Heriot-Watt University, Edinburgh

Janet Stack a former chair of WiC and an active campaigner for women in Science and Technology

Soheyla Tavakol, who designed the posters for both this and the 1997 conference and the cover for this book. She is a designer and senior lecturer at the School of Computer Science, Middlesex University

Pam Wain for her administrative assistance and moral support. Pam is President of the Women's Engineering Society and Champion of MentorSET, which provides mentors to women in computing as well as other parts of SET.

Conference Programme Committee

Alison Adam	University of Salford, UK
Jacqueline Archibald	University of Abertay Dundee, UK
Nanda Bandyopadhyay	University of East London, UK
Christina Björkman	Blekinge Institute of Technology, Sweden
Sue Black	London South Bank University, UK
Annemieke Craig	Deakin University, Australia
Cecile Crutzen	Open University of the Netherlands
Judy Emms	Independent consultant, UK
Claire Green	Sharp Laboratories of Europe Ltd, UK
Frances Grundy	University of Keele, UK
Edeltraud Hanappi-Egger	Vienna University of Economics, Austria
Sue Lees	University of Keele, UK
Greg Michaelson	Heriot-Watt University, UK
Rosa Michaelson	University of Dundee, UK
Christina Mörtberg	University of Oslo, Norway
Veronika Oechtering	University of Bremen, Germany
Janet Payne	Buckinghamshire Chilterns University College, UK
Ramanee Peiris	University of Dundee, UK
Margit Pohl	Vienna University of Technology, Austria
Helen Richardson	University of Salford, UK
Margaret Ross	Southampton Institute, UK
Heidi Schelhowe	University of Bremen, Germany
Britta Schinzel	University of Freiburg, Germany
Sigrid Schmitz	University of Freiburg, Germany
Angela Scollary	Victoria University of Technology, Australia
Linda Stepulavege	University of East London, UK
Eva Turner	University of East London, UK

Conference Organisation Committee

Jacqueline Archibald	University of Abertay Dundee, UK
Judy Emms	Independent consultant, UK
Rosario Gracia-Luque	University Of East London, UK
Frances Grundy	University of Keele, UK
Rosa Michaelson	University of Dundee, UK
Janet Payne	Buckinghamshire Chilterns University College, UK
Margaret Ross	Southampton Institute, UK
Soheyla Tavakol	Middlesex University, UK
Eva Turner	University Of East London, UK
Pam Wain	Women's Engineering Society, UK

Invited Papers

Juliet Webster

Wendy Faulkner

Lesley Ottery

Cecile K. M. Crutzen

1 Why are women still so few in IT?

Understanding the persistent under-representation of women in the IT professions

Juliet Webster

Work and Equality Research, London, UK

Juliet Webster specialises in research and policy advice on women's employment and gender equality, with particular emphasis on policies and practices within the EU. She has undertaken extensive research on sectors in which women are employed, including the IT sector, and on a range of issues facing women in employment. She is the author of Shaping Women's Work: Gender, Employment and Information Technology (Longman, 1996), and the co-editor (with Ken Ducatel and Werner Herrmann) of The Information Society in Europe: Work and Life in an Age of Globalization (Rowman and Littlefield, 2000).

Abstract

This paper examines some reasons for the under-representation of women working in IT professions. It is based on the findings of a two-year study of female IT professionals in seven EU member states, including the UK. The main purpose of the study was to examine this continuing under-representation of women in the IT professions across the European Union, and indeed to understand why this under-representation appears to be growing.

The paper looks first at the backgrounds of female IT professionals, many of whom excelled in maths and sciences at school, and upon coming into contact with IT for the first time, liked the technical aspects of computers – the problem-solving, the potential for experimenting and learning, and the creativity.

Despite this, women made up just 15% of IT professionals in the UK. Although companies want to recruit more women, they report a marked shortage of female applicants for technical jobs. The paper considers why, once working in IT, women do not progress on an equal footing with their male counterparts. It focuses particularly on the terms and conditions of the IT professions, and considers three major issues: working hours in IT, direct discrimination in promotion systems; and points of drop-out by female IT professionals. The paper concludes that the nature of work in the sector, coupled with current competitive conditions, create problems in increasing women's participation in IT.

1. Introduction

Employment in the IT professions has grown very significantly in recent years, both in the UK and internationally. Aside from the crisis of the dot.com crash in 2001, the IT sector has seen significant growth in the manufacturing of computer and related hardware, and particularly in software and IT services. In the European Union, for example, employment in computer services doubled between 1997 and 2001, and grew by 10% in 1998 alone.

This massive growth in employment overall has not been matched by a parallel increase in women's participation in IT work. In the IT sector, women's employment has remained resolutely around an average of 28% across the EU; in the professional areas of IT work (as opposed to clerical and other non-professional occupations within IT), women made up only 17% in 2001 and several surveys of the same period have shown that their representation is declining worldwide (Millar 2001; Millar & Jagger 2001; Webster & Valenduc 2003).

It is an issue of some concern to policy makers, employers and indeed gender equality practitioners that, despite more than 20 years of attempts to attract women into this comparatively well-paid and privileged area of the labour market, women remain such a small and, worse, apparently declining, proportion of IT professionals. Many recent research projects have set out to address this problem, among them the project on which this paper reports.

Project WWW-ICT (Widening Women's Work in Information and Communication Technologies) set out to understand the reasons for the under-representation of women in ICT in the EU, and to make recommendations to various practitioners and agents of change on what might be done to improve this. The focus of the project was on seven EU countries: Austria, Belgium, France, Ireland, Italy, Portugal and the UK. The research took place between 2002 and 2004.[1]

The empirical study had two main elements. In the first, we examined the biographies of individual women IT professionals as a means of considering the personal, educational and career trajectories of these women, and in order to check for the kinds of common characteristics which are frequently referred to in other literature (for example, the importance of strong role models in the family or school). In the second, we conducted case studies of employing organisations in the IT services sectors, in order to understand the nature of working life in IT and the issues of importance for women's participation in the profession. It is on this aspect of the study that this paper particularly focuses. First, however, it looks at the backgrounds of female IT professionals, and the routes through which they enter IT work.

2. Getting into IT

The backgrounds of women IT professionals and their entry routes into the work are more diverse and less predictable than is perhaps generally supposed. Our research focussed on today's IT professionals, and these are women who are generally too old to have encountered computers in school, certainly not at primary level. Mainly, their first encounter with computing was at university or even afterwards. However, they are women who generally excelled in maths or sciences at school, and this is important in countries like France because excellence in school grades affords access to a career in science or technology. In the UK, a considerable number of successful women IT professionals in our study went to single sex schools. Indeed, subsequent research carried out by the Girls Schools Association (*The Guardian*, 11 November 2004), shows that girls in single sex schools are less likely to be steered away by parents and teachers from what are still perceived to be boys' subjects.

Most women enter the IT professions with a degree, but not necessarily a degree closely related to their employment. Less than 20% of our informants had degrees in computer sciences, software engineering or information systems. Several had degrees in mathematics or physics, but there were also women with degrees in economics, journalism, marketing, chemical engineering, biology and even environmental studies.

Although most of our informants entered their computing jobs directly after higher education, a significant proportion came into the work through very different routes. Some entered through journalism or information management, others through marketing or after careers in teaching. With developments in web technologies, we found several cases of women who discovered the Internet and web design, and who developed their skills through self-teaching or through training programmes. We also found several cases of women who drifted into computing work by chance, for example, through temporary employment which became permanent. So there are no clear-cut trajectories or pathways that we can point to, in relation to the points of entry into IT work.

However, a common characteristic of women in IT professions is that they are generally motivated and indeed stimulated by the problem-solving and the technical side of the work. Contrary to research which has emphasised the alienation of women from technology (see, for example, Faulkner & Arnold 1985; Cockburn 1985; Hacker 1989; Wajcman 1991), our study suggests that women can be strongly attracted to technological work, because it is challenging, offering opportunities for creativity and personal development, because it requires analytical skills, and because it often involves working with customers or users, and translating their needs into a technological outcome. In fact, our informants emphasised the creative aspects of IT work, although by this they were referring to varying and different aspects of the work, from development to client relationship management to business management. By contrast with men's relationship to computing, though, they distanced themselves from the 'love stories' of their male colleagues with their computers. So, although many women find computing work attractive in itself, the culture and organisation of computing companies are fraught with obstacles for women's employment, retention and development, and consequently for gender equality in the sector, as we shall now see.

5

3. Employment Conditions in IT

IT professionals are typically male, young (in their mid twenties), and without domestic responsibilities. The majority of women working in this sector are also most likely to be young and without children. Employees in the IT sector are among the most favoured in the labour market, in terms of wages and employment contracts. Wages are relatively high, and many IT workers are paid in a combination of cash and share options. Moreover, employment contracts involving individually agreed pay, terms and conditions replace the fixed pay grades traditionally found in other sectors. Performance-related pay or bonus schemes are common.

Employment is predominantly on full-time permanent contracts. Part-time employment and flexible working arrangements are very much an exception in this sector, though they are more common among female employees. Full-time working often means long working hours. Project work can be unpredictable, involving tight deadlines, so evening and weekend working is not unusual. Working hours certainly often exceed those laid down in employment contracts, though overtime is rarely paid for. Indeed, as Mermet and Lehndorff (2001) have noted and as our study confirmed, long hours are often self-imposed by the employee. In practice, they can arrive at and leave work according to their own preferences, and this tends to translate into extended working hours. Consequently, in France, the implementation of the 35-hour working week has been very problematic in this sector, where even the imposition of the legal limit of 39 hours was fraught with difficulties. It is perhaps not surprising that, given these kinds of working patterns, the sector employs predominantly young men who seem able (and apparently willing) to provide the total availability needed by their employers.

This is the state of affairs for employees. However, conditions are less favourable for the 'buffer' of temporary and contract workers in the IT sector. There is a significant level of self-employment and contract employment in computing (though we could not collect statistical data on this aspect of work in all countries). In Austria, for example, 20% of people working in the sector are self-employed or working in a company owned by a family member. Self-employed computing professionals are not as advantaged as their counterparts in the core IT workforce. Although their working time patterns seem to be similar to those of their permanently employed counterparts, they are more vulnerable to redundancy and have been hit hard by the recent worldwide downturn in the sector. Equally, entrenched ageism throughout the sector has made workers over 50 particularly vulnerable to redundancy.

In terms of employment and industrial relations, the IT sector is a world away from traditional companies. Even in countries with strong collective bargaining frameworks (for example, Belgium, France), employment relations are highly individualised. This has been described as a 'non-union human resource model'. At its centre is a lack of trade union membership and collective bargaining, underpinned by corporate antipathy or hostility to unions. This is especially so in the case of US multinationals, which are present in every national IT sector and particularly prominent in countries like Ireland and the UK. There are very low levels of unionisation on US-owned green-field sites. Equally important is employee indifference to unions which are seen as irrelevant to their already relatively privileged circumstances. The fact that computer services employees are young, and highly skilled, and up to now operating in a tight labour market where unemployment and labour market disadvantage are unknown, militates against trade unionism. Even in countries where union membership is high, membership figures for the sector (which are difficult to obtain) seem to be comparatively low. Collective employee relations are replaced in computer services by individualised employee relations, personnel management by human resource management. Pay and conditions are agreed bilaterally (and often kept confidential from other employees). Pay is based partly on performance assessed through individual appraisals carried out periodically by line managers. Training and development needs are usually assessed at the same time. Communication – not consultation – is carried out on a one-to-one basis between employers and employees.

4. Organisational Practices

4.1 The organisation of work

IT companies, whether large multinationals or small companies, tend to favour flat structures with few hierarchical layers, reflecting a more generalised organisational trend towards 'de-layering' which has been in process since the late 1980s. Such structures are often accompanied by a rhetoric of closeness to management, yet in the context of global strategic decision-taking, management decisions are usually very far removed from individual employees. It is common for IT professionals, development staff for example, to be organised into project teams, led by a project team leader or project manager. These teams may be temporary, operating only for the duration of the project, or semi-permanent. They may also consist of interdependent workers with complementary skills, or individuals with the same skills working independently of one another but within a group known as a team. Previous research has suggested that women are often under-valued in interdependent teams, where their technical skills are taken for granted relative to the interpersonal or team-working skills of their male counterparts (Woodfield 2000).

4.2 Working time and work-life balance

IT work is predominantly done full-time and more. Much of it is deadline-driven, particularly where it is governed by project timetables or client demands. Long working hours are the norm, as is availability to the company and to clients, and this is imposed by employees on themselves as well as by their employers. Hot-desking and client-based working are common among IT professionals. Home-based working is also common, with infrastructures provided by employers. Client-based working involving long distance travelling can be problematic for managing childcare or other family responsibilities, but home-based working can by contrast be very family-friendly. Again, however, there are numerous examples of what Lehndorff calls 'self-exploitation' by IT professionals: such as dealing with emails at what might be considered to be 'unsocial' working hours – late at night after children are in bed, or very early at weekends.

> Working hours? They are exaggerated because no one can say a simple 'no' to the client. This is the company's policy. You have to give all your availability and energy to the firm: working overtime and sometimes also at home after work [Marta, Italian IT company].

Part-time working is very unusual in this sector, but where it does exist, it is principally done by women returning from maternity leave. We found that in some cases it severely limited their progression prospects, with companies demoting part-timers from management roles and excluding them from particular client relationships. Other forms of family-friendly working or work-life balance arrangements were almost non-existent in the companies studied for this project. Some participating companies regarded families as problems that would divert employees from their work. One employer saw family-friendly policies simply as devices to be used in a tight labour market to attract a wider pool of job applicants. In recessionary conditions, there was felt to be no need for such arrangements.

Informal flexible working arrangements do exist; employees are often allowed by their companies to take time off when they need to, as long as their work is done. In practice, however, this usually means more time spent at work, rather than less. In general, it would seem that reconciliation between professional and private life is difficult for employees (of both sexes) in IT professions. Most of our informants, however, were young, unmarried and without caring responsibilities, so were largely unaffected by this issues. The question remains, however, of whether the industry attracts such workers because they are the only people who can manage these types of working time demands, or whether the working time arrangements have evolved in response to the type of employees who predominate in the sector.

4.3 Employee development and women's progression

The women working in IT professions in our study entered their work almost universally through a computer science education, and we found this still to be the main entry route for professional jobs, for example, in development, programming, design work, and project or business management. A significant minority entered the profession through other disciplines, however, including other natural sciences and management studies. Many of our informants also had higher degrees. On-the-job learning and skills maintenance are considered critical in the IT professions as the means by which professionals develop their capabilities in the most recent technical developments. In addition, business and management skills take on increasing importance in the career development of IT professionals, and technical skills and tasks seem to become less prominent as professionals progress.

In large companies, there are widespread employee development opportunities, particularly in comparison with smaller organisations which have fewer resources for this. However, increasingly we found a tendency across the sector for training and development to be individualised, that is, for training to be managed and conducted by the individual employee using computer-based learning technologies, the Internet, and interaction with peers, and low levels of intervention by the employing organisation. The individualisation of training and learning is common to many sectors and is not exclusive to the IT sector. It is a departure from an excessively bureaucratic, supply-driven approach to training, focusing more on the individual learning demands and needs of employees, and placing much more autonomy in their hands. However, it also poses problems for employees who find it difficult to allocate time for learning outside of their normal working routines, particularly people with domestic or caring responsibilities. IT work is often highly pressured and can involve long hours: time for training and learning is often scarce. It would seem that it is no accident that the majority of IT professionals are young and without domestic responsibilities.

> *Quand je vois les informaticiens, enfin les programmeurs, ils doivent continuer à se former tout le temps … Je pense que ce côté-là est difficilement conciliable avec une vie de famille. (..) Enfin, ceux qui le font ne sont pas mariés, n'ont pas d'enfants [Computer graphic artist, Belgium].*

The women in our case studies were generally very much attracted to technical work and enjoyed performing it. Many reported that the use of problem-solving skills was one of the most satisfying aspects of their work because they saw this as creative. For some, creative work meant being engrossed in coding and programming; for others, it meant designing and developing a website or service, or developing an overview of a project through their project management work.

The IT sector is a relatively privileged place for women to work. Pay and autonomy are high, and there are considerable opportunities for progression, along two basic career trajectories: a technical career path and a management career path. The latter is the most common career pattern for IT professionals, and includes possibilities to move into project management, team management or business management. Employers often assume that women are more comfortable in management than in technical roles. In fact, we found that women are sometimes directed away from technical work and towards project or business management, on the assumption that this sort of work is particularly closely compatible with their assumed interpersonal and organisational skills. Moving into management with even a relatively junior promotion was a clear disadvantage for some of the women we encountered, because they resented being moved from technical work.

> *I would love to be able to make a career just writing code, but it seems like you can't. You have got to move away from that in order to progress, which I think is a shame.*

(..) I am now looking round and thinking 'What do I do next?' I don't want to let go of the coding, but it sounds like in order to progress, you have to. I know I don't want to be a people manager, but I think the next role for me is probably project management. I am kind of doing a lot of that now [Software engineer in the UK].

Nevertheless, women remain significantly under-represented in managerial and particularly executive positions in IT. The WWW-ICT project identified several factors which contribute to this state of affairs. First, company promotion practices vary from formal and transparent progression arrangements through to informal and opaque systems. In the latter group, we found discriminatory practices including what we might call 'promotion through visibility', in which participation in extra-curricula activities (football clubs and pub evenings, for example) and in informal networks raises visibility and so confers advantages on certain employees, usually men. The persistence of such networks indicates that these employers lack experience of working with women, and generally lack gender awareness. We also found several striking examples of direct discrimination against women by male managers, on the basis of assumptions about their availability for, and commitment to, their work.[2]

These kinds of practices should be contrasted with the very well-defined and transparent progression systems which exist in other organisations. Formal progression policies and practices have a major impact on women's participation in IT professions. Several organisations committed to the project of improving women's participation throughout their ranks also understood the need to implement consistent policies for recruitment, training, appraisal and development, and implemented these policies as whole packages. This coherence of approach communicated clear messages to women about potential career routes, and provided the infrastructural channels through which they could move. Some companies also run grooming schemes specifically designed to prepare employees with strong interest in and potential for senior positions. Such 'fast track' systems are often operated in conjunction with specific schemes for developing women in various ways. Mentoring and other confidence-building initiatives were also established in order to address a commonly-noticed tendency for women to understate their own skills and knowledge, and deselect themselves from eligibility for promotion opportunities. Women's reticence in showcasing their abilities and in advocating themselves was noted by several employers keen to pursue equality programmes.

In general, we found that these kinds of organisations – ones with awareness of how gender operates within and beyond their own spheres – were most likely to recruit and promote women into senior positions, but even here, women were massively under-represented. Even the most equality-conscious companies revealed internal conflicts between their equality agendas and their other organisational practices, particularly the organisation of working time and in situations of restructuring. It has been suggested that women IT professionals leave the profession in disproportionate numbers at maternity, and then again in mid-life, when they seem to be disproportionately targeted by organisational redundancy programmes or voluntarily leave large organisations in search of other working arrangements (George 2003). So, just at the point when they might be entering senior management and executive positions, many women are leaving large organisations or IT professional life, reducing the already small pool eligible for these.

A major obstacle to women's representation in IT professions – and one which cuts across very many well-intentioned corporate equality programmes – lies in the working time arrangements and culture of the profession. Long working hours particularly affect people in technical roles, who have to be available to their employers and their clients, and those in senior management. Moreover, it extends beyond the 'workaholic' UK to countries which do not generally have a similar culture of long working hours and in which the European Working Time Directive has been adopted without quibble. (Italy was the only country participating in this study in which working hours in the IT sector are regulated by collective agreement.)

Even in companies with strong gender equality programmes, promotion into senior positions appears to depend upon the ability and willingness to work long hours and thereby to demonstrate commitment to the work and the organisation.

Certainly in the company there would be an expectation that when you reach the senior level that you would be available all the time [Senior engineer in Irish IT company].

Often, implicit messages are transmitted from senior executives to more junior staff that such working patterns are necessary for career advancement – messages which fundamentally contradict those that they wish to convey through their organisations' other equality initiatives.

The UK General Manager told me that in 2002 he had 15 weekends at home. Now, his job is to ensure equality of opportunity for everybody in the company (...). Now I have some difficulty with that because I think actually that if large corporations are really serious about having more senior women, then there are going to have to be some more compromises at the top [Senior IT executive in multinational located in the UK].

This type of working may discourage people – of both sexes – who are unable to engage in it from pursuing promotion possibilities in their organisations. In general, of course, it is women who are primarily disadvantaged by long working hours.

It is quite clear from this and other studies that more than twenty years of public and private policy interventions appear to have had little impact on the rate of women's participation in the profession (although it is arguable that they may have had some positive impact on the *nature* of women's jobs in IT). In the concluding section of this paper, I would like to place the study findings in the wider context of developments taking place in the IT sector, and thereby to suggest some factors which I believe to be critical to an understanding of women's prospects in the IT professions.

5. The IT Sector: A Good Place for Women?

Since the early 1980s, when computing first emerged as a significant new area of work, there have been many and widespread attempts by public authorities, voluntary organisations and private sector employers, to attract and retain women into computing professions. Most of these initiatives were informed by a perspective which centred on the idea that simply 'adding women in' to technological jobs would provide a solution to the exclusion of women from technology (Henwood 1993). The context within which these initiatives were pursued – wider corporate strategies and practices concerning organisational and technological changes – were often, however, overlooked and, consequently, many initiatives were at best ineffectual and at worst, harmful to the very people they were designed to benefit.

At the beginning of the 21st century, the structural developments taking place in the IT sector have not provided a positive environment for improving women's representation in the IT professions. In the last few years, the sector has undergone an almost unprecedented downturn. Over 100,000 employees and contractors have been made redundant in the UK since the middle of 2001 (E-Skills Bulletin 2004), organisations have been restructured, while programming functions are now routinely outsourced to third countries (India, Israel, Romania, to name a few) and so on. Many of these organisational changes are extremely detrimental to both women's numerical representation and the quality of their working lives in IT.

Just as in her account of her work in AT&T, Hacker (1989) noted that the process of organisational and technological change within this large corporation ultimately undermined her and her colleagues' attempts to pursue equality initiatives, so too in the WWW-ICT project, we found that organisational and structural changes being wrought within companies at corporate level proved extremely hostile to more localised, decentralised equal opportunities programmes. Recessionary conditions seemed to prompt, in the large corporations at least, a reassertion of highly centralised decision-taking, authoritarian and bullying management styles, an abandonment of corporate commitments to equality and a return to conventional fiscal performance measures which allowed no leeway for longer-term projects.

In this context, training and development budgets were commonly cut back, with particularly negative consequences for employees, such as women, who said that they found it more difficult to pursue these activities in their own time. In corporate redundancy programmes, there was a suspicion that middle-aged women were being picked up more than their male counterparts (though there was no firm evidence for this). Competitive pressures wrought by an economic downturn cut across well-meaning and well-structured equal opportunities strategies and were ultimately more influential on corporate behaviour. The retrenchment by corporations also reduced the pressure on them – existing during periods of skills shortages – to draw from a wide a portion of the labour market as possible.

These are not merely temporary responses to contemporary competitive conditions. A fundamental change in the culture of IT organisations is taking place. Originating in the United States, this culture is now gaining ground in the European IT sector. It is, as I have already noted, characterised by long working hours, new forms of HR management involving individualised setting of pay and terms and conditions of employment, and weak or non-existent trade unionism (sometimes a result of explicit hostility to trade unions by employing companies). In recruitment and progression practices there is increasing emphasis on the employees' personal qualities, including self-direction, self-management and self-advocacy.

In my view, the 'new HR' has very ambiguous consequences for employees in general, and for gender equality in particular. Individualised pay systems, particularly the performance-related and bonus systems common in the IT sector, have been relatively lucrative for employees until the recent recession in the sector and the decline in share prices. Recently, however, these pay systems have made IT professionals of both sexes vulnerable to the vicissitudes of the stock market and labour market. Self-advocacy, although in principle empowering, has been found to be problematic for those who lack strong self-confidence, women in particular. It can also be problematic if these attributes, rather than their other skills and qualifications, increasingly form the basis on which employees are assessed and promoted. This risks re-introducing discrimination and preferential treatment on the basis of personal prejudice, personal knowledge or shared interests into employee progression practices.

This, then, is an organisational culture which carries the danger of overlooking the particular needs of women in IT professions. It is based on individualism and ignores social structures and sources of inequality. Equal opportunities may form part of an organisation's policies practices, but these tend to be undermined by its wider HR approach. Many of the companies we studied for this project had apparently democratised their employee relations, introducing more individually-governed working arrangements and practices: autonomy in arranging working hours, self-driven training and learning, team-based working, self-promotion. However, in doing so they overlooked persistent gender equalities, both in their own ranks and in society at large. In this way, gender became 'invisible' (Korvajärvi 2003) and company policies became gender-blind. These companies believed that because they had put in place practices which were aimed to attracting and retaining women, women's continuing under-representation surely reflected problems elsewhere – beyond the scope of company intervention. If this continuing inequality is to be tackled, we seem to keep coming back to questions posed over twenty years ago. Is it a worthwhile project in the first place? How is it to be achieved and by whom?

References

Cockburn, C. 1985, *Machinery of Dominance: Men, Women and Technical Know-how*, Pluto, London.

E-skills Bulletin 2004, *Quarterly Review of the ICT Labour Market*, London, e-skills UK.

Faulkner, W. & Arnold, E. (eds) 1985, *Smothered by Invention: Technology in Women's Lives*, Pluto Press, London.

George, R. 2003, *Achieving workforce diversity in the e-business on demand era*, IBM, Portsmouth.

Hacker, S. 1989, *Pleasure, Power and Technology*, Unwin Hyman, London.

Henwood, F. 1993, 'Establishing gender perspectives on information technology', in Green, E., Owen, J. and Pain, D. (eds) *Gendered by Design: Information Technology and Office Systems*, Taylor & Francis, London.

Korvajärvi, P. 2003, *Conceptual Considerations around Gendered Organizations*, paper presented to Gender, Work and Organization conference, Keele University, 25-27 June.

Mermet, E. & Lehndorff, S. 2001, *New Forms of Employment and Working Time in the Service Economy (NESY)*, Country Case Studies Conducted in Five Service Sectors, ETUI Report 69, Brussels, European Trade Union Institute.

Millar, J. 2001, *ITEC Skills and Employment – assessing the supply and demand: an empirical analysis*, Issue Report No 11, Socio-Economic Trends Assessment for the Digital Revolution (STAR) project report, Brighton, SPRU.

Millar, J. & Jagger, N. 2001, Women in ITEC Courses and Careers, Brighton, SPRU and IES.

Roche, W.K. & Gunnigle, P. 1995, 'Competition and the New Industrial Relations Agenda', in Leavy, B. & Walshe, J. S. (eds) *Strategy and General Management: an Irish Reader*, Oaktree Press, Dublin.

Wajcman, J. 1991, *Feminism Confronts Technology*, Penn State University, Pennsylvania.

Webster, J. & Valenduc, G. 2003, 'Mapping Gender Gaps in Employment and Occupations', in Vendramin. P. et al. *WWW-ICT Conceptual Framework and State of the Art*, WWW-ICT Deliverable No 1, published on www.ftu-namur.org/www-ict.

Woodfield, R. 2000, *Women, Work and Computing*, Cambridge University Press, Cambridge.

Notes

1 The project was co-ordinated by Patricia Vendramin and Gérard Valenduc at the Fondation-Travail Université, Namur, Belgium, and involved partners from the Institute for Technology Design and Assessment at the Technical University of Vienna, the Regional Foundation Pietro Seveso in Milan, the National Agency for the Improvement of Working Conditions in France, and myself in the UK. The project's website gives further details of the other country participants at www.ftu-namur-org/www-ict, from where downloadable project reports are also available. Responsibility for the arguments and analysis presented in this paper is my own.

2 In one case, an IT company manager expressed reluctance to recruit or promote women because he supposed that they would not cope well with travelling to clients' premises. In another example, a promotion to management was withdrawn from a woman after she asked to work part-time following her maternity leave, on the grounds that management work was necessarily full-time.

2 Becoming and Belonging: Gendered processes in engineering

Wendy Faulkner

Science Studies Unit, University of Edinburgh, UK

Wendy Faulkner is a Reader in the Science Studies Unit, University of Edinburgh. She was trained in biology and then science and technology policy studies (University of Sussex), but now considers herself a sociologist of technology. She moved to Edinburgh in 1988 where she has been heavily involved in developing and running the University's Masters and Doctoral Programmes in Science and Technology Studies. She has a long-standing interest in gender, science and technology issues starting with her involvement in Alice Through the Microscope (Brighton Women and Science Collective, Virago 1980) and Smothered by Invention (with Erik Arnold, Pluto, 1985). She is currently engaged in an ethnographic study 'Gender in/of engineering.' For many years she also conducted research on knowledge use in industrial R&D and innovation.

Abstract

The concept of 'gendered occupational cultures' can help explain gender inequality and gender segregation at work – beyond the obvious and widely acknowledged structural factors. It allows us to examine the more subtle and taken-for-granted factors which contribute to making an occupation like engineering more appealing, comfortable and supportive to (more) men than women. Two social phenomena are key to how occupational cultures are produced and, thus, gendered: the complex socialisation process by which people 'become' members of an occupational community, and the various markers by which they are understood to 'belong', as a 'real' engineer. The paper explores both these phenomena, by drawing on interview data from women and men engineers in Scotland. The data highlight various ways in which becoming and belonging can be gendered, in particular: the presumption of hands-on tinkering skills, the invisibility of women engineers as engineers, the informal social culture, and the masculine coding of engineering work (be it 'technical' or managerial). Overall, it seems, women engineers are more likely to suffer losses of confidence and may struggle more than men to gain 'membership' as engineers. The paper concludes that these issues are less significant amongst men engineers for the simple reason that engineering is a more 'gender authentic' career choice for them than for women. The implications for policies intended to recruit and retain more women in engineering are explored.

1. Becoming and Belonging

'Gendered occupational cultures' is a useful concept in seeking to understand continuing gender segregation and inequality at work. I am using the concept to capture factors which are not structural – important though these are especially in engineering (e.g. long hours and lack of flexible working practices). 'Occupational cultures' here includes many possible dimensions: shared ways of thinking and doing the job, the language and symbols used on the job, formal and informal social interactions with colleagues, shared humour and stories, shared identities, etc. The 'gender' focus obliges us to look at the men/masculinities of engineering as much as (if not more than) the women – since the majority group is likely to play the greater role in shaping an occupational culture. The key thing is to identify what aspects of a particular occupational culture render it more appealing, more comfortable and more supportive to particular genders (i.e., particular types of men and/or women). In spite of the label 'gendered', I am also seeking to identify aspects of occupational cultures which are gender*ing* – in the sense that they 'produce' or perform particular genders.

I propose that central to how occupational cultures are (re)produced, and thus gendered/gendering, are processes of *becoming and belonging*. Making the choice to be an engineer is only the first step to becoming one. Many years spent in education and subsequent on-the-job learning are necessary before would-be engineers 'arrive' as fully-fledged engineers. Becoming, in the sense I am using it here, is therefore an achievement, involving a lengthy and complex process of professional socialisation. Key to that *achievement* is that one's membership in the occupational community is established, that one is understood by the community to belong, as a 'real' engineer. Gaining engineering expertise (how to think and work in particular ways) is a necessary but not sufficient precondition to membership; there are several other markers of belonging in engineering.

Prior US work indicates some of the ways in which belonging in engineering is gendered – and some of the consequences. Engineer-turned-sociologist, Karen Tonso (1997; 1999) conducted a series of studies in a US engineering college. By analysing the labels engineering students have for one another, she demonstrated that women engineering students are visible as (sexualised) women but invisible as engineers. And through participant observation in design projects, she found that peer interactions and institutional practices further compound this invisibility, with the result that some very able women engineers are not recognized as such by their faculty and struggle to get good jobs. In an interview-based study of women men engineers in the workplace, McIlwee and Robinson (1992) concluded that 'To be seen as a competent engineer means throwing ones self into ritualistic displays of hands-on technical competence' *even when the job does not demand this competence*. In general, women engineers do not belong by this informal marker. As a result, in organisations where this 'engineering culture' is strong, and where promotion is not based on formal criteria, women engineers tend to lose out in terms of career progression.

In this paper, I explore further some of the ways that processes of becoming an engineer and belonging in engineering may be gendered. I draw on interviews with a cross section of women and men engineers working in Scotland, conducted as part of a study entitled 'Gender in/of engineering'.[1] Because this study is currently in-progress, the data and analysis presented here are partial and provisional. It should also be noted that, although ICT specialists were included in the study, some of the detailed points may be more relevant to the traditional engineering disciplines. Nevertheless, I am confident that all of the general themes explored here are salient to some degree, across both communities.

2. Becoming an Engineer

2.1 Choosing to be an engineer

There are notable commonalities and differences in the reasons why women and men opt for a career in engineering. All are motivated by a combination of factors. In most cases, these include the fact that they liked maths and science at school, see themselves as 'practical' people and wanted a good career. Maths and science are of course a necessary foundation for engineering, but it is notable that women engineers, like men engineers, appreciate the bounded, law-like character of these subjects, which they frequently juxtapose with subjects like English where 'there is no one right answer'. Most women engineers are also inspired and excited by engineering technologies, even if a slightly higher proportion of men engineers report what Ruth Oldenziel (1999, p. 9) calls a 'love of technology'. Predictably, the majority of men entering engineering degrees have some background of tinkering, where the majority of women do not.

This was not the most significant difference to emerge from this section of my interviews with engineers, however. Like Ulf Mellström's (1995), my interviews revealed that engineering is a more self-evident – or in my terms 'gender authentic' – choice for men than for women. The men who opt to be engineers are not exceptional, as men. Indeed, many of those I interviewed provided little or no account of their choice – precisely because there is nothing remarkable for a man about choosing to be an engineer. By contrast, virtually all of the women I interviewed have a story to tell about why they made the choice; like not having children as a woman, it demands an explanation. The reactions of outsiders are a constant reminder that being a woman engineer (whether young or old) makes them unusual, remarkable. Many relish being unusual, even rebellious; and many are extremely confident, the sort to seek out a challenge.

2.2 Engineering education

In this context, it was astonishing for me to discover that many women experience a rapid loss of confidence on entering engineering degrees. Both men and women students find engineering courses very difficult, and many are surprised at the high mathematical content. What is striking is that the women students often assume everyone else is better than them, that they are not good enough. With time, most come to realise that, as Jessica put it, 'We are all the same – good at some things and not others'. And with time, many do very well academically: it is common (in my own university at least) to find disproportionate numbers of women obtaining very good engineering degrees (also McIlwee and Robinson 1992).

Hands-on practical skills are a particular focus of low self-esteem for women engineering students – which is why experiments in gender-inclusive educational reform typically include greater attention to these aspects (e.g. Willoughby 1999). Women students are also conscious that they 'stood out as a female', especially those entering before 1990. Joanne's experience of university is typical of many women engineers:

> *The first year in particular, there was definitely that feeling of stepping beyond your comfort zone … and somehow assuming that everybody knew more than I did. [I discovered that] many of the men had soldering irons at home … it seemed alien to me!'*

Getting to build a radio and have it work was a big boost to Joanne's confidence, but she never came to enjoy hands-on work and is still (after 11 years working) sometimes teased by male colleagues for her lack of tinkering skills.

2.3 On-the-job learning

There are many things which engineers need to know but don't get from university education – especially experience related to work processes, work relationships and practical matters. This more rounded engineering knowledge is acquired on the job over a period of years. Fresh graduates are given discrete tasks, working closely with someone else. As they gather experience of different types of work, they progressively see more of the bigger picture and get given more responsibility – so gaining experience of the whole process. There is variation between firms as to how formal the supervision and how structured the training. How easy or not this period is depends hugely on how supportive and approachable the individual mentor or manager is.

Asking questions is a vital means by which engineers learn on the job. Graduate engineers are expected to ask questions of their more experienced colleagues, and get their work checked. Indeed, asking questions and reviewing each other's work is a routine part of engineering work, even amongst really experienced engineers. In practice, however, every new engineer discovers that there are some colleagues who you should not expose your ignorance to and others who are happy to answer questions. And in practice, some new engineers are bolder than others about asking what may appear 'ignorant' questions. Senior woman engineers report that they have learnt to always to ask questions, in the spirit of Karen's 'mantra', '*There's no such thing as a stupid question*!'. There is a hint that men engineers are less likely to declare that they don't know something – i.e., more likely to hide their ignorance – but always relieved that someone (else) has asked the question! This might also be linked to gender authenticity

– if as men they are supposed to be 'naturals', the women have more of an excuse for not knowing – or it may just be a continuation of the tendency for more girls than boys to ask questions at school.

Both men and women have to prove themselves in their early years as an engineer, and this brings a lot of anxiety at times. Fiona's first few years as a mechanical engineer working in a manufacturing company involved being moved around different parts of the operation. On occasion, this became something of a 'hazing' experience, where what she had to prove was not her engineering ability so much as her willingness to laugh along at rather uncomfortable sexual 'jokes' – in other words her ability to be 'one of the lads'. An equivalent gender performance is sometimes demanded of men – a 'proof of manhood' – especially in interactions with blue collar workers or technician engineers, e.g. on the building site or shop floor. Civil engineer, Hamish, once had to demonstrate his bravery by setting up an explosion in a potentially dangerous mine.

3. Belonging as an Engineer

Most people report that it takes anywhere from 4 to 7 years before they feel they've really 'arrived' as a fully-fledged engineer. Along the way there are a number of critical moments when engineers experience a step up in their professional confidence: realising that you are mostly getting it right and that people are asking you questions, getting positive feedback from external partners or clients, and running a whole project from start to finish. Becoming chartered often marks the end point of this process and is universally viewed as a serious landmark, worthy of celebration.

Whilst all engineers, women and men, struggle though these early years of socialisation to some degree, there are some clear gender influences on how easily one gains membership in the occupational community, which taken together are likely to make things harder for more women than men.

3.4 Visibility

The experienced women engineers I interviewed are well used to being visible as a woman first and an engineer second. Contrary to Tonso's findings, however, most claim any lack of credibility resulting from this is short-lived. Joanne, for example, says that 'Being taken seriously is a stronger challenge for women initially.' And Karen, reports that 'As a senior woman who is blond and girlie looking, there are people who don't take me seriously to start with. But once they realise I can do the job, it's over.' Such claims are of course very difficult to assess empirically.[2] At the very least, the visibility issue represents another layer of work which women and not men engineers need to do before they are taken seriously as engineers.

3.5 Informal social culture

The informal social culture of engineering workplaces can be quite 'laddish' – characterised by talk about men's sports, 'slagging' humour, swearing and sexual or heteronormative innuendo. One has to be careful not to overstate the case. The majority of the social interactions I have observed appear respectful. Even where the laddish culture is evident, there are other (potentially more gender inclusive) topics of conversation and ways of interacting. Not all women find the laddish culture uncomfortable, and not all men find it comfortable. Nonetheless, as indicated earlier, membership – for women and men – means becoming 'one of the lads', to some extent at least. The most extreme case of this I have observed is in an oil services company, where women and men alike widely acknowledge that women who don't 'adapt' and 'fit in' never really belong. And when the work is offshore, 'fitting in' can mean tolerating the widespread presence of pornographic TV and calendars. There is real hostility towards any woman who exerts her right to object; 'That's not fair, when there's only one woman and 150 men on the platform!'

The laddish culture is probably more marked in workplaces where there is a lot of interaction with blue collar workers, or where there are a lot of younger engineers. But it is by no means absent in engineering offices I have observed and been told about in the UK. The only place where I have not found a laddish culture was in a software development office of a very diversity-aware company in the USA. Here the informal culture is still gender normative, but it is a family-centred culture – so much so that women and men who don't have children sometimes find themselves working longer hours than those who do because they don't have the 'excuse' of leaving to attend to their children.

3.6 Authenticity

I have been told anecdotally that, where a group of woman engineers have had a drink or two, they commonly confess to feeling a fraud. (In my experience this is not confined to women engineers!) If this is indeed a widespread experience, it would be consistent with the issue of engineering being a less gender authentic occupation for women than men.

For some women engineers, it seems, the lack of confidence or sense of authenticity continues to be tied up with the issue of practical, hands-on skills. Sally had only just started her first job when I interviewed her;

When I came here there was quite a large practical element, so I felt quite stupid.
… There's so much you don't understand when you leave university.

For many experienced women engineers, the relative lack of hands-on skills is no longer a confidence issue. Like the women interviewed by McIlwee and Robinson, these women say they just aren't interested in the hands-on side of engineering and point out that tinkering skills are rarely required in professional engineering jobs. Theresa, for example, had an unusually strong background in car maintenance, but never became (or felt) as good as her male colleagues, especially those who had entered through apprenticeships. Like many such women, Theresa stresses the other things she is good at – in her case, business development – which some of the tinkerer men are not: 'People occupy their area of comfort don't they?'

3.7 What counts as 'real' engineering

A problem arises with Theresa's approach when different kinds of engineering work are not all counted equally as 'real' engineering. Typically, engineers have two discourses about this. One is a narrowly technicist version in which engineering is presented as the 'nuts and bolts', drawings and calculations. The other is a more heterogeneous[3] version, which encompasses also inter-personal relations and various aspects of business management. There are professional, corporate and gender tensions around these two versions of what counts as engineering.

One source of gender tensions is that the two versions of engineering are manifest in two very available versions of masculinity. One takes its marker from hands-on work with technology, and is modelled on the technician engineer – hence, 'nuts and bolts'. The other takes its marker from corporate authority and commerce, and is modelled on the senior manager or businessman (gender intended). Any man engineer who moves into these latter roles may lose his credentials as a 'nuts and bolts' engineer in the eyes of engineering colleagues, but he does not lose his credentials as a man. If anything, he gains in this regard, since the authority wielded as managers and the money made in business are widely applauded markers of achievement in men. In Bob Connell's terms, high level management and business roles provide powerful models of hegemonic masculinity (1987).

Significantly, *neither* version of engineering – the technicist or the heterogeneous – has strong feminine associations. On top of this, the ever-present technical/social dualism in engineering is another source of gender tension, since 'the technical' is so readily associated with men and 'the social' with women, and the two are deemed to be mutually exclusive (Faulkner 2000b). This situation creates a paradox for women engineers. On the one hand, moving *out* of narrowly technical roles is seen as more 'natural' (in the sense of gender authentic) for them than for men – because it is widely assumed that women engineers have better 'people skills' than men. On the other hand, moving *into* management and business engineering roles is seen as more 'natural' for men engineers than for women, especially at the higher levels. And because engineering is already pretty gender inauthentic for women, I suspect that those women who move up the hierarchy (so away from 'nuts and bolts' engineering) are in greater risk of losing their engineering credentials than are men who make the same move.

4. Two Cases: Claire and Karen

Many of the findings I have just reviewed are illustrated by the cases of Claire and Karen. At the outset, there were a lot of similarities between the two women. Both graduated in the 1990s, so are now in their 30s. Both are from middle class backgrounds. Both relished being a rebel by choosing a different career from their parents. Both chose mechanical engineering, though neither had any prior socialisation in 'hands-on' engineering. Both hoped engineering design would provide some outlet for their artistic talents. Both were motivated to do something socially worthwhile in their work. Both are career oriented and ambitious. In the event, Claire and Karen's experiences of becoming an engineer and their career paths have been rather different. However, each of them struggles in different ways around issues of 'belonging' as an engineer.

4.8 Claire

Claire was immediately disappointed when she started at university: 'it was all maths', and very little design. She found the maths 'very, very difficult', although she got to be good at it and afterwards felt proud that she had been able to rise to the challenge of the degree. Most distressing of all, she felt there was always a gap between the calculations and anything practical – she 'couldn't relate them to anything real'. Like many others, she was 'so unfamiliar with [hands-on work], I found it quite frightening and quite difficult to cope with'. The combined effect of this and the 'gap' she experienced was a damning indictment of her education: 'It erodes your confidence, because … I have this degree in engineering but actually I couldn't use it!'

In the event, Claire's first job was a research post at her university in computer-aided engineering, which led to a PhD. This helped to restore her confidence: her supervisor was supportive, and the project took her into machine tool companies, including six months abroad in a firm, which built up her practical experience. She says of herself that she is not very good at career planning. After the research job, she taught computer-aided engineering at other universities for four years. She quit because she was being asked to teach outwith her specialism.

Her current job was a considerable shift. For the last 5 years, Claire has been working in a start-up R&D firm developing medical technologies, where she is responsible for 'putting in information systems to support the business' on both the engineering and management sides. This includes a lot of programming and other technical work as well as process development, training and the supervision of four staff. In spite of the high technical content of this job, Claire presented herself to me as no longer doing 'a professional engineering job'. She has resigned her hard won membership of the Institute of Mechanical Engineers, which she feels 'a little bit' sad and 'a small regret' about. And she suspects the firms' engineers do not really see her as one of them. Nevertheless, she enjoys her current job and is now rising to the challenge of understanding the business side better by taking an MBA part time.

4.9 Karen

Karen chose a degree in architectural engineering, which was half taught by architects, so had 'more design and less maths' than a normal engineering degree. She had a happier time at university than Claire, though she 'hated' subjects like controls and microprocessors 'because they didn't involve people like building services do'. More of a career planner than Claire, she joined the head office of a multinational building design consultancy company with a graduate training scheme. Her first line manager undermined her confidence somewhat because he did not trust her to get on with jobs, but then she moved to another 'who assumed I could do it'.

Karen has been a high achiever. In her fifth year with the company, she was responsible for designing all of the mechanical building services in a major iconic building, incorporating many principles of sustainability. She subsequently won a prestigious national prize for this work, became chartered and got her first major promotion in the company, signalling that she was ready to bring in business and run projects unaided. And yet, Karen has recently left the company in which she has had such a brilliant early career, for a job in project management.

Her departure followed a move to a regional office of the company. In this office, the engineers are all expected to do a bit of everything, including the 'back room' job of detailed design. Karen resented this, on the grounds that she had already proved herself in detailed design, and that this is not where her personal strengths or interests lie. Although she was highly valued and respected for her 'up front' skills in concept design and winning new business, she was not allowed to concentrate on the work she enjoys. In addition, Karen's disinterest in doing detailed design work probably undermined her engineering credentials amongst some in the wider office. In spite of the fact that virtually all the staff do perform both up front and backroom roles, most of those I observed celebrate a practical, 'nuts and bolts' version of engineering. There were gasps of astonishment once when she admitted that she'd never 'sized' a gas pipe – 'You've got this far and never sized a gas pipe?!'.

5. Conclusions and Implications

My central argument is that the confidence and membership issues highlighted by the cases of Claire and Karen will in general be experienced less deeply amongst men engineers – precisely because engineering is a more gender authentic career option for them as men than for women. The evidence presented here highlights several elements which together conspire to gender the processes of becoming and belonging: the presumption of hands-on tinkering skills, the invisibility of women engineers as engineers, the informal social culture, and the masculine coding of engineering work (be it 'technical' or managerial). I believe that all of these elements are symptomatic of the fact that engineering has long been strongly male-dominated. More precisely, I believe they reflect a two-way, mutually reinforcing relationship between the presence of occupational cultures which favour or are more comfortable to men, and the continued numerical predominance of men in engineering.

The challenge, for efforts to recruit more women into engineering, is how to break that circuit. Vivian Lagesen (forthcoming) has recently argued that the 'strength of numbers' matters hugely, and I agree with her. Her close study of recruitment campaigns at the NTNU in Trondheim, Norway, demonstrates that the most crucial measures are those which *directly* increase the numbers of women entering computer science and engineering courses (like quotas), and which *make visible* the presence of women in these fields. I would argue that such measure are effective in so much as they move towards 'normalising' engineering as a career choice for women – so start to tackle what I believe to be the underlying gender authenticity issue.

Improving the retention and career progression of women in engineering fields raises different challenges and demands different sorts of measures. We have seen that support and intervention measures are needed at many critical points along the path of becoming an engineer. In university education, there is a need for greater attention to practical skills and design, and to relating the mathematical core teaching to real technological challenges. In companies, there is a need for better training of mentors and managers so that junior engineers are more consistently supported – e.g. through promoting a climate in which 'there are no stupid questions' – and so that engineers at all stages have appropriate, ongoing career reviews and advice.

Most if not all of these measures would be good for men engineers as well as women, and good for engineering as a profession. Somewhat more difficult to tackle are the issues surrounding the informal social cultures in engineering, and the troubled boundaries about what constitutes 'real' engineering. With respect to the former, there is arguably a need for careful diversity training, of the type used in some US firms, to encourage a more inclusive informal culture without generating resentment amongst the majority group. The latter will demand, in the language of feminist technology studies, new 'co-constructions' of both gender *and* engineering.

References

Bijker, W. E., Hughes, T. P., & Pinch, T. J. 1987, *The Social Construction of Technological Systems*, MIT Press, Cambridge, MA.

Connell, R. 1987, *Gender and Power: Society, the Person and Sexual Politics*, Polity Press, Cambridge, UK.

Faulkner, W. 2000a, 'The power *and* the pleasure? A research agenda for 'making gender stick' to engineers', *Science, Technology, & Human Values*, vol. 25, no. 1, pp. 87-119.

Faulkner, W. 2000b, 'Dualisms, hierarchies and gender in engineering', *Social Studies of Science*, vol. 30, no. 5, pp. 759-92.

Lagensen, V. forthcoming, 'The strength of numbers: Strategies to include women into computer science', *Social Studies of Science*.

McIlwee, J.S. & Robinson, J.G. 1992, *Women in Engineering*, SUNY Press, Albany, NY.

Mellström, U. 1995, *Engineering lives*, Technology & Social Change (Tema T), Linköping University, Linköping, Sweden.

Oldenziel, R. 1999. *Making technology masculine: Men, Women and Modern Machines in America, 1870-1945*, Amsterdam University Press, Amsterdam.

Tonso, K. 1997, 'Constructing engineers through practice', PhD thesis, University of Colorado at Boulder.

Tonso, K.L. 1999, 'Engineering gender – gendering engineering: A cultural model for belonging, *Journal of Women and Minorities in Science and Engineering*, vol. 5, no. 4, pp. 365-404.

Willoughby, L. 1999, *Changing the Curriculum - Changing the Balance?* Report of the EU Leonardo da Vinci programme Curriculum-Women-Technology project, Leeds Metropolitan University, Leeds.

Notes

1 An indication of the framing and research questions of the study can be found in Faulkner (2000a). I gratefully acknowledge the financial support of the Economic and Social Research Council for this study (ref: RES-000-23-0151). Thanks are also due to the many engineers who gave so generously of their time to share their experiences with me, and (in the case of those cited here) who agreed to their stories being published. In total some 50 engineers have been interviewed for this study, and observation was conducted in three engineering workplaces – one of them in software development. The interviews I draw on here were conducted in 2004; most took at least one hour and were taped.

2 Tonso's work is hugely important in this regard because, as an experienced engineer herself, she was able to follow interactions amongst engineers closely and identify when valuable contributions were not recognised.

3 I use the term heterogeneous in the sense coined by sociologists of technology: to convey the densely interwoven, 'seamless web' of social and technical elements in all technological artefacts and activities (Bijker, Hughes & Pinch 1987).

3 Bridging the Boardroom 'Divide'

A personal view

Lesley Ottery

Independent Consultant

After her degree Lesley Ottery trained as a computer programmer with the Ministry of Defence. She moved into IT management, initially with ICL, and then spent 14 years in the Electricity Supply Industry. Lesley was appointed IT Director for BNFL in 1992 and then Director of Information Services for British Gas in 1994. As Director of Business Services she ran all the internal services including HR before becoming Director of Business Development running the business transformation programmes including taking the company into the electricity market. During this time she established the Applications company AG Solutions. She moved to Switzerland in 2000 to join Sita, the airline telecoms & IT company, as Global CIO. She joined Fujitsu Consulting as European CIO before moving to the USA as Global CIO in 2002.

Abstract

During my thirty years at work it has always struck me as strange that there were so few women in senior management and executive positions in the companies I worked in and with. Certainly it did not reflect my perception of our abilities relative to our male colleagues. Was it the heavily male oriented industries that I worked in? After all, there are not many female power station managers or, for that matter, many women who would wish to take on that particular challenge. However, in IT companies this should not be the case. Was it that often discussed 'glass ceiling' or are women just not interested in reaching the top of the corporate tree?

As I moved through the management levels and entered the boardroom, female colleagues became more and more scarce. Where did they go? I have worked with many very talented women so why are we so poorly represented in the Boardroom? What impact, if any, is this having on women pursuing careers in IT?

At the conference I will offer my personal views on these questions illustrated by real examples from my own career and that of some of my female contemporaries. Also, I will reflect on how perceived, or real, gender bias can further impact us as we face the challenge of sustaining a career into our fifties.

4 Intelligent Ambience between Heaven and Hell: A Salvation?

Cecile K. M. Crutzen

Open University of the Netherlands

Cecile Crutzen is a senior lecturer at the Open University of the Netherlands in the School of Informatics specialising in 'People, Computers, Society'. She designs course material and e-learning environments for distance education in Informatics. Currently she is responsible for a virtual design room where students work in teams for the final part of their Bachelors courses. She is also preparing 'Ambient Intelligence' as a new topic for Masters courses. In her research, she investigates the relationship between computer science and gender studies with the aim of enriching informatics with a diversity of thinking and acting.

Abstract

Questioning gender is about taking an active, critical role in the technological design of our daily behaviour. It is a deconstruction of the oppositions that exist in the discourses of ambient intelligence designers, the ICT industry and computer scientists. What underlies the assumption that ambient intelligence will, by disappearing into our environment, bring humans both an easy and entertaining life? The gender perspective can uncover power relations within the promotion and realisation of Ambient Intelligence that satisfy an obvious wish for a technological heaven. The deconstruction of the promise of progress and a better life reveals what is overvalued, what is undervalued and what is ignored. This paper is a deconstruction of the view, currently prevalent in the discourses of Ambient Intelligence; a view of humans and the way they live. A view that will influence the way women and men will be allowed to construct their lives.

1. Introduction

Ambient intelligence sounds wonderful until one cannot turn on the television because one has not finished eating one's vegetables.[1]

Ambient intelligence (AmI) is a new buzzword from computer science. It is one of the key concepts being used to develop the information society aspects of the EU's 'Sixth RTD Framework programme'. With this theme industry, designers and scientists explore a vision of future daily life - a vision of humans being accompanied and surrounded by computerised devices, intelligent interfaces, wireless networking technology and software agents.

These technologies are planned to be embedded in everyday objects: mobile phones, cars, roads, furniture, doors, walls, household tools, animals, clothes and even food. Computing resources and computing services will be present anywhere and interconnected anytime. Ambient Intelligence research and development includes the older topics of 'Ubiquitous Computing' and 'Pervasive Computing'.

AmI as a 'crossover approach' is strongly related to a lot of computer science topics such as affective, mobile, situated, wearable, ensemble, invisible, context-aware, peripheral, smart, sentient and calm computing: embedded computers, attentive and knowledge-based user interfaces, personal technologies, interoperability and adaptability, multi modal communication protocols, real-time operation systems, remote sensing, robotics and multi-agent software. (Punie 2003, p.6; Schmidt 2004; Oulasvirta 2004)

The focus of AmI is to bring to life the everyday objects and tools of our daily environment. A comprehensive formula is given by Antti Oulasvirta and Antti Salovaara:

> ...This technology aims to provide services and control over processes, and support decision-making and other cognitive needs. Responsiveness and adaptation are based either on pre-programmed heuristics or real-time reasoning capabilities. (Oulasvirta & Salovarra 2004)

The purposes of this machine reasoning are:
- circumambient ways of monitoring the actions of humans and the changes in their environment using sensors of many types,
- using physical actors to react and pre-act in a way that is articulated as desirable and pleasant.

But the humans who are to live in this intelligent ambience are not asked for their views of what is 'desirable and pleasant'. For this technology it is the producers' and designers' visions of a better life that seem to dictate what will be provided.

2. The Short Term Future of AmI

A lot of ambient technology is already available, monitoring analogue physical processes, describing them with digital data and analysing this data using knowledge-based interpretation models. This technology is not new. Since the late 1970s in many farms the eating habits and milk yield of cattle have been monitored and engineered.

What is new is that now the public and the private environment of humans is permeated by an overwhelming amount of autonomous active devices, causing the inevitable employment of artificial intelligent agents to automate routine decisions and to provide against stupefying read and write collisions.

This penetration process has already started with remote recognition systems for facial expression, body tracking, and more (Turk 2004). With biometrics technology our hands, eyes, voices, faces, movements will be used to model and to control the way we live. (Boertien 2002; Jain 2004; Oviatt 2004) In the very near future humans will be overwhelmed by huge quantities of personalised real-time responses based on networking RFID tags.[2]

Related technologies for future ambient technology are smart materials for Multi-Application Smart Cards and wearable devices, MEMS[3] and sensor technology, embedded systems development technology, ubiquitous communication and I/O device related technology. For the reasoning part there is already much research and design devoted to adaptiveness and learning, media management and media handling, natural language interaction, and emotional sensitivity.

For the integration of all these components ISTAG[4] has identified three key layers:

- platform design,
- software and service architecture, design, engineering and integration,
- experience prototyping and simulation.

The integration and co-operation of several scientific disciplines within each of these layers is leading to open standards and interoperability, and to mastering the value chain from technology to exploitation. (IST Advisory Group 2003, pp. 14-16)

AmI implies a seamless environment of computing, advanced networking technology and specific (mainly remote and non tangible) computer interfaces for humans.[5] Many technological links for AmI are already available.

At the moment, the main effort is towards designing simple isolated appliances that might be acceptable to the consumers of this new technology. This prepares the ground for a complete infiltration of our environment with even more intelligent and interconnected devices. People should become familiar with AmI, slowly and unspectacularly, getting used to handing over the initiative to artificial devices. There is much sensing infrastructure already installed for handling security and road traffic. What remains to be done is to shift the domain of the intended monitoring just enough to feed the ongoing process of people getting used to these controls and forgetting the embarrassment of being permanently monitored, in other words – having no off-switch.

3. Questioning Gender

It is necessary to question gender in order to influence the process of AmI domestication, because of its impact on our daily live, especially on our routine activities and creative strategies. Gender and social aspects cannot be limited to only questioning the disappearance of the border between private and public, the changed meaning of 'home' or the promise of security as an alternative for the loss of privacy.

In the view of Judith Butler, questioning gender is a strategy that disrupts the obvious acting of every actor in worlds of interaction; designers, users and, especially in the case of AmI, the embedded routines of artificial devices:

> The abiding gendered self will then be shown to be structured by repeated acts that seek to approximate the ideal of a substantial ground of identity, but which in their occasional discontinuity, reveal the temporal and contingent groundlessness of this 'ground'. The possibilities of gender transformation are to be found precisely, in the

arbitrary relation between such acts, in the possibility of a failure to repeat, a deformity, or a parodic repetition that exposes the phantasmatic effect of abiding identity as a politically tenuous construction. (Butler 1990, p.141)

In every interaction world there is a continuity of ongoing weaving of a complex web of meanings in which we live, constructed by the interactions in that world. Gender is a web of meanings about women and men, masculinity and femininity, which is connected to other webs of dualistic values. Gender is a process[6] in which the meaning of masculinity and femininity are mutually constructed, situated at symbolic, individual and institutional levels of a domain. All social activities, practices and structures are influenced by gender. The meaning of gender is, and always will be, embedded in social, cultural and material constructions and is always dynamically linked to the meaning of many concepts such as technology or the constructed relationship between use and design. The performances of gender are mostly symbols or representations of power relations in a domain. A deconstruction[7] of the meaning of these kinds of power oppositions, such as the use-design opposition in AmI, reveals the gender aspect of the discourses of AmI and avoids the risk of reducing masculinity and femininity to fixed attributes based on biology and sex. AmI will influence the meaning of gender because AmI will be embedded in those daily environments in which specific gender meanings from the past are reinforced.

Questioning gender in AmI is asking: Could AmI be a technology that destabilises the fixed meaning of gender or will AmI stabilise the existing networks?

To take an active critical part in the technological design of our daily behaviour means to deconstruct meanings, especially the oppositions that can be found in the discourses of AmI designers and computer scientists, such as 'technical-human', 'secure-doubtful', 'invisible-chooseable'. A deconstruction could be the beginning of an articulation of the meaning of diversity in the discourses of AmI: diversity in use, in design and in the interaction between use and design. So the gender questions are: What has been overvalued, what has been undervalued and what has been ignored in the discourses that occur in the domain of AmI? Questioning gender is a way of uncovering the power relations within the promotion and realisation of AmI as something that could satisfy an obvious wish for a technological heaven. Analysing means the deconstruction of the progress and care pretensions related to this technology. The question is how can we see through the dazzling performances of smart and aesthetically designed objects, homes[8] and environments? How can we make scientists and designers take responsibility for not placing enough importance on privacy, cultural diversity and other ethical issues. Simply mentioning ethical issues at the end of a conference paper is an unacceptable substitute for failing to take on this responsibility.[9] It is a gender issue to ask what the price humans have to pay in the end by giving personal, including physical, data to facilitate the action of a surrounding technology. Is it still possible to resist and to distrust the overwhelming promises of a better life?

4. The Visions of Industry and Designers

The characteristics of AmI in many promotional publications are that smart objects will make our whole lives relaxing and enjoyable (Philips Research 2003). There are many attractive scenarios for the individual that represent a heaven on earth full of enjoyment: 'What will the future look like? Picture yourself relaxing at home on your couch. You're unwinding from a long day and want to play some music but you're too exhausted to move. Instead, you say 'Music where are you?' and hum your favorite slow tune. Luckily for you, your smart home entertainment system understands your needs. Not only does it play the song you were humming, it dims the lights to provide a more relaxing environment.'[10]

The gender question is urgent because industry claims that they apply female values and translate these into 'ease of use', 'experience of use', 'less complexity and more simplicity' (Manning 2002). This ease of use is based on the assumption that a perfect adaptability of the artificial devices for humans in their environments is possible and desirable. The costs of this adaptability are high – there will be continuous measurement and interpretation of our body data and body movement:

> One of the cornerstones of Ambient Intelligence is the adaptive behavior of systems in response to the user's mental or emotional state. In order to test the performance of such a system we obviously need to measure the physiological state of the user before and during the interaction with the system, especially if we also want to know if the user's state changes in the process. (Noldus 2003)

The AmI industry offers a service of 'personalisation': AmI is tailored to your needs and it can recognise you everywhere. As you move through an environment, AmI interfaces register your presence, self-initiatively perform tasks designed to make your life easier, and learn from your behaviour in order to anticipate your future needs. An ambient intelligent infrastructure 'will be aware of the specific characteristics of human presence and personality'. The promises of intelligent adaptability and anticipation are directed to the individual. AmI 'will be capable of meeting needs' and anticipating and responding intelligently to spoken or gestured wishes and desires without conscious mediation, and even these could result in systems that are capable of engaging in 'intelligent dialogue'. (Punie 2003, p.5)

In scenarios focused on the individual, human life is idealised and optimised (Punie 2003, p.6).[11] Social issues are only mentioned from an egocentric point of view (Punie 2003; IST Advisory Group 2001).

AmI designers see themselves as the creators of a better future; working along a straight line of civilising progress. They speak like heavenly fathers, creating a technological paradise, sensitive and responsive to people's vision of heaven on earth. They follow the ideal of creating devices which cause no disturbances and fit perfectly with their assumed expectations. They are convinced that digital environments, by acting on their behalf, can improve of people's quality of life.[12] 'Good' design is defined as making a product which will not create disharmony or doubt in the life of its users.

Their concept of 'usercentredness' is based on a notion of non-problematic interaction: '... which means technology that can think on its own and react to (or possibly even predict) individual needs so people don't have to work to use it'.[13] In such statements many subjective decisions on 'what is a better and easier life' are made. Having an 'easier life' is considered to be progress. An 'easy life', no time consuming distractions; no unnecessary disturbances are the qualities for that better life.[14]

This connection between technology and progress undervalues the subjectivity and situatedness of progress. It is very questionable as to whether or not human life will be better if artificial actors purposefully manipulate our behaviour and eventually gain control over it.

In many scenarios a 'better life' is visualised. These scenarios are extrapolations from the present, based on the designers' view of what should be better in their own lives. For industry and research these scenarios function as springboards for ideas about what kind of developments, technologies, society, economy, and markets are necessary to arrive at these scenarios. Describing scenarios is not an innocent activity. Incorporating the gender matrix of dualism is unavoidable because it is a repetition of actual beliefs. Scenarios are indicative and normative, they form the foundations of political decisions, which research topics will be financed and which not, which applications are developed and which not. So scenarios for a 'better life' for the prototype individual might become the standard way of living for everyone. In official EU scenarios 'Maria' and 'Dimitrios' (IST Advisory Group 2001)[15], who are both portrayed as very busy western people with almost no private life, the scenario-problem becomes evident.

The convergence of the designed domestication processes based on the assumption of a 'better life'[16] could become an apocalyptic trip of an automatic 'repression to normality', without the option of creative adventures or explorations. Why is it that in these scenarios it is only the advantages of AmI that are raised?

5. The Justification for AmI: Security and Care

One interpretation of the meaning of 'a better life' is 'taking away the worries' of a possibly unstable future. People are made vulnerable[17] and naked without an artificial skin of input and output devices. The world itself is already covered with an electronic skin

> ...that is already being stitched together. It consists of millions of embedded electronic measuring devices: thermostats, pressure gauges, pollution detectors, cameras, microphones, glucose sensors, EKGs, electroencephalographs. These will probe and monitor cities and endangered species, the atmosphere, our ships, highways and fleets of trucks, our conversations, our bodies – even our dreams. (Gross 1999)

Single-purpose AmI applications will be connected for continuous monitoring of the individual with the strong suggestion that this provides security and maintains health (Friedewald 2003)[18]:

> We trust less and we fear more. We will therefore be searching for reassurance and guarantees. Given this we will search for anything that helps us, nurtures us and keeps us safe. In other words we shall search for peace of mind. We will welcome tools that allow us to monitor the health of ourselves or our loved ones, that allow quick links with emergency services, or 'tag' our children so that we know where they are. In short how can our technologies look after us and our environments rather than us looking after our technology. (Philips Research 2003, p. 35)

Domestication of AmI will be forced by jumping on the bandwagon of some fundamental fears of the individual and society such as the present loss of security and safety because of terrorism, the necessary but unaffordable amount of care for the elderly (Braun 2004) and the sick, handling the complexity of combining professional and home work, difficulties in coping with the overwhelmingly obtrusive interactions and information of our society and being dependent on the gridlocked transport system. So-called 'Killer' applications are largely based on providing a bit more security and safety for the individual (Wahlster 2004).

Ambient Intelligence industries focus, too, on substitutes and prostheses for the human touch in the care of children, the elderly and the disabled: 'When daily contact is not feasible, the decision to move a senior is often driven by fear and uncertainty for his or her daily well-being. Our goal is to create a surrogate support system that resurrects this informal daily communication.' (Mynatt 2001, p.340)

Is it enough to outline health care scenarios 'to encompass societal, economic as well as technology developments and form a logical framework in which use cases can be fitted' with as goal 'managed care' in a health care system 'that uses organizational and management controls to offer patients appropriate care in cost-effective treatment settings'? (Riva 2003, p. 298) Can we counter-balance the risk of dehumanisation and depersonalisation by progressively disembodying patients, by reducing them to the sum of their biological and physiological functions and by identifying them with the collection of their vital parameters? (Gaggioli 2003, p. 84)

In particular, it is not enough to offer ordinary people, the consumers of the health industry, control only with an off-switch within their reach, with the argument that these technologies could very easily acquire the appearance of 'them controlling us'. Ambient Technology will no doubt control us, but in a situation where people are dependent on health care, for most of them a visible off-switch is not relevant. What is relevant is the availability of human-quality care as good as and as accessible as the intelligent prosthetic care.

So the development of AmI is and will be justified for several medical and ecological reasons and reasons of security. But these valid reasons should not lead us to shut our eyes to the ready-made abuse that could result from AmI.

6. The Deconstruction

In promoting the goodness and godliness of AmI, computer science and industry have not abandoned their overvaluation of objectivity, hierarchical structures and predetermined actions; values which ignore the beauty of ambiguity and spontaneous action and the claims for choosing and coupling our own support tools. They have only veiled it. Is AmI not a repetition of the old artificial intelligence (AI) dream of creating human-like machines? The differences between the human and the artificial are made invisible in many papers by speaking only of actors or agents and not making it clear if it is an artificial agent that is meant, or a human actor, or an embedded model of a human actor. Artificial agents are constructed and made to appear as if they have emotions and empathy.

It seems that in AmI the view of Heidegger has become reconstructed – that technology will enframe our world. People are made available as ready-made resources, reduced to cyber bodies producing data for input to the acting of artificial agents in their environment. A critical deconstruction should reveal the constitutional price we have to pay for this offer of an 'easy life', security, pleasure and support (Heidegger 1962, pp. 14-24).

6.1 Adaptability versus closeness

Within the discourse of AmI many mutually exclusive promises are made, justifying the future development of an ideal environment in which data about our bodies and our environment are used to create feelings of wellness; claiming that we will leave the period of one-sided adaptation by humans to the machine and move to a future in which machine action and human behaviour converge. Placing the user at the centre of AmI design contradicts the view that AmI technology should be mentally and physically invisible and unobtrusive, and should not require a steep learning curve (IST Advisory Group 2001, p.11). The overvaluation of 'design' by designers, industry and research has reduced 'design within use' to themes such as 'the adaptability of the technology' and 'the acceptance of these technologies by users'. The price of the promised adaptability of these intelligent devices is continuous measurement and interpretation of our body[19] data and movements:

> One of the cornerstones of Ambient Intelligence is the adaptive behavior of systems in response to the user's mental or emotional state. In order to test the performance of such a system we obviously need to measure the physiological state of the user before and during the interaction with the system, especially if we also want to know if the user's state changes in the process. (Noldus 2003)

This opening up of the private lives of AmI users is accompanied by closing off more and more opportunities for users to adjust AmI devices to protect themselves from unwanted actions. The price will be that the users will be limited in the options available to them to articulate their wishes.

6.2 Subject-object relations

A necessary condition for the realisation of AmI environments is not only monitoring in circumambient ways the actions of humans and the changes in their visible and invisible environment, AmI is also a pattern of models of chains of interaction embedded in things. Objects in our daily world – mostly inanimate – will be enriched by an intelligence that will make them almost 'subjects', capable of responding to stimuli from the world around them and even of anticipating the stimuli. In the AmI world the 'relationship' between us and the technology around us is no longer one of a user towards a machine or tool, but of a person towards an 'object-became-subject', something that is capable of reacting and of being educated.[20] Everyday objects such as doors, tables, books, lights or even the flow of air and water are transformed into computational interfaces (Ishii 1998). It is a future of artificial actors 'whispering' in the background of human life and awareness, interacting with each other and their environment. People become the objects of the ongoing 'conversations'.

People are in danger of losing within the activity of use the activity of 'design'.[21] In AmI the symbolic meaning of use and design is reconstructed as an opposition in which 'design' is active and virtuous and 'use' is passive and not creative. This dominance of design discloses and largely prevents the act of discovery of the users by the designer and acts of discovery on the part of the users. Design is focused on generalised and classified users. Users are turned into resources, which can be used by designers in the process of making ICT-products. They do not have sufficient room for starting their own design processes. Those who do not fit into regimented classes are seen as dissidents. In AmI, designers are creating an artificial play in which they have given the active and leading role to the artificial subjects. Users are ready-made sources of data for the technology in their environment. By interpreting 'usercentredness' in this way, the active explicit participation aspect is lost. As we can see in this architectural concept of AmI of Piva et al., the user is reduced to an observable object placed in a feedback loop that, in the opinion of the designers, converges to an optimal intelligent environment with an action/communication oriented smart space function in order to influence the user (Piva et al. 2005).

AmI reinforces the design and use dualism because the design of ambient intelligence is such that the use will be fixed to prevent in the interaction between artificial devices unpredictable conflicts of values and not solvable situations. Too much of such events will diminish the claim of ease of use. On the other hand, too much obvious acting on the part of artificial devices will make the lives of users dull and predictable. Travelling like 'Maria'[22] makes a stay abroad in a foreign culture like a stay in your own hometown. The individual is seen as cocooned in a womb of sensors, protecting them from unexpected dangers. Or they are seen as travelling, equipped with a wearable technical home shell, suppressing feelings of homesickness and hiding the AmI user's alienation from the ambivalence of the community.

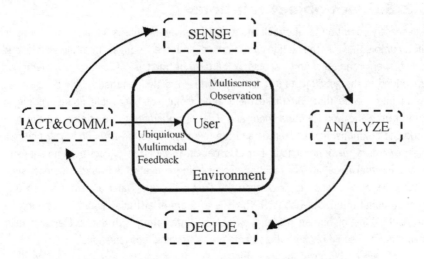

Fig. 1: User-centred ambient intelligence closed loop (Piva, 2005, pp 65-66)

6.3 Mental invisibility versus physical invisibility

In the vision of industrial designers AmI is embedded; many invisible distributed devices are hidden in the environment. A continuous process of miniaturisation of mechatronic systems and components will make this possible. Physical invisibility or perceptual invisibility mean that one cannot sense (smell, see, hear or touch) the AmI devices anymore; one cannot sense their presence nor sense their full (inter-)action, but only that part of interaction output that was intended to change the environment of the individual user. Many (inter-)actions between artificial devices will take place in the background of the life of the individual. According to Schmidt, our relationship to computer systems will change from 'explicit interaction that requires always a kind of dialog between the user and a particular system or computer, ...to implicit interaction'. (Schmidt 2004, p.162, p166)

The physical disappearance of AmI from our environment means that the whole environment surrounding the individual has the potential to function as an interface. Our body representations and the changes the individual will make in the environment, could be unconsciously the cause of actions and interactions between the AmI devices. This physical invisibility is a technological design statement. The hiding of AmI in daily aesthetic beautiful objects or in the infrastructure is like the wolf in sheep's clothing, pretending that this technology is harmless. Although 'not seeing this technology' could be counterproductive, it is suspicious that computing is largely at the periphery of our attention and only in critical situations should come to our attention. Who will decide how critical a situation is and who is then given the power to decide to make the computing visible again? Providing selective perceptivity to consumers could be counterproductive for the acceptance of AmI. Making technologies disappear, while assuming that this will reduce the tension for users could, on the contrary, make acceptance insoluble (Punie 2003, pp.40-41). Peterson thinks that the technology should reveal at least what the system has to offer in order to motivate users to relate the possibilities of the technology to their actual needs, dreams and wishes. 'For this purpose, domestic technologies should be remarkable rather than unremarkable' (Petersen 2004, p. 1446).

Visible ICT devices embed software objects, such as the implemented models of interaction, the user profiles, and the hierarchical and conditional procedures, which are always invisible. It is through the interface we sometimes can get a glimpse of these software objects. A glimpse indeed mostly decoded in metaphors. These metaphors are bridges for designing interaction by the users. A good metaphoric interface enables users to influence the actions of the ICT device without reading the software. It pretends that the user can steer and predict the actions of the ICT device. But the failure to build user-initiated interfaces of high quality so far, has led in most AmI projects to the bizarre conclusion that the software should be so intelligent that it can predict the user's intentions.

6.4 The meaning of invisibility: undervaluation and overvaluation of design

The goal of AmI is to produce an active and effective technology, mentally and physically invisible, integrated into our daily environment and routines. In and around the discourses and the implementations of AmI there are several meanings of the word 'invisibility'. There is a stubborn misunderstanding about physical and mental invisibility. The assumption that physical invisibility will lead to mental invisibility is wrong. So long as a tool is physically invisible, the process of mental invisibility cannot start. We could get used to the effects of the tool but the moment the tool acts outside the range of our expectations, it will only frighten us because we cannot control it.

According to Punie, mental invisibility could be one of the outcomes of a domestication process, which is not

... necessarily harmonious, linear or complete. Rather it is presented as a struggle between the user and technology, where the user tries to tame, gain control, shape or ascribes meaning to the technological artefact. This is not resistance to a specific technology but rather an active acceptance process. (Punie 2003, pp. 40-41)

Physical invisibility is contradictory to mental invisibility because the process of domestication is not a process initiated by the user. In our daily life a lot of things and tools become mentally invisible. Because of their evident and continuous presence they disappear from our environment. A door is mentally invisible when we open it as a matter of routine. But the moment we cannot open it, the door becomes very present in the action of trying to leave or enter the room. Most routine activity with ICT-tools such as word-processing can be classified as obvious and therefore mentally invisible. Dewey has called these unreflective responses and actions 'fixed habits', 'routines': 'They have a fixed hold upon us, instead of our having a free hold upon things. ... Habits are reduced to routine ways of acting, or degenerate into ways of action to which we are enslaved just in the degree in which intelligence is disconnected from them. ... Such routines put an end to the flexibility of acting of the individual.' (Dewey 1916, chapter 4: Education as Growth) Routines are repeated and established acting; frozen habits which are executed without thinking. Routine acting with an ICT-tool means intractability; the tool is not present anymore. The mutual interaction between the tool and the user is lost.

The claim of mental invisibility by AmI is that AmI will be settled in our fixed routines. Marc Weiser was one of the first who focused on this characterisation of computer technology: 'The most profound technologies are those that disappear. They weave themselves into the fabric of everyday life until they are indistinguishable from it.' (Weiser 1991) Mental invisibility is seen as a precondition for acceptance; the stabilisation of use and the domestication of AmI technology.

Mental invisibility can only be the outcome of an integration process on the part of human actors. Things, tools and technologies can become obvious. Humans use them without thinking in their routine acting. But this is only one way of dealing with technology. Not all our acting is routine acting. Using an ICT-product is negotiating, not only about its content, but also about what actions of the ICT-product are suitable for the actor's situation. In my opinion translations and replacements of ICT-representations must not fit smoothly without conflict into the world for which they are made ready. A closed readiness is an ideal which is not feasible, because in the interaction situation the acting itself is ad-hoc and therefore unpredictable. The ready-made behaviour and the content of ICT-representations should then be differentiated and changeable to enable users to make ICT-representations ready and reliable for their own spontaneous and creative use.

6.5 Mental invisibility versus doubt

A closer look at the relationship humans have constructed with their environment, how humans experience the things and tools in their environment, is necessary to analyse the influence of AmI. Actions and interactions always cause changes, but not all activities of actors are 'present' in interaction worlds. If changes are comparable and compatible with previous changes, they will be perceived as obvious and taken for granted. The change from a closed door to an open door normally is mentally invisible. Opening and closing the door is in most situations an unreflective act. The door is 'ready-to-hand' and subordinate to the action for which it is used: entering or leaving a room. These ready-to-hand interactions will not raise any doubts.

Doubt is a necessary precondition for changing the pattern of interaction itself. Heidegger gives several examples of how doubt can appear and obvious tools will be 'present-at-hand' again: when a tool does not function as I expect, when the tool I am used to is not available, and when the tool is getting in the way of reaching the intended goal. In this last case the tool is obstinate. In special situations, e.g. in urgent need of fresh air, – doubt arises as to how to act – and all doors and windows nearby pop up into mental visibility.[23]

According to Heidegger, the 'present-at-handness' (*Vorhandenes*) and the 'ready-to-handness' (*Zuhandenes*) of a tool are situated and they do not exclude each other. On the contrary, they offer the option of intertwining use and design activities in interaction with the tool itself. This intertwining makes a tool reliable, because it is always individual and situated.[24] According to Dourish, this can happen only through involved, embodied interaction. Intertwining of use and design needs the presence-at-hand of the ICT-representations (Dourish 2001, p. 125). Their readiness-to-hand should be doubtable.

With AmI we are in danger of losing this 'critical transformative room' (Crutzen 2003). In our interaction with the AmI environment there is no room for doubt between representation and interpretation of the ready-made interactions with our environment. The act of doubting is a bridge between the obvious acting and possible changes to our habitual acting. Actors and representations are only present in an interaction if they are willing and have the potential to create doubt and if they can create a disrupting moment in the interaction. In the view of Dewey, doubting is critical thinking: 'Thinking, on the contrary, starts, ..., from doubt or uncertainty. It marks an inquiring, hunting, searching attitude, instead of one of mastery and possession. Through its critical process true knowledge is revised and extended, and our convictions as to the state of things reorganized.' (Dewey 1916, Chapter 22: The Individual and the World)

According to Weiser and many of his successors, we should live in an AmI infrastructure without thinking about it. 'Hundreds of computers in a room could seem intimidating at first, just as hundreds of volts coursing through wires in the walls once did. But like the wires in the walls, these hundreds of computers will come to be invisible to common awareness. People will simply use them unconsciously to accomplish everyday tasks.' (Weiser 1991) However, is it justifiable to compare AmI devices with the infrastructure of electric power?

The traffic infrastructure has changed our vision of distance and flexibility. In spite of technical provisions and laws, many people are killed and injured daily and much psychological and material damage occurs – but this has become mentally invisible in society. People still think that we are free to choose our means of transport. Doubting the traffic infrastructure is not politically correct.

Will we be able to create actions of questioning and doubting in our future relationship with AmI? In simulating a perfect guardian angel we can arrive in a hell in which humans are punished when trying to change their routines, when not acting like the implemented simplistic models of human behaviour or when not fitting statistical normality. It is crucial how the AmI industry will provide within interaction with their products the facility to create for ourselves critical transformative rooms, and that AmI is 'intelligent' enough to cope with this type of user-initiated 'change of change'.

To enable doubt is a delicate action. Doubt should not lead to desperation. Continuous doubting will lead to 'obstinate' tools that will become an obstacle to mutual actability. Because of the developers' incompetence, instead of implementing proper doubt management into ICT-products, the room for mutual actability has become smaller and smaller during the last decades and user interaction was fenced in between forced routine and despair. AmI tends to shrink this room to an off-switch at least. But will not the option to use this switch be ruled out by the very infiltration of AmI in our daily environment? And if we remain competent to control our home lives, who will be in control of the AmI intelligence in public spaces? Who will have the power to switch that button?

7. Conclusion of the Deconstruction: Critical Transformative Rooms

What we want, what is possible, what is makable, comes more and more closer to each other. If these three melt, it let us be just as powerful as god. Modern people say: 'I want' and always more often it happens. If one wants something in former days, one had to sit down and work for it. That time is beyond. If modern people come home, they expect to be able to see in their dark house. The finger touches the light button, and there is light. The inclusion of that buttons and keys in our world makes believe that we all are wizards. [26]

In the future AmI things and AmI tools will be unavoidable. Western hightech society is developing into a world inhabited by cyborgs. However, can humans in AmI environments still act as cyborgs in the sense of Haraway, living in a symbiotic relationship with the machines, staying responsible for them by '... embracing the skilful task of reconstructing the boundaries of daily life', by '... building and destroying machines, identities, categories, relationships, space stories ...'? (Haraway 1991, p.180-181)

Can the cyborg image construct a way out of the maze of dualisms or should instead the cyborg be interpreted as an actor in the middle of these dualisms, creating critical transformative rooms; places in which, by questioning the performance of gender, the underlying ontological and epistemological assumptions of the actors (industry, designers, users) in the domain of AmI could be analysed? Is there still time to escape from the powerful push of the industry to introduce this all-enveloping server-technology? Is it still possible to claim for technology that is to be used under human conditions, where things that are technically possible are no longer necessarily seen as progress? Perhaps Haraway was right in her claim to be a cyborg rather than a goddess, because the technological heaven is an illusion.

In the process of a critical domestication of AmI technology, acting within the AmI-induced dualisms users should feel not only the comfort of being permanently cared for, but also the pain of giving away intimacy. We should feel that danger, but in feeling it should not be clueless. The critical transformative room that stands between the consumer and AmI should include a diversity of options to influence the behaviour, use and design of the technology. The off-switch is only one end of a rich spectrum of intervention tools. According to the experience of Rudolph: 'ubiquitous or pervasive applications are very fragile and any design paradigm must include ways in which the average user can fix problems'[27], designers and researchers feel this pain, too, but they compensate for this by the hard to beat satisfaction of building this technology. The core of their attraction to this lies in 'I can make it', 'It is possible' and 'It works'. It is the technically possible and makeable that always gets the upper hand. Who wants to belong to the non-designers? (Sloterdijk 2001, p. 375)

Acts of doubt in a critical consumer's approach are necessary. They need to envision several paradigms and critical strategies, concepts and realisations. According to a suggestion of Sloterdijk, 'immune systems' will become an important topic in a world in which integrity can no longer be thought of as something being given to enable worshipping a merciful surrounding, but only as the effort of an organism, taking care to separate it from its environment. Life preserves its existence, not primarily by participating in its environment, but stabilises itself even more by excluding and selectively refusing co-operation. Sloterdijk speaks about a technology driven by the 'self domestication of humans' (Sloterdijk 2002, pp. 109-110) and, according to Frank Mewes, this is not necessarily a bad thing:

> But ICT is definitely not the empowerment of mankind that it is often taken for. On the contrary, taken as an anthropotechnology it is restrictive. Even today the active badges and self writing appointment diaries that offer all kinds of convenience could be a source of real harm in the wrong hands. Not only corporate superiors or underlings but also overzealous government officials and even marketing firms could make unpleasant use of the same information that makes invisible computers so convenient. (Mewes 2002)

A model for 'informational immune spaces' with two-sided conditional borders is the 'bubbles' concept of Laurent Beslay and Hannu Hakala; this facilitates the management of an appropriate informational distance from other humans and from non-human AmI actors. 'A bubble is a temporary defined space that can be used to limit the information coming into and leaving the bubble in the digital domain. ... A bubble can be created whenever it is necessary for personal, community or global use. The bubbles can be shared between individuals or groups.' According to Beslay and Hakala, this model should be integrated with the identification tags model (Beslay & Hakala 2005).

From the viewpoint of Sloterdijk's philosophical tetralogy 'Spheres', the bubbles concept is a chance for survival of the diversity of the human individual. But it could destroy our 'being-in-the-world' (*Dasein*) as 'being-together-with-others' too. (Heidegger

1926, §63) Bubbles could be seen as safe places to share views and experiences, but the boundaries of bubbles will easily lead to marginalisation and isolation too. Technical devices such as location-based services, radio frequency identification tags, body implants, ambient intelligence sensors cannot be confidential agents that will build and maintain the bubble-leaks between the individual and other actors, between the digital and the physical world (Beslay & Hakala 2005). A bubble approach is only feasible if access to bubbles and acting in bubbles can be determined by the bubble owner, whether an individual or an organisation.

A promising architectural approach is the concept of a 'gadget world'. People configure use and aggregate complex collections of interacting artefacts. The everyday environment is a collection of objects with which people can associate in ad-hoc dynamic ways. In this approach more complex artefact behaviour can emerge from interactions among more elementary artefacts. According to Irene Mavrommati this approach can scale both 'upwards' (towards the assembly of more complex objects, i.e. from objects to rooms, up to buildings, cities and so on) and 'downwards' (towards the decomposition of given gadgets into smaller parts, i.e. towards the concept of 'smart dust'). In taking this approach people are active shapers of their environment, not simple consumers of technology. (Mavrommati 2002) Albrecht Schmidt argues for an AmI interaction model in which users can always choose between implicit and explicit interfacing: 'The human actor should know ... why the system has reacted as it reacted' (Schmidt 2004).

Should humans, as Heidegger proposed, take a detached stance to AmI, letting the technology 'turn itself'? (Heidegger 1962, p. 41) Technology will bring the essence of its connection to people into the open. Approaching the danger will lead us to doubts and perhaps changes such as preparations for life-saving and opening up to design. Heidegger recommended that these reflections take place in art[28] because of its cognisance with technology and also the very deep differences with it (Heidegger 1962, p. 35). Experiments with interactive art in responsive environments can reveal the indeterminacy of audience participation[29]. 'Untitled events' that have taken place in the Black Mountain College, and initiated by John Cage, have emphasised the performativity of artefacts by presenting them as ready-made acting possibilities. Creating such opportunities gives room for a diversity of construction of meaning in the acting itself (Cage 1966). Especially places where women, art and technology come together could function as critical transformative rooms for AmI. According to Zoë Sofia, contemporary women technological artists are successful 'in shaping alternative futures that do not simply intensify the powers of the already strong but enlarge the influence of the values and interests of those not satisfied by the pursuit of the new as a good – or even a god – in itself.' (Zoë 2003, p. 518)

We need ICT-bubbles to protect us from being overwhelmed by the growing complexity of our technologically advanced lifestyle. A cluster of AmI companies offer us for the near future a new life-infrastructure as a salvation. This infrastructure will emulate our bodies and emotions very closely. The deconstruction of their current AmI development projects reveal: their ICT-bubbles will be governed from the outside and thus they will turn into a matrix of golden ICT-cages. Sloterdijk names this 'the domestication of the human' (Sloterdijk 1999). But there are independent approaches to building ICT-bubbles which can be ruled from the inside. These approaches will be our salvation from the threat of AmI, to make our lives happier. Or will we be travelling the cyborg road between heaven and hell instead?

Having a body in ambient intelligence environments will reconstruct the gender matrix of dualisms and show it to us in new guises. Questioning gender could reveal the old paternalistic assumptions and could suggest how we can take a design position ourselves in order to disrupt the AmI discourses – although we have to take that position between heaven and hell.

References

Becker, Barbara & Eckel, Gerhard 1994, 'On the Relationship between Art and Technology in Contemporary Music', http://viswiz.gmd.de/~eckel/publications/becker94c.html [2 April 2005]

Beslay, Laurent & Hakala, Hannu 2005, 'Digital Territory: Bubbles', to be published in the Vision Book 2005 http://europa.eu.int/information_society/topics/research/visionbook/index_en.htm http://cybersecurity.jrc.es/docs/DigitalTerritoryBubbles.pdf [28 Sept 2004]

Boertien, Nicky & Middelkoop, Eric 2002, 'Authentication in mobile applications' https://doc.telin.nl/dscgi/ds.py/Get/File-23314/VH_authenticatie.pdf [1 June 2004]

Bohn Jürgen, Coroama Vlad, Langheinrich Marc, Mattern Friedemann & Rohs Michael 2002a, 'Social, Economic, and Ethical Implications of Ambient Intelligence and Ubiquitous Computing', http://interval.hu-berlin.de/deutsch/rfid/kernprobleme_Security/socialambient_mattern.pdf [2 April 2005]

Bohn Jürgen, Coroama Vlad, Langheinrich Marc, Mattern Friedemann, Rohs Michael 2002b, 'Living in a World of Smart Everyday Objects - Social, Economic, and Ethical Implications',http://www.vs.inf.ethz.ch/publ/papers/hera.pdf [2 April 2005]

Braidotti, Rosi 1996, 'Cyberfeminism with a difference', http://www.let.ruu.nl/womens_studies/rosi/cyberfem.htm [2 April 2005]

Braun Anette, Constantelou Anastasia, Karounou Vasilik, Ligtvoet Andreas, Burgelman Jean-Claude, Cabrera Marcelino 2004, 'E-health in the Context of a European Ageing society', http://esto.jrc.es/detailshort.cfm?ID_report=1207 [30 December 2004]

Brunick, E. 1995/1996, Introduction to Linguistics and Critical Theory, http://tortie.me.uiuc.edu/~coil/contents.html [13 October 1999]

Butler, Judith 1990, *Gender trouble: Feminism and the subversion of identity*, Routledge, New York.

Cage, John 1966, 'Diary: Audience 1966'. Republished in *Multimedia from Wagner To Virtual Reality*, (eds) Packer, Randall & Jordan, Ken 2001, Norton & Company, New York, pp. 91-94.

Cantoni Rejani 2004, 'Bodyarchitecture: the Evolution of Interface towards Ambient Intelligence', in (Riva 2004) part 3, chap. 11, pp. 213-219, http://www.vepsy.com/communication/book5/11_AMI_Cantoni.pdf [2 April 2005]

Crutzen, C.K.M. 2000, Interactie, een wereld van verschillen, Een visie op informatica vanuit genderstudies, Dissertatie, Open Universiteit Nederland, Heerlen.

Crutzen, C.K.M. 2003, 'ICT-Representations as Transformative Critical Rooms', in *Agents of Change: Virtuality, Gender, and the Challenge to the Traditional University*, (eds) Kreutzner, G., Schelhowe, H., Leske+Budrich, Opladen, pp. 87-106.

Culler, Jonathan 1983, *On Deconstruction:Theory and Criticism after Structuralism*, Routledge and Kegan, London.

Dewey, John 1916, *Democracy and Education*, The Macmillan Company, used edition: ILT Digital Classics 1994, http://www.ilt.columbia.edu/publications/dewey.html [2 April 2005]

Dewey, John 1917, *Essays in Experimental Logic*, The University of Chicago Press, used edition Ratner 1939.

Dourish, Paul 1999, 'Embodied Interaction: Exploring the Foundations of a New Approach' http://www.dourish.com/embodied/embodied99.pdf [2 April 2005]

Dourish, Paul 2001, *Where the Action is,* The MIT Press, Cambridge.

Friedewald Michael & Costa, Olivier Da 2003, 'Science and Technology Roadmapping: Ambient Intelligence in Everyday Life (AmI@Life)' esto.jrc.es/docs/AmIReportFinal.pdf

Gaggioli Andrea, Vettorello Marco & Giuseppe Riva 2003, 'From Cyborgs to Cyberbodies: The Evolution of the Concept of Techno-Body in Modern Medicine', *Psychology Journal*, vol. 1, no 2, pp. 75-86, http://www.psychnology.org/article201.htm [2 April 2005]

Giráldez Marcelino Cabrera & Casal Carlos Rodríguez 2004, 'The role of Ambient Intelligence in the Social Integration of the Elderly', in Riva, 2004, part 4, chap. 14, pp. 267- 282.

Gross, Neil 1999, 'The Earth Will Don an Electronic Skin', Business Week Aug 30, 1999 http://www.businessweek.com/1999/99_35/b3644024.htm [2 April 2005]

Haraway, Donna J. 1991, 'A Cyborg Manifesto: Science, Technology and Social-Feminism in the late Twentieth Century', in Haraway, Donna J. 1991, *Simians, Cyborgs, and Women. The Reinvention of Nature*, Free Association Books, London.

Heidegger, Martin 1926, *Sein und Zeit*, used edition Heidegger, Martin, *Sein und Zeit*, Tübingen, Niemeyer , 17. Auflage, 1993.

Heidegger, Martin 1936, *Der Ursprung des Kunstwerkes*, used edition 1960, Philipp Reclam jun, Stuttgart.

Heidegger, Martin 1962, 'Die Technik und die Kehre', Verlag Günther Neske, Stuttgart.

Ishii F. I. Hiroshi a.o 1998, 'ambientROOM: Integrating Ambient Media with Architectural Space', in CHI-98, p. 18-23 April 1998, ACM ISBN I-581 13-028-7

IST Advisory Group 2001, 'Scenarios for Ambient Intelligence in 2010', edited by K. Ducatel, M. Bogdanowicz, F. Scapolo, J. Leijten & J-C Burgelman, IPTS-ISTAG, EC: Luxembourg, ftp://ftp.cordis.lu/pub/ist/docs/istagscenarios2010.pdf [2 April 2005]

IST Advisory Group 2002, 'IST Advisory Group - Trust, Dependability, Security and Privacy for IST in FP6' ftp://ftp.cordis.lu/pub/ist/docs/istag-security-wg61final0702.pdf [2 April 2005]

IST Advisory Group 2003, 'Ambient Intelligence: from vision to reality (For participation - in society & business)', pp. 14-16, http://www.ideo.co.uk/DTI/Catal-IST/istag-ist2003_draft_consolidated_report.pdf [2 April 2005]

Jain, Anil K./Ross, Arun 2004, 'Multibiometric Systems', *Communications of the ACM*, vol. 47, no. 1, pp. 34-44.

Krueger, Myron 1977, 'Responsive Environments', republished in Randall Packer & Ken Jordan (eds), *Multimedia from Wagner to Virtual Reality*, Norton & Company, New York, pp. 104-120.

Levinas, Emmanuel 1996, Martin Heidegger and Ontology, Diacritics 26.1, pp. 11-32
http://www.press.jhu.edu/journals/diacritics/v026/26.1levinas.html [19 November 1999]

Loenen, Evert J. van 2003, 'On the role of Graspable Objects in the Ambient Intelligence
Paradigm' in Proceedings Smart Objects Conference 2003,
http://www.grenoblesoc.com/proceedings03/Pdf/Van%20Loenen.pdf [2 April 2005]

Manning Andre 2002, 'Research into women's impact on technology' in Philips News 2002
http://www.newscenter.philips.com/about/news/section-13488/article-2235.html [2 April
2005]

Mavrommati, Irene 2002, e-Gadgets case description, in Doors of Perception 7: Flow
http://flow.doorsofperception.com/content/mavrommati_trans.html [2 April 2005]

McGinity, Meg 2004, 'RFID: is this game of tag fair play?' Communications of the ACM, vol. 47,
no. 1, pp. 15-18.

Mewes Frank, 2002, Regulations for the Human Park: On Peter Sloterdijk's Regeln für den
Menschenpark, in Gnosis, vol. VI, no. 1, September 2002.
http://artsandscience.concordia.ca/philosophy/gnosis/vol_vi/Sloterdijk.pdf [2 April 2005]

Mynatt, E. D., Rowan, J., Craighill, S. & Jacobs, A. 2001, 'Digital family portraits: Providing
peace of mind for extended family members', in Proceedings of the ACM Conference on
Human Factors in Computing Systems (CHI 2001), Seattle, Washington: ACM Press, pp.
333-340 http://www.cc.gatech.edu/fce/ecl/projects/dfp/pubs/dfp-chi2001.pdf [2 April 2005]

Noldus, Lucas 2003, 'HomeLab as a Scientific Measurement and Analysis Instrument', in
Philips Research 2003, pp. 27-29.

Oulasvirta, Antti & Salovaara, Antti, 2004, 'A Cognitive Meta-Analysis of Design Approaches to
Interruptions in Intelligent Environments', in CHI 2004, April 24-29, 2004, Vienna, Austria,
Late Breaking Results Paper, pp. 1155-1158.

Oviatt Sharon, Darrell Trevor & Flickner Myron (eds) 2004, 'Multimodal interfaces that flex,
adapt, and persist', Communications of the ACM, vol. 47, no. 1, pp. 30-33.

Petersen Marianne Graves 2004, 'Remarkable Computing - the Challenge of Designing for the
Home', CHI 2004, April 24-29, Vienna, Austria, pp. 1445-1448.

Philips Research 2003, '365 days - Ambient Intelligence research in HomeLab',
www.research.philips.com/technologies/misc/homelab/downloads/homelab_365.pdf [2 April
2005]

Piva, S., Singh, R., Gandetto M. & Regazzoni C.S. 2005, 'A Context- based Ambient Intelligence
Architecture', in Remagnino et al., 2005, pp. 63 – 87.

Punie, Yves 2003, 'A social and technological view of Ambient Intelligence in Everyday Life:
What bends the trend?', Key Deliverable, The European Media and Technology in Everyday
Life Network, 2000-2003, Institute for Prospective Technological Studies Directorate General
Joint Research Centre European Commission,
http://www.lse.ac.uk/collections/EMTEL/reports/punie_2003_emtel.pdf [2 April 2005]

Raisinghani Mahesh S. 2004, 'Ambient Intelligence: Changing Forms of Human-Computer
Interaction and Their Social Implications', in Journal of Digital Information, vol. 5, no. 4,
Article No. 271, 2004-08-24 http://jodi.ecs.soton.ac.uk/Articles/v05/i04/Raisinghani/ [2 April
2005]

Ratner Joseph (ed.) 1939, Intelligence in the Modern World, John Dewey's Philosophy, with an
introduction by Joseph Ratner, Random House, New York.

Remagnino Paola, Foresti Gian Luca & Ellis Tim (eds) 2005, Ambient Intelligence: A Novel
Paradigm, Springer, New York.

Riva Guiseppe 2003, 'Ambient Intelligence in Health Care', *Cyberpsychology & Behavior*, vol. 6, no. 3,

http://labstudenti.unicatt.it/doo/autori/Username%20n.%2007/p295_s.pdf, pp.295-300 [2 April 2005]

Riva G., Vatalaro F., Davide F. & Alcañiz M. (eds) 2004, 'Ambient Intelligence', IOS Press, 2004, http://www.emergingcommunication.com/volume6.html [2 April 2005]

Sloterdijk, Peter 1999, *Regeln fur den Menschenpark*, Frankfurt: Suhrkamp Verlag

Sloterdijk, Peter 2001, Kränkung durch Maschinen, in Peter Sloterdijk 2001, *Nicht gerettet, Versuche nach Heidegger*, Suhrkamp Verlag, Frankfurt am Main, pp. 338-366.

Sloterdijk, Peter 2002, *Luftbeben. An den Quellen des Terrors*, Suhrkamp Verlag, Frankfurt am Main.

Schmidt, Albrecht 2004, 'Interactive Context-Aware Systems Interacting with Ambient Intelligence', in Riva et al. 2004, part 3, chap. 9, pp. 159-178.

Smalley, Eric 2004, 'Rules aim to get devices talking', TRN Magazine http://www.trnmag.com/Stories/2004/060204/Rules_aim_to_get_devices_talking_060204.html [2 April 2005]

Svanæs, Dag 1999, 'Understanding Interactivity, Steps to a Phenomenology of Human-Computer Interaction', http://www.idi.ntnu.no/~dags/interactivity.pdf [2 April 2005]

Turk, Matthew 2004, 'Computer vision in the interface', *Communications of the ACM*, vol. 47, no. 1, pp. 60-67.

Wahlster, Wolfgang et al. 2004, 'Grand Challenges in the Evolution of the Information Society' ftp://ftp.cordis.lu/pub/ist/docs/istag_draft_report_grand_challenges_wahlster_06_07_04.pdf [2 April 2005]

Weiser, Marc 1991, 'The Computer for the 21st Century', in: *Scientific American*, vol. 265, no. 3, September 1991, pp. 94-104, reprinted in IEEE: *Pervasive Computing*, January-March 2002, pp.19-25 http://www.ubiq.com/hypertext/weiser/SciAmDraft3.html [2 April 2005]

Zoë, Sofia 2003, 'Contested Zones: Futurity and Technological Art', in *Women, Art and Technology*, Judy Malloy (ed.), The MIT Press, Cambridge Massachusetts, pp. 502-522.

Notes

1 A quotation from Larry Rudolph (Smalley 2004).

2 RFID (radio frequency identification): A generic term for technologies that use radio waves to remotely identify people or objects carrying reactive tags. See e.g. http://www.rfidjournal.com/article/articleview/207 [2 April 2005] or (McGinity 2004).

3 For more information Micro-Electro-Mechanical Systems (MEMS) see http://www.memsnet.org/mems/what-is.html [2 April 2005]

4 Information Society Technology Advisory Group. ISTAG has been set up to advise the European Commission on the overall strategy to be followed in carrying out the IST thematic priority and related activities of research as well as on the orientations with respect to the European Research Area by helping to stimulate the corresponding European research communities. http://www.cordis.lu/ist/istag.htm [2 April 2005]

5 Named 'implicit HCI' in Schmidt (2004, p.164).

6 Judith Butler sees gender as a daily performance of each individual: *'Gender ought not to be constructed as a stable identity or locus of agency from which various acts follow; rather, gender is an identity tenuously constituted in time, instituted in exterior space through a*

stylized repetition of acts.' (Butler 1990, p. 140).

7   On deconstruction see e.g. (Culler 1983 p. 155, pp. 213-215, p. 228; Crutzen 2000)

8   For an overview on smart homes see under topic 'Smart Rooms, Smart Houses & Household Appliances' of the American Association for Artificial Intelligence (AAAI) http://www.aaai.org/AITopics/html/rooms.html [2 April 2005]

9   This is mostly the case in publications in which the technological realisations are highlighted. For instance, in (Riva 2004) ethical and social aspects have a prominent place. See also for social implications: (Raisinghani 2004; Bohn 2002a, 2002b; IST Advisory Group 2002)

10 Philips Research - HomeLab http://www.research.philips.com/technologies/misc/homelab/index.html [2 April 2005]

11 For a critique of scenarios see also: (Giráldez 2004, p. 274)

12 The Ambience project: http://www.extra.research.philips.com/euprojects/ambience/ [2 April 2005]

13 Philips Sustainability Report (2002), www.philips.com/Assets/Downloadablefile/sustainability-2153.pdf [2 April 2005]

14 European Foundation for the Improvement of Living and Working Conditions, sector future (2003) *The future of IT – now it's getting personal,* http://www.emcc.eurofound.eu.int/publications/2003/sf_ict_1.pdf [2 April 2005]

15 An animated scenario for 'Anya' (corporate creative knowledge worker who works equally from home, the office and whilst travelling; she has one teenage son, Paul, from her previous marriage to Joe and a four year old daughter, Minnie, with her current partner, Marcus) is to be found at http://www.eurescom.de/public/projects/P1300-series/P1302/ [2 April 2005]

16 Evert van Loenen is aware that this domestication is not easy, because humans are used to 'buttons, dials and remote controls'. He sees that 'intelligent objects and devices, can form attractive bridges from the graspable to the ambient world' in the form of 'tangible robot' and a 'magic wand' with 'somewhat mysterious looking pens', and the twinkling sound of a bell tree. Visible and touchable objects are seen as transfer objects to assist the domestication of users in an ambient invisible world. (Loenen 2003)

17 The meaning of 'vulnerable' is a subjective construction process and is linked to the physical construction process of tools and devices and their breakdowns.

18 For an overview of the medical applications see (Gaggioli 2003).

19 Rejani Cantoni calls the related research platform '*Bodyarchitecture*': '*... for investigating different forms of natural, multimodal human-computer interaction. It involves the research and development of computer vision, speech and gesture recognition systems that connect media and physical spaces to what its inhabitants are, and do and say*' (Cantoni 2005)

20 Statement by Stefano Marzano in 'newvaluenews number thirteen - Philips Design - July 2002', p. 16 http://www.design.philips.com/assets/Downloadablefile/New_value_News13-12820.pdf [2 April 2005]

21 Heidegger's meaning of 'design'. He uses the word '*Entwurf*' (project-in-draft): 'The German terminology shows us clearly the opposition that there is in Heidegger's thought between dereliction and the project-in-draft – between *Geworfenheit and Entwurf. ... 'Entwurf'*: does not mean, ... , to contemplate this beyond as an object, to choose between possibilities as we choose between two paths that intersect at a crossroads. This would be to deprive possibility of its character of possibility by transforming it into a plan established beforehand. Possibility must be seized in its very possibility - as such it is inaccessible to contemplation but

49

positively characterizes the way of the being of *Dasein*. This way of being thrown forward toward one's own possibilities, of adumbrating them throughout one's very existence, is a crucial moment of understanding.' (Levinas 1996; Heidegger 1926, §31, pp. 145-148).

22 Maria is one of the scenarios in (IST Advisory Group 2001).

23 *Real world objects were either 'ready-to-hand' or 'present-at-hand'. When objects are ready-to-hand, we are unaware of their presence. When objects are present-at-hand, we are aware of their existence because they are not present, or they do not function as we intend. [...] When we experience the 'ready-to-hand', we are in a position of 'thrownness', which Heidegger explains as being immersed in a situation.* (Brunick 1995/96, III. A. Deconstructing the Rationalistic Tradition), (Heidegger 1926, §15, §16.)

24 For a definition of 'present at hand' and 'ready to hand' see (Heidegger 1926, §15, §16.): http://www.lancs.ac.uk/depts/philosophy/awaymave/405/glossary.htm [2 April 2005] and (Svanæs 1999, pp. 45-46; Dourish 1999, p. 12; Dourish, 2001, pp. 106-110; Crutzen 2003) Heidegger calls this kind of reliability: 'Verläßlichkeit'. He used it with two meanings: leavable and trustworthy (reliable) (Heidegger 1936, pp.28-29). The presence of all diversities of use between these extremes makes a tool reliable and the use of it situated.

25 Dewey calls this kind of doubt 'an intruder, an unwelcome guest' (Ratner 1939, p. 838; Dewey 1917)

26 A quotation from an interview with Peter Sloterdijk by Wouter Kusters and Dimphy Smeets: 'Dan wil je wel juichen: Es geht, es geht, es geht!', http://home.wanadoo.nl/wku/Sloterdijk/Interview.html [2 April 2005]

27 A quotation from Larry Rudolph (Smalley 2004)

28 Rosi Braidotti sees the inter-connectivity of art and technology as a move away from technophobia, towards a more technophilic approach. (Braidotti 1996) According to Barbara Becker and Gerhard Eckel, art should express nonstandardised, individual views and therefore it is opposed to the current habit of using and installing technology (Becker & Eckel1994)

29 Early experiments were done by Myron Krueger (1977)

Gender Politics

Katherine R.B. Greysen

Frances Grundy

Rosa Michaelson

Johanna Sefyrin

Linda Stepulevage,
Miriam Mukasa

Jutta Weber, Corinna Bath

Eva Turner

5 An Initial Investigation of Students' Self-Construction of Pedagogical Agents

Katherine R.B. Greysen

The University of New Mexico, Albuquerque

Abstract

This paper investigates the questions of how race and gender affect the design of pedagogical interface agents. The ultimate aim of the research is to provide design guidelines for pedagogical agents that go beyond the current 'one size fits all' mentality to encompass issues of race and gender in a way that provides meaningful learning experiences for a greater number of people. Specifically, this paper explores how the design of embodied pedagogical agents, with regard to race and gender, affect participation and identification with online tutorials and multi-media programs.

1. Introduction

This paper examines the design and utilization of interface agents from a multicultural perspective of race and gender. As 'real-time' interactive agents, the general or popular description of interface agents includes the constructs of social interaction, guidance and feedback, which can include non-verbal gestures and body language. As such, it follows that if based on human social interaction, the animated behaviours and response of a constructed agent will fall within the same socially constructed paradigm of the user that created them.

Beginning with a brief overview of interface agents and their design, I then describe a pilot project that investigated the design of agents created by users themselves. Finally, I will discuss the results of the study and talk about implications for future research. It is assumed that by examining the issues of race and gender, we may gain a broader or more comprehensive view of the effectiveness of interface agents.

1.1 Statement of the problem

Although there is a fair amount of information about gendered multimedia interfaces and gendered behaviour in online chats, etc. the Artificial Intelligence (AI) field has barely begun to explore gender or issues of race in the design of their Intelligent Agents or ECA (embodied communication agent). Authors such as Adam (1998) have presented the field with excellent critiques and resources regarding the issues but, as yet, the AI field as a whole has been resistant to acknowledge that differences even exist, much less that they impact on access to computer technology. As noted by Cassell (2001), 'As humans interact more with software agents, and come to rely on them more, it becomes more important (not less) that the systems rely on the same interactional rules that other humans do' (p.80). Given that the United States' system of education is based on dominant cultural norms of construction (white and male), it follows that racism and various cultural stereotypes will integrate into all forms and methods of multimedia education. Therefore the purpose of this project is not to examine the tutorial construction design or the internal architecture of embodied pedagogical interface agents but to look at the outward design of the agent itself.

1.2 Theoretical framework and research questions

My theoretical perspective is based within a constructionist, feminist orientation (Turnbull 2002) which essentially means that I believe knowledge is created within the constructs of a dominant social and education system. In addition, I believe that our individual realities are based on prior knowledge and interaction with others which build on previous understandings of new and existing frameworks and applications. In order to explore the intersections of race and gender and how these cultural variables fit into the relatively new field of embodied pedagogical interface agents, the research project was guided by the following questions: Do women and men design agents differently? and Are there differences in design with regard to the designer's racial or ethnic identification?

2. Literature Review

My noted themes of gender and race have popped out several times during the investigation of this topic. These themes, or design factors, have led to the question of how race and gender affect the design of pedagogical interface agents and consequently access to multimedia educational programs and systems. Reeves and Nash (1996) have found in several studies on human interaction with computers that humans interact with computers using social rules appropriate to interactions with other humans. In fact, during evaluation of the interface agents, users tended to protect or spare the feelings of the animated agents. Taking these actions into account, we then turn to Rickel, Marsella, et al. (2002) who state 'While our goals are ambitious, the potential payoff is high: Virtual humans that support rich interactions with people pave the way toward a new generation of interactive systems for entertainment and experiential learning' (p.37). The question that remains is 'entertainment and experiential learning' for whom? If programs are not accessible and/or designed for use with women or for different races and cultures then the only people being entertained and educated via technology are replications (white and male) of the same people who designed the interface systems in the first place.

2.1 What (and who) is an interface agent

An intelligent agent, in a very brief summary, works from a multimodal interface that incorporates natural movements and expressions of human communication. An embodied communication agent (ECA) is a 'virtual human capable of carrying on conversations with humans by both understanding and producing speech, hand gestures and facial expressions' (Herring 1994, p.1 of 4). Because concepts of human social discourse are applied to a computer interface it is important to specify and design a framework for the representation of discourse that integrates several modalities of human communication into an interface design.

An interface agent goes by many titles, as well as names. There are Animated Interface Agents, Embodied Interface Agents, Embodied Conversational Agents and Animated Pedagogical Agents, to name just a few. However, in spite of the title and some primary differences of interactions, the goal of the agent is essentially the same which is to facilitate a better understanding of concepts and educational modalities in interactive learning environments (Cassell 2001, 2002; Johnson et al 2000; Rist et al. 1997).

However, with regard to the external features of an Embodied Conversational Agent (ECA), male and female agents tend toward stereotypical gender designs. For example many of the male ECAs have well-defined, muscular upper bodies, broad shoulders with narrow waists, and are quite tall. The male agents are dressed in tradition male clothing: white long-sleeve t-shirt or sweater, and black slacks. In addition, the vast majority of male ECAs have light complexions with dark hair (Cassell 2001, 2002; Johnson et al 2000).

Female agents tend toward a similar form of cultural referencing. However, these agents tend to be portrayed as para-professional entities, i.e. physician's assistants or real estate agents, etc. Typically these female agents are white and are stereotypically female. Programmed with attributes associated with feminine behaviours, i.e., eye gaze, head tossing, body posture and hand gestures, female agents tend toward a conservative style of dress which is, however, flattering to her figure even when wearing a white lab coat . In addition female agents tend to be holding accessories i.e. sunglasses, pointers, clipboards (Cassell 2001, 2002; Johnson et al 2000).

Although there are many other interface agents, these are common representations of men and women on the internet. The point of describing them is to point out first that they have stereotyped gender characteristics of dress and gestures and that the majority were white, or at best, racially ambiguous.

2.2 Race and cultural differences in multimedia design

Among the many issues that differentiate countries from one another are the basic differences in cultural norms. There are different national languages, different foods and styles of dress. With regard to multimedia interface design, it is important to consider the effects of layout and colour. Colour variations among cultures have been well researched and documented. White in some cultures can imply 'death' while in western cultures white indicates 'purity'. The colour red has multiple meanings just in western cultures. Red can mean angry when placed as a feeling, as a deficit in business or, a red sign can infer danger and a high level of alert. Some countries have different colour schemes; Asians prefer softer, pastel colours while citizens of the United States tend toward more bold, primary colours (Evers and Day 1997).

Other primary issues in intercultural interface design are the layout and language used in the design. Some cultures read right to left, while others begin on the left side of a document. For instance, when combined with the layout of the screen, the placement of the primary text determines where the menus and screen icons are placed. A western type layout, i.e., left to right, could be disadvantageous for those from non-western cultures who read right to left. In addition Scott (1999) questions whether conformity and acceptance of the western style internationally 'illustrates a bias toward western culture and perhaps a touch of cultural imperialism' (p.6) due to the influence of the United States in software development.

Unfortunately while some of the general cultural differences are being addressed there is very little on race issues within the field of animated or embodied interface agents. In fact, there is essentially nothing that looks at or investigates the differences in response or access of the Black/African American, Latino/Hispanic, Native American and Asian populations, to name just a few of the many cultures that participate within the education system of the United States. What is surprising about this overt lack of research is that the concept of the Digital Divide (see Term Definitions) is well known and often cited within the research (National Telecommunications and Information Association 1994, 1997, & 1999).

2.3 Gender

In their book, The Media Equation (1996), Reeves and Nass stress 'all people automatically and unconsciously respond socially and naturally to media' (p.7). If that is true, then it is imperative that the ECAs people deal with are as human-like as possible. As embodied conversational agents become more and more familiar to the general user population, it will become increasingly important to have appropriate designs to facilitate and meet a user's need. Therefore the goal of interface design is to enable social skills that decrease interpersonal distance, increase trust and make possible social relationships.

The above point is noted in a type of Question and Answer article by Cowley and MacDorman (1995). In this article the authors are answering questions about the creation of 'chatterbots' (an online conversation simulator). Although chatterbots and ECAs are distinctly different in their programming and design, chatterbots were essentially the first ECAs. In the information given by the authors regarding whether or not the chatterbot should have a gender, the authors' state:

Yep – gender and sexuality is a very difficult theme. If your bot is female you must expect a lot of questions about 'bra size' and undergarments and more funny or not so funny intimate details like this...there are some very horney and girlish chatterbots around the net...if you are a man (and mostly all programmers are men)...

I use the above paragraph to bring attention to the way the images of women are perceived and treated in virtual environments. As Reeves and Nass note in *The Media Equation*, stereotypes of gendered behaviours are important to consider in design because 'people try to know the gender of those they interact with because it cues them about how to behave, what to say and how to say it . . . (p.168). In a culture of gendered social roles, the ease with which Reeves and Nass write regarding communication interactions brings an entire new framework to the foreground as ECAs are increasing being designed as assistive, subordinate females. In addition Cassell (2002) points out that the attitudes held by researchers and investigators, also influenced by social norms, unwittingly reinforce the very gender inadequacies they are attempting to expose. Specifically, Cassell emphasizes the 'binary' nature of viewing gender.

We have become used to seeing 'masculine' and 'feminine' as natural dichotomies – a classification that mirrors the natural world (p. 402).

It is a generally recognized fact that racism and sexism exists within the educational systems in the United States. It is also generally accepted that more or less value is attached to different social groups culturally. In fact, the value placed on different social groups is assigned by a ranking hierarchy of race, gender and class (Mindell 1995). These assertions are supported by Lipman (1998) who states, 'Racism (as well as sexism and class bias) intersects with the ideology to elevate attributes and characteristics that favour White, middle-class males over other races and ethnicities' (p. 26).

Concerns regarding design or research bias are also voiced by Scott (1999), in her study, 'Interface Design: Ethical Considerations'.

Design of the interface and the workplace environment [where it is created] can introduce bias and this in turn can disadvantage or offend users because of gender, disability, age, or culture (p. 2).

In addition, a 1992 study by Huff, Fleming & Cooper indicates that software designers have different expectations of female and male users and tend to design differently where the system is for one gender. However, where the system was to be used by both genders, male and female designers tended toward design characteristics typical of software designed for males.

Given the above information concerning issues of race and gender within multimedia design, the basic hypothesis behind this paper is that if individuals are given the opportunity to design their own pedagogical interface agent, they will design an agent who looks much like themselves. Fortunately, technology has evolved to the point where it is relatively easy for students to design their own pedagogical agent or at least to choose features such as gender, skin tone, facial features, etc. Giving individuals this choice would potentially provide them with more control over their learning experience and allow them to interact with an agent with whom they feel most comfortable. For example, individuals who are not of the dominant culture group, white and male, may elect to design a pedagogical agent which is of the same gender and/or ethnicity they are/or belong to. However, as far as I am aware, no study has been carried out which examines the factors associated with allowing individuals to design their own pedagogical agent, the types of agent constructed and why they are of that type.

3. Research Methods

At this point of the project the designs of seven university students' pedagogical agents have been evaluated. Utilizing a free design program ([V]Host at HYPERLINK "http://www.mysitepal.com" http://www.mysitepal.com) participants were able to create an animated character, choosing the character's hair colour, clothing, accessories, etc. With the sitepal.com program[1] participants were also able to perform quite subtle manipulations on the appearance of these characters, for example, ageing the characters, changing skin tone, modifying the size of the character's facial features, etc. After completing their design participants were asked to complete a survey and brief interview.

3.1 Method/rationale for choosing participants

Pilot study participants were recruited on a voluntary basis from a graduate level computer simulation class at a Southwestern University. Students were offered extra credit for participation in the research project. Once recruited, participants met with the researcher in her office for instructions and information. Using a computer in the researcher's office, the participants were directed to the 'sitepal' website and given directions on how to design an agent.

Of the seven students who initially participated in the project only five were selected for analysis at this time. The elimination of two students was based on outlying factors: the only male of seven and the only international student. After the elimination of these two students from the initial seven, the project was left with five American females of differing ethnicities and ages. Ethnicities of participants included Native American, African American, Latina and two white women. Ages of the participants ranged from early thirties to the early fifties. All the five women use the computer for email, research and general word processing. Two use the computer professionally; two considered themselves advanced users and one identified herself as an intermediate user. All participants stated they had comfortable experiences online except the intermediate user who stated she did not 'have the time to learn the programs' or to respond appropriately in emails, 'It takes time to send and read messages. I use an old computer and it is very slow. So, sometimes I don't even read them [email messages].'

3.2 Data collection techniques

Data collection for this project followed basic ethnographic techniques and included an analysis of each printed design or design artefact, a short (10-15 minute) survey which requested personal demographic data (e.g. gender, race, etc.), a description of their agent, and the decisions governing their choice of agent design. Following this phase, participants were asked to take part in an individual interview where the decision making process was discussed in more detail. Utilizing the three methods of data collection, artefact design, surveys, and interviews, allowed for triangulation of the data which enabled the corroboration of the data from different perspectives or 'angles' (Mason 2002, p.33). All participant names are pseudonyms.

4. Findings and Data Analysis

Findings from the data are discussed by addressing each of the research questions with information given on the surveys and in the individual interviews. This basic analysis of the data is followed by a discussion of the agent designs and then summarized by an overview of the findings to address the data that identified broader concerns and implications for the field.

Research question #1: Do women and men design agents differently?

Because there were no men included in the final analysis, correlations between demographic data and agent type is not possible with regard to gender. However, there is a fair amount of information regarding the five female participants' preferences in the design of pedagogical interface agents. Within this context, there are three primary themes that were identified in the surveys and interviews: comfort/trustworthiness, intelligence, and a stated preference for a female gender.

4.1 Comfort/trustworthiness

All five women explicated a preference for comfort which often included the features of trustworthiness. Excerpts that demonstrate this theme are as follows:

> Andrea: *I feel like if you are going to have an agent you want to have somebody who is going to be trustworthy to not just me, but, trustworthy to a larger audience. A pedagogical agent has to have a high level of trustworthiness.*

> Sylvia: *...to look friendly and nice because I care and to feel like a person and she is important, and I always feel that first impressions are important.*

> Mary: *it is just a comfort level for me. Like with a doctor, I prefer a female doctor especially with examinations.*

4.2 Intelligence

The concept of intelligence was the second most common desired trait for a pedagogical agent. Intelligence, or demonstration of knowledgeable behaviours, is also recognized in the literature as an important component of an agent's behaviour, '[we] give the impression that the agent is knowledgeable, but if the agent is unable to answer student questions and give explanations, the impression of knowledge will be quickly destroyed' (Johnson et al 2000, p. 48). In the following examples, two of the women were very explicit about this feature in their agent.

Sharon: *the first thing I would flush out is their intelligence factor. Umm...I can't stand that anyone would be intimidated by me. Intelligence is very important to me. I don't want anything, anyone, appear to not know the answer to my questions*

Andrea: *To me she looks smart, she looks capable, like she is ready to go... she is capable of making intelligent decisions*

4.3 Decisions regarding gender of agent

When answering the questions both in the interviews and on the surveys, all of the women gave specific reasons for choosing a female pedagogical agent. Analysis of these responses will be further addressed in the section Agent/Artefact Designs.

Andrea: *Female. As a female web developer, I am fed up with the predominately male culture of the tech world. I feel that men have frittered away their moral capital.*

Sharon: *Female - a friendly, approachable figure that could help me and not intimidate me.*

Sylvia: *Female. Myself.*

Mary: *Female, as I am female and that is my comfort level. Also, I feel women are more dedicated and show more passion*

Kim: *Female...I am most comfortable interacting with women in general, so my agent mirrors that.*

Research question #2: Are there differences in design with regard to the designer's racial or ethnic identification?
Differences in the designs with regard to racial or ethnic identification were more prominent in the oral and written narratives than in the designs themselves. The themes that surfaced for three of the women during the analysis of this section combines the racial or ethnic choices made with the belief that skin colour did not matter. This analysis contrasts sharply with the other two women, one white and one African American. The African American participant, Mary, stated that agent was 'Caucasian, because I could not find any female ethnic figures' [in the design program[1]]. And Sharon, the white woman, wrote on the survey her agent was 'white - [because it is a] common visual reference.' When asked during the interview to elaborate, Sharon replied, 'it means that I, now that you made me reflect upon it, I don't think I have ever

been taught by a woman of colour....I don't think she looks anything different than me...really white (Sharon page 2, lines 23-25).' For the three women who combined racial or ethnic choices with the belief that skin colour did not matter stated:

Andrea: *she has dark skin and a big nose which could be anything. I guess as time goes by the world just gets browner and browner and I wanted somebody who could be just about anybody. It is not some kind of purebred person. I mean she could be Latina, she could be Jewish, she could be a light skinned African American, she could be a number of different ethnicities and I feel it is just more reflective of the world we live in...it is much more that just white people with white hair* (Andrea page 2, lines 1-6).

Kim: *Woman of colour (undefined ethnicity, - probably African American or Latina or multiple races). And, again, when discussing her design in the interview stated, really, the race or ethnicity does not matter to me* (survey).

Sylvia: *I don't mind who teaches as long as I learn something* (survey).

4.4 Artefacts/agent designs

Themes, or common aspects, that that are identifiable when looking at the design artefacts include: the use of dark hair, casual/business attire (open neck blouses or tank tops), and the wearing of jewellery (necklaces), see fig.1.as an example. Statements describing the reasons behind the designs were asked both on the survey and in the taped interviews, some of which were addressed in the above section. Other responses included decisions regarding dress, jewellery, hair and eye colour, as well as race or ethnicity.

However, as the literature suggests (Cassell 2002, p. 402) the women did exactly what white male designers have done which is essentially, a self portrait of how they see themselves, or perhaps, rather how they would like to be seen. On this note, I will return to the last statement made by Sylvia that provides a perfect segue to the analysis of the agent designs

Sylvia's statements caught my eye because of contradictions between the survey, the taped interview and the design itself. Sylvia's description of the design on the survey states: 'Brown skin colour, Native American.' On the survey Sylvia wrote: 'I don't mind who teaches as long as I learn something'. Contradicting that statement is one that was made in the interview:

Kate: *what about that same question with regard to race or ethnicity...do you feel more comfortable with someone of your same background?*

Sylvia: *no. no.*

Kate: *no?*

Sylvia: *I would rather have someone of, and I wrote that and I erased it, I would ....*

Kate: what was that?

Sylvia: I would like someone who is not Indian.

I focus initially on this participant because I feel that her responses and her design, while contradicting each other, support the underlying assumptions for the project given on page 4 of this paper, 'individuals who are not of the dominant culture group, white and male, may elect to design a pedagogical agent which is of the same gender and/or ethnicity they are and/or belong to. In this case, Sylvia's design (fig.1.) featuring a conservatively dressed (v-neck shirt with blazer), 'Brown skin colour, Native American', was further described by Sylvia on the survey as:

My agent is like me. I am female. I have brown eyes and hair colour. I wear my hair up in a bun, or let it hang. I wear eyeglasses ... I dress conservatively, not too dressy or too plain.

In the taped interview, Sylvia continued along the same vein by stating:

I gave her black hair, and I tried to show some grey because my hair has some grey and I wear eye glasses so I gave her eye glasses. Her eyebrows are arched and mine aren't anything like that and her eyes have makes up, and I rarely wear makeup. I like her to always smile and to look friendly and nice because I care, and to feel like a person, and she is important, and I always feel that first impressions are important and I always try to do things right ... And if you look at her outfit, that is the way that I dress [missed this...] nice shirt, a necklace, I made sure that the neck didn't have a low cut like on some of the clothes I saw (Sylvia page 1, lines 6-13).

fig.1. Sylvia's design (published with the permission of the student)

The concept of self-portraits has surfaced in every agent design at this point in the research. Self-portraits, defined by Donald Kuspit (2004), are a 'presentation of himself [sic] as an autonomous, free-thinking, self-conscious person, as distinct from an obedient, faceless servant of a dogmatic establishment' (p.10). Supporting this definition, Flo Leibowitz (2003) states, '[self-portraits] functions as a kind of equalizer: that is, self-portraiture is a form that is accessible to painters of all genders and social classes ...' (p.289). On this note, the agent designs by the women function not only as an 'equalizer' but also as a presentation of self, as Kuspit asserts, 'distinct from an obedient, faceless servant of a dogmatic establishment'. Accordingly it follows that in a field represented by the white pedagogical agents of white male developers to have dialogue and demonstrate a voice in self-portraiture could be a transformational and emancipatory act (Freire 1970).

Looking at the agent designs of women as a form of self-portraiture, the function of the use of self as a model becomes clear and allows for expanded analysis of the designs. For instance, Kim's design features a 'female with brown skin and hair coincides with Kim's overall appearance and Latina ancestry. Kim continued saying that she thought the agent 'was not so much an 'alter ego' but more, 'how I would like to see myself.' In addition, Kim wrote on her survey that she thought the agent, 'looked funky cool, something I am not, or at least I don't see myself that way.'

Sharon's agent design also fits with the concept of self portraiture. In her statement describing the agent she wrote, 'My agent is female, 30-35 yrs of age, hip clothing, feminine, youthful appearance.' Sharon continues describing her agent in her taped interview by stating,

I don't think she looks anything different that me...really white and, you know, something I had never noticed is that I never think of myself as forty, I think of myself as thirty. I have this constant theme running through my head and I think that comes from the coaching world... Constant reference to what you have to be, to get approved (Sharon page2, lines 23-28).

Finally, Mary, who is the African American participant, also provides a glimpse into the use of self-portraiture as a voice for self-identification. Mary's written description of her agent states, 'my agent was a Caucasian female and the features tilted toward French decent (hair style). The agent has dark hair, green eyes with very basic and comfortable clothing and basic jewellery; *such is my preference* (italics added). When asked during the interview why she chose certain features Mary stated,

She is a Caucasian female, with what I consider French features and I chose the roses [background] because that represents me, I love roses. And the style of clothing I choose was more casual because that is also my comfort level outside of the work environment. And real basic jewellery, very little jewellery, very basic. And, um, I felt this agent was someone I would be comfortable with (Mary page 1, lines 6-10).

And, when asked why she chose an agent who was Caucasian when she is African American, Mary replied

> [Race] really doesn't matter to me. Especially here in Albuquerque I have been so far removed from my culture. I have become more homogenized here than in my hometown . . . you are a product of your environment (page 1, lines 22-26).

Mary continues on the same thought in her interview when discussing how she feels about her agent (page 2, lines 6-10),

> Mary: I was told I was trying to be white but that was not my fault, that was how I was raised and not that you try to be a certain way but, you assimilate [the culture] around who are with. I tell people I am homogenized.

> Kate: why do you choose that word?

> Mary: a blending, I feel like a blending. Like the colour palettes in the program.

Although the analysis of Mary's agent and transcripts appear to represent a reversal of the other designs in the sense of a self-portrait as a transformational tool, the analysis does continue to utilize the pattern of self-portraiture as illuminated by Kuspit (2004), as a presentation 'as an autonomous, free-thinking, self-conscious person.' Specifically, in her decision to name her reality as 'homogenized' and as 'a product of her environment', Mary actually demonstrates the core of Freire's constructs for emancipatory learning in the 'naming' of her own truth (1970, p. 77) which leads to a critical awareness, 'The more active an attitude men take in regard to the exploration of their thematics, the more they deepen their critical awareness of reality and, in spelling out those thematics, take possession of the reality' (p. 97).

However, while I would not presume the authority to label any of the participant's self-portraiture as the beginning of a revolution, I will assert that it is the dialogue of identification that instigates change (Freire 1970). As noted in the abstract for this paper, 'The ultimate aim of the research is to provide design guidelines for pedagogical agents that go beyond the current 'one size fits all' mentality to encompass issues of race and gender in a way that provides meaningful learning experiences'. I believe the project has accomplished that task in that the data demonstrates, essentially, one size fits only one. And, more importantly, that the accepted generality of white and predominantly male pedagogical agents limit access to online programs and tutorials for women and people of other races or ethnicities by lowering comfort levels and constructs of trustworthiness.

5. Limitations of the Study

The limitations to this study are several. The first limitation, and most identifiable is trying to do a comparison project that is gender based with only one gender. That there were no males in the final analysis contributes to a feeling of 'incompleteness' with regard to the project. The choice to eliminate the only male respondent was based on the desire to avoid 'tokenism' of his opinions if comparisons were made to the five female participants.

The second limitation is based on the lack of substantial population at this time, for analysis. I feel that to obtain the necessary corroborative evidence for this topic, a wide range of participants are needed as the study continues.

The third limitation of the research is directly correlated to the sitepal.com design program with regard to the skin colour palettes. Three of the five women stated they felt the skin tones were not representative of what they wanted to achieve and that the colours available did not look realistic.

6. Discussion

To answer the general question of 'what does this all mean?' I respond by stating this research means that tutorials and multimedia education programs need to approach design from an inclusive position which will provide increased access for women and people of different races and ethnicities. The issues of learner control within the programming is of paramount importance when looking at design of tutorials or programs that need to reach a large numbers of people, as in a national crisis or just a few people in a distance education classroom.

This project supports what is already known regarding the 'personification' of pedagogical agents in multimedia education. However I believe the results of the project take what is previously known one step further. Not only is it important to have engaging and intelligent agents to work with but it is important to have agents that represent the students who are working with the program. The possibility of 'individualizing' multimedia programs by including 'agent options' is not out of reach financially or technologically and needs to be considered as part of the viability of each new tutorial or multimedia program.

This project demonstrates the need for future research in the areas of agent design, interface design and multimedia programming with respect to issues connected to race and gender. I sincerely encourage replication of this study in larger numbers with an equal representation of men and women. Another suggestion for future research would be to place an agent design program within a multimedia tutorial (i.e. how to fix a printer, etc.) and observe the agent designs 'in action' so to speak with their creator/participants as the tutorial progresses. Finally, I encourage continued investigations and research with gender and race issues to insure equal access and voice in the field of interface and technology design.

References

Adam, A. 1998, Artificial Knowing: Gender and the Thinking Machine, Routledge, London

Cassell, J. 2001, 'Embodied conversational agents: Representation and intelligence in user interface', AI Magazine, vol 22, no 3, pp. 67-83. Retrieved electronically 2/19/03: gn.www.media.mit.edu/groups/gn/pubs/AI.magazine.cassell.pdf

Cassell, J. 2002, 'Genderizing HCI' in Jacko, J. and Sears, A. (Eds.), The Handbook of Human-Computer Interaction, pp. 402-411. Lawrence Erlbaum, Mahwah, NJ.

Cowley, S.J. & MacDorman, K.F. 1995, Are machines able to think?: An artificial intelligence living inside my PC, http://www.abentenermedien.de/jabberwock/chatterbotfaq-en.html [February 2004]

Evers, V. & Day, D. 1997, 'The role of culture in interface acceptance' in HCI Conference', Interact 1997, pp. 260-265

Freire, P. 1970, Pedagogy of the Oppressed, Seabury Press, New York.

Herring, S. 1994 'Gender differences in computer-mediated communication: Bringing familiar baggage to the new frontier'. Keynote talk at 'Making the Net*Work*: Is there a difference in gender communication?' American Library Association Annual Conference. Miami, June 27, 1994. http://www.eff.org/Net_culture/Gender_issues/cmc_and_gender.article [17 February 2003]

Huff, C.W., Fleming, J.H., & Cooper, J. 1992, 'Gender differences in human-computer interaction' in In Search of Gender Free Paradigms for Computer Science Education. Eugene, OR: International Society for Technology in Education, eds. Martin & Murchie-Beyma.

Johnson, W.L., Rickel, J.W., & Lester, J.C. 2000, 'Animated pedagogical agents: Face to face interaction in interactive learning environments', International Journal of Artificial Intelligence in Education, vol 11, pp. 47-78.

Kuspit, D. 2004, 'The art of being seen: The art of self-portraits', Art New England, April-May.

Leibowitz, F. 2003, 'Images of the female and of the self: Two recent interpretations by women authors'. Hypatia, vol 18, no 4.

Lipman, P. 1998, Race, Class and Power in School Restructuring. State University of New York Press, Albany, NY.

Mason, J. 2002, Qualitative researching (2nd edn.). Sage Publications, London.

Merriam-Webster Unabridged Online Dictionary. Retrieved electronically at: http://www.m-w.com/home.htm

Mindell, A. 1995, Sitting in the Fire: Large Group Transformation Using Conflict and Diversity. Lao Tse Press, Portland, OR.

National Telecommunications and Information Association, 1994, Falling through the net. http://www.ntia.doc.gov/ntiahome/fttn99/html [16 November 2001]

National Telecommunications and Information Association, 1997. Falling through the net: Internet access and usage http://www.ntia.doc.gov/ntiahome/fttn99/html [16 November 2001]

National Telecommunications and Information Association, 1999. Falling through the net: Defining the digital divide. http://www.ntia.doc.gov/ntiahome/fttn99/html [16 November 2001]

Reeves, B., & Nass, C. 1996, The Media Equation: How People Treat Computers, Television, and New Media Like Real People and Places, Cambridge University Press, Stanford, CA.

Rist, T., André, E. & Müller, J. 1997, 'Adding animated presentation agents to the interface',

Intelligent User Interfaces, pp.79-86, www.iuiconf.org/97pdf/1997-001-0011.pdf [19 February 2003]

Rickel, J., Marsella, S., Gratch, J., Hill, R., Traum, D., & Swartout, W. 2002, 'Toward a new generation of virtual humans for interactive experiences'. *IEEE Intelligent Systems, July/August*, pp. 32-38.

Rickel, J. & Johnson, W.L., 2000, 'Task-oriented collaboration with embodied agents in virtual worlds' in Cassell, J. Sullivan, J. & Prevost S. (eds.), *Embodied Conversational Agents*, MIT Press.

Scott, J. 1999, 'Interface design: Ethical considerations'. Paper presented at *Australian Institute of Computer Ethics Conference*, July, Lilydale. www.businessit.bf.rmit.edu.av/aice/events/AICEC99/papers1/SCO99051.pdf [19 February 2003]

Turnbull, S. 2002, 'Social construction research and theory building', *Advances in Developing Human Resources*, vol 4, no 3, pp. 317-34.

Notes

1 The sitepal.com design program actually has at least five embodied images that reflect various ethnicities and races. In addition, the program allows for altering skin colour, eye colour, basic styles of hair, dress, and colours as well as features that can alter body shape and size.

6 Some Ideas on Constitutive Ethics for Information and Communication Technologies

Frances Grundy

School of Computing and Mathematics, University of Keele, UK

Abstract

Kramer and Kramarae have identified four sets of masculine gendered ideas that are used in conceptualising the Internet; anarchy, frontier, democracy and community. These are constitutive ideas as opposed to regulative ones; in other words they constitute the Internet. I suggest two alternative constitutive ideas, but not necessarily 'feminine' ones, that might be used as constituent parts of the Internet. These are reflexivity, or examining what we are about, and pluralism. The adoption of these two principles as constitutive ethics would have a profound effect on teaching and practice of using not just the Internet, but developing and using ICT more generally.

1. The Big Issue[1]

In their excellent article 'Gendered Ethics on the Internet' Jana Kramer and Cheris Kramarae (1997) identify four sets of ideas that are used in conceptualising the Internet. Each of these sets of ideas includes an ethical component that is deeply gendered in favour of men who are still the dominant group of Internet users. They contrast these ethical components with such ethics as the rules for computing professionals regulating their duty to their clients including property issues such as copyright protection (p. 228).

I use these ideas as a jumping off point. The Internet is a crucial and large component of our use of ITC and in some senses symbolic of this use. If there are ethical problems with the Internet, then this is going to have ramifications for much of our living and working with and learning about ITC.

What I offer first is a codification of Kramer and Kramarae's distinction between the two types of ethics, a distinction that is wider in scope than the Internet and which embraces practices in academic disciplines related to ITC. I should then like to offer some thoughts on contributions that could be made to the gender debate on ethics and ITC, particularly by those championing the interests of women.

2. Regulative and Constitutive Ethics[2]

Let me first illustrate the difference between these two sorts of ethics by looking at two non-computing case, the game of chess and the medical profession. Chess is defined by, or constituted by, a series of rules, like what counts as checkmate; that each player takes it in turn to move; that the pieces can only be moved in particular ways and so on. On the other hand, there are rules like 'do not deliberately distract your opponent' which do not define or constitute the game but which regulate the behaviour of those engaged in it.

To turn now to the medical profession, when people talk about the ethics of a profession like medicine, they usually have in mind rules like doctors should not seduce their patients or get them to alter their wills in the doctor's favour. Other regulative rules are, for example, doctors should respect confidentiality and fully inform patients if they are being used in experiments. These are obviously very important rules; without them, many patients would suffer and not go for the treatment they need. But, in principle, and however much in practice the medical profession needs to be regulated, it could in theory still exist without these rules which (merely) regulate the practice of medicine.

But there is another type of ethic, without which the medical profession could not be conceptualised. The profession could not exist if it were not for value-laden talk of illness and cure. Medicine is an applied science meant to intervene in the world and to promote the good: health, longer life, less pain etc. If there were no value-laden principles such as these, there would be only the morally neutral sciences such as physiology and psychology and an intellectual pursuit of the knowledge of what causes what. To intervene in the world to reduce illness and pain is to recognise a system of values that helps to define or constitute the profession of medicine. We cannot conceive of this profession without these constitutive rules; they necessarily enter into our very conception of this profession.

So, although the *regulative* rules like doctors should not seduce their patients are very important, they only regulate the activity of the medical profession. Other values are needed for it to exist - however vague. Not so 'obvious' is the kind of value judgement made when saying that for a woman to become menopausal below the age of 30 is a condition that might require treatment. But the same would not be said of a woman over 50. Or, again moral judgements are being made when it is said that a person who grieves for a close relative or friend for a period of a year is quite normal and would not call for treatment. On the other hand, to grieve in an incapacitating way for a person for 20 years or more might be thought by many to be a form of mental illness. The profession of psychiatry could not exist without this kind of *constitutive* moral value judgement.

3. Regulative and Constitutive Ethics of the Internet & ITC in general

In a similar way the ethics of the Internet cover not only regulative rules governing the activity of Internet users - rules about *how* they do what they do - but also constitutive moral principles which define *what* they do.

Amongst regulative rules for the Internet and ITC there are rules, which may or may not be legal ones, for example rules against theft of passwords, flaming, grooming children for sex, maintaining confidentiality, ensuring the integrity of safety critical software.

Turning now to constitutive rules, Kramer and Kramarae point out that, to a large extent, we have to conceptualise the new in terms of what we already have. They examine four main ways in which the Internet has been conceptualised: anarchy, the frontier, democracy and community. They include in each case a set of principles that help to define the Internet (I am concentrating on the Internet for the moment and will extend this to ICT more generally later).

Let's start with the view of the Internet as a frontier. They quote Frank Connolly's view that 'Cyberspace, the electronic frontier, is the realisation of the American fantasy - the ultimate in freedom and rugged individualism' (p. 232).

Freedom is conceived as absence of interference, a conceptualisation which they quote Virginia Held as pointing out, works better for men than for women, who have by law and custom not been thought to be able to fend for themselves.

The frontier is the promise of new beginnings. It is male, adventure, boldness, daring, restless energy, independence, rough, violence, strength, heroic exploits, and danger. It is not female, intimacy, caring, vulnerability, meaning in daily customs, or artistic. (p. 231)

Kramer and Kramarae continue by pointing to the fact that to bring in this model means 'using one's own judgement and accepting sole responsibility for decisions and actions.' Here possibly lie risks equivalent to those undertaken by traditional 'frontiersmen'. Why did these frontiersmen take risks? To discover new lands, new life styles, gold, riches and so on. The goals for our rugged Internet user are usually far more modest. They are to get the better of things already manufactured by man. And, what risks do Internet users face according to this conceptualisation? By and large they are not physical. Women and, more particularly girls, possibly run more physical and emotional risk than boys and men from use of the Internet through flaming and grooming for example. Hackers were originally all male, although now there is an increasing number of female hackers. All hackers face risk of prosecution and punishment and this possibility may well be one that inspires a feeling of frontiersmanship and derring-do amongst other emotions.

We have allowed this notion of the Internet as a frontier with its connotations of rugged individualism, heroism and bravery into the constitution of the Internet. What counts as a constitutive ethic of the Internet depends on how people see it. If not enough people see its constitution in a certain ethical light, for example as a frontier to be conquered, then to that extent it loses its claim to be a constitutive ethic. But this notion of the Internet as a frontier seems to me to have taken hold. It is male and has had a profound influence.

Kramer and Kramarae write in a similar vein about the other three ways in which the Internet is conceived: anarchism, democracy and community. Each has an ethic, or perhaps 'ethos' would be a better word for something so diffuse, that runs counter to feminist ethics, even the conception of the Internet as a community. They quote Marilyn Friedman's view that the model of community tends to be 'focused particularly on families, neighborhoods and nations. These sorts of communities harbor social roles and structures that have been highly oppressive for women.' (p. 237)

Our problem is that, if these are the constitutive ethics that define the Internet, can we possibly change this constitution by defining new ethics? I quoted Virginia Held's list of supposedly[3] female characteristics which are not part of the constitution of the Internet. It is extremely difficult (as always) to see how the Internet could have ever been formed from such values, or even transformed incorporating such values. Male characteristics are always 'there' and gutsy, female characteristics are either 'not there' or, if they are there, they are often fluffy.

4. The Internet as a Democratic Forum

Kramer and Kramarae, rightly, have mixed views of the Internet as a democratic forum. Although, on the one hand, everybody has a voice, on the other hand, 'as in any democracy, the majority rules'. While the gender gap for Internet usage was wide in the 1990s, the average gap for 12 countries worldwide is now 8% (UCLA World Internet Project 2004). However, the picture of usage by gender varies from country to country. For example, another study in the US found the gender gap in 2003 to be 2.5% (Center for the Digital Future 2004, p. 31). Furthermore, the 'one person, one vote' principle, which is embodied in democracy, is compromised by the fact that women and men have different styles of communication which give away the gender of participants and if they are female they are ignored (p. 235). Yet another report suggests that, while the gap had closed even by 2000, interestingly women were less intense and less frequent users than men (Federal Reserve Bank of Atlanta 2002).

In a sense, some components of Kramer and Kramarae's constitutive ethics are disappearing. Things are changing - 'The 'Geek-Nerd' Perception of the Internet is Dead' (Center for the Digital Future 2004, p. 22). However the influence of these early ethics has by no means gone and we must remember that the formative time for the Internet was a period in which men unquestionably dominated it.

I use here the example of the world of computing and allied topics, or ICT. If women are going to work at all, they have to work in a male dominated industry. So, forums have developed on the Internet within which women can air their views and discuss the difficulties they encounter as women, for example, the email lists systers and bcswomen. To be a member of the latter group, for example, one has to be a member of the British Computer Society (BCS) and female. It exists under the umbrella of the BCS and has to conform to its rules. So, in fact, all this provides is an environment in which women can come to terms with and learn to live in the prevailing male dominated environment. Anyone who falls into these two categories can join this group and have their say. But although these criteria clearly define the constituency, it does not necessarily follow that it will be a force for radical change; in fact this is quite unlikely. These forums do not, by their very nature, provide platforms for radical voices – these are disenfranchised.

5. The Need for Reflexivity

I should like to suggest two new elements in an adequate conceptualisation of the Internet and the work involved in developing and using ITC more generally. These are reflexivity and pluralism. I use 'reflexivity' in the sense that Anthony Giddens uses it (1984, 1990) and which for him marks the difference between modern and traditional society. In traditional societies things continue without challenge as the way they have always been; whereas the modern society is one in which self-conscious reflection on activity and institutions is constantly being fed back into the justification and/or changing of those institutions.

Giddens holds that the social sciences 'are actually more deeply implicated in modernity than is natural science, since the [continuous] revision of social practices in the light of knowledge about those practices is part of the very tissue of modern institutions'. (Giddens 1990, p. 40) Even allowing for this, there is a reluctance to conduct self-examination in the mainstream of pure and applied sciences. The situation in the disciplines of ICT is parallel in some ways to what feminist philosophers, such as Sandra Harding, argue about pure sciences like physics and its refusal to allow itself to be examined. She talks mockingly of 'Sacred Science' (1986). Science holds itself above and beyond other disciplines. A science like physics claims to exemplify an empirical method of investigation that will give a true explanation of any other form of social activity, but it will not subject itself to this method. In other words it is above its own law. Thus it does not allow attempts to explain scientific activity in the way that science itself recommends we explain all other social activity. But hypotheses about science's role in social affairs should be open to the same kind of investigation as physics itself uses. Harding states that

> ... these [hypotheses] appear blasphemous to the vast majority of both scientists and non-scientists – not bold hypotheses that should be scientifically investigated to determine whether or not they can be refuted but psychologically, morally, and politically threatening challenges to the Western faith in progress through increased empirical knowledge. (p. 38)

Harding continues

> *Why is it taboo to suggest that natural science ... is a social activity, a historically varying set of social practices? that a thoroughgoing and scientific appreciation of science requires descriptions and explanations of the regularities and underlying causal tendencies of science's own social practices and beliefs? that scientists and science enthusiasts may have the least adequate understanding of the real causes and meanings of their own activities? To what other 'community of natives' would we give the final word about the causes, consequences, and social meanings of their own beliefs and institutions?* (p. 39)

In a footnote Harding reports an observation by Pauline Bart 'that in speculating about the comparative resistances that different disciplinary fields offer to feminist insights, we should not underestimate the comparative levels of personal and political threat to the leaders of these fields - primarily men ...'. Harding then continues 'This line of reasoning would support my argument that feminist critiques of the natural sciences meet even greater hostility than critiques in other areas, scientific rationality is directly implicated in the maintenance of masculinity in our kind of culture.' (pp. 33-34)

Computing isn't a science in the sense that physics is, but nevertheless aspires to be in order to benefit from the various features that give science its kudos (Grundy 2000). Calling itself a science facilitates the use of arguments like those used for physics even if it doesn't stand up to scrutiny in the detail. So those who criticise the tenets of computing are told simply 'It's not computing', the strong implication being that such criticisms have no place in the computing canon and indeed ought not to be happening at all within the discipline of computing. In other words, we are being denied the opportunity to conduct these examinations and, at the same time, to be allowed to remain 'in the fold'. Those who deny us this opportunity have clearly lost sight of the Socratic dictum: 'The unexamined life is not worth living'.

Computer scientists and other, real, scientists have no problem in 'allowing' social scientists to examine what they do. But the boundaries that exist between the disciplines (for whatever reasons) are such that, although the sociologists note what is happening in the sciences (they are bound to), scientists on the other hand pay little attention to what the sociologists say. In short, such views are immoral and a cop out as far as any remedial action is concerned.

Having said this, it is important to acknowledge that there are schools, institutes and departments both in this country and abroad where what social scientists have to say is not only listened to but also taught within the organisation. Notwithstanding this there are plenty of traditional computing departments and schools to which my previous paragraph applies. (Grundy 2004)

I would like to suggest that openness to self-examination and what people in other disciplines, especially the social sciences, have to say, should be a constitutive rule of the Internet, and more broadly, of all the disciplines allied to ICT.

Why can't there be conventions that authors of all academic reports have to give their standpoint, to give their gender, and give the reasons for being involved in that research as is done sometimes elsewhere, for example in anthropology and to some extent in critical discourse analysis? It would be part of this ethic of openness that people under all circumstances, not just authoring, did not shelter under the cloak of anonymity that the Internet, for example, can provide. Applications for research grants from the EU require any evidence that women are involved in the research and are certainly enhanced if outcomes will improve gender mainstreaming.

6. The Ethics of Pluralism

It is almost inevitable that those women who succeed in reaching the top, in what was so recently an almost exclusively male preserve, think they have discovered the way to enhance their positions without confrontation with men in power. Naturally they are keen to pass on their ideas and see other women follow their lead and take up their attitudes – after all they clearly have the secret of success.[4]

One ramification of this hold that the present power structure maintains is a continued reluctance to examine the discipline in the way I have suggested at the end of the previous section. This leads to monistic thinking, not only directly in respect of the detail of ICT and computing facilities and the way they are implemented, but certainly in respect of the social context in which it all takes place, including the very important one of gender. This makes those in power feel that there really ought to be only one voice; that to have more than one voice is to be divided and ruled. To have dissenters from this is to dissipate effort, to 'rock the boat' and to jeopardise progress.

But it is monistic thinking that jeopardises progress; it prevents discussion and in this case, insofar as the social aspects are concerned, a real unearthing and revelation of what actually occurs as the patriarchy maintains its hold.[5]

It is by no means clear that to be effective women must speak with one voice. To quote Biddy Martin (1988) paraphrasing Foucault

Power and authority are no longer vested in a central point ... nor does resistance arise from a central point. For that reason, a very different form of political organisation and struggle suggests itself, an alternative to the frontal attack on the state. (pp. 9-10)

She goes on to say that the women's movement has been criticised for its '... fragmentation, lack of organisation, absence of a coherent and encompassing theory, and the inability to mount a frontal attack'. But she suggests that these alleged features may very well represent fundamentally more radical and effective responses to the deployment of power in our society than would a unified attack. Efforts towards centralisation and abstraction are, she suggests, misguided.

To listen and speak with one voice is not only unnecessary but is both unrealisable and ineffective. I would like to see as a constitutive principle of the Internet and ICT disciplines the principle that all voices be encouraged.

It is said that some do not like this pluralistic situation; they suggest that feminists can only succeed in this arena of computing and ICT if we speak with only one voice or, at least speak with only an approved number of voices. In the nature of things, it is difficult to produce evidence for these efforts to prevent some types of views being expressed.

What does pluralism include? It includes allowing the publication and dissemination of articles examining the social construction of computing and the way that this has influenced its development as occurring in conferences such as this one. It also includes these radical articles being read and argued about in the most technical of departments. In other words, such discussion should become a component of, or a constitutive element, of these departments. And obviously it should be taught to students learning about ICT – as already occurs in some institutions much to their credit.

7. Two Constitutive Ethics for ICT

A combination of reflexivity and pluralism would make a very considerable difference at all sorts of levels in ICT work. It would for a start greatly enliven undergraduate work in many raw computer courses; too many of these are non-discursive and do not encourage debate. Students are set to learn and reproduce too many things for which they are led to believe there is only one right answer. Incorporation of these ethics, particularly pluralism, would also allow for different approaches and styles of thinking which this still young, nervous and defensive discipline so often abhors.

It was often claimed that having women at the top would present a new view of relationships within the organisation, a new view of corporate aims and so on. Some people wonder whether they are in fact putting forward a different point of view, and one way of seeing things as they really are would be to encourage challenge and discussion. Reflexivity plus pluralism where everybody's views are respected would help decide this sort of issue and also stimulate a great deal of debate.

References

Center for the Digital Future 2004, *The Digital Future Report Surveying the Digital Future Year 4 – Ten Years, Ten Trends,*
http://www.digitalcenter.org/downloads/DigitalFutureReport-Year4-2004.pdf
[25 September 2004].

Federal Reserve Bank of Atlanta 2002, *Gender and the Internet,*
http://www.frbatlanta.org/filelegacydocs/wp0210.pdf [25 September 2005].

Giddens, A. 1984, *The Constitution of Society: Outline of the Theory of Structuration,* Polity Press, Cambridge.

Giddens, A. 1990, *The Consequences of Modernity,* Polity Press, Cambridge.

Grundy, F. 2000, Where is the science in Computer Science? Paper presented to Women, Work and Computerization Conference, Vancouver, BC., http://www.keele.ac.uk/depts/cs/staff/a.f.grundy/home/science.htm [20 September 2004].

Grundy, F. 2004, 'Arbeiten an den Grenzlinien – Möglichkeiten und Probleme der Interdisziplinarität' in Grenzgänge. *Genderforschung in Informatik und Naturwissenschaften*, eds. Sigrid Schmitz & Britta Schinzel, Ulrike Helmer Verlag, pp. 13-29. Also available online in English as 'Working at the boundaries: Opportunities and problems facing interdisciplinarity' at http://www.keele.ac.uk/depts/cs/staff/a.f.grundy/home/publications.htm [1 January 2005].

Harding, S. 1986, *The Science Question in Feminism*, Open University Press, Milton Keynes.

Kramer, J. & Kramarae, C. 1997, 'Gendered ethics on the Internet', in *Communication Ethics in an Age of Diversity*, eds. Josina M. Makau and Ronald C Arnett, University of Illinois Press, Illinois, pp. 226-243.

Martin, B. 1988, 'Feminism, criticism and Foucault', in *Feminism & Foucault: Reflections on Resistance,* eds. Irene Diamond & Lee Quinby, Northeastern University Press, Boston, pp. 3-19.

Searle, J. R. 1969, *Speech Acts: An Essay in the Philosophy of Language*, Cambridge University Press, Cambridge.

UCLA World Internet Project 2004. First Release of Findings From the UCLA World Internet Project Shows Significant 'Digital Gender Gap' in Many Countries, http://www.ccp.ucla.edu/downloads/UCLA_World_Internet_Project.doc [20 September 2004]

Notes

1   The Big Issue is a street newspaper sold in the UK by and on behalf of homeless people - 'the most successful social business in the UK'.

2   I owe these terms to John Searle (1969), although I am applying them in a new area.

3   Why is it that when we talk about male characteristics we never seem to run the risk of being accused of essentialism, but when we talk of 'female characteristics' we have to guard ourselves against such charges by, for example, using words such as 'supposedly' as I have done here?

4   I have been somewhat alarmed recently in my trade union work by the number of men and women who brought complaints to me about bullying by more senior women (although these have not necessarily been from the world of ICT). What I would argue here is that many of these women (some of whom I know have suffered themselves) are not being reflexive enough about their new and powerful roles.

5   I vividly recall sending the abstract of a paper that challenged the normal view of computing as a science and relating this to the recruitment of women to the editor of an influential computing journal. Not only did he reject my paper outright on the basis of the abstract, but he also wrote that it was not suitable for his *or any other* computer journal (my italics). This is the kind of active censorship that women who don't want to rock the boat collude with. When I showed this to a departmental colleague, he offered to write protesting on my behalf, but then retracted his offer because he thought he might want to submit something to that journal!

7 Gender Mainstreaming in FP6: experiences from an IST project

Rosa Michaelson

University of Dundee

Abstract

There is no female science waiting in cupboard to be discovered. We have to make it happen. - Nicole Dewandre, Director of the Women and Science Unit, 3rd Gender Equality in HE Conference, Genoa, 13-16 April, 2003.

In response to the lack of women at all levels in EU funding processes, the 'leaky pipeline' of female scientists, and a growing awareness of gender equality issues, the European Commission has adopted Gender Mainstreaming as the means to promote gender equality in the Framework 6 (FP6) research program (Rees, 2002b; Osborne et al., 2000; Rees, 1998). In a gender impact assessment of the Information Society (IST) programmes of framework 5 it was noted that "gender issues do not appear to be systematically considered in the policy-making process" (Gender in Technology, 2001). FP6 is now in its second year, and the impact of this policy is yet to be evaluated by the commission. It is difficult to predict the effect on gender equality of this novel policy implementation, which requires every Integrated Project (IP) and Network of Excellence (NoE) to have a gender issues plan. These plans are twofold: consortia are asked to describe gender actions that will take place to support women within the project, and encourage more females to participate in the group; and are expected to consider the impact their research will have on gender equality. This paper presents the experiences of a computer scientist working on both computer science research and gender issues for the European Learning Grid of Excellence (ELeGI) Integrated Project[1]. ELeGI is a consortium of 23 groups investigating the use of GRID technologies for new educational services.

Introduction

In response to the lack of women at all levels in EU funding processes, the 'leaky pipeline' of female scientists, and a growing awareness of gender equality issues, the European Commission has adopted Gender Mainstreaming as the means to promote gender equality in the Framework 6 (FP6) research program (Rees, 2002; Osborne *et al.*, 2000; Rees, 1998). This paper presents the experiences of a computer scientist working on both computer science research and gender issues for the European Learning Grid of Excellence (ELeGI) Integrated Project. ELeGI is funded with €7.5m under the Information, Society and Technology (IST) Framework 6 programme from 2004 until 2008. The consortium consists of 23 partners investigating the use of GRID technologies for new educational services.

Firstly, I present a brief history of gender mainstreaming in EU research funding, followed by an outline of how gender mainstreaming policy has been translated into a process in FP6 by the addition of a B.10, Gender Action Plan (GAP) section within Integrated Project (IP) and Network of Excellence (NoE) bids. I give an outline of the ELeGI Integrated Project in section 3. Then my dual role as researcher and a member of the equality group with ELeGI is discussed, with an overview of my background in gender equality. In the next section, the ELegI GAP and an overview of the Gender Issues Management Plan are described. In conclusion issues that arise from this experience are given. The responses from members of the consortium, those in the IST directorate, and the Women and Science unit, to gender mainstreaming in this context are also considered.

Shortcomings and possible problems with gender mainstreaming are already well detailed by those involved in the process of policy change (Pollack, 2000; Rees, 2002a). My role as gender equality co-ordinator with an integrated project comes with the dangers of tokenism, and a corresponding shallow response from the group. There are also misunderstandings concerning where gender and ICT research fits within the funding process: should it sit in a project as a designated work package, or should it be a separately funded strand from another directorate?

Do these problems matter? I would argue that the gender mainstreaming experiment is worth conducting despite these caveats, if only because the process has produced more discussion, both within the secretariat, amongst funding bidders, and the associated university services such as UKRO. It has highlighted cultural differences about ideas of gender equality across Europe. It has also allowed those of us who felt split between our roles as ICT researchers and feminists to play to both strengths.

Gender Mainstreaming in FP6

Mainstreaming is the systematic integration of equal opportunities for women and men into the organisation and its culture and into all programmes, policies and practices; into ways of seeing and doing (Rees, 1998).

• Background

The history of European policy with regard to Gender and Science from 1950 until the late 1990s is documented by Rose, amongst others (Rose, 1999). Following the UN Beijing Conference on women in 1995, the importance of 'mainstreaming', or integrating gender equality, was highlighted in EU policy. Gender Equality is enshrined in the Treaty of Amsterdam, Article 2: "The Community shall have as its tasks... to promote ... equality between men and women...." (Degraef, 2004). In 1998, an important report on Mainstreaming Gender in the EU was produced by Teresa Rees (Rees, 1998). Then in 1999, following the adoption of the "Women and Science" Commission, the Council of the European Union also adopted a resolution concerning women and science that led to a 40% target for women's involvement at all levels in FP5 (Women and Science, 1999). The ETAN report of 2000 suggested how Gender Mainstreaming could be adopted to increase involvement of women in science across Europe (Osborne et al., 2000). During the FP5 period data on women in scientific research across the EU was amassed and analysed, and a number of useful reports were published (Rees, 2002). However, in a gender impact assessment of the Information Society (IST) programmes of framework 5 it was noted that "gender issues do not appear to be systematically considered in the policy-making process" (Gender in Technology, 2001). To counteract the current under-representation of women in scientific professions, the EC has adopted gender mainstreaming in its sixth Framework programme (FP6), which runs from 2002 to 2006 (EC Resolution, 2001). Here Gender Mainstreaming has been defined as "a long term strategic approach to gender equality designed to complement the legal right women have to equal treatment with men, and positive action measures, designed to address some of the disadvantages they face" (Osbourne et al., 2000, p. 2).

• "Programmes and practice"

Rees describes three ways of implementing gender mainstreaming: (i) equal treatment which ensures men and women are treated the same; (ii) positive action with special actions to redress disadvantage; and (iii) mainstreaming equality by integrating gender equality into systems, structures, institutions, programmes, policies and practices (Rees, 2001). During FP5 a Women and Science Unit was created within the Directorate General of Research and Technological Development, and projects were initiated to monitor data about women in science across Europe (Degraef, 2004; Rees, 2002; SHE figures, 2003). How has gender mainstreaming policy been interpreted within the programmes and practices of FP6?

A general objective of the Commission (referred to in the introduction of all specific programmes of FP6) is as follows:

This work programme attempts, where possible, to reinforce and increase the place and role of women in science and research both from the perspective of equal opportunities and gender relevance of the topics covered (Vademecum, 2004).

Various EU instruments may include a task to oversee the promotion of Gender Equality in the project management. These include the Specific Support Actions (SSA), the Specific Targeted Research Projects (STREP), the Co-ordination Actions (CA) and the

Integrated Projects (IP). Of particular interest for this paper are the IP and Network of Excellence (NoE) where gender mainstreaming has been interpreted as follows:

1. IP and NoE proposals must design a gender equality action plan (Part B.10.1: Gender Action Plan).
2. Once funded, a project must show how the Gender Action Plans are conducted within the research period.
3. These plans are evaluated as part of the project evaluation.

In section 5 below I discuss the ELeGI GAP in more detail. An interesting point, which I did not at first appreciate, is that there is scope for social science/gender research within an IP or NOE via the work packages.

The 40% target for women's participation in evaluation panels applies in FP6 as in FP5. It has also been suggested that in parallel to this target setting, it would be appropriate that members of the panel have gender expertise as well as their main field of expertise (Vademecum, 2003, p.5).

Cross-sectional evaluation of all of the above will be conducted via the Women and Science Unit (as with impact studies of FP5) as described in the guidelines for Scientific Officers/Project Officers who work in the DG RTD:

> The implementation of gender issues will be followed during the whole 6th framework programme by collecting statistics (on work force) and making them accessible to the public. For the NoE's and IP's, the implementation of the action plans will also be followed. These data will be stored in a new strategic database, which includes all relevant information on gender issues in EC projects under FP6 (Vademecum, 2003, pp. 6-7).

FP6 is now in its second year, and the impact of this policy implementation is yet to be evaluated by the commission, though funding for impact analysis has been announced.

The ELeGI Project

ELeGI (the European Learning Grid Infrastructure) project is funded under IST FP6 (Technology-Enhanced Learning and access to Cultural Heritage) with €7.5m from 2004 until 2008. There are 25 partners, with approximately 60 people involved, of whom five women. This continues my involvement with exploring the potential of GRID technologies for new learning technologies, which began with the EU-funded LeGI Working Group, a Network of excellence funded under IST Framework 5.

The ELeGI project aims to develop software technologies for effective human learning. The group wishes to promote and support a learning paradigm focused on knowledge construction using experiential based and collaborative learning approaches. We are interested in the ideas of context-based, personalised and ubiquitous computing. The term "ubiquitous" here does not refer simply to "anytime/anywhere", but more generally to the ability to support multiple diverse learning contexts and automatically adapt to them. This is in contrast to the current information transfer paradigm which focuses on content and the key authoritative figure of the teacher. The team is concerned with "human centred design", rather than the applicative approach to developing e-learning tools.

The ELeGI project has three main goals:
- to define new models of human learning enabling ubiquitous and collaborative learning, which merges experiential, personalised and contextualised approaches;
- to define and implement an advanced service-oriented Grid-based software architecture for learning. This will allow us to access and integrate different technologies, resources and contents that are needed in order to realise the new paradigm. This objective will be based on pedagogical needs, by the requirements provided by test-beds (SEES), and informed by the experience gained through implementing the demonstrators;
- to validate and evaluate the software architecture and the educational approaches through the use of SEES and demonstrators. This builds on work already done, creating new learning environments rather than creating new learning resources per se (ELeGI, 2004).

The view of the consortium is that learning is a social, constructive phenomenon (Vigotsky, 1962; Hein, 1993). Knowledge construction occurs through new forms of learning based on an understanding of concepts through direct experience of their manifestation in realistic contexts (such as providing access to real world data) which are constructed from sophisticated software interfaces and devices, and represented as services. Knowledge is also constructed through "social learning" – active collaboration with other students, teachers, tutors, experts or, in general, available human peers.

The Grid is an emergent technology which was first proposed by Foster and Kesselman in 1994/95 in a selection of essays on distributed computing which describe new computing architectures to integrate the world wide web and a range of specific software resources (Foster, 1995). One analogy used by those who are developing Grid systems is with an electrical grid: the idea of information on tap, with no need for source details. Those who wish to develop Grid technologies claim that it will facilitate collaboration, allow the use of very large data sets and large-scale remote experimentation, and hence underpins much of the e-science research base.

The impetus for the distributed systems Grid is that of high energy computing, astrophysics and quantum physics, and micro-biology and bio-informatics. In Europe, CERN, and in the US, NASA, are interested parties in the use of the Grid. Commercial interest in Grid technologies is shown by Sun, Intel, Microsoft, IBM, Logica, BAE, Rolls-Royce, Roche, Pfizer and GlaxoSmithCline. Software developed to meet Grid specifications are available from Globus and Condor (Global Grid Forum, 2004). In the UK, the DTI and research councils have funded various e-science centres, the three super-computing sites and a number of large-scale research projects to investigate the use of Grid technologies. The grant allocated is £120M for three years (e-science, 2003). Examples of problems that are required to be solved by Grid technologies include (i) SETI@home (regarded by some as embarrassingly parallel[2]) which involves screen-saver code running on many workstations and is not time-dependent (SETI, 2004); and (ii) Weather forecasting, which requires the integration of very large data sets, and the querying of large distributed data sets on small number of very powerful machines. The ELeGI consortium is interested in the potential of the Open Grid Services Architecture as a means to investigate existing and new educational resources (Foster, 2002). This view is reinforced by investigations into successful e-learning software which offers a service, rather than static content delivery (Michaelson, 2004).

Within ELeGI, I have a dual role; firstly to conduct my own research, and secondly, as a member of the Equality Group, I have responsibilities for the project Gender Issues Management Plan. The next section describes both of these roles in more detail.

A dual role within the IP

• Research in ELeGI

Finesse *(finance education in a scaleable software environment)* addresses problems associated with the teaching of finance courses in the U. K. Higher Education sector by constructing a networked, web-based portfolio management game which delivers real-time stock market data for group-based learning (Power et al., 1998; Helliar et al., 2000, Michaelson et al., 2003). It was designed as a subject-specific resource within a software framework called TAGS (tutor and group support) which allows the project group to design and test various educational systems (Allison et al., 1999; Allison et al., 2001). TAGS and Finesse are part of collaborative project work between educators and computer scientists, which started in 1995. In ELeGI we will use Finesse as a demonstration by moving it from TAGS to a Grid-compliant architecture (Allison, 2004).

• Gender Equality Background

In 1999 I was appointed to the post of National Co-ordinator for the Scottish Higher Education Funding Council (SHEFC) Women in Science, Engineering and Technology initiative (WiSET). In 2002 I was re-appointed as the SHEFC Gender Equality Co-ordinator for a further 18 months. My duties under WiSET included co-ordinating institutional representatives based at each Scottish Higher Education Institute. In 1999 I identified relevant issues by visiting each institution where I met with senior managers, Vice Principals, Deans of Science and Engineering, personnel officers, academic women in SET and staff developers. My post also involved dissemination of suitable materials, and networking with other interested groups, such as AWISE and WiC

(AWISE, 2004; WiC, 2004). These duties continued within the wider remit of Gender Equality. I liased with those in the SHEFC Widening Access Funding and Strategic Policy groups, and evaluated gender equality aspects of the 2002 Scottish higher education strategic planning process. From 1999 until 2003, I was a member of the Advisory Group of ATHENA, a Women and SET initiative administered by the Equality Challenge Unit of Universities UK (previously known as the Committee of Vice-Chancellors and Principals).

During this period, I attended Scottish, UK and European group meetings associated with Equal Opportunities, Gender Equality in HE, and Women and SET - this included those working in the EU CORDIS directorate. I was responsible for advising SHEFC, and the sector, on all relevant policy issues such as Gender Mainstreaming and Government Science Policy. I responded, on the funding council's behalf, to major UK consultations such as the 2001 Quinquennial Review of the UK Research Councils and the Equal Opportunities Council of Scotland education strategy. Most recently, I was a member of the advisory team for the Baroness Greenfield's Report, 'Set Fair', commissioned by Patricia Hewitt, Minister for the DTI, which led to the setting up of the UK Resource Centre for Women in SET (see UKRC, 2005).

• ELeGI Gender Equality role

Within ELeGI I have various gender equality roles. During the bidding process I was involved with writing the B10 section, and those work packages that reflected my computer science research interests. I also drew to the attention of the executive the need to integrate the B10 with work packages and management plans, where appropriate. Management responsibilities include membership of the Equality Group, dissemination and networking, and the administration of meetings. The planning and reporting process are also my job. In addition I organise and attending events associated with gender equality action and research. I am a member of the organising committee of the WiC 2005 Conference on Gender Politics of ICT. I am organiser of two Scottish Hopper Colloquia, one in May 2005, the other in 2007 as a member of the women@cl project which is funded for three years by EPSRC. Scottish Hopper colloquium are modelled on the American Grace Hopper Conferences and are professional meetings for women in computer science research. I will continue to attend and present at Gender and IST/ICT conferences which are sponsored by the EC, and will encourage ELeGI colleagues to attend these events. We have decided to set up a Gender Research & e-learning group within ELeGI and hope to present at the first ELeGI conference in Salerno in July 2005.

The ELeGI Gender Action Plan

The Commission recognises a threefold relationship between women and research, and has articulated its action around the following:
- Women's participation in research must be encouraged both as

scientists/technologists and within the evaluation, consultation and implementation process
- Research must address women's needs, as much as men's needs
- Research must be carried out to contribute to an enhanced understanding of gender issues (Guide, 2003).

A B.10 Gender Action Plan has two sections, the second of which has a further refinement into two. The first section details actions such as mentoring, networking and making links to external groups such as schools and professional bodies. The second section is where the relevance of gender research must be detailed. This is more obvious in the case of Biological research or health fields. In the GAP section a consortium must detail activities intended to support women in the project, and discuss the impact of the research on gender equality, and the way that the research will consider gender issues, where appropriate. The B.10 should refer to sections in the rest of bid via details in the Work Packages, the evaluation process, and as part of the project management objectives. Thus, in deciding to create an equality sub-committee as part of the project management team, we had to explain when this group would meet and the expected remit of the group. In the management deliverables section of the B part of the bid we detailed a deliverable in the form of a Gender Issues Management Plan, which was completed in the first half of the first project year. It is interesting to note that the B.10 section of part B of the current FP6 bidding process is only one page out of, typically, more than a hundred. This follows the style of the previously adopted Ethics section, B.11, which is also mandatory within the bidding process. Unusually, the EU intends to publish the B.10 sections of all successful bids (Vademecum, 2003). As a result I have sent copies of the ELeGI B.10 to several colleagues seeking EU funding, and have presented it at an UKRO workshop on Gender Action Plans in FP 6 (Paisley University, 28 October 2003).

In the ELeGI GAP, section 1, we gave details of dissemination, networking and events; in section 2 we discussed the need to think about how to research gender and e-learning (See Appendix A). My experience of various support groups for women in computing, such as WiC, was useful for section 1. The GAP was the basis for the subsequent Gender Issues Management Plan.

The Gender Issues Management Plan was produced by myself and the project officer, who is a member of the Equality Group. This deliverable has required us to make some modifications from the GAP. The process of obtaining funding took over a year since the bid was lodged with the Commission. Several changes have occurred since the B.10 was written. For example, the Equality Group is smaller than proposed and will meet annually. More networks and conferences have emerged as time goes by. Mentoring is not going to be easy to organise, partly due to the lack of women in the group, partly due to differences in cultures (both different countries and different types of organisation), and partly because the women's needs are not identical (only 2 of the 5 women are in computing, for example). Gender awareness questionnaires have been designed to help group leaders identify each group's organisational support for gender equality. This method of scoping gender equality needs was not detailed in the original plan. It is hoped that this will make some of the cultural differences more explicit. We have strong UK contacts in gender equality (such as the conferences that I am linked with), but are still identifying more European contacts. Though members of the consortium are happy to support gender equality, there is as yet, little evidence of mainstreaming. I am happy to report an increase from four to five in the current numbers of women in the project.

Conclusion

Some issues have emerged during the process of writing a GAP and the management plan for gender issues for ELeGI. I have already discussed some of the problems with mentoring women in ELeGI. A major worry is to what extent this process is mainstreaming gender. Though colleagues are supportive of gender equality, there is a desire to leave much of the fine detail to me, and this is shown in the 50% allocation of my role to management duties for gender equality, and no such allocation to any other member of the consortium. In other words, I am concerned about tokenism in the process.

In trying to create an Equality Group, it became clear that we had been over ambitious in choosing biannual meetings. The project has a strong management ethos, and there are several meetings in Luxembourg and Brussels which I and others cannot attend. It was also apparent that this group would self-select and it has 5 members. My overall research presence is small compared to the rest of the consortium, and unfortunately funding cuts were easier to apply in no-core areas. However, though I drafted the first version of the Gender Issues Management Plan, the project manager has been very helpful in correcting the draft, and disseminating the report. Some of the women have welcomed the women-only mail group, and have commented on feelings of isolation within the consortium.

Another concern is that the evaluation of the GAP and the process within the period of the funded instrument is seen as a cross-cutting exercise, and not one that is conducted in the normal way via the research directorate. In retrospect asking for a short self-reflective report to be a deliverable could make the process more meaningful.

Problems of understanding the process from within the directorates, and consortiums have also emerged in the last year. At a roundtable discussion during GIST 2004, Dr. Zobel of the Directorate of IST said that there had been a lack of gender research work packages in proposals. I mentioned the mixed messages that had emerged from EU project officers and evaluators concerning the appropriateness of work packages with gender research aspects (GIST, 2004). There were also fears about the vulnerability of such work packages to any funding cuts during the negotiation stages, since they were not regarded as core research by most of the consortium. It was obvious from the discussion that specialised researchers in gender and ICT had not been contacted by computing consortiums, and integrated within their proposals.

There are also more general issues that arise from considerations of the nature of social interventions of this type.

...merely adding gender and stirring will be neither a theoretically nor politically adequate substitute for feminist approaches (Rose, 1999, p.43).

What is the 'correct' feminist approach to science? Is Gender Mainstreaming only about 'adding in gender'? Feminist approaches are by no means uniform, and diversity is seen as a strength of the many forms of feminist theory. There are several feminist views of gender policies with regard to science, engineering and technology. For example, there are those who wish to create a feminist science by questioning the epistemological basis of science in general, in contrast to those who wish to increase the numbers of women in SET (see Anderson, 2004 for an overview of feminist epistemiology and philosophy of science). Mainstreaming has been criticised by those who worry about changing the status quo (usually in terms of 'positive discrimination doesn't work'); it has also been regarded as a rhetorical device with no practical implications for change, and is thus open to attack from many points of view.

As a measure of the policy process for FP6, from the Research Directorate it would be useful to know to what extent the expectations of a target of 40% female evaluators for evaluation panels, and the actual gender equality expertise amongst members of the evaluation panels for FP6.

In my opinion, the current working through of gender mainstreaming policy in FP6, is an interesting way of dealing with the perceived dichotomy of responses to the 'Women in SET problem'. Research groups are encouraged, firstly to think about the support mechanisms for women in SET, secondly, to explicitly address the possible effect of their work on gender equality, and thirdly, to deal with the possibility of gendered research. The process has produced more discussion of gender equality in science, engineering and technology, both within the secretariat, amongst funding bidders, and the associated university services such as UKRO. It has highlighted cultural differences about ideas of gender equality across Europe. It has also allowed those of us who felt split between our roles as ICT researchers and feminists to play to both strengths.

Acronyms

AWISE	Association of Women in Science and Engineering
CA	Co-ordination Actions
CERN	*Conseil Europeen pour le Recherche Nucleaire*
	(European Laboratory for Particle Physics)
ELeGI	European Learning Grid Infrastructure
ETAN	European Technology Assessment Network

EU	European Union
Finesse	Finance Education in a Scalable Software Environment
GAP	Gender Action Plan
GIST	Gender perspectives for the design of Information Society Technology
HEI	Higher Education Institute
IP	Integrated Project
OGSA	Open Grid Services Architecture
NoE	Network of Excellence
SET	Science, Engineering and Technology
SETI	Search for Extraterrestrial Intelligence
SSA	Specific Support Actions
STREP	Specific Targeted Research Projects
UKRC	UK Resource Centre for Women in Science, Engineering and Technology
UKRO	UK Research Office
WiC	Women in Computing
WiSET	Women in Science, Engineering and Technology

References

Allison, C., Bramley, M., Michaelson, R. and Serrano, J. (1999) An Integrated Framework for Distributed Learning Environments in *"Advances in Concurrent Engineering", 6th ISPE International Conference on Concurrent Engineering,* (Bath, 1999), 345-354.

Allison, C., Ruddle, A., McKechan, D. and Michaelson, R. (2001) The Architecture of a Framework for Building Distributed Learning Environments in *Advanced Learning Technologies,* (Wisconsin, 2001), IEEE Press, 29-35.

Allison, C., Michaelson, R. (2004) Design Considerations for an EleGI Portal, *3rd Intl. LeGE-WG Workshop: Towards a European Learning Grid Infrastructure,* Berlin, 3rd December 2003. EWIC at www.bcs.org/ewic. ISSN 1477-9358

Anderson, E. (2004) Feminist Epistemology and Philosophy of Science, *The Stanford Encyclopedia of Philosophy (Summer 2004 Edition),* Edward N. Zalta (ed.) plato.stanford.edu/archives/sum2004/entries/feminism-epistemology/

AWISE (2004) www.awise.org

Brown, J. S., Duguid, P. (2000) *The Social Life of Information,* Harvard Business School Press, Boston, Massachusetts. 1-57851-708-7.

CERN (2004) http://gridcafe.web.cern.ch/gridcafe/whatcando/compu-problems.html

Degraef, V. (2004) *Presentation on Gender Action Plans in FP6,* UKRO Workshop, Paisley University, 28 October 2004.

EC Resolution (2001) Council Resolution on Science and Society and on Women in Science, 26 June 2001 (10357/01) europa.eu.int/comm/research/science-society/documents_en.html#back

ELeGI (2004) www.cordis.lu/ist/directorate_e/telearn/fp6_elegi.htm

EOC Research and Resources Unit (2000) "A checklist for Gender Proofing Research", UK Equal Opportunities Commission.

e-science (2003) www.escience-grid.org.uk/

Foster, I., Kesselman, C. (1995) *The Grid: Blueprint for a New Computing Infrastructure*, Morgan Kaufmann, San Francisco.

Foster, I., Kesselman, C., Nick, J. M., Tuecke, S. (2002) *The Physiology of the Grid: An Open Grid Services Architecture for Distributed Systems Integration.* www.globus.org/research/papers/ogsa.pdf

Gender in Technology (2001) *Gender Impact Assessment of the Specific programmes of Framework Programme 5: User Friendly Information Society (IST)*, European Commission, Information Society Directorate-Generale.

GIST (2004) *Gender as a Category in the IST Priority of the 6th and 7th Framework Programme? Building Alliances for Future Collaborations.* Minutes of the roundtable discussion, The International Symposium "GIST - Gender Perspectives Increasing Diversity For Information Society Technology" June 24 to 26, 2004. Bremen, Germany. July 15 2004. kitkat.informatik.uni-bremen.de/new/egist/html/dl/euroundv1.pdf

Global Grid Forum (2004) http://www.gridforum.org/

Guide (2003) Annex 4, Integrating the Gender Dimension. *IST Priority, Continuous submission call: Guide for Proposers.* Co-ordination Actions, Final Edition. IST Director General. December, 2002. Revised edition, March 2003 Reference: B_PGCA_20020C_EN.DOC. www.cordis.lu/ist/

Hein, G. E (1993) The Significance of Constructivism for Museum Education", in *Museums and the Needs of the People*, Jerusalem. Israel ICOM Committee. www.gem.org.uk/hein.html

Helliar, C.V., Michaelson, R., Power, D.M. and Sinclair, C.D. Using a Portfolio Management Game (FINESSE) to Teach Finance. *Accounting Education*, 9 (1). 37-51.

Michaelson, R. (2004) Closely observed initiatives: or How I learnt to speak fluent JISC, Understanding Sociotechnical Design workshop, Napier University, Edinburgh, June 2004.

Michaelson, R., Helliar, C. V., Power, D. M., Allison, C. (2003a) *Group Work and the Web: FINESSE and TAGS*, D. Hawkridge, R. Kaye, (eds.) *Learning and Teaching for Business: case studies of successful innovation*, Kogan Page. June 2003. ISBN 0 7494 4025 2.

Osborne, M., Rees, T., Bosch, M., Hermann, C., Hilden, J., McLaren, A., Palomba, R., Peltonen, L., Vela, C., Weis, D., Wold, A. and Wennerås, C. (2000) *Science Policies in the European Union: Promoting excellence through mainstreaming gender equality.* A report from the ETAN Network on Women and Science, Luxembourg: Office for Official Publications of the European Communities. 92-828-8682-4

Pollack, M. A., Hafner-Burton (2000) Mainstreaming Gender in the European Union, *Journal of European Public Policy*, Vol. 7, No. 1 (September 2000) www.jeanmonnetprogram.org/papers/00/000201.html

Power, D.M., Michaelson, R. and Allison, C. (1998) The Finesse Portfolio Management Facility, in the *9th CTI-AFM Conference*, York, CTI-AFM, 119 -125

Rees, T. (1998). *Mainstreaming Equality in the European Union: Education, Training, and Labor Market Policies* (New York: Routledge).

Rees, T., (2001) 'Mainstreaming gender equality in science in the European Union: The ETAN Report' *Gender and Education*, Vol. 13, No. 3, pp. 243-260

Rees, T. (2002a) 'The politics of "mainstreaming" gender equality' in E. Breitenbach, A. Brown, F. Mackay and J. Webb (eds.) *Changing Politics of Gender Equality* Basingstoke: Palgrave. pp. 45-69.

Rees, T. (2002) *National Policies on Women and Science in Europe: a report about women and science in 30 countries*, The Helsinki Group on Women and Science, D.G. for Research / RTD-C5, Women and Science, March, 2002. 92-894-3579-8

Rose, Hilary (1999) A fair share of the research pie or re-engendering scientific and technological Europe? *European Journal of Women's Studies*, Vol. 6, pp. 31–47.

SETI (2004) setiathome.ssl.berkeley.edu/

She Figures (2003) *"She figures", Women and Science: Statistics and Indicators*, European Commission Directorate-General for Research: Science and Society europa.eu.int/comm/research/science-society/pdf/she_figures_2003.pdf

Shirts, M., Pande, V. S. (2000) Screen Savers of the World Unite! *Science Magazine*, Volume 290, Number 5498, Issue 8, December, pp. 1903-1904. The American Association for the Advancement of Science. folding.stanford.edu/papers/SPScience2000.pdf

UKRC (2005) www2.shu.ac.uk/nrc/index.cfm

VADEMECUM (2003) VADEMECUM: Gender Mainstreaming in the 6th Framework Programme – Reference Guide for Scientific Officers/Project Officers, DG RTD, Unit C-5: Women & Science, March 2003. ftp://ftp.cordis.lu/pub/science-society/docs/gendervademecum.pdf

Vigotsky, L. V. (1962) *Thought and Language*, Cambridge, MA. MIT Press

WiC (2004) www.wic.org.uk/index.htm

Wilkinson, B., Allen, M. (1999) *Parallel Programming: Techniques and Applications using Networked Workstations and Parallel Computers,* Prentice Hall, New Jersey, 1999. ISBN 0136717101

Women and Science (1999) *Women and Science: Mobilising women to enrich European research*. Communication of the Commission adopted on 17 February 1999.

Appendix A: Example B.10 for the ELeGI consortium bid.

B.10 GENDER ISSUES

B.10.1 GENDER ACTION PLAN

Gender Equality is an important issue for the Computer Science Community. Not only are there few women studying Computer science and IT at university level, there are fewer women academics in university departments, especially in promoted posts. This gender imbalance is reflected in the IT industry across Europe [1]; it also mirrors the European-wide issue of the representation of Women in science, engineering and technology [2].

Employment and participation in the project will aim to involve both genders without bias. This means using equal opportunities in the selection of staff; while we cannot mandate practices in partner organisations, the project will act as an advocate for equal opportunities within the partnership. Each of the members of the ELeGI consortium has and actively pursues an Equal Opportunities Policy, which includes Gender issues.

The ELeGI project will design and implement a project-level action plan able to act synergistically with the members policies to promote gender equality within the frame of the project. Following guidelines from the D.G. Women and Science Unit, mainstreaming activities will be undertaken via gender action plans appropriate to each project [3]. These will be defined during the Management WP with the help of specific experts. The action plans will include measures to encourage the involvement of women at all stages of research and development such as:

1. disseminating best practice across the projects in the area of gender equality, and distributing the results of the evaluation of the action plans to the consortium;
2. making links with networks of female scientists in the field of the project via organisations such as:
   - the British Computer Society Women's Group,
   - the Scottish Hopper Colloquium for Women in Computer Science,
   - the Femconsult Database (see www.cews.uni-bonn.de),
   - the Network of Women in Computer Science, Mathematics and Physics of the Netherlands;
3. organising an European colloquium for female scientists on the proposal topic using the model of the American Grace Hopper Conference for Women in Computer Science (see www.gracehopper.org/);
4. investigating training programs for female researchers and junior administrative staff;
5. linking with European researchers in Gender Equality via the Research in Gender Equality in Higher Education Conferences and the D.G. Research for Women and Science of the European Commission.

Once these plans are finalised, the Equal Opportunity committee will monitor any project activities and ensure that the interests and needs of both genders are taken into account. The committee will meet on a biannual basis and will report to the project co-ordinator on the state of the application of the plans, will express advice on project activities, will promote new actions where necessary, will suggest revisions of the policy and will evaluate the impact of each plan.

Measures relating to these action plans will be performed during the project duration. A gender action report concerning the progress and implications of the plans will be delivered at the end of the project.

B.10.2 GENDER ISSUES

Gender issues in IT and education are still under-researched. Some regard the current uses of ICT as a barrier for women whereas others see it as potentially liberating; many are concerned that the status quo will be maintained, or re-enforced, by any changes in technologies for education [4].

This proposal is concerned with designing new forms of technology to support learners and educators. It is necessary to ask whether the structured projects enable women as well as men to make sense of their experiences, to find their voice, and to take positive action on their worlds. Rather than promoting the latest technology to connect learners with teachers, and with each other, it is necessary to consider whether these technologies are equally available to women and men, and whether women and men are likely to approach and experience these technologies in the same way.

The project will investigate ways in which learning and educating is a gendered activity. The questions that must be posed go to the heart of how educators see their tasks. For example, the question, "How do adults learn?," is transformed into "How do women and men learn?" The question, "What sorts of conditions must we create for learners so that the open door does not become a revolving door?," becomes "What sorts of support do women and men need in order to succeed as learners?"

In the framework of ELeGI we will ensure that methodologies and technologies we produce are not biased towards either gender by doing the following:

- developing inclusive design techniques at all levels of the project process;
- selecting pedagogic models that favour both men and women,
- ensuring that assumptions made about learning or knowledge are carefully examined for any gender bias,
- developing guidelines for technology that is even-handed with respect to gender,
- evaluating all systems with respect to gender,
- ensuring that global partnerships are even handed with respect to gender,
- ensuring all participants in test-beds are selected uniformly with respect to gender.

These research issues will be monitored at the management level. Moreover, gender issues will be an important part of the evaluation workpackage for both the work

93

methods of the project teams and in the nature of the research that is carried out.

Throughout ELeGI, gender issues will be seen as part of the more general issue of equal opportunities which also covers race, ethnicity, national origin, sexual orientation, religion, age, veteran status and disabling condition. Equal opportunities, and specifically gender, are important both within the operation of this project, and for the intended beneficiaries of this project. All results coming from E-LeGI will be multi-cultural, multi-lingual and gender non-specific and we will ensure that the interests and needs of both genders are taken into account, and the dissemination is made to both groups.

References

[1] Panteli, N., Stack, J., Ramsay, H. (2001) Gendered patterns in Computing work in the late 1990s, *New Technology, Work and Employment*, 16, 1, 3-17.

[2] Rees, T. *National Policies on Women and Science in Europe: a report about women and science in 30 countries*, The Helsinki Group on Women and Science, D.G. for Research / RTD-C5, Women and Science, March, 2002. 92-894-3579-8

[3] *Science Policies in the European Union: promoting excellence through Mainstreaming Gender Equality.* The ETAN expert working group on Women and Science Report for the European Commission, 2000. 92-828-8682-4

[4] Brown, J. S., Duguid, P. (2002) *The Social Life of Information*, Harvard Business School Press.

Notes

1 ELeGI is funded with €7.5m under the Information, Society and Technology (IST) Framework 6 programme from 2004 until 2008.

2 'Embarrassingly Parallel Computation' is a well-defined term used in the context of cluster computing, parallel processing and distributed systems. References for the use of this terminology include: Wilkinson, Allen, 1999; Cern, 2004; and Shirts, Pande, 2000.

8 Understandings of Gender and Competence in ICT

Johanna Sefyrin

Mid Sweden University

Abstract

Developers' understandings of gender have been shown to influence their development of software; viewing competence in information and communication technology (ICT) as masculine probably affects the construction of e-government services as well. This work is a study of understandings of gender and competence in ICT, among two groups of individuals who use ICT daily in their workplaces. The main focus of the work is on understandings of gender and competence among the participants in the study, along with social processes which produce, confirm or change those understandings. In the groups studied, competence in ICT was viewed as a question of interest in ICT, where men were seen as more interested in ICT than women. Furthermore, situated understandings of competence and gender in ICT were developed in the groups and were negotiated among individuals in the groups, and then used as norms with which individuals understood themselves and their behaviours. In the discussion section, the conclusions are related to the development of e-government services.

1. Introduction

Faulkner (2003) talks about the division of work in technology as gendered in a way that is partly based on an understanding of men as technically competent. Cockburn (1985) has examined how technical competence is related to masculinity, and describes the mechanisms that reproduce men as technologically more competent. According to Cockburn, the mechanisms are based on a 'continual redefinition, sub-division and fragmentation' of work processes (ibid. p. 231). In this way, every time a woman enters an occupation previously held to be male, the occupation lose status, and men move away from it, keeping a distance from women by moving to other occupations; the occupation is redefined as non-technological, or requiring less technological competence. In this way, according to Cockburn, men keep their status as technologically competent, and maintain their difference from women. Cockburn's studies shows that technological competence is nothing natural or self-evident, but that it is socially constructed. Following this line of thinking, Vehviläinen (1997) has studied the social construction of technological knowledge, though in terms of expertise. Vehviläinen (ibid.) concludes that expertise cannot be measured in objective terms, but is shaped through social and political processes and practices; thus, expertise as well is socially constructed. Mellström (2003) brings similar questions into focus as essential for the construction of competence, asking who has the power to define what is valid and relevant as technological competence. Corneliussen (2003) studies how individuals position themselves in relation to a hegemonic discourse of computers, and concludes that it is easier for men to be associated with computer competence. According to Corneliussen:

> Men are expected to have more interest, experience and knowledge about computers than women. Men are expected to be motivated by playing with or being fascinated by the technology, while women are expected to be motivated by an understanding of computers as something useful, practical and needed (ibid. p. 2)

All the informants in the study referred to this discourse, which is to say that it is hegemonic. One of the informants even said that she couldn't understand computer programming, because she is a woman. The informants in the study thus used a discourse they all knew of, to make their own behaviour legitimate. They did not do this in a similar manner though; they used different strategies to either follow the discourse or protest against it; that is, they chose to position themselves in different ways related to the discourse.

Understanding technological competence as something masculine has consequences in several areas; among them is the current development from government services to e-government services in Sweden as well as internationally (Følstad, Jørgensen & Krogstie 2004). E-government services are public services given by municipalities as well as government agencies at different societal levels through electronic channels like the Internet (Følstad, Jørgensen & Krogstie 2004; Bakry 2004). The aim of e-government, according to Grönlund (2001), is to make public services accessible to the citizens 24 hours a day, seven days a week, resulting in higher accessibility, quality, and at a lower cost to the taxpayer. This aim is usually reached by decreasing manual services in local offices, and replacing this by increasing self-services via the web, automated telephone systems and call centres (Wiberg & Grönlund 2002). Examples of services are the option of making income-tax returns via the web offered by the Swedish Tax Authority, the facility to search for new employment in databases on the web offered by the Swedish National Labour Market Administration, and the option to fill in forms for sick leave on the web offered by the Swedish Insurance Office.

Assuming that the discourse Corneliussen (2003) describes above indeed is hegemonic, this probably does play a part in understandings of gender; also among those who are developing e-government services. A study made by Huff and Cooper (1987) showed that program developers had certain gendered ideas about the intended users of the software, ideas that made them develop different software for boys, girls and students. Rommes, van Slooten, van Oost and Oudshoorn (2004) conclude that developers often rely on gender stereotypes when they take gender into account in their software development. Another method frequently used among software developers in their study was the 'I-methodology', where the developers use themselves as user representatives, assuming that they are representative of users (Rommes, van Slooten, van Oost & Oudshoorn 2004). These findings indicate that understandings of gender do influence the software that is being developed. Since e-government services are aimed at all citizens, which is a large and heterogeneous group when it comes to e.g. age, ethnicity, education, occupation, gender and class, relying on gender stereotypes or the I-methodology is probably not a good idea.

In this work, the focus is on the social processes constructing competence in ICT as gendered in a certain way, and more specifically, social processes during everyday conversational interaction within groups of individuals. I have used the term 'understandings' to refer to ideas about how things are or should be in a certain area. My use of the term 'understanding' is very close to the concept of discourse used in the meaning of 'a particular framework of ideas or way of understanding' (White 2004, p. 9). Elvin-Nowak and Thomsson (2001, p. 410) talk about dominant discourses as something individuals use as 'standards against which to understand and evaluate their own experiences and construct their own ideas'. This means that those constructions are normative, and affect individuals' practices and thinking. The study is inspired by the approach of 'doing gender' (Kvande 2003; Korvajärvi 2003), and of discourse analysis as it is used in social psychology (Winther-Jørgensen & Phillips 2000). In 'doing gender', gender is seen as something emerging in people's activities, and as produced and reproduced in everyday interactions between individuals (Kvande 2003; Korvajärvi, 2003). The focus is on individuals' active production of meanings and understandings. With this perspective, gender becomes performed in different gendered practices, rather than being biological in origin. Gender is thus seen as produced in social processes and activities, and among those activities are speech, conversations and thinking (Acker 1997, in Kvande 2003). Different understandings and practices for doing gender are connected to a specific location and to a specific context, limited by the certain conditions, individuals and circumstances in that context (Kvande 2003; Haraway 1991).

West and Fenstermaker (2002) report findings from a study of a University of California Board of Regents meeting, where participants while speaking, repeatedly referred to themselves in terms of gender, race and class, in order to make their own and others' statements and behaviours meaningful as certain types of persons. In this way, the participants referred to implicit understandings, assumed to be acknowledged by the others present, of how a person of a certain gender, race and class, should act in such a context. This meant that individuals referred to these shared understandings to validate and make sense of their own and others' behaviour, much in the same way as the participants in Corneliussen's study (2001) referred to a hegemonic discourse of computers to legitimate their own positions. In this way, the participants in the study 'did' gender, race and class.

Based on this theoretical ground, the purpose of this study was to describe some understandings of competence in ICT and its relation to gender, and to describe how these understandings are reproduced and changed in interaction between the individuals participating in the study. An important question raised in the study was how understandings would be developed and used as – in Elvin-Nowak's and Thomsson's (2001) words – standards against which individuals understand and evaluate their experiences and construct their ideas.

2. Method

I wanted to explore understandings of gender and ICT in the context of everyday interactions at work, among individuals interacting with each other on a daily basis, individuals who are working with ICT in some way. Focus group interviews seemed an appropriate technique to use for this purpose, preferably with existing work groups, i.e. people who interact on a daily basis in their workplaces. I conducted focus group interviews with two different groups each consisting of about seven persons, mixed men and women. One group consisted of economists in a large Swedish industrial company, and the other of systems analysts in a large Swedish service company. In traditional terms these two groups consist of, on the one hand, users, i.e. the economists and, on the other hand, people who in some way are involved in the development and construction of ICT[1], i.e. systems analysts.

I met each group twice. In the first meeting I told the participants about the study, the background, purpose and so on, and they were given a questionnaire with questions about their views on gender and competence in ICT. In the questionnaire I also gave a definition of ICT, which was about ICT as a set of technical artefacts, but also of programs, systems and services around these artefacts. The questionnaire was used mainly to prepare the participants for the focus group interviews, to give them an opportunity to think the matter through in order for them to have something to contribute during the focus group interviews.

The second time we met was when the focus group interviews were actually taking place. During the focus group interviews, in which I played the role of moderator, we discussed the same topics as the questions in the questionnaire. I focused on questions about if and how the participants thought that competence in ICT has anything to do with gender. The purpose of the focus group interviews was to make the participants talk about gender and competence in ICT, and to express their everyday understandings of the topic. In this way I wanted to analyse how they talked about this gender and competence in ICT. The focus group interviews were recorded on digital video. When I had transferred the video recordings to computer files, I watched them and transcribed to text every section in which the participants talked about gender and competence in some way. I then analysed the discussions with the help of a number of analytical concepts.

2.1 Analytical concepts

My primary areas of interest when it came to analysis was whether the participants in the focus group interviews understood gender as difference or as sameness, or if they discussed gender in terms of gender neutrality (Magnusson 1998; Hedlin 2004), if they discussed gender at a personal, group, or symbolic level (Fahlgren 2002), if gender had become normative in the group, and if there were several different, and perhaps opposing, understandings (Magnusson 1999).

2.2 Analysis of the interactive process

When I watched the recordings, I discovered things that the analytical concepts did not cover, things that had to do with a dynamic interactive process taking place in the discussions. I noticed how the participants developed a common understanding of gendered competence in ICT, how they tested and added different concepts and experiences in order to develop their understanding, and how they positioned themselves in relation to this understanding. It was also clear that the participants negotiated different positions as valid depending on the understanding of gendered competence in ICT that was developed in the group. This was an unexpected find but gradually the focus of the study slid over to the social processes in the group. The analysis of the interactive process was inspired by the theoretical perspective of doing gender, with its focus on the negotiation of meanings (Kvande 2003), and Donna Haraway's concept of located knowledge (Haraway 1991).

3. Results – Analysis of the Interactive Process

In this section the results are presented, with a focus on the analysis of the interactive process. However, the questions discussed during the focus group interviews, and the results of the analysis using the analytical areas are interwoven in these results. All names are fictitious.

3.1 The economists

The economists' group consisted of four women and three men, the oldest in their fifties and the youngest in their thirties. In this group there was an apparent wish to reach a consensus, to agree upon understandings on the topics that were discussed during the interviews. The economists from the industrial company discussed ICT in terms of mobile phones and their use, programming VCRs, using computers, the Internet and search services on the Internet. They related this to their private lives and not to their work, although I asked them about their tasks at work several times. Indeed, they appeared to be using computers and the Internet all the time in their work. For this group, competence in ICT had to do with interest in ICT, and they saw this interest as more common among men than among women. Some of the participants saw this as biological, meaning that boys from birth are more interested in technology than girls are. Others saw this as a matter of upbringing and talked about it in terms of gender roles, the roles of schools, computer games for boys, and culture. However, there was a general consensus that it *should* be as easy for women as for men to achieve competence in ICT. However, they saw that in reality there are differences in how women and men are engaged in technical education and the professions, but they could not really explain this.

In this group, computer games were seen as something that men, but not women, engage in. Also, there was an understanding that men are more interested in 'technological stuff', and this included the Internet. The participants saw women as less interested in and less frequent users of the Internet, including the downloading of music. These are the general understandings that were developed in this group, but even within the group there were individuals who did not conform to these understandings, i.e. who did not follow the group norm.

One such example was Svante, a man in his fifties, who said that he was not very interested in technology in his private life. Svante said that he was tired of computers when he came home from work and did not want to sit in front of the computer, since he had done it all day at work. Svante told us that his wife, a teacher, spent a lot of time in front of the computer in her private time, and she also programmed the VCR in their home. Svante seemed to think that he did not conform to the understanding of a man's interest in technology that had been developed in the group. According to this understanding he, but not his wife, should sit in front of the computer, and he, and not his wife, should program the VCR. Here, Svante seemed to make an exception to the understanding of gender and competence in ICT that was taking shape in the group, and he seemed to feel a need to explain his position, to defend his actions, since they did not conform to the dominant discourse. He used his age to explain that he was not as interested in the computer and the VCR as he, as a man, was supposed to be according to the group's ideas. He said that maybe it is age that determines interest in computers and technology, and that he, belonging to an older generation, is not included in the group for which this discourse is valid.

In this way, Svante added an explanatory factor in the group's understanding of the area, and deepened their understanding of gender and competence in ICT. Svante's experiences became part of the experiences that were used to develop an understanding of the area in the group. This also means that individual participant's different understandings were used to shape and develop a general understanding, or to develop several different understandings, in the group. Furthermore, it is obvious that the understanding in the group worked as a normative discourse, which the participants used to understand themselves and their behaviours. The result of the negotiation is not clear; there was no statement that one behaviour was better or more valid than the other. Instead, it seemed like they simply left it at that, either that both behaviours (to as a man be uninterested in computers and programming of the video in the private life, and as a man be interested in these things) were seen as valid, or that there was no resolution of the matter.

Another example of how the participants negotiated meanings of gender and competence in ICT, is related to the area of downloading music from the Internet. As stated above, there was an understanding in the group that women are less interested in the Internet, including the downloading of music. However, this was questioned when Maria, a woman, stated that she in fact does download music and burns it onto CDs. When she said this, she seemed a bit embarrassed and the others laughed a little; it is obvious that she was an exception in the eyes of the others; a few moments before another participant stated that only guys download music from the Internet. This was followed by a discussion between Cecilia and Maria, who were both in their thirties, but who acted totally differently when it came to downloading music from the Internet. Cecilia said that she usually asked her boyfriend, who, she claimed, was very interested in 'all that Internet stuff', to download the music she wants. Cecilia claimed she had no time and no interest in learning how to do it, she said she had other things to do that were more important. Maria said she had other things to do too, but she downloads music anyway, she finds the time to do this. This is obviously a small conflict about whose behaviour is the valid behaviour, from the point of view of the discourse developed in the group. In the eyes of the group women are uninterested in doing this, and Cecilia's position was unquestioned until Maria said she downloaded music. When Maria admitted she does download music, she felt a need to explain her behaviour, which seems odd and deviant in the eyes of the others present. When she did this, Cecilia's position was no longer self evident, and then she felt a need to explain and defend her right to be uninterested and ignorant of this area. This can be seen as a negotiation of valid positions related to the discourse of women as less interested in computers. At first, there was a general consensus about how the area should be understood, but when Maria told the group about her acting, it was no longer self-evident how the matter should be understood. This was followed by a discussion about the validity of different behaviours related to how women can and should act when it comes to downloading music from the Internet. Cecilia claimed her right – as a woman – to be ignorant of and uninterested in downloading music, and Maria claimed her right – again as a woman – to be interested and competent in this area. One can see how the participants used the understanding developed in the group to understand themselves as women and as men.

3.2 The systems analysts

The group of systems analysts consisted of three men and three women, aged about thirty to fifty, a slightly younger group of individuals than the economists. In this group the participants were not as talkative as the group of economists, and I could not detect the same wish to reach a consensus. The participants in this group were more individualistic and did not try to agree on the matters discussed. One other thing was that this group consisted of systems analysts, which made their position in relation to ICT somewhat different from that of the economists.

Also in this group, competence was perceived as something that comes from an interest in and time spent with ICT, and this interest was seen as something that men have more than women. Everyone agreed on this, and a variety of phenomena that supported this view were discussed. Such examples are that, in their own company there was a programmers' section, apart from their own section which consisted of analysts, and there were more female analysts than there were programmers. Here, programming was seen as a more technical activity than analysis, and the distribution of women programmers and analysts thus confirmed their view of women as less interested in technology and technical activities. Also, according to their own standards, they reported that they knew few women whom they regarded as highly competent in ICT. In their view, competence in ICT has to do with the ability to configure hardware and software in different ways. One of the participants said he knew a woman who had built her own computer network at home out of pure interest, and he seemed very impressed by her; for him she was a striking exception in his experiences of men and women and their relationship to ICT. When I asked the participants about their image of a person who is competent in ICT, none of them thought of a woman, although two of the female participants explicitly tried to find an example of a woman competent in ICT in their own past experiences. This shows how the participants in the group used their own personal experiences and knowledge to shape an understanding of gender and competence in ICT, how their personal experiences in this area were limited, and how these limitations affected their understandings of the area. This I interpret as an example of located knowledge (Haraway 1991).

The participants talked a lot about gender differences, but on several occasions claimed that there should be no gender differences when it comes to the conditions that they saw as prerequisite for acquiring competence in ICT. In the end, one male participant, Gunnar, tried to summarise the discussion by saying that the discussion had made it clear that gender differences are biological in their origin. Another male participant, Jonas, did not agree, and there followed a discussion that showed that there was no consensus at all on this matter. Three of the participants started to argue that interest in technology is biological and more common among boys, and one argued that it is a question of culture and upbringing. Then one participant changed her opinion, so there were two people on each side (the remaining participants did not take sides). Obviously there was no consensus on the matter of gender and competence in ICT, and individual participants in the group interpreted the discussion of gender differences in very different ways. Some interpreted it as a proof of the biological origin of gender differences, and others as a proof of how girls and boys are brought up in different ways by families and the surrounding society. The same discussion thus was interpreted in the light of totally different frames of reference, and thereby acquired totally different meanings.

4. Conclusions

The participants in the study expressed the view that competence in ICT has to do with interest in ICT, and that men are more interested in ICT than women. In this way, both groups related to a discourse of men as more interested and competent in ICT than women, a discourse based on gender difference. However, their opinions were based on different explanations of the origins of the perceived gender differences.

During the focus group interviews the participants developed an understanding of competence in ICT as gendered, an understanding I perceive as specific to this particular situation and this particular constellation of individuals. This can be seen in that the participants used each other's concepts and experiences to understand and convey their own understandings. In this way the group represents a limited amount of knowledge, concepts, words and experiences to discuss the particular topic, and these conditions limited and characterised the understandings presented. As I interpret it, they did gender and gender differences, in a particular way in these two groups, based on experiences and knowledge available among the individual members of the groups.

It is also clear that the participants tested different understandings and models of explanation in order to develop a mutual understanding of gender and ICT. These different understandings were tossed in to the discussion, sometimes as a matter of trial and error, and sometimes in a way suggesting more grounded beliefs that the individuals want to convey to the others. All theses ideas affected the understanding developed, sometimes more, sometimes less; some were accepted by the others, and others were discarded. An interesting question would be to study this phenomenon in more depth; why some understandings or statements were regarded as valid and important, while others were not. Was it because of the originator's position, status or charisma, or was it related to a hegemonic discourse of ICT as something that is more interesting for men than for women?

There are obvious examples of negotiations of meanings between the participants, and of how the understandings in the groups were normative in that the participants used them to understand themselves and their behaviour. This sometimes had the consequence that their own behaviour was questioned as odd or deviant, as in the cases of Svante and Maria. I would say that their examples show how understandings can affect individual's behaviour in that they are used as normative discourses that individuals position themselves in relation to. This is shown by Cecilia who stated that she was not interested in computers and that she let her boyfriend download the music that she wants from the Internet, and claimed her right to be uninterested and prioritise cleaning and other domestic tasks before spending more time on the Internet and learning about downloading music. She used a discourse which says that women are uninterested in computers in order to validate make her own behaviour. Corneliussen (2003) notes similar behaviour among the participants in her study of how male and female students position themselves in relation to computers.

A final conclusion is that there were several different understandings of the gendered interest in ICT existing at the same time within one group. This is apparent from the examples of women downloading music from the Internet among the economists, and on the origin of perceived gender differences among the systems analysts. A possible interpretation is that the understandings are local and contextual. Another interpretation is that there is no dominant discourse of how to explain or view those questions, and that the field is open for different interpretations. This can be interpreted as cracks in understandings (Elovaara 2004), that is, openings for change.

5. Discussion

It is clear that the understandings in the groups studied were normative, based on gender difference, and that the individuals used them to understand and motivate their own actions. To me the most interesting findings of this study are the different situated understandings that were developed in the focus group interviews, and the ways these were reproduced and changed in the interaction between the individual participants. There was an overall understanding of ICT as being more interesting for men, and hence, of men as being more competent in ICT, but there were differences in the way this was interpreted. I would like to relate the conclusions of the study to some reflections related to e-government services, by formulating some questions as interesting for further studies:

- How are understandings of gender and competence in ICT reproduced and changed among people working with the development of e-government services?
- How do understandings of gender and competence in ICT among developers of e-government services affect the public services they develop?
- How can general understandings of men as being more interested and competent in ICT be changed into an understanding of women and men as equally interested and competent in ICT?
- How can the IT-society *for all* (Government Bill 1999/2000:86) be communicated, not using the starting point that men more than women are interested and competent in ICT?
- How can ICT be constructed in a manner that doesn't discriminate against women (or men) but that still takes into consideration that women and men live under different circumstances and conditions?

References

Acker, J. 1997, 'Foreword' in Gendered practices in working life, eds. L. Rantalaiho, & T. Heiskanen, Macmillan, Basingstoke.

Bakry, S. H. 2004, 'Development of e-government: a STOPE view, International Journal of Network Management, vol. 14, pp. 339-350.

Cockburn, C. 1985, Machinery of Dominance: Women, Men and Technical Know-How, Northeastern University Press, Boston.

Corneliussen, H. 2003, Negotiating gendered positions in the discourse of computing, paper presented at the conference Information Technology, Transnational Democracy and Gender – RELOADED, Luleå University of Technology, 14-16 November.

Elovaara, P. 2004, Angels in Unstable Sociomaterial Relations: Stories of Information Technology, PhD thesis, Blekinge Institute of Technology, Sweden.

Elvin-Nowak, Y. & Thomsson, H. 2001, 'Motherhood as idea and practice: A Discursive Understanding of Employed Mothers in Sweden', Gender & Society, vol. 15, no. 3, pp. 407-428.

Fahlgren, S. 2002, Genusperspektiv i undervisning och lärande: rapport från ett pedagogiskt genusseminarium vårterminen 2002, paper presented to a pedagogical gender seminar, Östersund, Spring 2002.

Faulkner, W. 2003, 'Teknikfrågan i feminismen', in Vem tillhör tekniken? Kunskap och kön i teknikens värld, ed B. Berner, Arkiv förlag, Lund.

Fern, E. F. 2001, Advanced Focus Group Research, Sage Publications Inc., Thousand Oaks.

Følstad, A., Jørgensen, H. D. & Krogstie J. 2004, User Involvement in e-Government Development Projects, Proceedings of the third Nordic conference on Human-computer interaction, Tampere, 23-27 October.

Government Bill 1999/2000:86, Ett informationssamhälle för alla.

Grönlund, Å. 2001, 'En introduktion till Electronic Government' in Elektronisk förvaltning, elektronisk demokrati: Visioner, verklighet, vidareutveckling, ed Å. Grönlund, & A. Ranerup, Studentlitteratur, Lund.

Haraway, D. 1991, Simians, Cyborgs, and Women: The Reinvention of Nature, Routledge, New York.

Hedlin, M. 2004, Det ska vara lika för alla så att säga... En intervjustudie av lärarstuderandes uppfattningar om genus och jämställdhet, Bachelors Thesis, Kalmar University, Sweden.

Huff, C. & Cooper, J. 1987, 'Sex Bias in Educational Software: The Effect of Designers' Stereotypes on the Software They Design', Journal of Applied Social Psychology, vol. 17, no. 6, pp. 519-532.

Korvajärvi, P. 2003, 'Doing Gender as Theory and Practice' in Where Have All the Structures Gone? Doing Gender in Organisations, Examples from Finland, Norway and Sweden, eds E. Gunnarsson, S. Andersson, A. Vänje Rosell, A. Lehto, & M. Salminen-Karlsson, Center for Women's Studies, Stockholm.

Kvande, E. 2003, 'Doing Gender in Organizations: Theoretical Possibilities and Limitations' in Where Have All the Structures Gone? Doing Gender in Organisations, Examples from Finland, Norway and Sweden, eds E. Gunnarsson, S. Andersson, A. Vänje Rosell, A. Lehto, & M. Salminen-Karlsson, Center for Women's Studies, Stockholm.

Magnusson, E. 1998, 'Vardagens könsinnebörder under förhandling – om arbete, familj och produktion av kvinnlighet', PhD Thesis, Umeå University, Sweden.

Mellström, U. 2003, 'Teknik och maskulinitet' in Vem tillhör tekniken? Kunskap och kön i teknikens värld, ed B. Berner, Arkiv förlag, Lund.

Rommes, E., van Slooten, I., van Oost, E. & Oudshoorn, N. 2004, Designing Inclusion. The development of ICT products to include women in the Information Society, Report from SIGIS; Strategies of Inclusion: Gender and the Information Society, http://www.sigis-ist.org [30 March 2005]

Vehviläinen, M. 1997, Gender, Expertise and Information Technology, PhD Thesis, University of Tampere, Finland.

West, C. & Fenstermaker, S. 2002, 'Accountability and Affirmative Action: The Accomplishment of Gender, Race and Class in a University of California Board of Regents Meeting' in *Doing Gender, Doing Difference: Inequality, Power and Institutional Change*, eds S. Fenstermaker, & C. West, Routledge, New York.

White, R. 2004, 'Discourse analysis and social constructionism', *Nurseresearcher*, vol. 12, no. 2, pp. 7-16.

Wiberg, M. & Grönlund, Å. 2002, 'e-Government in Sweden: Centralization, Self-Service and Competition', in *Electronic Government: Design, Applications & Management*, ed Å. Grönlund, Idea Group Publishing, Hershey PA.

Winther Jørgensen, M. & Phillips, L. 2000, *Diskursanalys som teori och metod.*, Studentlitteratur, Lund.

Notes

1 According to themselves, as systems analysts, they are involved in the analysis of activities or organisations in the early stages of systems development, not in programming and implementation, although they are also skilled in programming.

9 Implementation of Large Scale Software Applications

Possibilities for end-user participation

Linda Stepulevage, Miriam Mukasa

University of East London, UK

Abstract

This paper focuses on the integration of generic software such as enterprise resource planning [ERP] into organisational life. These applications have gained prominence as the IT systems of choice in many organisations. The perspective that dominates the literature studying these applications reflects a rationality based on alignment of the software and organisational processes and fails to consider aspects such as the existing knowledge and skills, contingent practices and work experience of end-user groups.

Drawing on the strand of research that studies implementations of new technologies as social relations, this paper considers the experiences of end user groups as they engage in adaptation of the software and embed technology in contexts of local use. Design and use activities are complex and multifaceted and the embedding of software for local use represents an overlap between them. This paper explores whether the shift towards large scale generic software allows for a blurring of the boundary between design activities and those of use in applications for office work. Office work is gendered female in the UK where clerical and secretarial work is usually done by and considered to be suited to women.

The paper draws on a case study of the introduction and integration of a generic software application for supporting the administration of student records at a UK university to explore the possibilities for end-user participation in the embedding of these software packages. The paper presents an analysis of the implementation activity, IT-office worker relations, and the different constructions of skills and knowledge understood to be required as the workers attempted to deal with this software application.

1. Introduction

Since the mid-1990s many organisations have opted to purchase integrated, enterprise-wide configurable software systems known as enterprise resource planning [ERP] systems (Kumar & van Hillegersberg 2000). ERP systems 'are designed to integrate and optimize various business processes such as order entry and production planning across the entire firm' (Mabert et al. 2001, p. 69), automating core activities such as manufacturing, human resources and finance (Gibson et al. 1999). The rationale for such systems is usually presented in terms of reduced costs, greater control over business processes, and lower technical risk. (Gibson et al. 1999; Holland et al. 1999; Vowler 1995). Research on ERP implementations, however, has found organisational results to be disappointing, even if the software itself works well technically (Gibson et al. 1999). The literature on ERP notes that a significant proportion of implementation projects overrun budgets in both time and cost (e.g. Gupta 2000; Sprott 2000). Some of the literature claims that 'ERP not only provides an accurate view of an organization, but also allows for a more efficient response to the increasingly competitive manufacturing environment' (Gupta 2000, p. 117). Other research notes that these packages can be a straitjacket on the company forcing it to work in the way that the package is designed (Vowler 1995). The qualitatively different nature of ERP systems, where change is demanded across the whole organisation, may involve re-engineering of an organisation's core business processes to take advantage of the software (Gibson et al. 1999, p. 3).

The literature indicates that a key problem centres on end-user acceptance. Gibson et al. note that one company found that they underestimated the culture shock from having a new IT system (1999, p. 8). A number of case studies of ERP implementations show that the need for training was underrated. One study showed that training 'was generally the most underestimated component of the process' and that the most successful firms had involved users in the process from the start (Mabert et al. 2001, p. 75). Gupta notes that planning for and providing end-user education/training is 'one of the primary challenges' in ERP implementations (2000, p. 117).

Another common problem centres on customisation of the generic packaged software. One of the key decisions is whether or not to customise it. The amount of customisation depends on whether an organisation wants to change their business processes to fit the software or to change the software to fit their business (Gibson et al. 1999, pp. 4-5). The literature implies that this is a high level management decision and stresses that a strategy is needed to inform the selection of software and plan the implementation to ensure an alignment of business processes with software packages. This research notes the importance of stakeholder consensus and user involvement in order to implement these changes in organisational structure, work processes and/or software (Gibson et al. 1999).

We interpret some of this research as being grounded in a rationality which assumes that the packaged software can meet the needs of an organisation and/or that the work of an organisation can be re-engineered to align with generic sets of tasks represented within the software. The research identifying user training as a key issue is representative of this strand. This perspective draws on a conceptualisation of development of a new computer-based system as a closed technical artefact with end-user involvement a function of the operation of the system, not its development.

Some of the research moves deeper into the software-organisation relationship to explore mismatches between underlying data and process models and the organisational structure implicitly embedded in the software. ERP systems provide reference models that claim to embody the current best business practices, but as Kumar and van Hillegersberg note, 'While at the abstract level the idea of "universal" best practices may be seductive, at the detailed process level these mismatches create considerable implementation and adaptation problems.' (2000, p. 25). Some literature on the mismatches between software and organisation focus on misfits in terms of data, processes and output (Soh et al. 2000); others explore mismatches in terms of organisational culture (Krumbholz & Maiden 2001).

This research, however, still implies a separation between the technical and the social, even though it recognises a close relationship between them. The perspective we draw on in this paper is that of the social construction of technology. From this perspective the technology is one of the many constituents of a social system, rather than separate from it. Social construction views the relationship between the technical and social groups as a dynamic one, in which the construction of a technical artefact is an ongoing negotiation with no clear boundaries between design, implementation and use (MacKenzie & Wajcman 1999). Implementation, therefore, can no longer be considered a straightforward stage in systems development but rather an ongoing negotiation amongst the various participants at the site of use (e.g. McLaughlin et al. 1999).

When we consider the literature that takes gender into account in the development of computer-based office systems, we add another layer of analysis concerned with issues of user involvement and the relationship between IT implementers and the users of the applications – those of power and influence, positioning in relation to the development of the technology, and technical expertise and knowledge of the larger work system. For example, research carried out during the implementation of packaged software at a further education college shows that office workers learned and used SQL to develop an acceptable work system for themselves in a situation where the systems manager knew little of this database query language and was never available when things went wrong (Ramsay et al. 1997, pp. 87-88). Other research shows clerical workers independently gaining technical expertise in a software package and enhancing their work systems by designing accounting applications (Stepulevage 2003). More typical cases, however, are those in which user involvement in design coincides with patterns of gendered work in terms of power and influence. Stepulevage analyses how a work system based on the same software was constructed differently at two sites. Where the intended users were male accountants, they participated in its development to fit their local requirements; where the intended users were women clerical workers, however, the same software was intended to be implemented without any participation from users, even though the context of use and the position of the women workers was different from that of the male accountants. A survey of office workers in the Netherlands shows that there has been little progress in their participation in decision-making regarding IT systems (Tijdens 1999, p. 54), and while a body of work was published in the early 1990s regarding women's participation in design, there is currently little research oriented towards questions of gender and participation in design by office workers (see Green et al. 1993; Howcroft and Wilson 2003).

2. Background

Surveys year after year in the UK show that women remain the majority in secretarial, clerical, and administrative work, while men remain the majority in professional IT work (see EOC 2003). This gendered division of work is represented in the development of the packaged software system we study in this paper. The development of office applications has been explored in papers at many WiC and IFIP conferences in the 1980s-90s mostly with regard to bespoke technical systems. These papers have noted the lack of communication between in-house developers and user groups, disregard for worker skills, knowledge and contributions, imposition of inadequate technical systems, and poor training in these systems (e.g. Grundy 1994; Holtgrewe 1994; Ramsay et al. 1997). We question whether these problems which exemplify a divide between development and user activities are evident in the large-scale packaged software implementations.

In order to explore this question, this paper analyses research data on the implementation of a large scale software package for student record administration at a public sector UK university. The overall objective of the original research carried out by one of the authors was to provide detailed case study evidence describing what happens in practice when packaged software is implemented in a different organisational context to that of private businesses and industry, upon which most of the ERP literature is based. As in the private sector, packaged software is becoming the computer-based system of choice in Higher Education institutions (HEIs). Within the context of increased student numbers, financial constraints, and an obligation to keep records of information for legal and other reporting purposes such as the annual reporting for universities to the Higher Education Statistical Agency (HESA) and the Universities and Colleges Admissions Service (UCAS), many institutions have been implementing discrete pieces of packaged software as a way of meeting the need for effective student administration.

A few empirical studies have since been published that focus on the implementation of packaged solutions for supporting student record administration in HEIs, but we found that these studies lacked an analysis that recognises the gendered nature of the work in these institutions and the experiences of different user groups in this context (McLaughlin et al. 1999; Scott & Wagner 2003). We therefore decided to analyse the research data to explore whether large scale packaged software implementations confirm earlier work on bespoke technical systems or whether new opportunities have arisen for women office workers to construct more effective work systems in a university setting.

At the time of study [2000], the university that is the subject of this case study had just over 6,800 full and part time students, with approximately half the students studying for postgraduate degrees, and about 1000 management, academic and support staff. The majority of support staff were women. The packaged software that is the focus of this research, which we refer to as SIS (Student Information System), provides support for student record administration at course and unit level for undergraduate degree programmes and at course level for other programmes. It is comprised of three different modules, a Marketing and Admissions module, a Student Registration module, and a Credit Management module. These modules are designed to reflect the yearly cycle in HE which includes various activities, e.g. students register, they add/drop modules, class lists are generated, enrolment reports are produced, student bills are printed and student grades are recorded. The software is not designed as a resource-planning tool, but since the system holds the entire university's course and student information, the data it produces goes forward to the financial and strategic planning units and also to the higher education funding bodies.

3. Research Methodology

The research used qualitative methods to explore the culture and practices of the institution and to collect data that was used to evaluate the implementation process and use of the system. Various techniques were employed. They included meetings, internal document reviews (including newsletters, user manuals, and reports generated by the system), questionnaire investigations (for end users and the project team), informal observations of the software in use, and semi-structured interviews. Nine interviews were conducted at this university, each lasting 45-90 minutes. The interviews were with the Head of MIS [man], 5 Department Administrators [women], a Secretary [woman] and a Trainer [woman].

Questions were asked about the IS policy regarding choice of application, organisation of IS, development methodologies, constraints to development, maintenance and training. Functional issues such as ease of use, design features, user interface, response times and the critical success factors specific to the different faculties together with details regarding level of user participation and level of information requirements and information support were also sought. The history of the evolution of IS within the institution and within higher education institutions in general was also a subject of enquiry. All the interviews were recorded and transcribed and written notes were taken. The interviews were supplemented by informal conversations with two heads of departments and academic staff. For this paper, we draw on the data from the MIS Manager and the five Department Administrators [D1 through D5].

4. Implementation of New Software

It has been argued by some researchers (see, for example, Lippincott 1997) that the approach taken for the replacement of administrative systems in colleges of higher education and universities, in many cases, has been driven by an institutional commitment to business process re-engineering and the need for more flexible systems, e.g. for interfacing with the World Wide Web. Cuts in funding have also created pressure to rationalise and be more business-like. Allen and Wilson claim that organisation in HEIs is moving from one of collegiality to direction from the centre, and that information strategy formulation is based on a mechanistic rational approach taken from the private sector in its crudest form. They argue that, while a formal, logical strategic planning process may be relevant to the private sector, it does not apply to HEIs where the decision-making process is more democratic and tends to be focused around committee structures and upon consensus building (1996, p. 246). Universities are essentially political institutions and a top-down rational approach ignores the political nature of the process where there are a number of 'powerful stakeholders in any university who can either be pacified or who may affect the process positively if included in it or can sabotage the process if they are excluded from it.' (p. 246) Earlier research into the implementation of a management and administrative computing system at a UK university demonstrates these points in its analysis. It shows that initially secretaries were not involved in the development of their work system; management, recognising their resistance to it, then took steps to bring the secretaries on board (McLaughlin et al. 1999, pp. 89-90). In our study, an organisational culture of democratic decision-making can be implied in that the administrators interviewed expected to be involved in design decisions. They said that they were ready to offer criticisms and suggest enhancements. Their experience shows, however, that they had little opportunity to do so. An investigation of the culture of the institution is beyond the scope of this study, and the experiences of these workers should not be taken as representative of all the clerical, secretarial and administrative staff at the university.

Another aspect we explore is concerned with large scale packaged software as incorporating 'best practices'. This question informs decisions regarding customisation – whether to re-engineer work processes or modify software. Allen and Wilson state that the 'information strategies' of universities tend to focus on the technology and technological systems in isolation (1996, p. 247). The software is conceptualised as a complete system and management decide on levels of local customisation. Therefore, we explore the social relations of customisation and ask whether the technical system and groups associated with it play a dominant role in what the ERP literature refers to as the alignment of the software and work processes. We choose the terms practices and activities rather than 'processes' since processes, in this context, might imply that tasks can be abstracted from the actual experience of workers carrying out the tasks.

Both of these aspects, user involvement in the implementation process of the new software, and the positioning of the software, whether as a technical system in isolation or a recognised constituent of a larger work system, are considered through a gender lens informed by feminist literature on gender/technology relations. This literature argues that there is a privileging of knowledge of the technical artefact over local knowledge of work activities. It also identifies a divide between IT professionals and management who are assumed to hold knowledge of the technical system and/or who have the authority to coordinate and drive its implementation; and administrative workers who lack authority in implementing technical systems, yet hold local knowledge about work activities, (Bodker and Greenbaum 1993; Webster 1996). In exploring whether women in administrative positions might have more opportunities for development as regards these packaged software systems, it is vital to establish whether they participate in decision-making activities, and whether knowledge of work requirements and practices, as well as technical knowledge, is valued.

5. User involvement: Experiences of Consultation and Training

5.1 Consultation

Like most major projects, SIS started with a process of competitive tendering based on a specification document describing the university's requirements. The MIS Manager told us they used conventional project management methods, e.g. a project plan, milestones, and critical path analysis of tasks. And, consistent with mainstream IS project methodologies, a project team was set up to manage the implementation. The project team was comprised of a broad range of stakeholders: academics, support staff including a clerical person from each main office, key departmental administrators and MIS staff, e.g. programmers responsible for hands-on implementation. According to the MIS Manager, the team met every 4-6 weeks and agreed the project plan, monitored and reviewed progress, and 'trouble shoot any problem areas.'

Project team meetings did not serve as a site where department administrators interviewed in this research participated in decision-making as none of them were on the team. One of the five administrators said she thought 'the consultation bit was fine' but further questioning indicated that this consultation for her was about being asked her views at a large open meeting at the short listing stage. She characterised the social relations of involvement as almost non-existent: 'as users we are marginalised; nobody consults us.'[D1] Another administrator [D4] characterised consultation as sporadic, 'as an afterthought.' She said, 'there is a feeling that we are just boring typists – it should not matter but it does matter the label you have.' A third administrator [D5] said she was never consulted and to emphasise her point, she said 'we are not even informed about enhancements.' She gave an example of coming in one morning and 'all of a sudden screens were changed.' She ended the description with 'no one has told you in advance, no email [was sent stating] that we [MIS] have updated the system.' Involvement was referred to by an administrator [D5] in relation to asking staff to fill in a questionnaire.

They sort of tried to involve everybody but, you know, filling in a questionnaire is one thing and people don't always know what they want...I can assess everything from an administrative point of view and I was clear about what I wanted, but I didn't know that what I wanted would be in a different format that made my job harder

The method of involvement was inadequate for this administrative worker who was clear about what she wanted, i.e. she was confident about her information needs and her knowledge of work activities. There was a clear mismatch between the work system she had envisioned and that which was presented to her.

These experiences reflect a low level of formal involvement in the decision-making consistent with conventional approaches to the design of bespoke systems (Gibson et al. 1999). However, more informal day to day interactions between MIS staff, management, and administrators can also be significant sites for development of the work system. One of the administrators [D5] gave an example of what we would consider a design negotiation, that of attempting to have changes made to a listing by module or degree, '[the listing was] pretty good but it comes out in numerical order which is totally unhelpful.' When she questioned MIS about it, they said it was to do with how the table was structured and how the code was written, and that they couldn't change it.

Another example given by two administrators [D1, D2] concerned a screen for producing address labels. Workers provided knowledgeable feedback to technical developers about the screen design, but their attempt to participate in development was ignored, as this quote shows

We asked them to modify the [address] label screen with two more fields because it would save us the extra work but nobody listens to us ... we have to go through this extended process

The extended process the worker refers to is a procedure whereby they use another application to extract the information they need, export it to a spreadsheet, then to mail merge, followed by more steps described in detail to the interviewer. This locally improvised process takes administrative workers about 20 minutes to do. It is an essential work task, and they have the knowledge and motivation to develop the procedure. They would prefer, however, that the SIS screen be modified as it would make their work more time efficient. Their willingness to improvise when their needs are not met is an act made in desperation as the work must be done, in this case at the high cost of their time. The suggestions made to MIS can be considered as attempts to participate in development. All the suggestions [there were many others made in interviews] are concerned with more effective engagement with the software and an associated more efficient use of their time. Even though one of the reasons given for generic application systems being the current software of choice is that they enable more effective and efficient work processes, here is a clear case of administrative workers' time not being used effectively, and their knowledge of work processes which could positively inform the development of the software was disregarded.

5.2 Training

From interviews, it seemed the training session served as a significant site in which administrators' lack of involvement became evident. According to the MIS Manager a new appointment was made to oversee implementation of the system and to do the training 'on business procedures, e.g. how do you change a degree programme?' Four of the five administrators we interviewed attended a formal training session. All expressed negative views of it, e.g. 'a two hour introduction to screens; not specific to the work we do' [D1]; 'training was pretty close to useless' [D4]; 'the trainer is scatty; she jumps from here there everywhere' [D5]. All the administrators interviewed criticised the lack of an overview of the software that would enable them to have an understanding of how the information was held and processed, for example

I have no idea where it starts and where it ends; I would like to know what it can do and how bits relate; I want to know the scope of it [D4]

We needed a much more comprehensive understanding of the whole system but were not given it.... They need to have an information officer perspective on training to implement what is there [D1]

The administrator [D3] who chose not to attend formal training, but instead browsed through a copy of notes about the system, expressed the lack of an overview as follows

The difficulty is always asking the right question when interrogating a system like that and knowing how to structure your question to be able to do that so you do need a certain amount of knowledge and to be able to interpret the results that you get back. ...You need an awareness of how other parts of the system impinge on the results you get back.

These comments support earlier points made in the literature about training being a key issue, and one that is often underrated. We interpret the administrators' comments as demonstrating what studies such as Suchman's research in a law office argue, that their work involves wide ranging knowledge, knowledge about how the data they work with is processed and is interrelated throughout the university (Suchman 1994). The administrators' criticisms of the training, however, demonstrate that their work activities were conceptualised as a set of routine tasks to be carried out on new software, and the training was designed to show them how to operate the software in order to carry out these tasks.

6. Positioning of the Software: An Intransigent Relationship with Administrators

Their training experiences are an indicator of the administrators' involvement in the implementation, but they also help in analysing the positioning of software. In this case, administrators' experiences of training show that the software was presented as a non-problematic tool. One of the administrators [D1] characterised the training as — 'basically, here is the system, go use it.' This implies that they were expected to operate but not necessarily understand how the new software fit into the organisation. The training reflects patterns identified in work on systems development, that of a gendered divide between design of computer-based work systems and their local use (Stepulevage 2003). The women administrators are treated as operators of the software and the software's recognised site of construction is distant from the women workers' location. This separate site for design was noted directly by administrators and indirectly by the MIS manager.

The administrators noted that MIS did 'the design work', and that MIS did it in isolation from local use. One administrator [D1] stated '[MIS] are designers interested in developing the system; they are not interested in the users' point of view'. Another administrator [D5] expressed her frustration at MIS's lack of response to a list of problems about the interface: 'It is not the users that are the designers; a lot of designers themselves do not use what they make.' One of the administrators [D2] explained

We produced reports and some of them were all wrong.... and MIS, well they are good but they don't understand registry work and when you ask them...they say, why don't you change the way you do things?

This administrator, grounded in her local knowledge of registry work, characterises MIS staff responses as distant from their work. MIS seems to position the software as the central actor in this enterprise and expect the users to adjust to it. The MIS comment as reported by the administrator, that registry should change the way it does things, privileges the software's construction of the activity over the administrator's knowledgeable assessment of registry needs. Other comments made by administrators, e.g. regarding the numeric list of modules, indicate that MIS staff were unable and/or unwilling to make changes suggested by administrators to the software.

This privileging of the software places the MIS professional in the role of knowledgeable guide to the software, the user as an operator of a machine, and the work as routine, context free and easy to replicate. These examples should not, however, indicate that there was no customisation of the software. As the MIS manager notes

Buying a package solution, you are always going to have to make compromises, but we were quite fortunate because with our profile and influences, we could bring to bear on the package and the company was quite happy to make the changes that we specified.

He goes on to explain a problem with the relationship between module code and title, where the university wanted the module code to remain unchanged if its title was modified. Changes in data structure were requested to enable the module code to be year stamped and therefore various titles could be stored for one code.

The suggested changes for the module listing, the address label screen and many others described in administrators' interviews were not implemented when initially requested, while the change to the module code was implemented. These outcomes coincide with both a gendered divide and a technical/office work divide. The change described by the MIS manager is described in technical terms, i.e. how it is represented in the data structure. The administrators describe their suggestions in the context of their local work activities. Without making the suggested changes to the software, they would still be able to do their work, even if it did take them more time.

A separation between the technical and the social can be identified in the question of user acceptance. The manager highlighted the positioning of the software in a technical domain when responding to an interview question about user acceptance. He responded in terms of choice of software, i.e. if he had to choose again, he would choose the same system. He added that 'if [he] were choosing today, [he] would choose something more integrated such as....' This opinion of 'user acceptance' is in stark contrast to the administrators' comments when asked about acceptance. All five administrators expressed strong dissatisfaction with what they experienced as a very inadequate system. One administrator [D2] said

Every student that came to see us was complaining about something, and it could all be traced back in one way or another to the implementation. Because of so much negativity, staff couldn't stand it anymore. We lost half the admissions team.

While the MIS manager considers user acceptance in relation to an isolated technical artefact, administrators express their acceptance in terms of their experiences of the software as embedded within the social relations of the organisation.

7. New Opportunities?

One of the administrators [D1] talked about her use of another software package which we refer to as RG, a report generator.

Fortunately I go beyond the standard reports. ...Standard reports are limited in what they can do, e.g. I need to find out how many students in the departments are taking our modules so to get that information, I have to use [RG]. Also not everybody wants standard reports.

She developed the 'extended procedure' for address labels, as well as for these non-standard reports. We interpret these actions as improvisations carried out under stress in order to get the work accomplished. They might not be empowering experiences of participation in the development of the work system, but for this administrator the SIS implementation did serve as an occasion for her to extend her skills and increase her knowledge about the university's software applications. This administrator also said

I am not supposed to be interested in computers. There is an issue here that women over 35 are particularly seen as incapable and it's a waste of resources trying to train them up. But that is not my background. I am very used to trying to use computers and trying to satisfy the needs of my boss who wants specific information.

This woman had confidence in her computing skills and had previously worked in other jobs where she was involved in implementations. For another one of the administrators [D4], however, though she was initially in favour of getting a new system 'when it finally came, it was a disappointment.' At interview, after she described her experience of training, she said, 'Since then I think that I am a Luddite and I don't know anything about computers.'

8. Closing

The possibilities for end-user participation in this packaged software development seem limited in that the MIS management conceptualised the software as a complete and completed software system. Local customisation was presented to the interviewer by the MIS manager as non-problematic, but it is beyond the scope of the research to explore the politics of the software purchase and details of decision-making about customisation and who would carry it out. The administrative workers described a number of interactions with MIS staff regarding the design of the software so there was the possibility of negotiation with them regarding the local customisation of their new work system. These possibilities were not realised, however, and any development efforts made by administrators to embed the software were done independently rather than in collaboration with MIS staff. This implementation was experienced by the administrators interviewed as a top-down process rather than a negotiation with MIS or any other project team members. The implementation practices can be characterised as techno-centric, with administrators expected to receive a completed system rather than engage in negotiation about its development.

The administrators' experience demonstrates the continuance of a designer/user divide that coincides with the gendered divide between IT work and office work. This research provides evidence of the skills and knowledge and commitment to effective work practices that the women workers have at their jobs, but it also indicates that their knowledge is not as highly valued as that of MIS and management. The administrators demonstrated that they are committed to and concerned about providing relevant and accurate information for at least three different user groups: managers, academics and students. Their positioning enables them to be very knowledgeable participants in the university-wide information network, and if they had been included as equal partners in the project their suggestions may have contributed to the construction of a more effective work system for administration. More research is needed on these large scale implementations to analyse the nature of the projects in terms of the dynamics of embedding technical artefacts within sites of locally gendered work and the extent to which end-user groups participate in these activities.

References

Allen, D.K. & Wilson, T. 1996, 'Information Strategies in UK Higher Education Institutions', *International Journal of Information Management*, vol. 16, no. 4, pp. 239-251.

Bodker, S. & Greenbaum, J. 1993, 'Design of Information Systems: Things vs People' in *Gendered by Design? Information Technology and Office Systems*, eds E. Green, J. Owen & D. Pain, Taylor and Francis, London.

Equal Opportunities Commission 2003, *Facts about Women and Men in Great Britain*, EOC, Manchester.

Gibson, N., Holland, S. & Light, B. 1999, 'Enterprise Resource Planning: a business approach to Systems Development' *IEEE Proceedings of the 32nd Hawaii International Conference on System Sciences* pp. 1-9.

Green, E. et al. (eds) 1993, *Gendered by Design? Information Technology and Office Systems*, Taylor and Francis, London.

Grundy, F. 1994, 'Women in the Computing Workplace: Some Impressions' in *IFIP Transactions Women, Work and Computerization*, eds A. Adam et al, Elsevier, Amsterdam.

Gupta, A. 2000, 'Enterprise resource planning: the emerging organizational value systems' *Industrial Management & Data Systems*, vol. 100, no. 3, pp. 114-118.

Holland, C. & Light, B. 1999, 'A Critical Success Factors Model for Enterprise Resource Planning Implementation', *IEEE Software*, vol. 16, no. 3, pp. 30-36.

Holtgrewe, U. 1994, 'Everyday Experts? Professionals' Women Assistants and Information Technology' in *IFIP Transactions Women, Work and Computerization*, eds A. Adam et al, Elsevier, Amsterdam.

Howcroft, D. & Wilson, M. 2003, 'Paradoxes of participatory practices: The Janus role of the systems developer', *Information and Organization*, vol. 13, no. 1, pp. 1-24.

Kumar, K. & van Hillegersberg, J. 2000, 'ERP Experiences and Evolution', *Communications of the ACM*, vol. 43, no. 4, pp. 23-26.

Krumbholz, M. & Maiden, N. 2001, 'The implementation of enterprise resource planning packages in different organizational and national cultures', *Information Systems*, vol. 26, no. 3, pp. 185-204.

Lippincott, J. 1997, 'Current Issues for Higher Education Information Resources Management' *CAUSE/EFFECT*, Spring, pp. 4-7.

Mabert, V., Soni, A. & Venkataramanan, M. 2001, 'Enterprise Resource Planning: Common Myths Versus Evolving Reality', *Business Horizons*, May-June, pp. 69-76.

MacKenzie, D & Wajcman, J. 1999, *The Social Shaping of Technology* 2nd edn, Open University Press, Buckingham.

McLaughlin, J., Rosen, P., Skinner, D. & Webster, A. 1999, *Valuing Technology: Organisations, Culture and Change*, Routledge, London.

Ramsay, H., Panteli, A. & Beirne, M. 1997, 'Empowerment and Disempowerment: Active Agency, Structural Constraint and Women Computer Users' in *Women in Computing*, eds R. Lander & A. Adam, Intellect, Exeter, U.K.

Scott, S. & Wagner, E. 2003, 'Networks, negotiations, and new times: The implementation of enterprise resource planning into an academic administration', *Information and Organization* 13, pp. 285-313.

Soh, C., Kien, S. & Tay-Yap, J. 2000, 'Cultural Fits and Misfits: Is ERP A Universal Solution?', *Communications of the ACM*, vol. 43, no. 4, pp. 47-51.

Sprott, D. 2000, 'Componentizing the Enterprise Application Packages', *Communications of the ACM*, vol. 43, no. 14, pp. 63-71.

Stepulevage, L. 2003, 'Computer-Based Office Work: Stories of Gender, Design, and Use', *IEEE Annals of the History of Computing*, vol. 25, no. 4, pp. 67-72.

Suchman, L. 1994, 'Supporting Articulation Work: Aspects of a Feminist Practice of Technology Production' in *IFIP Transactions Women, Work and Computerization*, eds A. Adam et al, Elsevier, Amsterdam.

Tijdens, K. 1999, 'Behind the Screens: The Foreseen and Unforeseen Impact of Computerization on Female Office Worker's Jobs', *Gender, Work and Organization* , vol. 6, no. 1, pp. 47-57.

Vowler, J. 1988, 'Buy or Build: it's your choice' *Computer Weekly* p. 62.

Webster, J. 1996, *Shaping Women's Work: Gender, Employment and Information Technology*, Addison Wesley Longman, Harlow, U.K.

10 'Social' Robots and 'Emotional' Software Agents:

Gendering Processes and De-gendering Strategies for 'Technologies in the Making'[1]

Jutta Weber, Corinna Bath

Institute for Philosophy of Science, University of Vienna

Abstract

In this paper we analyse prominent visions of social and emotional machines and put aside these visions with some prototypes and commercial products that currently came into use. We ask how traditional feminist critiques of technology might be applied to these recent developments in the field of 'social' Artificial Intelligence. The arguments will lead us to point out some basic problems and viewpoints in the development of de-gendering strategies for 'technologies in the making'. Finally, we map dimensions and strategies for a contemporary feminist critique of technology.

Over the past years we can observe profound reconfigurations of the boundaries between human beings and machines in the field of artificial intelligence and computer science. Particularly software agents and robots attest to an ongoing paradigm shift from machine-oriented concepts, algorithms and automats towards "interaction". (See Wegener 1997, Crutzen 2003) While early approaches sought to model rational-cognitive processes and to solve problems using formal structures, the emphasis is currently shifting to human-computer and human-robot interaction.

Recently artefacts such as software agents and robots are often conceptualised as friendly, understanding and believable partners which communicate "naturally" with users and support them in everyday life. "Sociable", humanoid robots are designed to take care of old or sick people. Software agents are expected to obtain information independent. In order to serve users and give them advice, they appear human-like on the screen.

In this paper we will first analyze prominent visions of social and emotional machines and put aside these visions with some prototypes and commercial products that currently came into use. From this illustrating introduction, we will refer to feminist critiques of technology and ask how these approaches might apply to these new artefacts. The arguments will lead us to point out some basic problems, questions and viewpoints in the development of de-gendering strategies for 'technologies in the making'.

1. The Vision of Sociable or Social Intelligent Robots and Software Agents

Cynthia Breazeal from the Massachusetts Institute of Technology (MIT) is one of the leading researchers in the field of social robotics. Her vision of a sociable robot is a good example that clarifies the robot researchers' promises:

> *"For me, a sociable robot is able to communicate and interact with us, understand and even relate to us, in a personal way. It should be able to understand us and itself in social terms. We, in turn, should be able to understand it in the same social terms - to be able to relate to it and to empathize with it. Such a robot must be able to adapt and learn throughout its lifetime, incorporating shared experiences with other individuals into its understanding of self, of others, and of the relationships they share. In short, a sociable robot is socially intelligent in a human-like way, and interacting with it is like interacting with another person. At the pinnacle of achievement, they could befriend us, as we could them."* (Breazeal 2002, p. 1)

Figure 1: Cynthia Breazeal with Kismet

She stresses that social artefacts that become part of our daily life must be able to adapt in a natural and intuitive manner – not vice versa. Her 'masterpiece' – as she calls it – the robotic creature Kismet is designed to interact physically, affectively and socially with humans, in order to learn from them. The man-machine-relation (or should one say the woman-machine-relation?) is modelled according to that of a human infant and a caregiver. Similar attempts we found in software agent research. Researchers stress that they aim at building *"emotional relationships by long-term interactions wherein the two parties pay attention to the emotional state of the other, communicate their feelings, share a trust, feel empathetic, and establish a connection, a bond."* (Stern 2002, p. 336f). In some commercial computer games like 'Virtual Petz' or 'Virtual Babyz' (figure 2) the characters are constructed to seek the users attention in order to interact with them, to get 'care' and to get 'socialized' by the users.

Figure 2: Virtual Babyz
[Source http://www.babyz.net]

To realize these envisioned social behaviours of machines researchers use models and theories from the fields of psychology, cognitive science, and ethnology, thereby aiming at the implementation of social and emotional competencies.

2. Anthropomorphism and Gendering

If we take a look at the first prototypes and commercial products that are intended to be social we have to admit that they do not appear very innovative, at least with regard to the predominant gender concepts - if not to say stereotypes – used. Cyberella, a presentation agent created at the German Research Center for Artificial Intelligence (http://www.dfki.de/cyberella), and the robot "Valerie, a domestic android" (http://www.androidworld.com/prod19.htm) for instance, were given a kind of super feminine shape (shown in *figure 3*).

Figure 3: Cyberella and Valerie
[Sources http://www.dfki.de/cyberella, and http://www.androidworld.com/]

Other software agents chat with users in a strongly gender stereotyped or even sexualised manner. Even though some of the new social artefacts appear more 'neutral' or less gender-stereotyped at a first glance they are nevertheless modelled on the ground of questionable ontological presumptions. Think for example of the reshaped wo/man-machine-relation that is constructed in analogy to the infant-caregiver-relation (e.g. Kismet).

The visions and realizations of social artefacts in software agent research and robotics give raise to many questions:

What and whose understanding of sociality and emotionality is realized in these new artefacts? Is it desirable from a critical, feminist perspective to develop 'emotional' artefacts we are supposed to empathize with? Do artefacts modelled in terms of infant-caregiver-relationships represent our understanding of social behaviour?

Or, more general: Is it desirable and promising to model human-machine-relationships according to those between humans? Are artefacts like Valerie, Cyberella and the like based on anthropological and ontological premises concerning human behaviour, relationships and emotions that we can identify with from a critical, feminist perspective?

But however we judge about these developments 'social' artefacts, we have to take seriously today's researchers dream of a new and potent generation of socially intelligent artefacts. The implementation of sociality and emotionality into artefacts has become a centre of attention in numerous research & development projects in the field of robotics and software agents. We now have research laboratories called 'affective computing', 'social computing' and the like. Robots are developed which rely on the interaction with humans for their socialization and 'education'. Some websites, e-commerce or electronic tutor systems and computer games are already populated with software agents that are said to be endowed with a rudimentary personality and show simple forms of emotional behaviour.

We now want to reflect these developments in the light of feminist critiques of technology.

3. Feminist Critique of Technology: Against Abstraction, Disembodiment, Decontextualisation and the Lack of the Social Dimension

In the last decades feminist scholars as well as other critics pointed toward the lack of embodiment and situatedness in AI research (e.g. Dreyfus 1963; Becker 1992). They pointed toward the fact that researcher did not take into account the social dimension of technology. They questioned the limited orientation towards rational-cognitive models and symbol processing. The critique often focussed on the reductionist modelling of thought, on the simple understanding of human planning and acting as a merely rational-cognitive process and on approaches to problem solving constrained by the use of formal structures (e.g. Suchman 1987)[2].

While much of the argumentation aimed against abstraction, disembodiment, decontextualisation and the lack of the social dimension, it seems as if these critiques were now recognized by emergent technosciences such as embodied cognitive science, embodied robotics (See Pfeifer & Scheier 1999) and intelligent software agents research (e.g. situated and reactive agents) and translated into action[3].

Having this paradigm shift in AI in mind it might help to rethink the critique of the feminist science studies scholar and sociologist Bettina Heintz. In her paper "*Papiermaschinen. Die sozialen Voraussetzungen maschineller Intelligenz*" ['Paper machines. The Social (Pre-)Conditions of Machine Intelligence'] she pointed towards the social and societal preconditions and implications of the mechanization of thought and every day life through AI. On the one hand she claimed that first of all it was human beings who adapted themselves towards the machine. Otherwise our unimaginative machines would not work at all. For example, think of the secretaries who are instructed to use a very simple language avoiding any ambiguities in order to enable software programs to translate their texts into another language. The abilities we regard as genuine ones of computers are often the result of our own efficient work. And often we unconsciously compensate for the deficiencies of the machines, while at the same time our readiness to perceive machines as intelligent stems from our tendency to interpret our reality as loaded or even structured with meaning. (See also Collins 1990)

On the other hand Bettina Heintz pointed out that a kind of mechanization of everyday life must have already taken place before the computer comes into this process. The translation of problems into algorithms only becomes possible when humans already act rule-oriented. A standardization of human behaviour is necessary to model and develop software applications. Following these arguments, the critique should not challenge primarily the claim that computers might become intelligent, but has to question the conditions that make us believe in the intelligence of machines. What is the background in our society that elicits rule-oriented behaviour that can be found so frequently?

While this critique referred to rational-cognitive intelligent machines, we are now faced with the vision of 'social machines'. Researchers want to develop machines beyond the limits of rational-cognitive grounded intelligence. They discover social behaviour as the basis of "real" intelligence. Can the shift from rational to social behaviour be perceived as a departure from masculinist technology design? Or is it more a continuation of old hierarchical patterns? Will chances for feminist intervention arise along these changes or will the envisioned dissolution of the dichotomy of human beings and machines cement the existing gender order?

The illustrations of robots and software agents we gave in the introduction of this paper already referred to our sceptical stance towards the 'innovative' potential of these so-called social machines. We ask ourselves: Why are the promised helpful, believable and trustworthy artefacts modelled according to crude gender stereotypes? Why is the mother-child relationship assumed to be a good model for the human-machine-relationship? And what should we think of this now so popular concept of social intelligence in technoscientific discourses and practices[4]?

There is another point that makes us feel uncomfortable: Sociality and emotionality have been deeply gendered categories in western thought that have traditionally been assigned to the feminine realm. And it is not by chance that we find a relatively large number of women who develop social robots and software agents, while there are only very few women who work in old-fashioned, symbol-oriented AI or biomimetic robotics. For example, most of the few female roboticists are now found in the field of 'social' robotics - as if their so-called 'natural' competencies of sociality, communication etc. predetermined them to work in such a field. What could be more appealing than a nice-looking woman like Cynthia Breazeal who embodies a true loving caregiver for a helpless infant robotic creature that needs training and caring to develop intelligence, social behaviour, emotions and a personality?

Having feminist critiques in mind, we ask ourselves: what does it mean when technoscientists want to anthropomorphize machines and discover sociality and emotionality as the cure for our still unimaginative, rational-cognitive grounded machines[5]. It seems that traditional strategies of wo/man-machine-communication are turned upside-down. While for a long time humans had to behave rationally and rule-oriented to make symbol-oriented machines successful, now machines are to become social in order to increase their usability and make them more helpful for human users. It's the machine now which is supposed to mimic or even learn those abilities and characteristics which were until recently regarded as purely and typically human and beyond the grasp of machines.

On this ground we want to contribute to feminist critique of AI, especially in rethinking Heintz' critical approach in the light of socially intelligent machines. This does not means to ask whether and how machines can be or become social, but what makes us think of machines as social. What concepts of sociality and emotionality are predominant in today's AI and why? And what are the societal conditions under which machines are regarded as social and emotional?

Every socially intelligent machine we can dream of is still based on rule-oriented behaviour, since this is the material ground and fundamental functionality of these machines. Therefore it is rule-oriented social behaviour that is at the core of the theoretical approaches, concepts and practices of software agent researchers and roboticists. The kind of rules might differ in diverse strands of AI, but a standardization of human behaviour is a precondition for every computer model and software application. Anthropomorphized machines are intended to operate by simulating *social* norms, supposed gender differences and other *stereotypes*. The starting point of these prototypes and implementations is rule-based social behaviour that is said to be performed by humans. Researchers often use folk psychological and sociological approaches about sociality and emotionality to model human-machine-relations. Especially those theories from the wide range of psychology and sociology are chosen for the computational modelling that assume that social behaviour is operational.

And it is not by accident that software agent research and social robotics are working with sociological and socio-psychological approaches that explicitly use gender dichotomies and stereotypes. For example, we found a case where researchers used a feminist approach to improve the construction of believable artefacts: The computer scientist Daniel Moldt and the sociologist Christian von Scheve (2002) point out the value of roles, class and sex/gender differences in social interaction and their usefulness to minimize the contingency and to maximize the prediction of the behaviour of the alter ego – of the human or machinic partner in social interactive processes. According to the viewpoint of Moldt and von Scheve roles, class, gender and other differences are ideal categories in order to construct anthropomorphized software agents. In the realm of human interaction it is regarded to be helpful to use emotions to influence users, to direct the intentionality of others and to smooth interactions. Referring to feminist sociologist Arlie Hochschild they claim, that emotions are based on a system of values and norms. They are influencing the development and performance of emotions to match the expectations of the alter ego. Inspired by these ideas Moldt and von Scheve strive for software agents that express emotions based on this system of values and norms. They hope that this would help to make software agents appear as intelligent, social and endowed with a personality (See Moldt & von Scheve 2002).

Not all of these new approaches that aim to implement sociality into machines exploit critical theories and feminist approaches in such a way. Nevertheless, this example shows that the paradigm shift from rational-cognitive to social machines does not lead to a departure from masculinist technology design. This and other models rather point to the fact that gender stereotypes are instrumentalised in order to build "better" machines that are perceived as socially intelligent.

Obviously, recent research in the field of software agents and social robotics is not primarily about making machines social as most researchers suggest. Rather it seems to be about training humans in rule-oriented social behaviour. Only relying on the latter can make the interaction with these machines intelligible: As much as secretaries have to use an impoverished language to be able to use computer translation software, it will be necessary to use impoverished ways of interacting to respond to these social robots and artefacts. And while researchers use social norms and stereotypes to make their artefacts more consistent, convincing and believable, training humans in stereotypical behaviour supports ways of acting which are predictable and therefore more exploitable in economic terms.

4. De-gendering Technologies: Dimensions and Strategies of Critique

Regarding recent developments in software agent research and social robotics it becomes obvious that we need a broader and deeply differentiated feminist critique of artefacts and processes in AI and computer science. In the rest of this paper we want to sharpen our analysis of de-gendering technologies from the insights given so far. Our intention is neither to develop a step-by-step recipe for necessary feminist interventions into technology design nor to give an overview on possible political practices, but to rethink strategies, tools and dimensions of feminist technoscience studies that are up to recent developments in the field of socially inspired Artificial Intelligence and computer science.

4.1 Gender Representation

Rethinking sexist images or strongly gender stereotyped speech patterns used in social robotics and software agent research it is clear that we need a critique of these stereotypes, patterns, norms and roles. This kind of critique of technology design targeting at *gendered representation* is found most often and is even shared by some (male) computer scientists. But what we wanted to show here is that it is not sufficient only to revise the design of technology in the sense of wiping out its explicit or implicit gender stereotypes only. Nor it would be satisfying even to eliminate these and other social norms, roles and stereotypes like those of class, of age, of race, of sexuality etc. Gendered ontological, anthropological and epistemological claims are also encoded in theoretical concepts that form the base for technological construction and software applications. For example, the changing understanding of the social and the conceptualisation of the human-machine relation in these fields show that we need to regard further epistemological, ontological and societal dimensions of critique.

4.2 Social Theory

The relation between 'social machines' and the standardization of everyday life should be explored from a *social theory* perspective. It is the question whether we live in a society where social relations in general or at least in specific realms are already enacted in terms of rule-oriented behaviour. Think for example of the standardization of the health care for elderly people where every little service - like e.g. combing the hair, washing the back, etc. – has standardized time schedules (minutes) and prices. In these realms the idea of social robots taking care of elderly people lies at hand. At the same time the standardization of social behaviour through agents and robots might also lead to more rule-oriented behaviour.

Another relevant aspect is linked to the question whether social machines are expected to fill in personal and relational vacancies that emerge with new social and work requirements in the age of globalisation. Are personal agents and robots that empathize with us and to whom we are befriended the substitute for personal human relations in the age of mobility and change? Which deficiencies of our social life in the neo-liberal economy are supposed to be "repaired" by those artefacts?

4.3 Anthropological and Ontological Dimensions

From a critical perspective questions of anthropological and ontological groundings arise on which technoscientific concepts in the fields of AI and software agent research are built. What is the underlying understanding of society, sociality and human interaction? How is the relation of human-machine conceptualised?

Look for example at the concept of sociality in many – especially Anglo-American - approaches of the social and behavioural sciences. Their sociality is regarded as the outcome of the interaction of individuals, which are understood primarily as self-interested. Thereby,

"'social' refers to the exchange of costs and benefits in the pursuit of outcomes of purely personal value, and "society" is the aggregate of individuals in pursuit of their respective self-interests." (Carporeal 1995, p. 1)

These (reductionist) concepts are partly translated into action by social robots and software agents and often become even more trivialized and simplified through software implementation processes. For example, in software agent research human behaviour is commonly standardized by no more than five personality traits and six basic emotions.

Other ontological and anthropological claims of Artificial Intelligence and Human-computer Interaction can easily be illustrated by the concepts of human-machine relationship, especially in the new field of 'social' Artificial Intelligence. The relationships of owner-pet, parent-baby or caregiver-infant relationship are kind of pedagogical relationships that afford a lot of time, patience, engagement and work to function properly. Are these the kind of relationship desirable for human-machine interaction? Do we really want to educate our machines?

To summarize and to return to our starting question about what strategies are necessary to design 'de-gendered technologies', we would argue that we need a deconstruction of gender representation as well as a critique of fundamental anthropological and ontological claims that cannot be easily translated into alternative technology design. We think that there are no ready-made prescriptions for de-gendering technologies on the level of technology design. Instead such an approach needs fundamental revisions of societal structures, politics of representation and technoscientific discourses and practises.

References

Adam, Alison 1998, *Artificial Knowing, Gender and the Thinking Machine*, Routledge, London/New York

Becker, Barbara 1992, *Künstliche Intelligenz. Konzepte, Systeme, Verheißungen*, Campus, Frankfurt

Breazeal, Cynthia 2002, *Designing Sociable Robots*, MIT Press, Cambridge, Mass.

Cassell, Justine et al. 2000, *Embodied Conversational Agents*, MIT Press, Cambridge, Mass.

Caporael, Linnda R. 1995, 'Sociality: Coordinating Bodies, Minds and Groups,' *Psycoloquy* 6(01), Groupselection 1, [Online], Available: http://www.psycprints.ecs.soton.ac.uk/archive/00000448, [September 30, 2004]

Crutzen, Cecile 2003, 'ICT-Representations as transformative critical rooms,' in: Gabriele Kreutzner & Heidi Schelhowe (eds.), Agents of Change. *Virtuality, Gender and the Challenge to the Traditional University*, Leske + Budrich, Opladen, pp. 87-106

Collins, Harry 1990, *Artificial Experts. Social Knowledge and Intelligent Machines*, MIT Press, Cambridge, Mass.

Dreyfus, Hubert 1963, *What computers can't do. A critique of artificial reason*, Harper & Row, New York

Duffy, Brian 2003, 'Anthropomorphism and the Social Robot', *Robotics and Autonomous Systems* 42 (2003), pp. 177-190 (See also [Online], Available: http://vrai-group.epfl.ch/socialrobots/papers/4-duffy.pdf [September 3, 2003]

Fausto-Sterling, Anne 1985, *Myths of Gender, Biological Theories about Women and Men*, Basic Books, New York

Fong, Terrence & Nourbakhsh, Illah & Dautenhahn, Kerstin (eds.) 2003, 'A Survey of Socially Interactive Robots,' *Robotics and Autonomous Systems* 42 (2003), pp. 235-243

Gratch, Jonathan et al. 2002, 'Creating Interactive Virtual Humans: Some Assembly Required,' *IEEE Intelligent Systems*, Vol. 17, No. 4, pp. 54-63

Heintz, Bettina 1995, ,Papiermaschinen. Die sozialen Voraussetzungen maschineller Intelligenz', in Werner Rammert (ed.), *Soziologie und künstliche Intelligenz. Produkte und Probleme einer Hochtechnologie*, Campus, Frankfurt a.M., pp. 37–64

Hubbard, Ruth 1979, 'Have only men evolved?' in R. Hubbard & M. Herifin & B. Fried (eds.), *Women look at biology looking at women*, Schenkman Publ. Comp, Cambridge,.

Moldt, Daniel & von Scheve, Christian 2002, 'Attribution and Adaption: the case of social Norms and Emotions in Human-Agent Interaction' in: Marsh, S. et al. (eds.), Proceedings of *The Philosophy and Design of Socially Adept Technologies*, workshop held in conjunction with CHI'02, 20.4.02, Minneapolis/Minnesota, USA, pp. 39-41

Pfeifer, Rolf & Scheier, Christian 1999, *Understanding Intelligence*, MIT Press, Cambridge, Mass.

Sengers, Phoebe 1999, 'Practices for Machine Culture. A Case Study in Integrating Cultural Studies and Artificial Intelligence,' *Surfaces*, Volume VIII, 1999

Suchman, Lucy 1987, *Plans and Situated Action. The problem of human-machine communication*, Cambridge University Press, Cambridge

Suchman, Lucy 2002, *Replicants and Irreductions: Affective Encounters at the Interface*, published by the Department of Sociology, Lancaster University at: http://www.comps.lancs.ac.uk/sociology/soc106ls.htm, [October 5, 2003]

Stern, Andrew 2002, 'Creating Emotional Relationships with Virtual Characters,' in: Trappl, Robert & Petta, Paolo & Payr, Sabine (eds.), *Emotions in Humans and Artifacts*, MIT Press,

Cambridge, Mass., pp. 333-362

Wegener, Peter 1997, 'Why interaction is more powerful than algorithms,' *Communications of the ACM*, Vol. 40, No. 5, pp. 80-91

Notes

1   This paper is an extended version of our paper given at the international symposium *Gender Perspectives Increasing Diversity for the Information Society Technology* (GIST), *June 24-26, 2004 in Bremen, Germany*

2   see Adam 1998 for an overview of feminist critique of AI

3   For a discussion of philosophical and feminist influences on AI see Sengers 1999, for example

4   The concept of social intelligence was developed at least partly because of the feminist critique of androcentric conceptions of evolution; see (Fausto-Sterling 1985; Hubbard 1979)

5   While roboticists and software agent researchers often point towards the tendency of anthropomorphisation in the human-robot or human-computer interaction (Duffy 2003; Fong & Nourbakhsh & Dautenhahn 2003.; Gratch et. al 2002; Cassell et al. 2000), they rarely reflect on the additional work of humans to make sense of machinic behaviour (see e. g. Suchman 2002 on the relationship between Breazeal and Kismet)

11 New Europe – New Attitudes?

Some initial findings on women in computing
in the Czech Republic

Eva Turner

Dept/School, University of East London, UK

Abstract

This paper was born out of my personal interest in the Czech Republic and my research in questions of gender and computing. After many years I returned to the Czech Republic to find out what the levels of awareness are in political and education circles of issues related to my research area. This paper investigates attitudes and data related to women in computing in the Czech Government, computing education, computing industry and gender research and concludes that the low numbers of women in computing education are accompanied by not only a lack of awareness, but also a great lack of interest in, what I perceive as, extremely important issues. This paper gives little in a way of comparisons to other countries; it is the beginning of what I hope will become a more in depth research.

1. Introduction

In August 2004 I spent a week in the Czech Republic trying to find information about the position of women in computing. I collected statistical data and publications and interviewed the member of parliament heading the Council for Equal Opportunities of Women and Men. I met the workers responsible for questions of gender equality at ministries most relevant to the questions of women in computing, sent a questionnaire to the Minister responsible for Informatics, and spoke to two members of a Commission for Informatics and Telecommunication – an advisory body on questions of policy in informatics to the ruling Czech Social Democratic Party. I also spoke to women interested and working in the field of gender equality and some working in the computing industry.

The reason for this interest is my own experience as a Czech woman growing up under communism and later working as a researcher in gender and computing issues in capitalist Britain. The journey from a girl and then a young woman not even aware of gender issues to where I am now has for me a dream-like quality. I believe that such a process is now happening in some strata of Czech society. In this paper I have taken some steps in finding whether I can draw a parallel between my personal process of transition and that of the Czech nation in the issues of women and computing. I hope to continue this work for some time to come.

2. Development of Gender Awareness in Czech Republic

2.1 Before and after the Velvet Revolution

The Czech Republic (then part of Czechoslovakia) became a 'capitalist country' in the change of regime that occurred during the Velvet Revolution of November 1989 and subsequently became a member country of the European Union in May 2004. In preparation for its entry to the EU and as a reaction to direct criticism by the United Nations, the Czech political leadership was forced to follow gender equality movements and EU legislation and include gender equality on the country's political agenda. For explanation we need to bear in mind that the Czech Government was very keen for the country to become a member of the EU.

In the years 1948 – 1989 the old communist regime professed gender equality, guaranteed the right to work for every citizen, stated quotas for women's employment and guaranteed women's rights in the constitution. While the majority of women were in employment, they were also responsible for running homes, families and holding together the care systems for the sick and elderly in the home. The general population had no opportunity, nor the necessity, to discuss the meaning of gender or women's equal rights. Taking this 'guaranteed equality' for granted, the population slipped deeper into accepting biologically and socially deterministic gendered views of the roles of men and women in society. This supposed equality applied also in further and higher education. Though the politicians and the needs of the planned economy imposed quotas for the numbers of students accepted into each field, the 'equal access' of men and women to further and higher education was guaranteed through a system awarding points for political 'acceptability' and entrance examinations. While women worked in administration, education, services and caring professions, men worked in fields of engineering, technology and were represented in large numbers in specialist medicine, politics, university education and research and development, in this way a situation probably not dissimilar to UK. While the first international agreement for removal of all discrimination of women was signed by the communist government in 1981 (Czech Helsinki Committee 1999), the gendered composition of higher education continued to mirror the gendered makeup of the society.

During my school, teenage and early adult years under the communist regime I did not feel, think about or understand my position as a woman in my native society. Neither did, I think, my mother who spent most of her adult life in full employment, caring for two children in very difficult financial and living circumstances, being married to a man who, while being a loving and caring husband and father, never stopped for a minute to think about the unequal lives she and he were living. Her life style was exactly the same as that of all her female friends and colleagues. While questioning women's position was extraordinary and acceptance was the norm, my mother's frustration often turned to rage and anger.

In school I was good at mathematics, enjoyed chemistry and physics and enrolled to study electrical engineering at Prague Technical University. The choice of this subject area was partially a result of pressure exerted by my mother as 'she knew someone' at the faculty. Her working life was spent in a feminized administrative world and she, as well as I, never questioned the gendered nature of the subject area she had chosen for me. The overwhelming memory I have of that short period of my life was the uniqueness of my position. I was one of very few women amongst about 400 male students. Without realising why, I dropped out very early and took a different route to adulthood (in fact ended up working for nine years with mostly women and very few men in the Prague University Library).

When the communist regime was overthrown, gender initiatives sprung mainly from the former dissident movement, the Czech Sociological Institute and interested individual academics. The Czech Sociological Institute had begun making numerical empirical studies of the position of women in the Czech Republic immediately after the Velvet Revolution in 1989. Based mainly on their findings, the Czech Helsinki Committee reported in 1996 about the human rights situation in the Czech Republic. This very lengthy report contains a section on 'Some aspects of women's rights in the Czech Republic' which mentions sexual harassment and unequal treatment in places of employment, advertising, unequal pay and the existence of glass ceilings. All this was described as almost a 'Czech cultural norm' (a term coined by Hana Havelkova). By then the British had an Equal Pay Act from 1970 and Sex Discrimination Act from 1975.

In 1990 the famous sociologist Dr Jirina Siklova founded The Gender Studies Centre, a women's NGO, then only an educational institution. This Centre is now also an information and advice centre for equal opportunities with its own library and website, a large number of publications and participation in a number of national and international research projects. During a brief examination, I found that this library contains little about women in science and technology and nothing on women in computing.

By 1996 the Czech government was forced to begin the debate on equal rights for men and women in Czech society. This debate was mainly influenced by the need to conform to EU standards, by open criticism from the United Nations on the absence of a gender agenda and by the pressure from pressure groups taking part in world initiatives – e.g. Beijing and Beijing+5. In Aril 1998 the Czech Government agreed its 'Action Plan of Priorities and Activities for Enforcement of Equality of Men and Women'. The Government decreed that each of its departments (or ministries) had to co-operate with women's organisations of which there are estimated to be 30, mainly of charitable status (MPSV May 2002).

I arrived in England in February 1978, took a degree in Computing and Statistics and then a masters in Computer Science. I noticed that there were many more men than women and particularly at the master's level I was one of four among 40 students. While I felt rather inadequate and shy, particularly as I had no female lecturers, I still did not question my situation, I accepted it and worked extremely hard to prove myself (to them and to myself). After my studies I accepted a position in a large city firm as the first and only female programmer and only then realised that I was meeting frequent gendered discrimination. The concepts connected to my own situation had only begun to slowly dawn on me, when my first daughter was born and I was not allowed to return to work on a part time basis. I took up university lecturing in Computer Science – again then as the only female lecturer. It was the university environment, which slowly enlightened me and helped me to understand my own position in the world of computer science.

I believe that the awakening of gender awareness in the Czech Republic is going and will continue to go through a slow and 'dream-like' process similar to my own. While the pressure groups and a few of the younger generation are already questioning the situation of women in their society, the majority and officialdom are still going through the motions of following directives without critical analysis. There is a very strong and loud opposition to gender and feminist movements (see reports on Gender Studies Centre website) and only personal and personalised experiences and the pressure from below will translate the concepts into actions.

2.2 Women in computing in the development of government gender policies

The ministry, which has been charged with collecting and publishing gender information and advising the Government is that of Work and Social Affairs. It has established a Department for Equal Opportunities for Women and Men which publishes (since 1998) an annual 'Aggregate Report on Fulfilment of Priorities and Activities of the Government for Enforcement of Equality of Men and Women'. Feeding into this aggregate report are reports from each ministry, or government department.

In October 2001 the Government established its advisory body The Council for Equal Opportunities of Men and Women with members representing ministries and NGOs and headed by a woman member of parliament (MPSV 2004). The one ministry, which is not represented, is the Ministry of Informatics. The Aggregate Reports are only presented to the Government after individual ministerial reports have been debated and accepted by the Council.

The Ministry of Work and Social Affairs publishes a range of reports containing gendered statistics, EU regulations and policies in the field of equal rights and opportunities, reports on fulfilment of international agreements and recommendations (e.g. Beijing+5) and EU calls for participation in gender relevant projects. There appears to be no specific interest in women in science and technology and of course none in computing in all these publications. Most of them stress that equal rights and opportunities at work are all covered by national legislation and thus guaranteed in the Czech Republic. By such reports the Ministry is trying to prove to the EU that gender inequality at work does not exist.

This appears to be in strict contrast with situations reported by the Gender Centre, e.g. a court case lost by a 50-year-old women refused employment on the basis of her age, or a Czech Sociological Institute Study on paternity leave (2003) reporting that paternity leave take-up is minimal and that it needs to be *seriously publicised in the general press without vulgarization and derogation.*

Using various EU grants the government published material prepared for educating national and local government workers in the questions of gender equality. There are booklets outlining how to deal with project applications, how to plan for equality, a booklet on gender mainstreaming (a principle encouraged by the EU in all its activities) and a training booklet on gender budgeting. I understand that these booklets have been distributed to a variety of government departments and local councils, but have not been able to gather any evidence about them being used in practice. There seems to be no evaluation of their direct influence on decision making in official circles. They were not in evidence during my interview at the Ministry of Informatics.

In my search for evidence of understanding of questions of gender and computing I sent a questionnaire to the Minister for Informatics, Mr Mlynar. His response can be summarised as follows: he believes that women and men have equal opportunities in the workplace and in access to higher education in the Czech Republic. If they are not represented in the IT industry then it is because they do not choose the field. He believes that a stronger impetus needs to be put on IT education, which he sees as the responsibility of the Ministry of Education. For him the whole area of equal opportunities is the responsibility of the Ministry of Work and Social Affairs and the role of Ministry of Informatics in this question can be judged in their offering money for training courses in ICT literacy (National Programme). His statistics show that in 2003 and 2004 women showed more interest than men in these courses, but the Minister did not give me any reference for this information, nor did he offer any analysis of such results. He believes that higher computer literacy can subsequently influence the choice of women's employment. The ministry see no need to collect statistics on women's employment in the ICT industries. He wrote 'the experience from abroad shows that it is specifically ICT that enables women to work around their responsibilities of caring for their families and women will use these opportunities more in the future' - a statement that appears to contain unquestioned assumptions of women's caring responsibilities. I need to add that in my interview with Mrs Curdova (see below) she criticised the National Programme in ICT literacy as not being particularly beneficial to women, because the courses are often held too far from their homes or at places not accessible by public transport.

In August 2004 I had a short interview with Mrs Curdova, the Member of Parliament heading the Council for Equal Opportunities of Women and Men. From this and an interview she gave for the Gender Studies website (2004) it is evident that she faces an uphill struggle with prejudice and inequality. She is impatient with the speed of progress in understanding of gender and equality issues in the political circles and the media, while acknowledging the positive work of non-governmental organisations. She confirmed that little has been done or written about women in technology and in ICT. She also confirmed that this year the ministerial report from the Ministry of Informatics had to be returned as inadequate, and also that the Sub-committee for Women in ICT of the Parliamentary Commission of the EU Council had to be dissolved because representatives of all political parties had expressed their surprise at such a 'nonsense'. While the government has recommended financing programmes (projects) with gender initiatives, no calls have been issued for equal opportunities in technology. Dr Niklova from the Ministry of Finance confirmed (in an interview in August 2004) that she knows of no request submitted to the government for financing initiatives to increase the numbers of women in the technology sphere, though the Ministry of Finance does not make decisions, it merely allocates money to other ministries.

One of the most interesting interviews was with two male founding members of the Commission for Informatics and Telecommunication – an advisory body on questions of policy in informatics to the ruling Czech Social Democratic Party. This body comprises 30 members of whom just one is a woman. Both my interviewees told me that the question of gender and equal opportunities never entered the agenda. The first person I interviewed said he knew that glass ceilings do not exist in the Czech Republic, women do not wish to be competitive, 'collect trophies' and thus have no need to enter higher management positions. He also knew that women do not have the ability to manage technical university education, particularly mathematics, as they possess different logical skills and, as a result, drop out of the universities. It is not difficult to imagine that some of this gender stereotyping passes directly into political advice. The other was more 'careful', he gave me two examples of women in management in the industry and did not see the point of making women work in an industry in which they do not want to be. He gave me a CD with the whole of the 5th Framework EU wide SIBIS (2002) project (Statistical Indicators Benchmarking the Information Society) in which the Czech Government participated. A quick examination of the data confirmed that gender mainstreaming was not on the agenda of any of the national participants in this project.

2.3 Women in computing in higher education

In general Czech universities are divided into technical universities and humanities universities. Both types offer some teaching in information technology. However it is the technical (and economic) specialist universities that students would choose to study computer science and informatics. A brief study of the web pages of computer science / informatics / engineering faculties (last accessed 10.9.2004) revealed that no gendered statistics of staff and students are published. Most universities either do not publish lists of students or have secure access to these lists. As the Czech language differentiates clearly between male and female names, I was able to do a head count of men and women staff and PhD students in a sample of appropriate universities and departments.

University	Acad staff total	Acad staff women	PhD total	PhD women	U/grad total	U/grad women
Czech Technical University Prague Dept of Computer Science and Engineering http://cs.felk.cvut.cz/webis/	69	3	81	0	Not available	Not available
Czech Technical University Prague Dept of Cybernetics http://cyber.felk.cvut.cz/	2	4	47	0	Not available	Not available
Charles University Prague Faculy of Mathematics and Physics Dept of Software and Computer Science http://www.mff.cuni.cz/	11	3	5	1	Not available	Not available
Charles University Prague Faculy of Mathematics and Physics Dept of Software Engineering http://kocour.ms.mff.cuni.cz/lidi.php	22	3	13	0	Not available	Not available
Technical University Brno Faculty of Information Technology http://www.fit.vutbr.cz/info/	12 men in academic management of the faculty, no list of staff or students otherwise available					
Masaryk University Brno Faculty of Informatics http://www.muni.cz/	24	2	33	0	1390	97 (7%)

None of the women academics above is in a position of faculty management (dean) or professorial (school / department) management

Table 1: Staff and students at Czech universities

The Czech Statistical Office (2003) publishes gendered statistics of students at individual universities and also nationally by subjects. It also publishes the total numbers of men and women students and academic staff, but not broken down by individual schools or subject areas.

University	Men students	Women students
Czech universities total	114,322	105,192 (48%)
Technical University Prague	17,925	3,357 (16%)
Technical University Brno	12,329	2,765 (18%)
Charles University Prague	17,743	23,180 (57%)
Masaryk University Brno	9,678	12,543 (56%)

Table 2: Data for 2001/02 for same universities as in Table 1

Czech Statistical Office data (2003) show that there are, on average, equal numbers of women and men entering university education (see Table 2) and that the numbers of women students and staff are rising. They also indicate that some fields, like pedagogy or nursing, have overwhelming numbers of women students. Table 2 documents the difference between technical universities (Prague and Brno) and those primarily concerned with humanities (Charles and Masaryk). The Charles and Masaryk Universities have much higher numbers of women in traditional female fields and thus the statistics hide the low numbers of women in their departments of computing or informatics (see Table 1). For the whole of the Czech Republic these statistics show the numbers of students for the field of 'Electronics, Telecommunication and Computer Technologies'.

	Total students	Total women students	Men graduating in 2001/02	Women graduating in 2001/02
2001/02	11,875	458 (3.9%)	1,413	32 (2.2%)
2002/03	14,859	678 (4.6%)	1,619	64 (3.8%)

Table 3

Table 3 documents further the very low proportions of women in the fields which are of interest to us. British government statistics indicate 20% of women students in computer Science in 2001 (DTI 2004) and Martin et al (2004) indicate 5% in Eastern Europe, 10% in Australia and 14% in the USA.

The Ministry of Work and Social Affairs (December 2003, p 38) states that '…it is mostly women that study social sciences and services fields, most frequently medicine and pharmacy. We find few women in technical and natural science fields and also at military universities'. They also say (p36) that while there are slightly more women in bachelors' degrees, women only account for about one third of all PhD students. Certainly among these there are almost none in computing or informatics (see Table 1). Again while observing the shortages, the Ministry have no analytical explanation of these findings, nor suggestions for improving the situation.

I had a short telephone interview with Ms Kralikova, who works part time for the Ministry of Education with specific responsibility for equal opportunities for men and women. She informed me that 'The Ministry does absolutely *nothing* on questions of gender equality in Informatics' (her emphasis). Recently they undertook a survey of 'training school teachers in IT literacy' and the results show that, while Czech education is almost totally feminized, the trainers and trainees on these courses were 100% men. The Ministry is now embarking on a new long-term gender research on transfer of pupils between educational levels (equivalent of secondary to sixth form and sixth form to university). This research will investigate success and dropout levels. The schools will be separated into field groups, but individual subject areas will not be indicated. This year the Ministry of Education has not issued any calls for applications for financing projects in the field of gender and the Ministry's collaboration with other ministries in the field of gender is minimal.

There exists in the Czech Republic a Centre for the Study of University Education, established in 1991 as a state-funded institution of the Ministry of Education. 'Its mission is to collect, analyze, collate and disseminate information concerning higher education and research policy'. This Centre has published a report evaluating dropout rates from technical universities in the Czech Republic (Menclova, Bastova & Konradova 2004). There is a section entitled Sex at the bottom of page 9 of this report, which translates as follows:

'Because we are investigating technical fields of university studies, the substantial majority (73.5%) of men over women (26.5%) is quite natural.' The report offers no gendered data, no gender analysis and no proportions of men and women in the 50% dropout rate.

In her survey of women in academic management Ms Bastova (2004) states that they have little time for their own research, and find the career requirements difficult to reconcile with their family responsibilities. Most had very short career breaks and managed mainly thanks to extended family help. They entered their management careers later than equivalent men. The paper does not compare different academic fields.

As a government advisory body, this institution may be able to influence political decisions. I have not yet examined evidence that the reports are being actively used. If that is the case, then it will be necessary to embrace the questions of gender and technology in greater analytical depth, and to question social conditioning, stereotyping and prejudices and its influence on equal access of women to technical studies and subsequent careers.

2.4 Women in Computing Employment

While it is difficult to find data on women in computing in the Czech education system, it is almost impossible to find data on the numbers and positions of women in the computing and informatics industry. In 2002 there were 194 000 people who worked in Information and Communication Technologies (ICT). This represents 4 % of the total labor force in the Czech Republic (source http://www.czso.cz, provided by M. Kristova). As elsewhere in the world the definition of 'the industry' is not stated and thus some may argue that for 4% the questions of equality are not substantially important.

The Czech Statistical Office has two classification categories which relate to computing and ICT: 'Technical, Health and Pedagogic workers' and 'Research and Specialist Professional workers'. In both of these categories women earned less then men, 71.5% and 70.8% of men's wages respectively in 2001, and both combined contained 30% of all employed in the national economy. 30% then becomes important. The Czech Sociological Institute (2003) reports that during 'last few decades' of all employees 45% were women, who worked on average 43 hours a week while men worked 48 hours. The British Department of Trade and Industry (DTI 2004) reports that women in SET areas earn on average 80% of men's wages and as Computer Analysts and Programmers 90% of men's wages.

An interview with Mr Masek from the gender department of the Ministry of Work and Social Affairs confirmed that, while the Ministry is responsible for the National Gender Action Plan, the questions of equal opportunities for women and men in employment are of no interest to the Ministry. It is predominantly interested in women's unemployment, i.e. women's access to employment, and sees no reason for collecting statistical or other data on women employed in any particular field. Thus data on women in ICT or computing industries are not available.

I had a telephone interview with the personnel director of the largest Czech software house and one of the five largest Czech IT companies. She collects some gender statistics, the latest for 2001 revealed that the company employed 350 workers, of these 74% were men and 69% had university education. However of the 26% of women in the company only 1/3 had a university education, most of them were not working in technical jobs. The company employed 241 non-administrative / technical staff for whom gendered statistics are not collected. 'At a guess', there was a maximum of 30 women among them. The company employed 2/10 women as top managers, 4/18 women in middle management and 6/35 as team managers. The director assured me that the situation now (August 2004) is the same. She expressed her belief that gender differences are socially constructed ('boys take alarm clocks to bits, girls comb dolls' hair') but did not see any problems with the majority of technical workers in her company being men. 'As the projects we work on are not gendered – e.g. medical databases / oncological registers – there does not seem to be any difference in the results of teams lead by men to teams led by women'.

I also spoke to an acquaintance of mine who leads the Systems Department at the Prague School of Economics. She is a systems specialist with a degree in informatics who has been working in the ICT industry for the past 30 years. She believes that women in the Czech Republic enjoy equal opportunities in the computing profession, but they work harder and earn less money (this in my mind is a contradictory statement, but it did not appear as such to her). She also believes that the individual disciplines within the industry are gendered, in the sense that men choose systems, networks and servers, women programming, analysis and methodologies. She does not mind that there are few women in the industry, she *gets on better with men*. However, she has had to learn how to communicate with them as they have *problems with communication*. For her the word 'feminist' evokes an image of an *unfeminine woman, who wants to enter male professions and does not look after her family*.

2.5 Women in computing research

The gender debate and most research in the Czech Republic focuses on issues of domestic violence, trafficking, reproductive health and gender equality education, and has not engaged with ICT issues (Symerska, Fialova 2004).

I met one PhD student studying at Gender Studies in Prague whose PhD thesis will be on gender and computing (just beginning) and one Gender Studies Centre researcher, Dr.Lenka Simerska, who is the ICT & Economy project manager. Dr Simerska informed me about her own participation in international ICT projects specifically aimed at women. In particular she participates in the Women Networking Support Programme, Gender Evaluation Methodology Project (GEM) for Central and Eastern Europe and is a co-author of a report 'Bridging the Gender Digital Divide in Central and Eastern Europe'. This report concludes that women are under-represented at all levels within ICT initiatives in CEE/CIS, there is an inadequate integration of gender and/or women-specific issues, lack of gendered statistics and unequal access to ICT training. Dr Simerska is highly critical of the ministerial initiatives, seeing them as wholly ineffective.

Following the European Technology Assessment Network (ETAN) report on Women and Science in 1999 Promoting Excellence through Mainstreaming Gender Equality, the Czech gender specialists have also published an explanatory booklet on the glass ceiling for women in science (Linkova, Saldova & Cervinkova 2002). This booklet is meant for educational purposes, however, the women at Ministry of Informatics I interviewed had never seen it.

Women in Science is a 'National Contact Centre' with a web presence, which elects a woman scientist every month, publishes Czech and international news on women and science and a quarterly magazine called Kontext. The latest issue (April 2004) contains an article about, among other women, Ada Lovelace. I am not clear what political influence this Centre has and how widely it is known among the population. This initiative is rather similar to attempts by the British Department of Trade and Industry (DTI), which has failed to make successful women in the field of scientific research popular among the British public.

An important contribution to a critical debate on gender politics is the Shadow Report on Equal Opportunities (Bouckova et al. 2004), which is a unique and welcome publication. The Shadow Report is highly critical of the official Aggregate Reports mentioned earlier. The Shadow Report accuses the government of inaccuracies, misreporting, little pro-activity, misusing statistics to paint a rosier picture of the position of women in the Czech Republic and its own activity in this field, and of not acting on its own recommendations. In the field of education, the report is highly critical of the lack of gender sensitive education and of the Ministry of Education for not fulfilling any of the 'gender priorities' set for 2003. In science and research the report states that while there are many problems (e.g. brain drain, lack of money) there are no gendered statistics, low gender awareness in science and research organisations, lack of support for research in the areas of gender, stereotyping of researchers, financial discrimination and lack of equal opportunities. The report makes suggestions and recommendations for improvement, however, as it has only been published in 2004 there is not yet any way of assessing its impact. In none of my interviews did a government official mention it.

3. Conclusion

Under pressure from and the influence of the EU the Czech government appears to expend a great deal of activity on promoting equal rights for women and men. A Committee under the leadership of a member of parliament, annual reports and a dedicated person at each ministry all now exist. My own short survey and the Shadow Report (Bouckova P et al. 2004) show that, while there are plenty of data in general categories and statistical confirmations as a proof of success of Government policies in the field of gender equality, little evidence exists that these make any real change to public opinion or to people's behaviour. There is an overwhelming impression that the Czech political circles publish gender equality reports to satisfy EU requirements and directives only.

In the field of women and technology in general and computing specifically there is no evidence that the political circles have even begun to perceive the shortage of women in technology and ICT as a problem. While I have been told by Dr.Simerska that a grant application for a gender and ICT project had been turned down, the ministries are not aware of any application and do not issue any calls for project applications in this field. There appears to be a belief that higher levels of general IT literacy will automatically lead to more women choosing ICT technology fields to study and to work in. There is also no awareness of any need for critical evaluation of social conditioning and technological gendered prejudices and stereotypes as reasons for the unequal position of women in technology education and profession. The Ministry of Education and the educational establishment has no agenda connected to women in science and technology or any dedicated approach to increasing the numbers of women students. I only know of one Czech university lecturer at the Czech Technical University in Prague, who is research active in the field of women and computing.

Every person connected to Government and education I spoke to expressed surprise that such a field should be investigated at all, or that statistics should be collected. Perhaps stereotypically, Ministry of Informatics and the people advising the party in government on policy on Informatics have proved to be the most ignorant in this respect. One of the interviewed officials informed me that he would accept a 'typical smelly anorak' for a job in his software company because he knew that the said anorak understands his job. But he would not accept him if he came to an interview in a suit and a tie. When I questioned whether he would therefore not accept me, I was wearing a trouser suit; he replied he would as I was not wearing makeup.

To the political response I perhaps need to add that when I requested an interview with the Minister for Informatics and explained that I am interested in questions of

Gender and Computing, the minister's secretary said to me 'I can already envisage what you look like' *(tak to uz si Vas dovedu predstavit)'*. I did not ask what his image of me actually was.

Looking through some of the ministerial statistics and reports, gender mainstreaming has not been widely instituted and the Shadow Report confirmed that only about 30% of political officials at all levels have so far undertaken equal opportunities training.

There is a group of researchers affiliated to the Gender Studies who are aware of the situation of women in science and technology in general and ICT and Computing in specific. The research in this field is very bitty and small and very sincere. Unsupported by money or officialdom, this research may seem rather difficult. In the material I briefly evaluated there are some facts and figures on gender access to ICT, but connected social analysis is missing. Perhaps the most disappointing is the fact that while their research is published in English on international websites, I had no indication from the official government circles that they are aware of it.

This report is only a taster of what I hope will become a full-scale research programme. An in-depth investigation of the real effects of the Czech government initiatives on changing perceptions and in-grained social stereotypes is needed. Thin on the ground is the feminist debate on innovation, development of technology and the use of ICT. The Czech Republic is a country with a very specific economic, political and gender history and is therefore extremely interesting for a gender and computing research. The process of awakening to these issues in the Czech society (akin to my own) is yet to arrive.

References

Bastova Jarmila 2004, Zpracovani ziskanych dat k ukolu 'rovne prilezitosti' – rizene rozhovory, work in progress.

Bouckova P et al. 2004, Stinova zprava v oblasti rovneho zachazeni a rovnych prilezitosti zen a muzu, Gender Studies Centre, Prague.

Czech Helsinki Committee 1996, Nektere aspekty zenskych prav v Ceske Republice (Some aspects of women's rights in the Czech Republic),
http://www.helcom.cz/index.php?p=2&rid=100&cid=373 [28 August 2004]

Czech Statistical Office 2002 & 2003, Focus on Women and Men, Comprehensive Information, in house publication.

Czech Sociological Institute 2003, Study on Use of Parenting leave by Men,
http://www.mpsv.cz/files/clanky/712/pruzkum.pdf [20 September 2004]

Czech Sociological Institute 2003, Study of public opinion on Women at Work,
http://www.mpsv.cz/files/clanky/712/zprava.pdf [20 September 2004]

DTI 2004, Gender + Innovation Summary,
http://www2.set4women.gov.uk/set4women/statistics/04_index.htm [28 December 2004]

Gender Studies, Faculty of Philosophy, Charles University,
http://soc-prace.ff.cuni.cz/gender/menu.html [28 August 2004]

Gender Studies website <http://www.feminismus.cz/historie.shtml [20 September 2004]

Gender Studies Centre 2004, An interview with Mrs Curdova,
http://www.feminismus.cz/fulltext.shtml?x=168464 [20 September 2004]

Linkova M., Saldova K. & Cervinkova K. 2002, 'Glass Ceiling, position of women in science',
National Contact Centrum - Woman and Science.

Martin, Ursula, Liff, Sonia, Dutton, William & Light, Ann 2004, 'Rocket science or social
science? Involving women in the creation of computing', Oxford Internet Institute.

Ministry of Work and Social Affairs and Czech Statistical Office, December 2003, Women and
Men in Data, in house publication.

Ministry of Finance and the Ministry of Work and Social Affairs (2004), Gender Budgeting, in
house publication

Menclova L, Bastova J, Konradova K (2004), Neuspesnost studia posluchacu 1. rocniku
technickych studiejnich programu verejnych vysikych skolv CR a jeji priciny, Ministry of
Education in house publication, Prague, Brno
http://www.csvs.cz/projekty/Neuspesnoststudia.pdf [14 September 2004]

Ministerstvo Prace a Socialnich Veci website containing reports in the area of equal opportunities
of women and men, http://www.mpsv.cz/scripts/clanek.asp?lg=1&id=712 [20 September
2004]

Ministerstvo Prace a Socialnich Veci May 2002, Narodni Zprava o Plneni Pekingske Akcni
Platformy, (National Report on Fulfilling the Beijing Action Plan), in house publication,
http://www.mpsv.cz/scripts/clanek.asp?lg=1&id=698 [28 August 2004]

Ministerstvo Prace a Socialnich Veci 2004, Satus Rady vlady pro rovne prilezitosti muzu a zen
(Constitution of the Council for Equal Opportunities of Men and Women), in house
publication, http://www.mpsv.cz/scripts/clanek.asp?lg=1&id=3138 [28 August 2004]

Ministerstvo Prace a Socialnich Veci all, Aggregate reports on Equal Opportunities of Men and
Women, http://www.mpsv.cz/scripts/clanek.asp?lg=1&id=696 [28 August 2004]

Simerska L, Fialova K 2004, Bridging the gender Digital Divide, extract on <http://www.witt-
project.net/article46.html> [13 September 2004]

Women Networking Support Programme, http://www.apcwomen.org/about/ [28 August 2004]

Women in Science, http://www.zenyaveda.cz [14 September 2004]

Communications:
Exploiting Technology

Tanja Carstensen,
Gabriele Winker

Tess Pierce

Margit Pohl,
Greg Michaelson

Gabriele Winker

12 A Tool but not a Medium

Practical use of the Internet in the women's movement

Tanja Carstensen

Hamburg University of Technology, Germany

Gabriele Winker

Hamburg University of Technology, Germany

Abstract

This paper deals with the question of the democratising and the influential potential of the Internet for women's policy networks. The paper examines to what extent the Internet produces new forms of participation in women's policy. We shall first develop a theoretical framework, within which women's networks are conceived as subaltern counterpublics (subordinate public arenas). On this basis, we differentiate between three areas of Internet use which can be used to strengthen the power and influence of such arenas: information, interaction and political action. We present the findings of an analysis of websites of women's networks in Germany and of interviews with women's policy activists carried out as part of the research project 'E-Empowerment. The Use of the Internet in Women's Policy Networks'. These findings are evaluated on the basis of the three above areas. The paper shows that women's policy networks use the Internet particularly for finding and providing information, but that interactive options such as forums and chats, and thereby potential for discussion and opinion-forming, are little used. Political action via the net is almost completely non-existent. Thus, women's networks are only beginning to exploit the technical potential of the Internet for strengthening subaltern counterpublic spheres, showing definite room for improvement.

1.Introduction

A lively theoretical and political debate on the potential of the new information and communication technologies and their influence on democratic processes arose with the increasing use of the Internet. The Internet per se was euphorically ascribed with democratising characteristics. Internet advocates optimistically anticipated that it would widen direct participation in political processes, accelerate the reduction of hierarchies and promote varied forms of interaction. Sceptics, on the other hand, feared the Internet would endanger democracy and intensify existing inequalities, through a digital divide of society.

Feminist research also discussed the implications for gender relations on and through the net. Questions of subject and identity construction – referred to as gender swapping – were the subject of much attention (Bruckman 1993, Turkle 1995). It seemed possible to dissolve bipolar gender arrangements and shift boundaries between human and machine (Haraway 1991).

The initial euphoria has since faded away, and it has become clear that, in Germany at least, active Internet users had also been involved in political activities previously, rather than being activated by the Internet itself. Moreover, hierarchies are present on the net, as in all areas of society. Education, income, and with them also gender, as well as age still determine access to the net (Winker in this volume). Identity constructions on the net also frequently repeat conventional gender attributions, meaning that active gender swapping has remained a peripheral phenomenon in practice.

However, the Internet does open up new possibilities for information, communication and participation that can also be used for women's policy activities. Information relevant to women can be circulated faster, and interactivity via synchronous and asynchronous communication channels can make it easier for women to be included in political activity. New forms of political actions and networking via the net are also suitable for women's groups (Harcourt 1999, Floyd et al. 2002, Paulitz 2003, Travers 2003).

Our research project 'E-Empowerment, The Use of the Internet in Women's Policy Networks',[1] funded by the German Federal Ministry of Education and Research, therefore examined to what extent the Internet can promote empowerment securing women's presence in political public spheres. We specifically asked which of the new, media-conveyed information and communication possibilities are used by women's networks, and whether new forms of political participation are becoming visible.

In this paper, we will investigate this question by referring to Nancy Fraser's concept of subaltern feminist counterpublics. Our first step will be to outline some concepts of feminist publics and relate these to the Internet. As a second step, we will present the findings of our research project. We will examine the results of our evaluation of the websites of 200 women's policy networks and of interviews with 20 feminists about their Internet use. We will use a selection of examples from other areas to point out potentials that are not currently exploited. Finally, we will provide a summary and develop some suggestions for improvement.

2. Theoretical Framework: Virtual Women's Policy Networks as Subaltern Counterpublics

2.1 Fraser's concept of subaltern counterpublics

Many concepts of the public sphere assume a single, universal, bourgeois public sphere, which is separate from the private sphere (Habermas 1991). Feminist researchers have been critical of such concepts from an early point in time, and have developed alternative concepts. Fraser (1993, 1997) in particular has concentrated on the exclusions in Habermas' model. She has focused attention on non-bourgeois or competing publics and the obstacles for equal participation in the bourgeois public sphere, such as status, ethnicity or gender. In her view, members of marginalized groups in a single public sphere have no place to exchange their needs, goals and strategies with each other. Therefore, these groups have always found it necessary to create their own, alternative publics. Fraser suggests using the term 'subaltern counterpublics' for this phenomenon. She defines the term as follows:

> parallel discursive arenas where members of subordinated social groups invent and circulate counterdiscourses, which in turn permit them to formulate oppositional interpretations of their identities, interests, and needs (Fraser 1997: 81).

Due to this diversity of arenas for different groups of society, assumptions and discussions that were previously excluded from debate, as they could not find an arena in the dominating political public sphere, can now be publicly debated, in principle. Fraser distinguishes publics according to their power. Hegemonic publics are influential and capable of setting the terms of debate for many others; these public spheres define what is political. Hegemonic publics are made up of the dominant groups in society. Although it is more difficult for subaltern publics to bring their subjects into political discourses than for the hegemonic publics, their emancipatory potential should not be underestimated. According to Fraser, the ambiguous character of subaltern counterpublics is the decisive factor:

> On the one hand, they function as spaces of withdrawal and regroupment; on the other hand, they also function as bases and training grounds for agitational activities directed toward wider publics. (...) This dialectic enables subaltern counterpublics partially to offset (...) the unjust participatory privileges enjoyed by members of dominant social groups in stratified societies (ibid. 82).

Fraser's concept of subaltern counterpublics eliminates the strict division between private and political matters, thus extending the concept of the political. The exclusion of 'private interests' from Habermas' public sphere, and the previous definition of the private sphere – in the sense of 'concerning personal and domestic life' and 'belonging to private property in a market economy' – discriminate against subordinate social groups (ibid. 85).

Fraser maintains that a plurality of public spaces supports the participatory equality of societal groups and broadens the subjects of political discourse. As there are no 'natural' limits to what is 'public', new subjects can be introduced into these discursive debates, thus calling for the removal of social inequality (ibid. 92). This model also places a different value on 'women's publics', as their multi-dimensional political character also becomes visible. They can thus succeed in making their opinions and discourses into general issues.

This potential also applies to political women's networks on the Internet. They can be understood as subaltern counterpublics within this theoretical framework. The term 'subaltern' should not be interpreted in the derogatory sense as 'inferior' or 'subservient'. Instead, the meaning of 'subaltern' introduced by Gramsci (1992) as 'of subordinate status' refers to the actions of the 'subordinates', that is those societal groups who are denied access to hegemonic power and defend themselves against the rule of elites.

2.2 Political women's networks on the Internet as subaltern counterpublics

In our empirical study on 'E-Empowerment', we understand women's policy networks as groups of women who regard themselves as political and feminist, independent of their concrete form of organisation (e.g. girls' projects, women's career networks, self-help groups, women's groups within trade unions, in political parties or women's centres of excellence). These groups all tackle social problems, communicate on women's issues and regard themselves as representing women's interests (Frerichs & Wiemert 2000).

The aims and objectives of women's policy networks are extremely varied. They support equal opportunities and equal rights for women and men in the fields of family and career, and thus for paid and unpaid activities; they are active against violence against women in public and domestic life; and they support women in all kinds of difficult social situations – to name but a few important aims and objectives. Women's policy networks arise in the course of debate on different societal subjects. They are usually in opposition to or critical of the hegemonic male-influenced public sphere, as they find other discourses, subjects and forms of political and social participation important, and thereby reveal the way in which social inequality is a dominant factor in the previously existing public spaces.

Women's policy networks do not, however, stop at providing individual support and help. Instead, their activists also analyse mechanisms of oppression, gender-specific division of labour or dichotomous gender stereotypes, with the aim of overcoming forms of discrimination. They have taken on very varying organisational forms, so as not only to inform or help women but also to achieve further-reaching socio-political changes. They are thus a part of feminist publics. However, as the hegemonic publics determine what is political, feminist publics tend to take on the role of subaltern counterpublics, in which alternative discourses enable critique and extension of the hegemonic discourse.

Previously, a range of media and activities was available for extending the dominant discourse, such as organisations' own magazines and leaflets, press releases, meetings and exchanges in person, petitions, demonstrations, etc. Today, these options are supplemented by the information, communication and participation potential of the Internet. The Internet - used in a targeted way - can therefore strengthen women's policy networks in their function as subaltern counterpublics. Women's policy networks can experience empowerment via the Internet, if the multi-dimensional potentials of the new medium are put to full use. The figure below shows how women's policy issues can be strengthened via the Internet (Drüeke & Winker 2005).

Aims of women's policy networks	In relation to information	In relation to interaction	In relation to political action
According to Frerichs/ Wiemert	addressing problems within society	communication, advice-giving, exchanging experiences	representing interests
According to Fraser	developing oppositional interpretations of identities and interests	creating spaces that allow withdrawal and re-groupment	representing interests outside their own spaces and exerting influence in larger arenas
Internet functions	publishing orientation knowledge, findability via search functions and links, cooperative provision of information	forums and chatrooms for exchanging and developing problem-solving skills	preparing and carrying out political activities on the net: - planning actions - signature lists - online polls

Table 1: strengthening subaltern counterpublics through women's policy Internet presences

Information: Women's policy networks address social problems. Described in terms of Fraser's analytical framework, women's policy networks develop interpretations of identities and interests in opposition to the hegemonic discourse, and offer new frameworks and meanings for social reality. As information can be quickly made transparent and accessible on the net, this aspect can generally be supported very well online. By using the Internet, women's policy networks can publish knowledge which can then reach a larger circle of interested women. Feminist discourses can be made accessible to a wider public. The possibilities of finding this information can be improved by search functions and links. Networks can refer to each other and bundle their resources. Finally, they can offer information co-operatively, i.e. by using tools in which every network can enter information on to a common platform.

Interaction: At the same time, women's policy networks have the function of creating spaces for withdrawal and regrouping, and using them to communicate about their issues outside the hegemonic discourse. In these spaces, they consult and encourage each other and exchange experiences. Internet services such as forums and chatrooms simplify communicative exchange between women's policy activists. They can improve the flow of information between women, support discussions and provide a means to develop solutions to problems together. Fraser's spaces for practising political activities can be created in interactive forums and chatrooms; the results of these interactions in Internet-based forums can then be transferred into larger arenas. Although there has been experience that face-to-face communication leads to further-reaching and more intensive exchange, communication on the Internet is a valuable addition to traditional forms of discussion, due to its greater flexibility with regard to time and space.

Political action Finally, aside from addressing problems within society and communicating on these problems in small groups, the goal of subaltern counterpublics is to represent their interests outside their own spaces. Fraser describes this as their main emancipative potential, because they are able to change political reality by influencing discourses and norms in larger public spaces. The new technologies offer opportunities for larger groups to participate in political activities. The Internet can be used as a platform to plan joint political actions, and to call for participation. In this way, more effective and outwardly perceivable publics can arise.

Fraser's analytical framework for creating public spaces through women's policy networks described above gives grounds for optimism for an increase in power and influence through the use of the Internet's technical possibilities, with women's networks additionally active online. The Internet can be an additional support and platform for creating counterpublics, particularly as the boundaries between the public and the private can be more easily overcome on the net. Exchanges can also take place between different publics with varying power, simultaneously interlinking publics with higher and lower status.

Our research project examined to what extent Internet use already contributes to an empowerment of women's policy networks, on the basis of the three areas of 'information', 'interaction' and 'political action' resulting from this theoretical framework. In the following section, we therefore start by looking at women's policy networks' web presences from this perspective. We then explain how women's policy activists use the Internet for their political activities. Thus, we examine the aspects of service on one hand and use on the other.

3. Evaluation of the Web Presences of 200 Networks

Taking the above assumptions as our starting point, we investigated women's policy networks in Germany to find out how they use the Internet for information, interaction and political action (Sude 2005). There are about 5000 networks for women in Germany. From this basic total we selected all those networks which state their target group to be exclusively women, are politically active on a national level and have their own homepage. The 200 networks which form the basis of the study can be divided into different subject groups; many of them fit into several different categories. The subject categories are as follows:

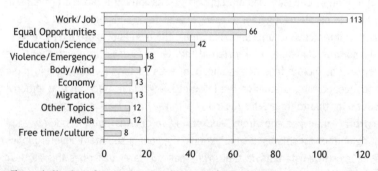

Figure 1: Number of women's networks per subject category

3.1 Provision of information

The first decisive factor for studying the creation of public spaces on the Internet is the information provided. Informed discourses require extensive and correct information to achieve functioning publics. The availability of many and well-structured indicators not only reflects the diverse technical possibilities of the Internet, it also provides the users with high quality information. On the basis of the existing women's policy websites, we classified the criterion of information into 19 indicators (cf. Table 2).

Indicator for Information	%	Indicator for Information	%
Self-presentation	88.5	Search functions	29.0
Links	79.0	Further education	25.0
Specialist information	78.0	Cooperation partners	22.5
Dates, tips on events	77.5	Appeals for funds	21.0
Media reports	61.5	Awards, scholarships	17.5
Exclusive offers	51.0	Job offers	15.5
News	43.5	Statistics	7.5
Archive	43.0	Help. FAQs. Sitemaps	7.5
Newsletter	36.5	Video streaming	1.5
Literature	30.0		

Table 2: Indicators for the category of information and their frequency in nationwide women's networks

The most important concern seems to be to introduce the network to interested web users. Networks therefore usually provide information on the history, the structures and the goals of the organisation in brief form. Link lists are also provided in many cases, most of which refer to sites on similar subjects. However, link lists in particular show large differences in quality. Thus, well-structured link lists are far less common than those offering simply a few unconnected references.

The women's networks' websites also provide extensive specialist information. One best practice example of this indicator is the website of the »Centre of Excellence Women in the Information Society and Technology«.[2] This website contains various references to studies and institutions, links to further specialised information and a wide range of very well structured and in part statistically processed data material. Dates of meetings and events are also announced on the homepages of over three quarters of the networks. These usually include information on activities, congresses, seminars, training courses, exhibitions, meetings and excursions.

It is remarkable that important specific media forms that are only possible via the Internet fall into the group of rarely used indicators. For example, search functions such as full text searches within their own website, or a sitemap which helps users to gain an overview of the total content and structure of the homepage tend to be uncommon.

As a result, we can establish that a wide range of orientation knowledge is provided, which is a basic pre-requisite for further political activities. However, the very varied possibilities of information provision that the Internet offers are not yet fully exploited.

Jensen (2004) comes to a similar conclusion in her study of media use by women's projects in various cities around the world. She establishes that Berlin-based projects often have no precise concept of the intended purposes of their own Internet presence. In contrast, her study found very precisely targeted and high quality websites based in Mexico City. For example, two organisations there offer information services on women's policy and news services. This clearly shows the Internet's potential for producing content against the mainstream of the established mass media. However, these possibilities are used to a varying extent.

3.2 Possibilities for interaction

Tools for interaction enable a reciprocal exchange of ideas and discursive communication, and consequentially collective action. Via relatively easy-to-use software, chatting provides users with the possibility of communicating in text form independent of location and, depending on data transfer speed, (almost) synchronously. This allows conversations and discussions on the Internet. Chatrooms can be used alternatively or additionally to offline discussions, in virtual workshops and working groups. One example of how a chatroom can be used in a very different way is the 'idee_it' network[3]. The activists involved in this programme host a chatroom at publicly announced chat times, enabling communication on the subject of IT and media professions. The chatroom of the virtual businesswomen's forum 'U-Netz'[4] offers a monthly expert-moderated chat on various career-related subjects. Users can also book their own chatroom for a small fee. However, only eight percent of the 200 women's networks in the study provide a chatroom.

Discussion forums can be used to publish news, which users can respond to at a later date. A longer discussion over days, weeks and months can develop. 27 percent of the 200 investigated networks offer one or more forums, but many of these forums are not regularly updated. The discussion threads are often very old, and in many cases there is no qualified moderation. One best practice example for the forum indicator is the web presence of the magazine EMMA.[5] On the website, launched at a comparatively late point in mid-2003, the 'women's political magazine' offers users the possibility of starting their own discussions and making contributions. According to the editorial team, this input also influences the magazine's print version.

3.3 Political action

Very few German women's networks offer joint political actions or facilities for immediate active participation on the Internet. In cases in which concrete activities are named on websites, users have to print out a PDF or Word document and submit it by post to participate.[6]

Whereas this Internet practice is still in its infancy in Germany, it is now common in the USA. US-based online political actions take place very frequently, for example

'ONLINE SIGNING OF STATEMENTS / PETITIONS' or specific possibilities to 'TAKE ACTION'. The US movement 'National Organization for Women'[7] (NOW) is one example of the strong virtual support for political actions in this context. NOW is the largest organisation of active feminists in the United States. According to its website, the organisation has 500,000 members. Founded in 1996, NOW's main objective is to achieve equal opportunities for all women. It also works on subjects such as discrimination (in the workplace, in schools), abortion rights, birth control and also reproduction rights for all women, the end of all forms of violence against women, racism, sexism and homophobia.

The 'TAKE ACTION' button on the NOW website leads to a long list of subjects specific to women and options for political participation. Users can become virtually active members of NOW by means of a simple procedure, and access regular information on details of important political actions and how to participate. To take part in ad hoc actions, particularly online, they simply have to fill in a contact form on the NOW net. Registering and highlighting their 'topics of strong interests' is all users have to do to regularly profit from the political actions of their choice and the automatic 'action alarm'.

4. Interviews with Feminists about their Internet Use

In a second step we interviewed 20 women who are actively involved in feminist politics and asked them how they use the Internet for information, interaction and political action (Carstensen 2005). Some of them work in a political network on a full time basis, others as volunteers. They are aged between 23 and 58, and have very different levels of experience with computers and the Internet. Some of them are responsible for the web presence of their network and spend a lot of time working with it; others use the net for several hours a week only, particularly for e-mail, and are not very comfortable with the Internet.

4.1 Motivations for networks' own web presence

Most of the women we interviewed now take a network website for granted. Different motivations were decisive in designing a homepage. One important reason was that they wanted to be 'modern'; they had the impression that it is essential to be on the Internet nowadays. Besides this, they wanted to present and position themselves and make their organisations better known. One woman said:

a project which hasn't got a website today only half exists. It is a kind of self-presentation, and presence has become very important. Without presence you don't get money. Another important concern is to make women more visible.

Some of the interviewed women regard their Internet presence as an aid and opportunity for saving time. The provision of information online saves distributing information, press releases, event promotion and brochures by traditional post, because interested parties can simply download it from the Internet. Furthermore, the web presence can be updated easier and faster than a CD or a book. Another reason was that the clientele prompted the networks to go online.

4.2 Information

The women interviewed use the Internet predominantly for searching for information. Most of them look for organisational information (e.g. train connections) and academic texts, an overview of current political discussions such as gender mainstreaming, etc., and for the specialist issues in their working fields. They often use the sites of ministries, research institutes, foundations and universities, legal-related sites, sites of trade unions or women's organisations to find this information.

When the women in our survey are looking for information beyond the websites with which they are familiar, they enter keywords in a search engine. The most frequently used search engine is Google. The satisfaction level with this strategy is extremely varied – the women interviewed often find the quality of the material found depends on the search terms selected. They also find that the quality, topicality and factual content of the information is not always reliable, and the huge number of hits and the resulting confusion and 'flood of information' can be too much for some of them. Others are extremely satisfied with the use of search engines; they describe how they vary their keywords in the course of each search, differentiate and restrict their searches and are thus successful. Other women, in turn, describe how they like to surf from one link to the next. They are not put off by the large number of search results.

The women state that they gain different benefits from using the Internet for searching for information: keeping up to date, gaining an overview of the activities of other groups and individuals, access to ideas, preparing events, texts, lectures and strategies of argumentation. But they also name disadvantages of the Internet, e.g. the lack of structure, too much information, no guarantee of quality and increasing time pressure because of the flood of information they have to cope with.

4.3 Interaction and political action

We also asked the women in our survey how they use interactive possibilities. The women interviewed stated that they use e-mails for all purposes, especially for making arrangements, organisational tasks, appointments and for working on joint texts by sending them as attachments. They also receive many enquiries or registrations via e-mail or send out information about events or news. For all of the interviewed women, the use of e-mail is now a normal part of their political activities. Thus, they do gain many benefits from interaction via the Internet. They feel better informed and consider this a strategic advantage, they are able to transfer information in a fast and simple way, and they can improve their public relations. Furthermore, they are able to reduce their administrative tasks, they can simplify their communication and exchange processes and have more contact with like-minded individuals. A very important point is the solidarity, networking, mutual aid and assistance they experience from other women on the Internet.

Mailing lists, forums and chats, however, present a different picture. Only few women use these possibilities. Most of the women interviewed state that the communication in such forms seems senseless, that they cannot see any use in the discussions there for their political work. They emphasize that they do not have enough time to spend so many hours on the Internet or they do not have the skills to do so.

Women's online communities that have arisen via the Internet itself present a completely different picture. Whereas most of the networks hold regular face-to-face meetings outside of the Internet, there are several women's organisations that communicate almost exclusively via the net. One example of a well-known women's online community is the Webgrrls.[8] The Webgrrls are a network for female specialists and managers working in or for the new media. They aim to promote women's career development, presence and influence within the industry. Online communication via forums, chats and mailing lists is a prerequisite for the existence and functioning of communities that have arisen online and focus on online forms of action. For networks that have been in existence independent of the internet, it is apparently of subordinate interest to become involved in intensive exchanges and discussions on the Internet. Hence, use of these interactive possibilities is crucially dependent on the other options for exchange and discussion available outside of the Internet (Schachtner & Winker 2005).

Furthermore, most of the women interviewed have little experience of political action in online form. Some of them are critical that no opinion-forming or development of political ideas takes place on the net. However, on the whole they do not consider the Internet suitable for political action. Most of them think e-mails are ineffective for political demonstrations; physical presence is still considered necessary. They distrust e-mail actions and time pressure bars them from spending more time on the Internet.

5. Conclusions

If we now consider the findings of both the evaluation of the web presences and the interviews with feminist users, we can summarize as follows:

The clear focus of the websites of German women's networks is currently on providing information. Websites tend to present the network itself, give information on upcoming events and provide background material on the subjects covered by the network. At the same time, interviews with women's policy activists confirm that they use the Internet primarily for searching for information. Professional and voluntary women's policy experts use the net to search for academic texts, information on current political discussions from a gender perspective and specialised women's policy subjects from their working areas, as well as for organisational support for their everyday tasks.

Thus, the women's policy networks use the medium of the Internet in the same way as they use the traditional media, especially for the purpose of public relations. A wide spectrum of specialised knowledge and a large amount of information is made accessible to a large audience via the Internet. A potentially large group of users therefore has the possibility of principally improved orientation. Many different subjects related to women's work and lives are made public by taking up the problems of society on the net. This certainly supports and strengthens the already existing subaltern publics.

However, the information is currently poorly linked and networked according to subject areas. Women's networks are also frequently difficult to locate on the web. The wide range of subjects resulting from the many different approaches among the networks is thus not made accessible to all interested parties via the Internet, but instead often only to insiders. This means that the information made available on the net is only used to a sub-optimal extent, and only finds its way into the process of political opinion-forming in fragmentary form.

In comparison to the information services – which could be improved but do at least exist – communication services with the aim of entering into lively discussion with the users on further activities are still distinctly under-represented. The Internet is very rarely used as an instrument of interactive opinion-forming. There are initial promising approaches in the area of forums and chatrooms, indicating that it is also possible to communicate and develop problem-solving skills online. However, in general, exploitation of the Internet's interactive potential is still in its infancy.

Similarly, very few visible women's policy activities such as petitions, online polls or public campaigns are being developed on the net. There are also no joint, inter-organisational projects in the women's policy arena, such as public conferences or future workshops that are jointly prepared and implemented on the web. A future workshop held online as part of the 'E-Empowerment' project showed that such forms of joint activities can certainly be carried out productively on the Internet. In this workshop, held on an online platform over three evenings, participants developed concrete ideas and demands on the future form of women's networking on the Internet.[9] The examples from the USA also show how virtual protest can be organised.

To summarise, we can state that the Internet is primarily used by the women's networks investigated as a one-way information channel, without exploiting the medium's interactive aspects. The women's organisations do not make full use of the Internet's basic potential as an information and communication medium, particularly for the creation of effective public spaces. Yet precisely such interactions, producing a link between different publics, can extend the influence and power of these publics.

We are convinced that new processes enabling a virtual linking and structuring of existing information and interaction services must therefore be developed, in order to create effective counterpublics using the technical potential of the Internet. One possibility is cooperation between women's networks. On the basis of an alliance of all interested women's policy networks into a 'virtual neighbourhood', various new search routes could make it easier and quicker for users to locate a large amount of information in a targeted manner. Simultaneously, a virtual neighbourhood would show and intensify the interwoven character of the networks and their focal points (cf. Taube & Winker 2005).

The challenge presented by the current situation is not in providing increasingly diversified information but in structuring all the information already available on the different women's policy websites, and making it easier to locate. Creating an online association of women's policy organisations would significantly improve the targeted search for women's policy-related information.

Should it be possible to organise support for the idea of a virtual neighbourhood, women's policy networks could pool their strengths and resources and strengthen and extend the content of subaltern publics. Such a women's online association would also present an opportunity to make the interests, requirements and identities represented within it accessible to many Internet users, thereby also influencing the hegemonic public discourse.

Acknowledgements

We would like to thank Katy Derbyshire for her translation, and Kerstin Sude and Ricarda Drüeke, who contributed to this investigation.

References

Bruckman, A. 1993, *Gender Swapping on the Internet*, http://www.mith2.umd.edu/WomensStudies/Computing/Articles+ResearchPapers/gender-swapping [24 January 2005].

Carstensen, T. 2005, 'Das Internet im frauenpolitischen Alltag' in *Virtuelle Räume - Neue Öffentlichkeiten. Frauenpolitik im Internet*, eds C. Schachtner & G. Winker, Campus, Frankfurt/New York, pp. 71-89.

Drüeke, R. & Winker, G. 2005, 'Neue Öffentlichkeiten durch frauenpolitische Internetauftritte', in *Virtuelle Räume - Neue Öffentlichkeiten. Frauenpolitik im Internet*, eds C. Schachtner & G. Winker, Campus, Frankfurt/New York, pp. 31-49.

Floyd, C., Kelkar, G., Klein-Franke, S., Kramarae, Ch. & Limpangog, C. (eds) 2002, *Feminist Challenges in the Information Age. Information as a social resource*, Leske + Budrich, Opladen.

Fraser, N. 1993, 'Rethinking the Public Sphere: A Contribution to the Critique of Actually Existing Democracy' in *The Phantom Public Sphere*, ed B. Robbins, University of Minnesota Press, Minneapolis, pp. 1-36.

Fraser, N. 1997, *Justice interruptus. Critical reflections on the "postsocialist" condition*, Routledge, New York & London.

Frerichs, P. & Wiemert, H. 2002, *„Ich gebe, damit du gibst": Frauennetzwerke – strategisch, reziprok, exklusiv*, Leske + Budrich, Opladen.

Gramsci, A. 1992, *Prison Notebooks*, Columbia University Press, New York.

Habermas, J. 1991, *The structural transformation of the public sphere: an inquiry into a category of bourgeois society*, MIT Press, Cambridge, Mass.

Haraway, D. 1991, 'A Cyborg Manifesto: Science, Technology, and Socialist-Feminism in the Late Twentieth Century' in Haraway D., *Simians, Cyborgs and Women: The Reinvention of Nature*, , Routledge, New York, pp.149-181.

Harcourt, W. (ed) 1999, *Women@internet. Creating new cultures in cyberspace*, ZedBooks, New York.

Jensen, H. 2004, *Die Informationsgesellschaft: Neue Chancen und Hemmnisse für geschlechtergerechte Entwicklung*, Available: http://www2.hu-berlin.de/ffz/pdf-files/jensen04.pdf [24 January 2005].

Paulitz, T. 2003, 'Productive Differences – Virtual Networks Call For Heterogeneity' in Kreutzner G. & Schelhowe H., eds, *Agents of Change. Virtuality, Gender, and the Challenge to the Traditional University*, , Leske + Budrich, Opladen, pp. 205-218.

Schachtner, C. & Winker, G. (eds) 2005, *Virtuelle Räume - Neue Öffentlichkeiten. Frauenpolitik im Internet*, Campus, Frankfurt/New York.

Sude, K. 2005, 'Internetpräsenz frauenpolitische Netzwerke in Deutschland' in C. Schachtner & G. Winker, eds *Virtuelle Räume - Neue Öffentlichkeiten. Frauenpolitik im Internet*, Campus, Frankfurt/New York, pp. 51-69.

Taube, W. & Winker, G. 2005, 'Virtuelle Nachbarschaften zur Unterstützung subalterner Gegenöffentlichkeiten' in C. Schachtner & G. Winker, eds, *Virtuelle Räume - Neue Öffentlichkeiten. Frauenpolitik im Internet*, Campus, Frankfurt/New York, pp. 107-123.

Travers, A. 2003, 'Parallel subaltern feminist counterpublics in cyberspace', *Sociological Perspectives*, vol 46, no 2, pp. 223-237.

Turkle, S. 1995, *Life on the screen. Identity in the age of the internet*, Simon & Schuster,

Notes

1 http://www.frauenbewegung-online.de
2 http://www.kompetenzz.de
3 http://www.idee-it.de/chat/index.html
4 http://www.u-netz.de
5 http://www.emma.de
6 e.g. on the website http://www.frauen-menschenrechte.de
7 http://www.now.org
8 http://www.webgrrls.de
9 http://www.zukunftswerkstatt-online.de

13 Blogging for Life

The role of the cyberconduit in everyday narratives, cyberfeminism, and global social change

Tess Pierce

Clark University, Worcester, MA, USA

Abstract

This paper calls for expanding the scholarship on gender and the Internet to include weblogs and utilises examples from ongoing research on the role of the Internet in women's everyday lives. Political Web Sphere analysis (Schneider & Foot 2002) forms the basis of an examination of weblogs produced by women from Iran, Afghanistan, and Iraq.

Weblogs mirror the Internet's culture of self-disclosure and community, are designed for audiences, and, in addition to providing a space for established voices to be heard, also create spaces for new voices. These *cyberconduits* are unique cyberfeminists who advocate for social justice on a local level, act as knowledge conduits by using digital media and technology such as blogging, and connect with activists on a global scale. This paper explores the usefulness of analysing cyberconduits' weblogs within the frameworks of Communities of Practice (Wenger 1998), Gender Performance Theory (Butler 1990, 1993, 1999), and Rhizome Theory (Deleuze & Guattari 1983, 1987).

Community of Practice (CofP) focuses on social interactions and place. Judith Butler's notions of performativity assist researchers in understanding how cyberconduits perform and subvert cultural gender roles and rules. Rhizome theory helps scholars to understand how the cyberconduit transforms her world while remaining true to her roots.

1. Introduction

A recent trend in feminist theory, scholarship, and practice addresses the emergent use of new communication technologies. Many label this trend *cyberfeminism*. Hawthorne and Klein (1999, p. 2) broadly define cyberfeminism as 'a philosophy which acknowledges, firstly, that there are differences in power between men and women specifically in the digital discourse; and, secondly, that Cyberfeminists want to change that situation'. But, just like feminism, a broad definition does not address the specificities and nuances of specific contexts. Therefore, we must specify narrow definitions that suit each application. Examples of contextual definitions include the use of digital technologies as political tools (Millar 1998; Plant 1996) as a means to subvert cultural institutions (Hall 1996) or as part of a liberating utopia (Haraway 1991). Cyberfeminism can help explain the reality of male controlled space that includes issues around harassment by males and 'women-only' sites/spaces (Borg 2000; Korenman 1999). In addition, context includes *who* the cyberfeminists *are*. For example, according to Faith Wilding, cyberfeminists are historical record keepers of activism or 'cybergrrls' who tend to be third wave feminists who 'generally seem to subscribe to a certain amount of net utopianism' (1998, para. 9-10).[1] In other words, cybergrrls are social activists who eschew theoretical critiques. Each of these cyberfeminisms links emerging digital technologies to the material lives and experiences of women despite any differences or similarities.

Despite this fluidity and adaptability, cyberfeminism depends on at least two conflicting narratives. One of these operates on a sophisticated theoretical level of feminism and technoscience, with Donna Haraway's (1991) cyborg as central character. The other integrates women's everyday lives with their actual use of communication technology for political organising. This paper, which is part of a larger work in progress, utilises the second narrative to argue for expanding the scholarship on gender and the Internet to include weblogs. The primary focus of this exploration is on the gendered discourse, personal narratives, and transformative cultural processes of weblogs by women from Iran, Iraq, and Afghanistan.

2 The Weblog as an Object of Research

2.1 Definition of the weblog

Weblogs (or blogs) are windows into a web of experiences and are the fastest growing communicative strategy on the Internet (Blood 2002a; Henning 2003; Rheingold 2003). Weblogs appear in several different forms but share several common characteristics. A blog website commonly includes:

- Dated entries with the most recent one on top (reverse chronological order).
- Hyperlinks to other websites.
- Internal links within the author's commentaries to other parts of the web site.
- Archives of previous posts.

Blogs can also include date and time stamps, comment sections, tracking software (to track references in other blogs), photographs and still images, or multimedia such as video or film clips, audio clips, and animation. Figure 1 is one of the weblogs discussed in this paper.

However, this does not really explain what a weblog is. Blogs are more dynamic than older-style personal home pages, more permanent than posts to an online discussion list, more private and personal than traditional journalism, and more public than diaries. Weblogs mirror the Internet's culture of self-disclosure, community, and potential for democratic participation. Blogs are designed for audiences. They provide a space for established voices to be heard and create new spaces for new voices. Weblogs have personality. They are an extension of the blogger herself and a connection to the blog visitor.

Weblogs are also reliable sources of information. '[T]he weblog editor can comment freely on what she finds. One week of reading will reveal to you her personal biases,

Figure 1: Home page from notes of an Iranian Girl
http://iraniangirl.blogspot.com/2002_10_27_iraniangirl_archive.html

making her a predictable source. This further enables us to turn a critical eye to both the information and comments she provides' (Blood 2002b, p. 12). Blood continues, 'These fragments, placed together over months, can provide an unexpectedly intimate view of what it is to be a particular individual in a particular place at a particular time' (2002b, p. 13).

2.2 Weblogs as cultural artefacts and communicative strategies

While weblogs are produced in many languages, this article focuses on the English language weblogs of women in, and from, Iran, Iraq, and Afghanistan. Research on English language sites is beneficial for three reasons. First, English is the language of origin for most of the current blog authors (Henning 2003). Second, free blog software programs rarely include non-English versions and, therefore, in order to reach the English-speaking audience, weblog authors rely on (often inadequate) translation programs.[2] This requires a moderate amount of programming expertise that not all bloggers posses. Third, our scholarly limitations as English speakers help us to identify and understand western influences on non-western cultural processes. In addition, the bloggers realise the importance of using English in their weblogs. As Iranian Girl (October 30, 2002) states in her weblog, 'This is my first english weblog. There are lots of Iranians that write weblogs. But their weblogs are in farsi & others in the world can't read them. So I decided to make a weblog to shout my words to the world from this little electronic page'.

The three weblogs used as examples are the Iranian insider's weblog, *Notes of an Iranian Girl* (http://iraniangirl.blogspot.com), a weblog of an Afghani living in exile, *Upper Echelon of Happiness* (http://theupperechelonofhappiness.blogspot.com), and the Iraqi weblog, *Baghdad Burning* (http://riverbendblog.blogspot.com). These three countries are important because of their political connections. Due to the current wars in the Middle East, they are commonly, and incorrectly, considered to be one cultural entity. This homogenisation is a form of cultural and gendered racism. This inquiry recognises their cultural differences while, at the same time, acknowledges their similarities. Research data is limited to a specific period - from March 19, 2003, the date of the first invasion by U.S. forces in the second Gulf War, through August 1, 2004. This period is significant because it encompasses the political web sphere from the war's beginning through Saddam Hussein's capture and the on-going transitions into democratic political states that follows. It is also a period of heightened social change that greatly affects the global women's movement. In her blog entry entitled 'Chaos' on August 31, 2003, Riverbend comments on Paul Bremer's controversial statement regarding the status of Baghdad.

[Iraq] is not a country in chaos and Baghdad is not a city in chaos. – Paul Bremer

Where is this guy living? Is he even in the same time zone??? I'm incredulous... maybe he's from some alternate universe where shooting, looting, tanks, rape, abductions, and assassinations aren't considered chaos, but it's chaos in *my* world.

Ever since the occupation there have been 400 females abducted in Baghdad alone and that is only the number of recorded abductions. Most families don't go to the Americans to tell about an abduction because they know it's useless. The male members of the family take it upon themselves to search for the abducted female and get revenge if they find the abductors. What else is there to do? I know if I were abducted I'd much rather my family organize themselves and look for me personally than go to the CPA. (Baghdad Burning, 2003)

Riverbend's comments exemplify how private lives differ from public perceptions. Her blog entry provides a glimpse of how women's private discourse, in a public space, informs the local while it transforms the global. It also exemplifies how cyberconduits, like Riverbend, intentionally change their language styles and narratives from private conversations into a public exchange of ideas. In addition, examining the Internet's role in how the language styles and narratives are unintentionally changed when they occur online provides insight into the discussions on policy-making and social movements.

This topic is particularly important because weblogs are unique communicative strategies. Communication on the Internet exists on at least three levels simultaneously - the interpersonal (1:1), mass media (1:many), and computing, such as search engines, (many:1). In addition, the Internet is unique in that it also exists on a (many:many) level through applications such as email boxes with multiple receivers, listservs, and public multicasts such as chat rooms or gaming web sites (Burnett & Marshall 2003). While blogs may seem to fall into the (1:many) communication level, they actually fit the (many:many) level better because of their interactivity. For example, the weblog author posts her thoughts and feelings in real time and conversations can simultaneously emerge between her and blog visitors while she is actively online. At the same time, visitors, using the comment sections of the blogs, can engage in conversations with each other. However, the interactivity is much more complex than real time conversations. Conversations can exist independently of the real time posts on the weblog. They continue long after the author logs off for the day. In addition, because weblogs connect to other weblogs, conversations about the original weblog may exist with, or without, the knowledge of the author. It is much like a vibrant party where everyone is part of the group, but, at the same time, they engage in individual conversations that change and flow depending on who enters and leaves the room. This multilevel communication model provides a unique perspective into women's everyday lives, while also providing the opportunity to examine the global consequences of their life experiences.

2.3 The cyberfeminist weblog

It is imperative that scholars examine cyberfeminism in order to cultivate discussions regarding access, inclusion, and gender. Feminist scholars must be compelled to examine how and why women, who choose to go online for personal and political reasons, navigate, challenge, and ultimately change their worlds. It is beneficial to understand how particular women use particular digital technology (in this case weblogs) in particular contexts. Interest in women with limited access, such as those who live in countries where laws and political climate specifically restrict Internet use, is particularly useful. More specifically, when we explore the lives of the women who act as connectors between those with restricted access and those with less restricted access, we can cultivate a deeper understanding of the implications of digital globalisation.

A cyberfeminist is more than a feminist who uses the Internet. Cyberfeminists link the historical and philosophical practices of feminism to contemporary feminist projects and networks to women's everyday experiences both online and offline. This paper calls for research that examines *cyberconduits* - cyberfeminists who not only advocate for social change on a local level but also connect to women globally creating a social movement. Cyberconduits are unique cyberfeminists who advocate for social justice on a local level, and who act as knowledge conduits by using digital media and technology, such as blogging, to connect with activists on a global scale. Key elements of a cyberconduit are nomadism, polyglossia, and rhizomatic transformation.

Rosi Braidotti's (1994) notion of a nomad figuration allows researcher to understand how cyberconduits move through established territories and challenge the cultural categories and values that inscribe them while blurring the conventional ideas of boundaries. In the virtual world, boundaries may appear not to exist, but they are, in fact, very real. They remain invisible until one chooses to acknowledge them. A cyberconduit not only 'sees' the boundaries, she has the intense desire to trespass them. Imperative to this effort is becoming a polyglot or a linguistic nomad. Cyberconduits, as polyglots, may speak many languages but take care to avoid translating a 'foreign' language into their 'native language'. In her seminal work on gender, culture, power, and identity, Ruth Behar (1993) advocates that scholars become bilingual and dual citizens in order to understand those who are different. This author agrees with her assertions. However, Behar falls short of what is needed in a technologically based culture.

Iris Young (1997) argues that bringing different perspectives into public life opens the channels of communication and builds coalitions that rely on differences and similarities to resolve community disputes. Therefore, becoming bilingual is not enough. It is only through the process of polyglossia where the woman, as cyberconduit, avoids translation and acknowledges her biases in order to understand the similarities she shares with the women with whom she interacts. This is extremely important in digital spaces. Not only do cyberconduits learn to understand and use spoken languages, improved blogging translation software allows them to write (or post) in more than one language simultaneously. As this aspect becomes more 'natural', boundaries fluctuate and multiply, and rhizomatic transformation occurs. Shadi's weblog, provides a good example of transformative language. Unlike the other two weblogs, the *Upper Echelon of Happiness* is written almost entirely as poetry (Shadi, 13 May 2004). Not only does Shadi use transformative language, she scrutinises how the changes in her life constitute a legacy for others to consider.

don't remember me when i'm gone!

remember me now!

leaving something behind is overrated.

it's to make us feel better about death. (Shadi, 2004)

Using Rosi Braidotti's (1994) and Deleuze and Guattari's (1983, 1987) figuration of the rhizome helps to understand how a cyberconduit, like Shadi, transforms her world. Just as the rhizome starts with a tap root that feeds and supports the plant as it grows, cyberconduits are rooted (or grounded) in feminist thinking and ideologies. As the rhizome grows, the tap toot is destroyed (or feminist thought is deconstructed) and an immediate, indefinite multiplicity of secondary roots grafts onto it and new feminist ideas build on the previous ones, developing something new. Paradoxically, by cutting the old, new plants/ideas grow, forming the foundation of a new feminist genealogy. Studying the online life experiences of cyberconduits is a way to see that cyberfeminism is a browser through which to view the world. But not all women who use digital technology or produce weblogs are feminists, let alone cyberconduits. Women are online for many reasons. This work does not claim that researchers ignore women who go online. This is far from true. What is true is that much of the research done about women online concerns business and e-commerce applications. Typical of this research is the marketing report that recommends e-commerce adjusts to accommodate the emerging group of online consumers consisting of teenage girls and women 55-and-over

(Rickert, A. & Sacharow, A. 2000). The problem is that studies like this one assume the same stereotypes seen in other forms of mass media - women's primary interests lie only in consumerism, beauty, and sex as the ingredients of power. Many feminist analyses of these stereotypes are available in media scholarship, and critics are quick to point out that the stereotypes reinforce a Western worldview that is white and heterosexual.[3] But women are going online for more than *buying* shoes; they are going online to advocate for human rights for the sweatshop workers *making* those shoes.

According to the U.N. Commission on the Status of Women (2003), citizens must cultivate leaders with the desire to challenge gendered restrictions in governmental Internet communication technology policies. Faith Wilding (1998, para.14 -15), in her treatise on cyberfeminism states, 'On the Internet, feminism has a new transnational audience …it must be remembered that the more this information can be contextualized politically, and linked to practices, activism, and conditions of everyday life, the more it is likely to be effective in helping to connect and mobilize people'. Therefore, it is imperative to examine the Internet, and the use of a personal computer to access it, from a feminist perspective.

3. Conceptual and Theoretical Frameworks

3.1 Community of practice

Community of Practice (CofP) is a methodological analytic framework that focuses on social interactions *and* place (Wenger 1998). Although first developed as a framework for examining business communities, feminist scholars find CofP useful in examining everyday behaviours (Eckert & McConnell-Ginet 1999; Hall 1996; Paechter 2002). Community of Practice is defined as 'an aggregate of people who, united by a common enterprise, develop and share ways of doing things, ways of talking, beliefs, and values – in short, practices' (Eckert & McConnell-Ginet 1999, p. 186). But it is more than shared repertoires; it contributes to the cultural identity formation of both the group and its individual members. Eckert and McConnell-Ginet stress the importance of examining the intersections of gender with age, ethnicity, sexual orientation, and/or class. Therefore, the study of CofP should not 'stand alone'; it must be examined in comparison with other frameworks to avoid the risk of generalising and, thus, perpetuating stereotypes.

A blogosphere (a set of related weblogs) is a Community of Practice. According to Nicholas Packwood, (2004, Virtual Geographies section, para. 4) 'The blogosphere is an environment in which new and unique trans-national and trans-cultural conversations and relationships emerge that are neither particular to locale, nor generalizable to commonplace abstractions of globalization'. Therefore, considering a blogosphere as a Community of Practice helps shift focus from group attributes defined by a physical space to group action and identity formation without the restrictions of geographical borders.

3.2 Performativity

Two theoretical frameworks inform this research: Judith Butler's (1990, 1993, 1999) concept of Gender Performativity and Gilles Deleuze and Félix Guattari's (1983, 1987) Rhizome Theory. For Butler, biological sex and gender are not only socially constructed categories, they are also the very apparatus of production of sexual difference. In other words, gender is both expressed *using* societal rules and it *produces* societal rules of expression. Gender performance can also be subversive because it imitates the 'natural' structure of gender at the same time that it disputes its naturalness. Butler advocates dismantling the rules that govern 'normal' gender construction because they are neither natural nor essential, are created within a specific historical context and may no longer apply, and performing them is an act of oppression devaluing the performer as deviant. Butler informs our understanding of the ways in which cyberconduits 'perform' gendered expectations even though they are in a space that does not require a physical body to exist.

Performativity helps us to address how gender is both invisible and visible in virtual space. The weblog serves as a bridge connecting online and offline lives. The weblog's purpose is the *act of blogging* – a gendered performance. If identity is situated, reciprocal, performative, and constituted in time in symbolic interactions of everyday life, then real life and virtual life are both fully actual (Schaap 2004, Presentation on the web section). In his examination of the Dutch Blogosphere, Schaap (2004) argues weblog authors perform both individual and collective identities in much the same ways online as they perform them offline. For example, bloggers are female or male, having a bad day at work, or living in a town - providing a unique vantage point from which to perform their everyday lives. Moreover, just as the concept of performativity informs us about gendered strategies of resistance, so too the use of the figuration of the rhizome helps to critically analyse online gender conformity.

3.3 Rhizome theory

Deleuze and Guattari (1983 1987) use the figuration of the rhizome to represent the constant process of transforming and the flux of multiple becoming. Using the rhizome figuration helps to establish connections. For example, in order to analyse language, researchers must look at it rhizomatically, viewing it not simply as language, but as everything related to language. By doing so one can see that political pressures or regional slang both compel change. A cyberconduit, as polyglossic nomad, not only hears and listens to women's multiple voices, she uses multiple voices herself in order to transform the old into something new.

However, in order to navigate the changing boundaries of language, one needs a road map. This road map helps the nomad to navigate the disjunctures and reconfigurations of language that occur in transformation. A map is a representation of a place with multiple entry points and multiple exits. It is not to be confused with tracing a picture of that same place. Tracing reproduces the old. Mapping, on the other hand, uses the cartographer's own experiences and talents to create something new. A map may be of India, but the map Joni Seager (1997) creates in her atlas about women's status around the globe, for example, is quite different than the map produced by Rand McNally to help navigate the streets of New Delhi. A cyberconduit not only acts as a road map of social activism for emerging feminists to follow, she creates this map through her relationships with them. She is both dynamic and interactive. But Packwood (2004) cautions us not to mistake the map for the territory. A cyberconduit may live in political areas mapped by government agreements but she can subvert state borders by re-mapping her physical worlds using digital technology such as blogging. The political map may represent a country's borders, but bloggers construct (virtual) personal maps that expand these borders. Both maps are real.

4. Political Web Sphere Analysis

Political Web Sphere analysis (Foot & Schneider 2002; Schneider & Foot 2004) is beneficial for exploring the political blogosphere, especially when focusing on hypertextual and personal narratives. A web sphere is a group of related web sites connected by hyperlinks and ideologies, and incorporates both structural and socio-cultural techniques (Foot & Schneider 2002).

In order to consider a blogosphere as a web sphere, one must consider how they are both dynamic and recursive (Foot & Schneider 2002, p. 226-227). Web sites and weblogs are dynamic in two ways. First, they are individually dynamic because of the hyperlinks embedded in each one. Second, researchers use these links to define and redefine the boundaries of the political web sphere that the individual web sites form. In addition, a web sphere is recursive. This concerns how and why web sites and weblogs reference other sites and how and why other sites reference them – with or without the others' knowledge or permission. 'Thus, as a web sphere is analysed over time (ideally via an archive that enables retrospective analysis), its boundaries are dynamically shaped by both researchers' identification strategies and changes in the sites themselves' (Schneider & Foot 2004, p. 118).

In addition, the notion of coproduction is essential to understanding how both weblog authors and their visitors are 'simultaneously users and consumers of the political Web' (Foot & Schneider 2002, p. 229). This is visible in four distinct areas. First, in the production of individual weblog features, comment sections on weblogs provide spaces where visitors and authors suggest additional links which, in turn, can turn up as part of related weblogs. Second, entire web sites can be co-produced. Although not the case with the three examples in this paper, many political weblogs are produced by multiple authors. An example of this is the *Weblog at Harvard Law* (http://blogs.law.harvard.edu/). The third area of coproduction is that which occurs across Internet applications. These could be email, bulletin boards, or chat applications. A recent post on *Baghdad Burning* (January 31, 2004) links to a discussion on cluster bombs hosted by Physicians for Human Rights. Finally, embedded links provide coproduction. Most weblogs include a sidebar that includes a friends list or links to favourite web sites. According to Foot & Schneider, 'these links enable visitors to get more information about the particular issues of concern to them from a range of perspectives, and in doing so, contribute to the coproduction of the political Web' (2002, p. 230).

Web Sphere analysis is also useful because it utilises both macro and micro analytic techniques (Schneider & Foot 2004, pp. 116-18). Macro-analysis allows for historical and inter-sphere comparisons. An example of this is Foot & Schneider's (2002) analysis of the U.S. 2000 elections. Their historical comparisons concerned how digital technology emerged as an integral part of the political process. The inter-sphere research compared the way different political campaigns, online news sources, advocacy groups, and related web sites functioned both independently of each other and cooperated in order to influence election outcomes. Their micro-analysis, on the other hand, examined texts, features and links (a discursive approach) while allowing for the relationships between the producers and the users. In addition, Political Web Sphere analysis addresses the weblog's uniqueness in that it is both ephemeral and permanent (Schneider & Foot 2004).

Weblogs and blogospheres are ephemeral because their construction and existence are transient and brief in nature. They are similar to performance media such as live TV, radio, or theatre. 'Web content, once presented, needs to be reconstructed or represented in order for others to experience it' (Schneider & Foot 2004, p. 115). Yet, the weblog also possesses a sense of permanence. Unlike performance media, blogs must exist in a permanent form to be transmitted much like film or video productions. In addition, a user must also have hardware (a physical, permanent machine) and software (such as a browser) to view the web pages and interact online. But, paradoxically, this permanence is also transient. 'Unlike any other permanent media, a web site may destroy its predecessor regularly and procedurally each time it is updated by its producer' (Schneider & Foot 2004, p. 115). This is the very nature of the Internet. After a web site is established, one can maintain the site's content, keeping the information updated, or delete the site altogether. The choice is up to the web site's author. A weblog is a unique web site because the archive feature makes it more permanent than a personal web page. Once a blogger adds a daily post, a visitor comments on an entry, or either of them adds a link to a related website, the information is stored as a permanent part of the blog. Therefore, different approaches are necessary to analyse web sites with these unique features.

4.1 Analytical approaches - structural

To assist in developing a Political Web Sphere analysis, Schneider and Foot (2004) suggest that researchers use discursive, structural, and socio-cultural approaches. These are especially helpful when considering gendered language styles. Recent scholarship supports the claim that stereotypical gender discourse patterns exist online (Coates 1993; Collins-Jarvis 1997; Herring 1994). For example, Herring (1994) and Coates (1993) claim gender is visible on the Internet even if the person who is gender swapping deliberately hides it. Collins-Jarvis (1997) argues that stereotypical power dynamics control the content and interactions in online discussions such as Internet Bulletin Boards.

Structural approaches, such as discourse analysis, look at individual websites as units of analysis. This includes examining the depth of the site (number of pages) and how they are organised (hierarchical elements). It also involves analysing the embedded features on the web site such as search engine functions, the privacy policy, or copyright information. A structural approach is useful in this research because it helps to determine the intended and unintended consequences of the links and connections that the web sites produce. For example, in an earlier study on two environmental web sites, a structural analysis revealed cultural, gendered differences that included a very hierarchical design in the web site produced by the male and a circular design produced by the women-run site. Also, the links on both web sites revealed unobvious connections. For example, the male-produced web site contained secondary and tertiary connections to the white supremacy movement in the United States and government conspiracy web sites that the author did not originally include (Pierce 2002).

4.2 Analytical approaches – technical media narrative

To analyse structural elements in weblogs, a technical media narrative analysis is also useful. Technical analysis methods (Roberts-Breslin 2003) address the tools and techniques of media sound and image production. These include, but are not limited to, visual framing, structure (linear and non-linear), and sound production (which also includes the absence of sound). Visual framing concerns more than the physical edges of an image or a web site. It addresses the way the visual narrative defines and shapes certain realities. Visual framing analysis considers who (or what) controls what is told, performed, or omitted.

Linear and non-linear aspects help understand the implications of structural designs. The Internet and the web blogs contain aspects of both. For example, a blog narrative may be produced as a linear story, such as a story of a day's events, but it is, at the same time, non-linear in that it can be experienced out of sequence. Distribution can also be non-linear in that different parts of the blog may be accessed at different intervals depending on the experiences and technological capabilities of the person interacting with the blogger. Finally, sound production can also be both linear and non-linear.

Most media productions, such as films and video, have simultaneous sound and image production. But this is not true of most weblogs. Although online streaming video with sound capabilities is gaining popularity, many web users do not have the hardware or software to support this technology. Technical media narrative analysis helps scholars to understand the impact of the message when sound is absent, or when sound is not available due to technical limitations. Also useful is the examination of the elements of sound design that include dialogue, narration, voiceovers, ambience, and sound effects. Structural analysis, therefore, provides the means to understand weblogs, but a critique of the structural approach is that it is inadequate to discuss their interactivity. Therefore, a socio-cultural approach is beneficial.

4.3 Analytical approaches – socio-cultural

The socio-cultural approach helps analyse 'multi-actor, cross-site action on the web' (Schneider and Foot 2004, p. 117). Socio-cultural analysis allows for examination of multiple web sites and the actions by both the users and producers performed on them over time. In order to paint a clear picture of weblogs and blogospheres, and to understand how online gender dynamics mirror offline dynamics, analyses must expand to include personal narratives.

4.3.1 Personal narratives

According to Walter Fisher (1987), our use of personal narratives is what makes us human. Personal narrative is defined as story-telling (oral, textual, and hypertextual), based on experiences and performed in social situations (both formal and informal). Within these social situations, we employ different modes and strategies in order to create meanings. In other words, personal narratives change depending on who is telling what, to whom, and where. Personal narratives are social processes with performance, context, and political praxis equally important. As social processes, personal narratives cross traditional boundaries such as written/oral and public/private. In performance, both the narrator and her audience's experiences influence meaning and understanding. The act of telling the story is a way of organising experiences. While it is important to consider performance, context must not be ignored. Where the story is told, and why, influences its meaning and understanding.

Personal narratives both reflect and constitute reality building a relationship between the narrator and her audience where meanings are negotiated and renegotiated. It is a muddy, complex process that often results in misrepresentation and misunderstanding. This is why personal narrative as a political strategy is important. As political strategies, personal narratives address the relationships between language, social institutions, power, and subjectivity. Dennis Mumby (cited in Langellier 1989, p. 266) asserts, 'That storytelling is not a simple representing of a pre-existing reality. But is rather a politically motivated production of a certain way of perceiving the world which privileges certain interests over others'. Therefore, personal narratives not only make meanings themselves, their political function also defines them. Research on personal narratives has primarily been situated in written and oral contexts. Studies, like the one from which this paper's weblog examples come, contribute to the emerging body of research that considers the importance of the hypertext narrative.

4.3.2 Hypertextual Narratives

Hypertext narratives, like those in weblogs, are more than stories; they are a system of/for storytelling with plots, characters, and settings resulting in both fragmented and limitless life stories. In more traditional linear narratives, such as oral storytelling, the author exercises a high degree of control over the chain of events that form the causal relationships of the plot line. She can define and order the reception of the events through her construction of the plot (the events as presented to the audience), and, depending on her narrative goals, she can manipulate the story to either increase or decrease its ambiguity. In interactive narratives she can present the same chain of events to her audience, but the dynamics can change because of direct audience interaction. Therefore, unique to hypertextual narratives, is the audience's manipulation and control of the story (Bizzocchi 2001; Bizzocchi & Woodbury 2003).

This is what Bizzocchi & Woodbury (2003) refer to as a conflict of two domains – the intended outcome of the storyteller and the actual outcome controlled by the audience's interaction. They claim, 'the design of [hypertext] narrative seeks a particular kind of outcome – a state of immersive surrender to the work. The reader engages in a suspension of disbelief, ignores the objective reality of the conditions of reception, and surrenders to the world of the story' (Bizzocchi & Woodbury 2003, p. 551). In hypertextual narratives, the audience no longer sits in the dark theatre watching the plot evolve, they become *part* of the plot.

5. Conclusion

Expanding research on gender and the Internet to include weblogs does not imply that weblogs are the 'killer app' that defines all cultural production. On the contrary, weblogs are just one aspect of the ever-changing Internet that should not be ignored. In addition, even though there is an emerging scholarly trend that addresses gender and technology, women are still under-represented in the scholarship that focuses on the Internet and World-Wide Web. Not only are women less likely to produce scholarly research in these areas, they are also less likely to be the focus of the research itself. For example, in their content analysis of weblog scholarship Herring et al. (2004) found male bias evident at all levels of scholarship – from conference participation to publication. Scholars of all disciplines, especially computer science and its related areas, must recognise the need to integrate global concepts of gender into already established perspectives, such as economics and software design heuristics, in order to create a solid basis for informed policy-making and to cultivate leaders with the desire to challenge gendered restrictions in transnational Internet communication technology policies. 'On the Internet, feminism has a new transnational audience ... it must be remembered that the more this information can be contextualized politically, and linked to practices, activism, and conditions of everyday life, the more it is likely to be effective in helping to connect and mobilize people' (Wilding 1998, para. 14-15).

This ongoing project is only a snapshot of three women's lives. Much more research is necessary that addresses the larger cultural implications of blogging. The women bloggers in this project's examples are engaged citizens working as part of the political process, educating each other, and creating political leaders. Using the emerging digital technology of today, bloggers, as cyberconduits, help shape the political worldviews of the new millennium. Therefore, it is imperative to examine the Internet (and the use of a personal computer to access it) from a feminist perspective. Because, after all, 'The personal computer is a political computer' (Wilding 1998, para. 7).

References

Behar, R. 1993, *Translated Woman. Crossing the Border with Esperanza's Story*, Beacon Press, Boston.

Berkman Center for Internet & Society at Harvard Law School, 2004, *Weblog at Harvard Law*, http://blogs.law.harvard.edu [18 January 2005].

Bizzocchi, J. 2001, Ceremony of innocence: A case study in the emergent poetics of interactive narrative, Master's thesis, Massachusetts Institute of Technology, http://merlin.capcollege.bc.ca/bizzocchi/dreams/Thesis_jb_pix_50.pdf [10 March 2003].

Bizzocchi, J. & Woodbury, R. F. 2003, 'A case study in the design of interactive narrative: The subversion of the interface', *Simulation and Gaming*, vol. 34, no. 4, pp. 550-68.

Blood, R. 2002a, 'Introduction' in *We've Got Blog. How Weblogs are Changing Our Culture*, ed J. Rodzvilla, Perseus, Cambridge, MA.

Blood, R. 2002b, 'Weblogs: A history and perspective' in *We've Got Blog. How Weblogs are Changing Our Culture*, ed J. Rodzvilla, Perseus, Cambridge, MA.

Borg, A. 2000, 'Why Systers?', *The Systers Online Community Home Page*, http://athena.systers.org/about.html [19 February 2002].

Braidotti, R. 1994, *Nomadic Subjects. Embodiment and Sexual Difference in Contemporary Feminist Theory*, Columbia University Press, New York.

BBC News UK Edition, 2003, 'Iraq 'needs tens of billions'', 27 August, http://news.bbc.co.uk/1/hi/world/middle_east/3183979.stm [17 January 2005].

Burnett, R., & Marshall, P. D. 2003, *Web Theory. An Introduction*, Routledge, London & New York.

Butler, J. 1990, 'Performative acts and gender constitution: An essay in phenomenology and feminist theory' in *Performing Feminisms: Feminist Critical Theory and Theatre*, ed S. E. Case, Johns Hopkins University Press, Baltimore & London.

Butler, J. 1993, *Bodies That Matter: On the Discursive Limits of Sex*, Routledge, New York.

Butler, J. 1999, *Gender Trouble. Feminism and the Subversion of Identity*, Routledge, New York.

Coates, J. 1993, *Women, Men and Language* 2nd edn, Longman, London.

Collins-Jarvis, L. 1997, 'Discriminatory messages and gendered power relations in on-line discussion groups', paper presented to the 83rd Annual Conference of the National Communication Association, Chicago, IL, 20-23 November.

Deleuze, G, & Guattari, F. 1983, *On the Line*, trans J. Johnston, Semiotext(e), New York.

Deleuze, G., & Guattari, F. 1987, *A Thousand Plateaus. Capitalism and Schizophrenia*, trans B.

Massumi, University Minnesota Press, Minneapolis.

Eckert, P., & McConnell-Ginet, S. 1999, 'New generalizations and explanations in language and gender research', *Language in Society,* vol. 28, pp. 185-201.

Fisher, W. R. 1987, *Human Communication As Narration: Toward a Philosophy of Reason, Value, and Action,* University of South Carolina Press, Columbia.

Foot, K. A., & Schneider, S. M. 2002, 'Online action in campaign 2000: An exploratory analysis of the U.S. political web sphere', *Journal of Broadcasting and Electronic Media,* vol. 46, no. 2, pp. 222-244.

Hall, K. 1996, 'Cyberfeminism', in *Computer-Mediated Communication: Linguistic, Social and Cross-cultural Perspectives,* ed S. C. Herring, John Benjamins, Amsterdam & Philadelphia.

Haraway, D. J. 1991, *Simians, Cyborgs, and Women: The Reinvention of Nature,* Routledge, New York.

Hawthorne, S. & Klein, R. (eds.) 1999, *Cyberfeminism: Connectivity, Critique and Creativity,* Spinifex, Melbourne.

Henning, J. 2003, 'The blogging iceberg - of 4.12 million hosted weblogs, most little seen, quickly abandoned', Perseus Development Corp, *White Papers,* http://www.perseus.com/blogsurvey/thebloggingiceberg.html [7 October 2004].

Herring, S. C. 1994, 'Gender and democracy in computer-mediated communication', *Electronic Journal of Communication,* vol.3., http://www.cios.org [8 November 1999].

Herring, S. C., Kouper, I., Scheidt, L.A., & Wright, E. (2004). 'Women and children last: The discursive construction of weblogs', in *Into the Blogosphere: Rhetoric, Community, and Cultures of Weblogs,* eds Gurak, L. Antonijevic, S. Johnson, L. Ratliff, C. & Reyman, J., http://blog.lib.umn.edu/blogosphere [26 October 2004].

Iranian Girl 2002, *Notes of an Iranian Girl,* http://iraniangirl.blogspot.com [1 November 2002].

Korenman, J. 1999, 'Email forums and Women's Studies: The example of WMST-L', in *Cyberfeminism: Connectivity, Critique and Creativity,* eds S. Hawthorne & R. Klein, Spinifex, Melbourne.

Langellier, K. M. 1989, 'Personal narratives: Perspectives on theory and research', *Text and Performance Quarterly,* vol. 9, pp. 243-276.

Millar, M. S. 1998, *Cracking the Gender Code: Who Rules the Wired World,* Second Story, Toronto.

Packwood, N. 2004, 'Geography of the blogosphere: Representing the culture, ecology and community of weblogs', in *Into the Blogosphere: Rhetoric, Community, and Cultures of Weblogs,* eds Gurak, L. Antonijevic, S. Johnson, L. Ratliff, C. & Reyman, J., http://blog.lib.umn.edu/blogosphere [26 October 2004].

Paechter, C. 2002, 'Masculinities and femininities as community of practice', *Women's Studies International Forum,* vol. 26, no, 1, pp. 69-77.

Pierce, T. 2002, 'Motherearth, connection, and gender: A metaphoric analysis of two environmental web sites', paper presented to the 25th National Women's Studies Association Conference, Las Vegas, NV, 9-12 June.

Plant, S. 1996, 'On the matrix: Cyberfeminist simulations', in *Cultures of the Internet: Virtual Spaces, Real Histories, Living Bodies,* ed. R. Shields, Sage, London.

Rheingold, H. 2003, *Smart Mobs. The Next Social Revolution,* Perseus, Cambridge, MA.

Rickert, A. & Sacharow, A. 2000, 'It's a women's world wide web. Women's online behavioural patterns across age groups and lifestages', *Media Metrix & Jupiter Communications.*

http://www.women.nsw.gov.au/ pdf/IT/it_framework/attach1.pdf [2 April 2004].

Riverbend, 2001, *Baghdad Burning*, http://riverbendblog.blogspot.com [4 October 2003].

Roberts-Breslin, J. 2003, *Making Media. Foundations of Sound and Image Production*, Focal Press, Boston.

Schaap, F. 2004, 'Links, lives, and logs: Presentation in the Dutch blogosphere', in *Into the Blogosphere: Rhetoric, Community, and Cultures of Weblogs*, eds Gurak, L., Antonijevic, S., Johnson, L., Ratliff, C., & Reyman, J., http://blog.lib.umn.edu/blogosphere [26 October 2004].

Schneider, S. M & Foot, K. A. 2004, 'The web as an object of study', *New Media and Society*, vol. 6, no. 1, pp. 114-122.

Seager, J. 1997, *The State of Women in the World Atlas*, Penguin, London.

Shadi, Z. 2002, *The Upper Echelon of Happiness*, http://theupperechelonofhappiness.blogspot.com [5 January 2003].

U.N. Commission on the Status of Women, 2003, *Women 2000: Gender Equality, Development and Peace for the Twenty-first Century: Implementation of Strategic Objectives and Action in the Critical Areas of Concern and Further Actions and Initiatives*, follow-up to the fourth world conference on women, http://www.un.org/ womenwatch/daw/csw/csw47/documents.html [19 April 2004].

Wenger, E. 1998, 'Communities of Practice. Learning as a social system', http://wwwco-i-1.com [19 February 2002].

Wilding, F. 1998, 'Where is the feminism in cyberfeminism?', *nparadoxa*, vol. 3, Summer, (n. p.), http://www.obn.org/cfundef/ faith_def.html [20 April 2004].

Young, I. 1997, *Intersecting Voices: Dilemmas of Gender, Political Philosophy, and Policy*, Princeton University Press, Princeton, NJ.

Notes

1 Cybergrrl is a trademarked name created by Aliza Sherman (1998). It is from her book, Cybergrrl®: A Woman's Guide to the World Wide Web. New York: Random House.

2 There are new programs that can simultaneously translate from Arabic into English, but these are expensive and often unreliable. The weblog authors discussed in this paper do not use them.

3 There are many critics that point to this. I recommend the work of bell hooks, Jeanne Kilbourne, Jackson Katz, and many others.

14 'I know that's not the topic we're on, but it is all linked isn't it?': Gender and Interaction in Email List Cooperation

Margit Pohl

Technische Universität, Wien

Greg Michaelson

Heriot-Watt University, Edinburgh, UK

Abstract

The birth of the Internet in 1989 was accompanied by warnings that women could easily be excluded from new mass communication technologies. Such fears now seem to be groundless: women are enthusiastic and proficient users and developers of Internet-based interaction systems. Nonetheless, concerns remain that patterns of computer mediated communication (CMC) might reflect gender stereotypes in embodied interaction that favour men, and hence CMC use might reinforce and perpetuate wider gender discrimination.

Our 1995 and 1998 studies of email use for paired problem solving suggested that gender biases in face to face interaction dissolve and that gender stereotyped behaviours no longer align cleanly with physical gender, echoing other investigators' findings. We hypothesized that this was because of the relatively private setting of one-to-one email. Here we discuss a new study of email list based interaction where participants cooperate to solve individual tasks in a shared setting. Our preliminary results again suggest that, even in this more public setting, overall gender stereotyped behaviours are absent and individual behaviours lie on a range of gender stereotypes regardless of actual gender.

1. Introduction

In her book The Psychology of the Internet, Patricia Wallace (1999, p.208) mentions that on the Internet people are often interested in whether the person they are talking to is male or female. She also points out that, in contrast to other personal features like skin colour or age, gender is very often visible on the Internet because it can be inferred from people's first names. It is well known that people play with gender on the Internet

179

but in many everyday situations they use their real name. Gender is presumably one of the few individual characteristics people can use for impression formation when they communicate on the Internet. It is, therefore, especially important to investigate how gender influences Internet communication.

Gender differences in face to face communication strategies have been thoroughly investigated. Tannen (1991) distinguishes the male favoured public "report" talk, to do with negotiating and maintaining status, from the female favoured private "rapport" talk, for establishing and maintaining relationships. Email's fundamental differences from face to face communication might be expected to modify some of these factors. Email messages are neither "spoken" nor "written" in the traditional sense (Herring 1996). Therefore, it can be seen as an entirely new form of communication. It reduces the awareness of personal and social standards and the awareness of the social context of communication (Matheson 1992). Internet interaction forms are, to some extent, male dominated. This probably reflects the social marking of all technology as male and the strong influence of male forms of behaviour on computer culture. Nonetheless, the Internet is a fluid medium which is, in principle, open to different forms of use by different social groups. It has often been argued that CMC is the modern form of the telephone. Spender (1995) states that the telephone is one of the most commonly reported "non-work" activities of women. CMC might provide women with the opportunity to chat even more easily over the Internet.

In the last two decades considerable research has been conducted to clarify this issue. In her investigation, Susan Herring (1996) found that in male-dominated lists posters tended to express opinions rather than share facts. This is contrary to the stereotypical expectation which posits that men communicate facts whereas women talk about their emotions, and that women act in a supportive manner whereas men tend to act more aggressively. Herring assumes that there are gender specific styles of email communication, with an aligned style predominantly used by women and an opposed style used predominantly by men. Herring, however, does not see these styles or variants as a strict dichotomy. Some women in her sample incorporated features of the opposed variant when participating in a discussion on a male-dominated list, whereas men behaved in a more 'aligned' manner on female-dominated mailing lists. Witmer & Katzmann (1997) found that women used more smileys than men and that, contrary to expectation, they wrote more inflammatory emails than men. Savicki, Lingenfelter & Kelley (1996) also investigated whether the composition of online discussion groups influenced styles of communication. Their results suggest that in male-dominated groups, subjects used more fact oriented language and more calls for action. In groups with lower proportions of men. subjects tended to self-disclosure and made more attempts at tension prevention and reduction.

Such results indicate that there are patterns in virtual communication which are influenced by gender. There has been considerable research in this area: for more extensive discussions of these issues see e.g. Rodino (1997), Wallace (1999) or Michaelson & Pohl (2001).

It must be noted, however, that the interpretation of these results is by no means straightforward. Savicki, Lingenfelter and Kelley (1996) point out that the findings of CMC investigations are highly context dependent. People behave differently in asynchronous and synchronous groups, the nature of the communication (task-oriented vs. informal) plays an important role. and the size and composition of the group will have an influence on results. Herring's (1996) assumptions that there are two different variants or styles of interaction, which are used very flexibly depending on group composition, implies that there is no strict gender dichotomy as regards virtual communication. 'Male' or 'female' behaviour is often adopted by the opposite sex depending on the specific circumstance, as Herring's (1996) study shows. Savicki, Lingenfelter and Kelley (1996) also point out that only part of their assumptions could be substantiated by their experiment. Several apparently obvious hypotheses (as, for example that in male-dominated groups more coarse language is used or in female-dominated groups more apologies and questions will appear) were not substantiated by results. Wallace (1999, p.209) expresses a similar opinion:

Research on behavioural differences between demographic groups is often controversial because results are so easily misreported, misinterpreted and potentially misused. They are also quite slippery, and differences that appear in one study can easily vanish in the next.

These difficulties have motivated some researchers to criticize studies of gender and virtual communication (see e.g. Rodino 1997). Rodino points out that "looking for binary gender differences in language helps recreate them." (Rodino 1997, p.2). Research on gender differences in communication often supports common stereotypes about female and male behaviour – the one being emotional and supportive and the other being aggressive and task-oriented. In contrast to this, Rodino tries to formulate an approach which transcends these dichotomies. Gender differences are not absolutely complementary and given but created in the process of communication. To describe such processes it is necessary to use a different approach of investigation. Rodino suggests a qualitative approach which she uses in an analysis of a continuous stream of conversation on an Internet Relay Chat (IRC).

While Rodino's approach is very promising, it might be argued that even if we assume that gender differences are not given but created in the process of communication, fairly stable patterns may still emerge. Discrimination against women pervades our whole society. This leaves women a rather constrained space in which to negotiate their position, even in the fairly fluid medium of CMC. On the other hand, the contradictory results described above can clearly be explained by the process of creation of gender described by Rodino. In our view, both approaches have their merits. The more traditional quantitative research looking for fairly stable patterns and the qualitative approach suggested by Rodino can contribute to clarifying the question of gender differences in CMC. We have adopted this integration of quantitative and qualitative analyses in our own research.

2. Email-mediated one to one cooperation

Based on the literature about gender differences in communication (for a discussion of this literature see e.g. Michaelson & Pohl 2001) we formulated several hypotheses about gender differences in CMC:

a) Men talk more than women (they send more and longer messages)
b) Women are more cooperative than men.
c) Men are more task-oriented than women.
d) Women tend to talk more about their personal experiences.
e) Women and their messages/topics are ignored more often then men and their topics.
f) Gendered behaviour is more pronounced in public than in private.

These hypotheses must be seen in the specific context of our experiments which take place in an academic setting. Subjects are students at our respective universities. The students always have to solve specific tasks. They also know that their conversation will be read by the university lecturers who conduct the experiment. As a consequence, certain kinds of behaviour do not occur, as for example flaming or the use of coarse language or other aggressive forms of behaviour. Therefore, we did not formulate any hypotheses concerning such topics although they are often investigated in other settings.

Our original experiments in computer mediated cooperation, in 1995 (Pohl & Michaelson 1997) and 1998 (Pohl & Michaelson 2000), focused on pairs of subjects using email in real time to solve problems, where each had domain expertise for the other's task. Full details may be found in (Michaelson & Pohl, 2001).

In analysing the email experiments, we introduced the notion of a measure of cooperation. Each subject's messages were analysed to identify the number of words involved in:

- *meta* discussion that expedites the interaction;
- *personal* questions or statements about the subject or their pair;
- *task* questions or statements about the subject (*own* task) or their pair's (*other* task) topic.

The cooperation measure for each subject is then the ratio of the number of words they utter about their own task to the number of words they utter about all tasks, including their own. A ratio of less than 0.5 indicates *altruism*, a ratio of 0.5 indicates *even handedness* and a ratio greater than 0.5 indicates *selfishness*.

We also used these measures to investigate the hypotheses that women react to men's utterances to a far greater extent than men react to women's, and that women and their topics are often ignored in communication processes.

To summarise, our analyses:

- did not identify any gross patterns of individual behaviour in email corresponding to prevalent gender stereotypes in face-to-face or telephone interaction;
- confirm Herring's suggestion (Herring 1996) that individuals display a range of gendered interaction styles;
- did not find any significant overall gendered differences in effort expended by subjects on their own and their partner's problem, with, on average, all subjects showing a similar degree of slight "altruism";
- found a slight tendency in mixed pairs for women to be more "altruistic" than men, but for Viennese women to be more "altruistic" than Edinburgh women regardless of their partner's gender.

We proposed a number of complementary explanations for the absence of gender effects:

- there is no bodily presence in email to reinforce gender stereotyped behaviours;
- asynchronicity of email interaction undermines successful male strategies for monopolizing face to face interaction;
- one to one email is private so the social/peer reinforcements of gender stereotypes in public interaction are minimized;
- the sample consisted of computer science students; it seems plausible to assume that female computer science students differ from other young women in that they are more self-confident and assertive. The work of Margolies and Fisher (2003) indicates that self-confidence plays an important role for those women who persist in studying computer science. They adapt to the prevailing culture in computer science departments which enables them to communicate with their male colleagues on an equal footing. Female students who are less self-confident and reluctant to adapt to this culture usually stop studying computer science very early.

In our studies, from the start we discounted cultural differences as problematic. While Austria and Scotland have different languages, histories and traditions, both are advanced capitalist countries immersed in the dominant global neo-liberal culture. In particular, University students in both societies are drawn from similar social milieu and enjoy comparable educations and lifestyles. Indeed, the email studies showed no significant differences between Austrian and Scottish participants.

It should be noted that references to "Austria/Vienna" and "Scotland/Edinburgh" are indicative of place of study rather than of citizenship. Both sets of participants included people born in the respective societies, first generation immigrants and those visiting to study.

3. Email List Cooperation

We are particularly interested in exploring our third explanation, that is the degree to which social/peer effects are important determinants of gender stereotyped behaviour in CMC. In order to investigate this further, we decided to generalise the one-to-one email scenario to group use of a shared email list. We hypothesised that there should be greater conformance to gender stereotyped behaviours in this setting as it is more public than one-to-one email.

As before, the experiments are conducted with subjects drawn from students on undergraduate or postgraduate computer science courses. The experiments are run independently of the courses students are taking, and participation is voluntary without payment in either cash or credits.

Each experimental session is based on up to four Vienna students and four Edinburgh subjects accessing a common email list in real-time. Sessions are conducted in English: in the 1995 and 1998 experiments we established that both native and non-native English speakers did not think that this compromised interaction.

Each subject in each location is asked to write a short essay on the attitudes of the people in the other location concerning a topical computing issue. We thought it important that, as before, each participant should have an individual task but that there should still be an element of paired cooperation through task commonality. Thus, while the subjects are not initially told so, ideally each topic is shared by a subject in each location.

The topics to be discussed were:

- Computer games
- Home computing
- Software copyright
- Artificial intelligence

Before each session, subjects give explicit permission for their email to be analysed in confidence. A session runs for around 90 minutes in small computer laboratories in both locations. After each session, subjects fill in a short questionnaire about their backgrounds.

Here we present preliminary results from a single session held in September 2004, involving three female subjects in Edinburgh, and two female and two male subjects in Vienna. Two earlier sessions are still being analysed.

4. Quantitative Analysis

A number of methodological problems arise in the new study in trying to categorise task utterances because of both the experimental design and the task topics.

First of all, subjects very quickly entered into general discussion about topics without discriminating between Vienna and Edinburgh attitudes. Where a subject expresses an opinion about a topic they share with another subject, it is difficult to tell if that opinion is prompting further discussion by the other subjects (i.e. is an own task utterance) or is providing information for the other subject with the same topic (i.e. is an other task utterance). Here, we have used the content and context of messages, including subsequent as well as previous messages, to identify interaction threads and to determine if utterances are responses (other) or prompts (own).

Secondly, the topics are very close and in general discussion there is considerable topic drift. Thus discussion of:

- software copyright included whether software was for home or work use;
- home computing included game playing, and vice versa;
- artificial intelligence included computer games.

Once again, we used the thread of messages to determine context and to impute an intention. Note that in writing their final essay a subject may use relevant material from a context different to their own topic in determining attitudes to that topic.

Bearing these caveats in mind, and noting that with only seven subjects it is impossible to draw significant conclusions, we now present a summary of quantitative measures.

	Ed women	Vi women	Vi men
subjects	3	2	2
messages	112	43	67
average mess no	37.3	21.5	33.5
wordno	2916	1264	1317
av. mess. words	26.0	29.4	19.7
own/(own+other)	0.39	0.37	0.42

Table 1: indicators for Edinburgh & Vienna women & men

Table 1 shows that on average:

- Edinburgh women and Vienna men sent more messages than Vienna women;
- Edinburgh and Vienna women sent longer messages than Vienna men;
- there are no differences in altruism between Edinburgh women, Vienna women and Vienna men.

	Edinburgh	Vienna	women	men
subjects	3	4	5	2
messages	112	110	155	67
average mess no	37.3	27.5	31.0	33.5
wordno	2916	2581	4180	1317
av. mess. words	26.0	23.5	27.0	19.7
own/(own+other)	0.39	0.39	0.39	0.42

Table 2: indicators for all Edinburgh, Vienna, women & men

Table 2 shows that on average:

- Edinburgh subjects sent more, longer messages than Vienna subjects;
- women sent slightly less but longer messages than men.
- There are no differences in altruism between Edinburgh, Vienna, women and men subjects.

Overall, all subjects are slightly altruistic in cooperation. This finding, while not significant, is very similar to that found in the email studies.

In this study, it is also useful to look at how much attention each subject's topic received, measured in terms of how many words other people expended.

	Ed women	Vi women	Vi men
subjects	3	2	2
other refs to own	1567	592	839
av others refs to own	522.3	296.0	419.5

Table 3: others contributions to Edinburgh & Vienna women's & men's tasks

Table 3 shows that on average there were:

- most contributions by others to Edinburgh women's tasks;
- more contributions to Viennese men's tasks than to Viennese women's tasks

	Edinburgh	Vienna	women	men	total
subjects	3	4	5	2	7
other refs to own	1567	1431	2159	839	2998
av others refs to own	522.3	357.8	431.8	419.5	428.3

Table 4: others contributions to all Edinburgh, Vienna, women's & men's tasks

Table 4 shows that on average there were:

- more contributions by others to Edinburgh than Viennese tasks;
- around the same number of contributions to female and male tasks.

We also analysed whether women got less attention than men from the other participants of the experiment. By this we do not only mean 'attention' in terms of strict question/answer sequences but also any comments a message gets. We assume that an indicator for this might be the reactions individual messages elicit. We categorised every message which is a reply to another message as a comment. This variable indicates that there are gender differences if there are significantly more comments made about men's messages than about women's messages. Table 5 shows that this is not the case.

women to women	men to women	women to men	men to men
95	53	60	5

Table 5: who reacts to whom (by gender)

Men make up approximately 29% of the sample and get about 27% of the answers of the other participants of the experiment.

A difficulty in the analysis is the fact that some of the topics which were to be discussed during the experiment appear to be more interesting than others. We decided to use four topics to be better able to distinguish between effort spent on one's own topic and effort spent on others' topics.

computer games	home computing	artificial intelligence	software copyright
91	41	51	34

Table 6: Preference for topics

Table 6 shows interest in topics measured in terms of the number of messages concerning them. Computer games was the favourite topic of all participants and nobody found home computing interesting. Note that the participants who had to treat home computing spent a lot of effort to maintain discussion about their topic. These participants were two fairly persistent women. The software copyright topic was only treated in 34 messages because only one participant was responsible for it.

We also analysed those email messages which elicited no response at all. It is difficult to be precise about this variable because in the end of the experiment some messages are not answered because of timeout. Approximately 25% of the messages which got no answer were sent immediately before timeout. Women sent 32 messages which got no answer and men 12. Given that men make up about 29% of the sample this distribution seems to be quite even. In addition, a few messages did not motivate any answer because they are only short acknowledgements of other people's statements (e.g. 'I like both'). If we consider the fairly confused nature of the conversation in this experiment we found it surprising that so many messages were answered. This also contradicts other studies in that area, e.g. Herring (1999) who describes a synchronous chat group where more than one third of all participants got no answers. This result also seems to indicate that the character of virtual communication depends largely on context. It seems plausible that in an academic setting where cooperation is part of the task people read and answer messages to a larger extent than in other situations.

There are some divergences as far as the total number of messages is concerned in the above tables. This is due to the nature of categorisation. Not all the messages are about a given topic and some messages are not answers to another person's message.

It is important to emphasise that these results, while characterising this cohort's behaviour, are based on far too small a sample to generalise. Individual behaviours are discussed in the next section.

5. Qualitative Analysis

The experiment we describe in this paper is part of ongoing research into gender differences in email communication. As noted above, our first experiments took place in 1995 and 1998. There is a noticeable difference between the interactions in these years and the interaction which took place in the year 2004. In 1995 we had serious problems with time lags in real-time email due both to relatively slow international email links and to instabilities with local networks and servers. Time lags, though reduced, were still present in 1998. In 2004 message exchange was substantially much faster which had a fundamental influence on the character of the exchange.

In 2004, participants sent many more messages which were much shorter than in 1995 and 1998. Most of the messages are no longer than one or two lines of text. We explicitly decided to use email software to make the results of the 2004 experiment comparable to the previous studies. Nevertheless, the conversation in 2004 took on the character of a chat group. This might also be due to the fact that messages in the 2004 experiment were directed to a group instead of a single person. In contrast to the previous experiments, this list interaction cannot be termed asynchronous anymore. One of the most salient characteristics of synchronous virtual communication is that the sequential nature and the turn-taking mechanisms of face–to-face communication are seriously undermined (Crystal 2001, p.152). In informal conversations, subjects told us that they felt confused by the number of messages and very soon only read those messages, which they found interesting. Nevertheless, the analysis of the interaction indicates that the subjects coped well with this situation. Although the discussion is sometimes very informal (despite the technical topics) some distinctive threads of discussion within a defined topic can be identified.

Another difference to the previous experiments is that there are almost no off-topic remarks. In the pair-experiments in 1995 and 1998 people felt free to exchange personal information and talked about individual interests which were not related to the task. There were very few personal messages in the 2004 experiment. At the beginning, two women introduced themselves and, in this way, offered personal information but there was almost no further discussion of personal topics. This is probably due to the public character of the situation, as opposed to the more private character of the pair-experiments in 1995 and 1998.

In the 2004 experiment, large individual differences can be observed. There is, for example, a noticeable difference between the two male participants. One of them wrote the maximum of messages (53) and the other the minimum (14). There are other counterintuitive observations. In a lengthy discussion, an Edinburgh female and a Vienna male participant exchange ideas about computer games. They especially talk about violence in computer games. It is commonly assumed that girls and women do not like violence in computer games (Cassell & Jenkins 1999). In contrast to that, Irma (all names are changed), the Edinburgh woman, is interested in violence in computer games and sends several messages about whether computer games can teach you to become a terrorist. Hugo, a Viennese male, asks Irma to stop talking about terrorists (spelling as in the original).

Irma: do you think that a if a game can teach you something, can also give ideas about something, like killing or becoming a terrorist?

Hugo: there are less terrorists beyond us as you think;-) please forget for some minutes the terrorists;-)

This interaction contradicts gender stereotypes in that it is the woman who insists on talking about violence in computer games and the man who tries to stop this topic.

Another noticeable feature is the insistence of the two women (one from Edinburgh and one from Vienna) who had to get input about home computing. As mentioned before, home computing was not an attractive topic but the two women were very persistent, so that in the end there was a considerable amount of discussion. During the last 20 minutes of the experiment they even found an interesting subtopic which initiated a lively but short discussion – addiction to computers and the Internet. Again, this contradicts gender stereotypes. The assumption is usually that topics introduced by women are ignored and that the women themselves are too polite to insist on their topics.

6. Conclusion

In the study described in this paper we investigated whether there are gender differences in cooperative problem solving via an email list. The samples we used for our experiments consist of computer science students. It is an open question whether the results obtained in this study are also valid for other contexts.

Initial results do not show any systematic differences between women and men, corresponding to results found in previous one-to-one email studies. Contrary to our hypothesis, the more public situation of group discussion did not result in any pronounced gender differences. Indeed, as in our previous studies, we found instances of female behaviour which correspond to stereotypical male forms of communication.

We assume that context plays an important for the explanation of these results. It might be argued that the composition of the group which was dominated by women had some influence on our findings. It should be noted, however, that in our previous experiments in a similar setting no gender differences were found either.

Research shows that gender differences depend very much on context. Considerable research has been conducted by passing observation of mailing lists or chat groups with large and anonymous groups of users, and no defined goal. Our experiments differ markedly from such a setting in involving the active construction of constrained scenarios. Thus it seems reasonable to assume that our results will differ from the results of passive research and that it will be difficult to generalise our results to other settings. Nonetheless, our research offers some support for the assumption that the use of mailing lists or chat groups in cooperative but unstructured e-learning does not necessarily lead to discrimination against women in terms of their participation and contribution.

We wish to emphasize that our results are only tentative because of the small size of our sample. However, our experiment is part of ongoing research and can, therefore, be interpreted in the context of other investigations. We intend to repeat this experiment with more groups of students to gain more reliability for our research.

7. Acknowledgements

We would like to thank our students for taking part in our studies. We are now in our tenth year of collaboration but have not met face to face since 1996; a tribute to the efficacy of electronic communication both by Internet and telephone.

References

Cassell, J. & Jenkins, H. (eds.) 1999, *From Barbie to Mortal Kombat. Gender and Computer Games*, The MIT Press, Cambridge, Mass., London, England

Crystal, D. 2001, *Language and the Internet*, Cambridge University Press, Cambridge

Herring, S. 1996,'Two variants of an electronic message schema', in S. Herring (ed.), *Computer-Mediated Communication. Linguistic, Social and Cross-Cultural Perspectives*, John Benjamin Publishing Company, Amsterdam/Philadelphia, pp. 81-106.

Herring, S. 1999, Interactional Coherence in CMC, in *Journal of Computer-Mediated Communication* (Online), Vol.4, No.4, http://www.ascusc.org/jcmc/vol4/issue4/herring.html

Margolies, J, Fisher, A. 2003, *Unlocking the Clubhouse. Women in Computing*, The MIT Press, Cambridge, Mass, London, England

Matheson, K. 1992, Women and Computer Technology. Communicating for herself, in M.Lea (ed.), *Contexts of Computer-Mediated Communication*, Harvester and Wheatsheaf, New York, London, Toronto, pp.66-88

Michaelson, G. & Pohl, M. 2001, Gender in email-based co-operative problem solving, Chapter 2 in E. Green & A. Adam (Eds), *Virtual Gender: technology, consumption and identity*, Routledge, June 2001, ISBN 0-415-23315-1, pp 28-44.

Pohl, M. and Michaelson, G. 1997, 'I don't think that's an interesting dialogue' - Computer-Mediated Communication and Gender, in A.F.Grundy, D.Koehler, V.Oechtering and U.Petersen (eds), in *Women, Work and Computerization. Spinning a Web from Past to Future*, Proceedings of the 6th International IFIP-Conference Bonn, Germany, May 24-27,1997, Springer, pp 87-97.

Pohl, M. and Michaelson, G. 2000, '(Just ignore the other message)': Alignment, quoting and iconic strategies in computer-mediated communication, Proceedings of 7th IFIP *Women, Work and Computerization Conference*, Simon Fraser University, Canada, June 2000.

Rodino, M. 1997, Breaking out of Binaries: Reconceptualizing Gender and its Relationship to Language in Computer-Mediated Communication, in *Journal of Computer-Mediated Communication* (Online), Vol.3, No.3, http://www.ascusc.org/jcmc/vol3/issue3/rodino.html

Savicki, V., Lingenfelter, D. & Kelley, M. 1996, Gender Language Style and Group Composition in Internet Discussion Groups, in *Journal of Computer-Mediated Communication* (Online), Vol.2, No.3, http://www.ascusc.org/jcmc/vol2/issue3/savicki.html

Spender, D. 1995, *Nattering on the Net. Women, Power and Cyberspace*, Spinifex , North Melbourne:

Tannen, D. 1991, *You just don't understand*. Virago

Wallace, P. 1999, The Psychology of the Internet, Cambridge University Press, Cambridge

Witmer, D.F. & Katzmann S.L. 1997, On-Line Smiles: Does Gender Make a Difference in the Use of Graphic Accents? in *Journal of Computer-Mediated Communication* (Online), Vol.2, No.4, http://www.ascusc.org/jcmc/vol2/issue4/witmer1.html

15 Internet Research from a Gender Perspective

Searching for differentiated use patterns

Gabriele Winker

Hamburg University of Technology, Germany

Abstract

The current scientific and political discussion on the under-representation of women within the Internet once again associates women with disinterest in technology in an essentialist manner. Gender-specific attributions are unquestioningly transferred to the new media, and it is assumed that women behave in unfailing conformity with existing gender stereotypes. The intention of this paper is to show that gender research has to use differentiated empirical studies. Gender studies can therefore make a concrete contribution to the task of shaping the Internet in the future.

I shall begin by briefly outlining the dilemma of gender studies in the technical area. In the second section I shall describe the reasons for the gender-differentiated Internet access data, using quantitative Internet studies from the USA, calling for a de-dramatisation of difference in this context. In the third section, I will overcome the dichotomous view of the digital divide and present a research framework for differentiated study of differing use habits and use requirements. This section illustrates that such an approach does not make the gender category superfluous, but challenges gender studies to present context-related studies, in which individual behaviour may be interpreted in the context of gender symbols and structures. My fourth step will be to explain how the new possibilities of online research can and should be used to gain further understanding in the sense of differentiated study designs. Finally, I will finish with a short outlook.

1. The Dilemma of Gender Studies in the Technical Area

Since the beginning of widespread public access to the Internet, numerous studies have indicated the under-representation of women within this new media. In Germany, women active in the fields of women's studies and politics have repeatedly called attention to this unsatisfactory situation, and Internet studies have uniformly identified this gender gap, prompting numerous activities on the policy side. Although regional women's Internet courses serve an important purpose, they also play a role in reproducing an image of women as deficit individuals in need of support. These activities are repeatedly justified using well-known gender-specific models of interpretation. Women's problematic relationship with computers is cited as an argument, as computer culture is considered masculine. Supporters of such projects often point out that women rarely select careers or degrees in information technology or technology in general, as there is a lack of female role models. They refer to women's lack of technical competence, claiming that this makes it more difficult for women to use the Internet. These arguments associate women with disinterest in technology in an essentialist manner.

This form of reification of gender stereotypes once again illustrates the dilemma that affects gender researchers when we work on technology-related issues. If we analyse the differences – in this case in Internet access and Internet use – between women and men within the context of technology stereotypes effective within society, we may well prompt positive political activity to support the underrepresented women. At the same time, however, our analysis reproduces the gender inequalities in this field and contributes to their continuing existence. If we ignore the differences and take up the position that gender only plays an insignificant role as a social category, in view of the dissolution of traditional societal structures and wide scope for action, we very obviously fail to acknowledge the empirical facts, for example in the area of the Internet.

2. De-Dramatising Gender-Specific Internet Access

To this day, the gender gap in Internet access has not been closed. In Germany, 47.3% of all women aged 14 years and above had access to the Internet in 2004, compared to 64.2% of all men (Eimeren, Gerhard & Frees 2004). In the other European countries, men are also more likely to have access to the new media than women, although the differences vary. The same also still applies to the USA, where women's online rate is 61%, slightly below the men's rate of 65% (Pew Internet 2003). It is striking that none of the German studies investigates possible reasons for this persistent access gap. Explanations seem to be of no interest, or the access difference seems to be sufficiently explained using the argument of women's disinterest in technology.

In contrast, US scholars demonstrate an empirical pragmatic approach. For example, Norris (2001) studies European Internet access data and poses the question of which socio-economic or individual factors may be significant for Internet access. According to Norris, gender is a significantly less important explanation for the probability of Internet access than age, education and income. This is also true of Germany, although the gender-specific discrepancies are still significant in contrast with Belgium, Denmark, France, Portugal, Great Britain and Finland. Bimber (2000) goes one step further with his study, which focuses, however, on the situation in the USA in 1999. Using regression analyses, his findings can be used to explain the differing online figures for men and women on the basis of socio-economic factors, such as education and income, and individual factors such as age. Gender plays a minor and insignificant role in this context. Ono & Zavodny (2003) reach a similar conclusion on the US situation in 2001, however they still establish gender-specific differences in access under a controlled gender variable for the years up to 1998.

Of course, these findings cannot be transferred one-to-one to the German situation. Gender researchers must assume that there are still gender-specific differences in specific age groups in Germany, in particular, that cannot be explained by differences in education and income alone. However, the effects of gender-specific division of labour and the resulting unequal distribution of education and income are also the primary explanatory factor for the distinctive access gap in Germany.

It would be an important task for the state financed institutes to make statistics available that do not stop at differentiating between men and women, but work with controlled inclusion of both gender and socio-economic and demographic factors, corresponding to good scientific practice. One first step in this direction is the gender mainstreaming evaluation of the (N)Onliner Atlas, published for the second time in 2003 (FTI 2004). This is a more intensive gender-based evaluation of the German Emnid research institute's findings on Internet access, on the initiative of the nationwide association 'Women Give New Impetus to Technology'. According to this study, the gender gap is no longer significant for 14 to 19-year-olds in Germany. 82.3% of all young men and 79.7% of all young women in this age group have Internet access. However, the statistics calculated in the study do not indicate to what extent the gender gap can become relative in other age groups, when taking income and educational differences into account.

The above findings do not mean that there is no longer a need for separate support for women's access to the Internet. In contrast, these programmes need to be extended to apply to women with low levels of formal education and low income. However, the focus of justification for such training programmes should change in future. It is not women's lack of technical understanding or the male stereotyping of computers which primarily prevent Internet access, but the continuing gender-hierarchical division of labour. Such an argument also illustrates, from a social policy point of view, that non-access to the Internet cannot be corrected primarily by women changing their attitudes to technology on an individual level, but that only a more gender-balanced educational and labour system and information programmes for varying life situations can be effective.

Socio-economic justification contexts also highlight the need for political action which goes beyond the politically declared objective of Internet access for all. It is important to investigate the inequalities within the net and to provide all citizens with Internet services corresponding to their varied and differing life situations and interests. However, a comprehensive analysis of the use and non-use behaviour, requirements and wishes of different groups of people is necessary to be able to make well-founded suggestions for these services.

3. Gender-Specific Inequalities in Internet Use

Studies carried out in various contexts reach the unanimous conclusion that men use the Internet more frequently and for longer periods than women. Women tend to be moderate users. In Germany, for example, male users spend an average 149 minutes on the net per day; female users reach an average of only 102 minutes, whereby the difference is particularly marked during the weekend (Eimeren, Gerhard & Frees 2004: 361). Gender-specific user frequency is also documented in the whole of Europe. For example, 49% of all male web-users in Europe use the Internet (almost) every day, but only 38% of all female users. The distribution in the groups 'several times per week' and 'once per week' is fairly balanced. 12% of all male users and 21% of all female users belong to the group of persons using the net rarely, i.e. once per month or less (EOS Gallup Europe 2002, p. 36). Bimber (2000) registers a similar distribution in the USA in the year 1996. Even in 1999, (almost) daily use was still significantly more common among male users. However, in the USA women have since overtaken men for moderate use and the group of rare users shows an equal gender balance.

There are currently few convincing explanations for this clear gender-specific use frequency and length, which does not appear to be resolved by the popularity of the Internet and almost balanced access rates for men and women, as can be observed in the USA or Scandinavia. The aforementioned study by Bimber (2000), which at least makes statements on the factors influencing these differences in the US situation, is only of limited use in this context. According to this study, along with education and, for men, full-time employment, gender is a decisive factor for frequency of use. This confirms gender-specific use, but the question remains as to why female web-users use the Internet less frequently and for significantly shorter periods than men.

Qualitative studies from a gender perspective attempt to find answers to these questions by passing them on directly to the users themselves. However, this approach tends to confirm existing stereotypes in society rather than finding differentiated answers for individual behavioural motives. For example, Heimrath & Goulding (2001) asked students and users of public libraries in Great Britain about the suspected reasons for differing use frequency, and received the corresponding stereotyping responses. Interviewees stated that men were primarily interested in technology for its own sake and women used computers for problem-solving. Due to more negative experience with computers in education and leisure, women were thought not to have a positive image of the new medium. Respondents also stated that very few women had begun to use the Internet on their own initiative, but the majority had been introduced by a man. In her survey of female Internet users in Australia, Singh (2001) revealed similar images. Respondents were asked about gender-specific differences in Internet use, and the study also reproduced the stereotype of women using the Internet as a tool for a broad spectrum of activities, with men tending to use it as a toy or trying to find out how individual hardware or software works in detail. It remains, however, unclear whether these results simply reflect gender stereotypes or are based on actual behaviour.

Thus, research has yet to fulfil the task of not only studying but also understanding existing images and stereotypes in society and concrete behaviour patterns. Researchers should bear in mind Bimber's (2000) point that access and use frequency are not influenced by the same factors and must therefore be studied separately. However, there could be an indirect connection, in that men have had Internet access for a longer time on average. People with longer experience of the Internet, referred to as early adopters, use the net more intensively, as Howard, Rainie & Jones (2003) elaborate, which could explain the gender gap to a certain extent.

These individual approaches at explanation are, however, insufficient for understanding the use patterns of individual groups of the population. For this reason, it is essential for the future to establish which factors influence individual use habits – as well as studying the digital access divide. Hargittai (2002) suggests that researchers distinguish access differences – the 'digital divide' – from use differences, which she refers to as the 'second-level digital divide'. However, this term maintains a dichotomous view of the digital divide. I am in favour of a more terminologically differentiating view of Internet use, and refer to 'dimensions of use' which research must investigate.

The first step is to create a research framework that does not reproduce dichotomous stereotypes of masculinity and femininity, but establishes the (differing) importance of the gender category in the respective context by studying individual groups. Studies should not only include quantitative data such as use frequency and length for differentiating use habits, but also qualitative data, such as reasons for the use or non-use of certain services, or the connection between use and everyday needs. I have drafted a research framework (see Fig. 1) based on a model suggested by DiMaggio & Hargittai (2001). These two authors differentiate between various levels in studying types of Internet use, on which social and thus also gender-specific inequalities may be manifested. There are inequalities in technical equipment, in autonomy of use, in skills, in social support and in purpose of use. All five of these factors can influence use habits.

The model of use dimensions I have developed is based on three dimensions that are important for Internet use. However, these three dimensions – autonomy of use, media competence and variety of use – are themselves influenced by further-reaching factors. Thus, the extent of autonomy of use not only depends on the technical prerequisites, but also on individuals' possibilities for deciding when and where to use the Internet. The second dimension is media competence, which is influenced by the users' individual skills and ability to find social support as required. Variety of use is the third dimension. This depends both on the interests of male and female web-users and on the available services that may be of interest to each user.

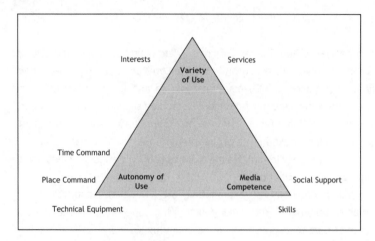

Fig. 1: Dimensions of Internet Use

3.1 Inequalities in autonomy of use

In my model, autonomy of use depends on technical equipment, place of access and time available. The European statistics do not indicate any great differences in technical equipment between men and women. However, men are significantly more likely to possess a fast DSL connection (15%) than women (10%) (EOS Gallup Europe 2002, p. 10). The same source shows differences in place of access. Although 74% of all male users in Europe have Internet access at home, this applies to only 67% of all female users. Women also have slightly fewer places of access (ibid, p. 32). This means that men's individual command over the place of internet use is greater than that of women.

Alongside technical requirements, which should be available in various places if possible, time available for Internet use is also very important. This factor is called time command in my model. There is no suitable data on individual command over time for Internet use. It is simply clear that people need time and peace and quiet to explore and permanently use the services of the Internet.

In the field of employment, there are indications that the existing horizontal and vertical segregation of the labour market can lead to differing amounts of available time. For example, researchers in the USA have established that, due to gender-hierarchical division of labour, men exhibit more intensive Internet use when in paid employment, because they carry out different jobs, and women use the Internet less, despite access at work (Nielsen & NetRankings 2002).

In this context, the new working hours survey carried out for the second time on behalf of the German Federal Ministry of Family Affairs, Senior Citizens, Women and Youth (BMFSFJ & Statistisches Bundesamt 2003) is interesting with relation to the situation in Germany. Whereas women work an average total of 43 hours per week, made up of paid employment (12 hours) and unpaid family work (31 hours), men work an average total of 42 hours, of which 22.5 are paid and 19.5 unpaid. Men therefore have more time at their disposal for activities of their choice. It is probable that this division of labour, only hinted at by these figures, has effects on autonomy of time and thus on Internet use. However, this assumption requires further empirical investigation.

3.2 Inequalities in Media Competence

The second dimension in the use triangle, which I refer to as media competence, consists of the indicators individual skills and social support. It is repeatedly supposed that men and women have different skills, which lead to different use habits. One supposedly responsible factor is female technical incompetence, as mentioned in my introduction. Although we should take this stereotype seriously as researchers, as it certainly has an influence on use behaviour, we should regard the effects of such stereotyped images on individual behaviour in a differentiated way.

For example, studies carried out by Vogel & Heinz (2000) and Minks (2000) clearly show that there is a group of people interested in and competent with technology, in which men are over-proportionately represented, and also a group of people not interested in and not very competent with technology, which is overwhelmingly female. At the same time, this also means that there is a broad field between these two poles, made up of people of both genders interested in and competent with technology in many different ways, who are neglected by gender-polarising studies although they actually represent the majority.

Furthermore – and in this context more importantly – scholars must clearly distinguish between media competence and technical competence in the case of Internet use. Technical competence is primarily required when the system breaks down, that is when technical defects appear. In such situations, computer or technology freaks are often better able to correct these defects. However, a lack of technical competence can be compensated in these situations by recall to social support networks. The findings of an empirical study on teleworking we carried out show that women organise such social support in the event of technical problems more frequently than men.[1]

No gender-specific differences have been established as yet in media competence. For example, a study carried out by Hargittai (2002) in the USA found that gender has no significant influence on research skills on the WWW. 54 test subjects were set five identical tasks. The tasks were finding local cultural events, online music, information on the positions of various presidential candidates on abortion, tax declaration forms and art produced by children. The test subjects' approach was recorded by means of screenshots of the websites they visited. Skills were measured on the basis of successful task-solving and the time required. The study found clear differences between age groups and length of Internet experience, but no gender differences.

Yates & Littleton (2001) point out that, even in a highly stereotypically charged area such as computer games, skills are equally distributed among boys and girls when the games are placed in a non-gender-specific context. The above authors carried out a study with girls and boys between the ages of 11 and 12, in which the context of a computer-based task was changed without making any changes to the software of the computer game. When the computer game was introduced as a 'game', the boys were significantly better at solving the tasks contained within it. When the computer game was declared an 'exercise' there were no gender differences, that is the skills for solving the task were equally distributed among boys and girls. A second study resulted in similarly surprising findings. Two structurally identical versions of an 'adventure game' were produced, including problems to be solved. One game was called 'King and Crown', the other 'Honeybear'. Both games required the same strategy. The bears in 'Honeybear' were depicted as gender-neutrally as possible, whereas 'King and Crown' contained more male characters. The girls' performance was significantly influenced by the software version; they were distinctly better at the 'Honeybear' version. In contrast, the results of the boys were similar in both versions of the game.

These examples illustrate that there are no indications as yet of unequal skills between men and women in gender-neutral applications such as online research. In areas which are strongly attributed to one gender, initially perceived differences in skills can become entirely relative if the whole extent of usage is taken into account. Studies from a gender perspective should pay particular attention to context. With this in mind, I find the research design and the findings of Yates & Littleton (2001) a pioneering model for the methodology of gender studies on the Internet.

3.3 Inequalities in Variety of Use

The third dimension in the triangle of Internet use is variety of use. This includes both the users' interests and the services available to meet these interests. There have been few analyses of what women and men actually do on the Internet. Market research institutes painstakingly attempt to trace the routes of women and men as consumers. However, firstly, Internet users are not only interested in commercially oriented websites, but also in further education and training services or careers support information, sites on health or bringing up children, and secondly, these market research analyses are not usually publicly accessible. Internet research is therefore still in its infancy as far as the concrete interests of both users and non-users are concerned.

The same applies to the evaluation of Internet services. My own study on e-government portals on federal, regional and local levels in Germany illustrates that Internet services are far from being designed in a gender-sensitive way (cf. Winker 2004). Our quality criteria of gender-sensitivity investigate whether the content and services are, firstly, of interest to people with varying life experiences and, secondly, whether they are easy to find by implementing suitable search functions (Winker & Preiß 2000). The intention of this test of gender-sensitivity was not to differentiate dichotomously between women's and men's areas, but to call attention to the fact that interesting or time-saving Internet services must also be developed for areas of work and life with female connotations. Mainly women, but also many men, for example those who engage in family work, could profit from this development.

The primary aim of this approach of heuristic evaluation of online services is therefore to examine the range and variety of information provided. The above study shows, for example, that fields of activity that take up a great deal of time for people with family commitments are still hardly supported by e-government programmes. To change this, it would be necessary to take subjects such as health, social matters, childcare and voluntary work into account alongside business and tourism. As a rule, the relevant portals contain only static HTML information on these subjects, but no updated dynamic information or even applications providing transaction possibilities for concrete life situations, and thus helping people save time.

I can illustrate this point using the example of the presentation of crèches, nurseries and after-school childcare facilities in Germany. Most cities and local authorities provide only an alphabetical list of all childcare facilities with addresses and telephone numbers, which provides no added value on the local telephone directory. In the best case, facilities can be sorted by area and additionally by type of service. Parents can only search for available childcare places in exceptional cases such as the city of Frankfurt. It is only this kind of further-reaching presentation of information which creates public transparency as well as practical advantages for parents – even if it cannot solve the many problems of state-run childcare.

There is also a need for research into how issues and problems frequently previously treated as private matters, such as violence against women and children, are made public via Internet sites. All too often, sites simply list the general emergency telephone numbers for police, ambulance and emergency medical care under 'Emergencies'. The website of the city of Hanover, in contrast, provides a positive example by listing the telephone number of the local women's refuge, an emergency number for rape victims and the telephone number of an organisation for the protection of abused women and girls on this same level.

I can illustrate the second criterion of gender-sensitivity, namely providing practical search functions within the portal itself, using the example of doctor databases. It is still impossible, in far too many cases, to search for female doctors in a larger database. There is a simple technical solution to this problem, as Bremen's 'Doctor Navigator' shows; however, programmers and designers have to think of this differentiation in the first place. Continuing education databases in which users can search for target groups show the importance of gender-conscious search possibilities. The city portal of Bremen, for example, is an excellent example. Users can further restrict the target group 'women only', meaning women's seminars, for instance to search for courses for 'returners to work'. But it is also possible to search for 'men only', i.e. men's seminars, so that women are not treated as the exception once again.

These examples show that both the empirically measurable content preferences and the range of service and its usefulness for various user groups must be included in further studies on use behaviour.

4. Gender-Sensitive Internet Research Using Online Research Methods

In order to achieve findings on the behaviour of various groups in differing contexts when using different Internet services, researchers must include quantitative and qualitative online research methods, for reasons of financial and time capacity alone. The two main data collection methods are online questionnaires and online interviews. Online interviews (Mann & Stewart 2002) and online questionnaires (Tuten, Urban & Bosnjak 2002) are particularly suitable for statements on users' use habits. Although the issue of representativeness is an unsolved problem in online surveys (Hauptmanns & Lander 2001), they can enable polls for which representativeness plays a minor role, such as evaluations of websites. These methods are also suitable for carrying out studies with an exploratory character.

In addition, further online research methods that allow insights into media-related behavioural practice on the Internet are particularly important for the current status of gender studies. These include possibilities of recording communicative sequences, such as exchanges in chats, forum contributions or e-mails within virtual groups. Another very interesting possibility on the client side is logfile analyses, with which individual surfing and searching strategies can be retraced and analysed. These online methods enable new insights into concrete means of use of the Internet.

All the digital documenting methods for data collection can be used to show individual behaviour data that could previously only be gathered using participatory observation. In contrast to participatory observation, the data material is neither transitory, nor the result of the impression of an individual researcher who perceives behavioural sequences through the filter of his or her own background of experience. Stegbauer correctly points out that previously non-existent possibilities of social research have arisen with the emergence of new Internet-based social spaces. Interactions are transitory, and are difficult to fully document in real social situations. Such problems do not apply to the study of asynchronous Internet-based social spaces. All communication processes in mailing lists and newsgroups are archived and can be made use of for studies. (Stegbauer 2001, p. 90)

The new documenting possibilities are also an important addition to the traditional instruments of social research. I am currently involved in a research project on the use of the Internet by women's policy networks (Schachtner & Winker 2005), and our experiences show how difficult it is to carry out polls on concrete online behaviour. Interviews with women's policy activists do provide very varied information on their assessment of the Internet, but their descriptions of their own use behaviour rarely go beyond the fact that most of them use Google for searching, and one or two frequently used addresses. This is hardly surprising, as no differentiated language or established structuring exist as yet. It is therefore difficult for individuals to become aware of their own information and communication behaviour. It is easier to find out individual attitudes to the Internet in an interview situation. The women's policy activists we have interviewed can be divided into three distinct groups that can be described as optimistic, sceptical and emotionless towards the possibilities of the Internet. However, actual behaviour on the web appears to be only loosely linked with these attitudes. The research project has documented the search strategies of a study group of 20 female students in answering 10 questions on women's policy, and established that their approaches were extremely varied. This is particularly remarkable as the Internet experience within the study group was on a fairly equal level (Carstensen & Winker 2005).

In addition, digital documenting methods are an equally important research focus with which 'collective orientation patterns' (Bohnsack 1997) can be reconstructed. The aim of this research is to establish explicit interrelationships of meanings, from which media-related behavioural practices of different groups, and thus also forms and styles of Internet use, result. Schäffer (2003) details these 'media use cultures' primarily in their generation-specific form. Buchen & Philipper (2002) focus on media cultures specific to types of schools and gender. Both studies succeed in reconstructing stereotypes towards which individuals orientate. For example, Schäffer describes the chat culture of school-age girls and Buchen & Philipper draw attention to the 'computer freaks' among young men at German intermediate secondary schools.

These media practice cultures are not, however, identical with concrete behaviour on the Internet, on the basis of which researchers can observe very different behaviour – although this is influenced by the symbolic settings and the structural conditions of division of labour. For example, the experience-linked knowledge represented within a group does not necessarily equate with the individual skills of the members of the group. As social scientists, we can only make statements on how 'doing gender' functions in practice and where tendencies of 'undoing gender' can be observed when we examine concrete online behaviour in differing contexts, in conjunction with revealing gender-stereotyping collective orientation patterns.

In future, due to the description of concrete Internet behaviour, male computer freaks will no longer be the focus of analysis, but more differentiated use behaviour by varied user types can be discovered. For example, young male chatters will appear, who were previously lost in the all too simple contrast of girl chatters and boy players.

It is therefore important to incorporate various perspectives into research designs in future, in keeping with the demands of triangulation. A practical approach is to reconstruct the collective orientation patterns within a group, as well as documenting and interpreting the Internet behaviour of the members of the group. Researchers can then make statements on how gendered subjects use the Internet, and thereby reproduce or even de-dramatise their own or outside gender-specific attributions. Hierarchies of power, institutional constraints and cultural attributions do, of course, limit scope for action, however cultural gender-specific orientations can also change through media behaviour. As social scientists, we must do justice to these processes of construction and deconstruction by using a suitable variety of methods.

In addition, new forms of online research can continue traditions of women's studies, in which it has always been important to show alternative routes of action in the sense of action research. In the research project on the significance of the Internet for women's policy networks mentioned above, the findings of a heuristic evaluation of web presences of German women's networks has been made available online (see Carstensen & Winker in this volume). This was simultaneously conceived as a prototype, so that new search strategies are not only described on the website, but can also be explored directly (Taube & Winker 2005). These and other possibilities were discussed on a national level by experts at a special future workshop that was conducted online. In this way, Internet research can make a concrete contribution to shaping the Internet itself.

5. Future Prospects

To sum up, one important future task of research is to study the varied process of co-construction of gender and Internet. This paper has shown that structural factors take effect in the case of the access gap, in connection with the gender-hierarchic division of labour. There is a lack of comprehensive data on gender-specific use of the Internet and particularly of analyses of explanations. Interests and requirements based on differing experiences of life and work certainly also have gender-specific effects in this case. At the same time, Internet use in particular shows collective behaviour patterns which are related to technology-related gender stereotypes. However, it is still extensively unclear in which concrete everyday situations these stereotypes are kept alive via processes of doing gender, and where they are at least partly deconstructed.

Particularly interesting for gender studies is the current process of transition, in which the Internet, with its previously technical connotations, is being transformed into non-technology. This is always the case when many women appropriate a technical artefact and integrate it into the contexts of their lives (Wajcman 1991). The Internet is currently still in a transitional situation; technology still emerges, especially in moments in which it does not work or in the case of more recent developments such as videostreaming or 3D animations.

The research concept for gender-sensitive Internet research I have presented here is ambitious and multi-facetted. It promises new findings through the consistent use of new online research methods and methodological scrutiny of dichotomous gender research. These findings do not stop at simply portraying the status quo, but lead to concrete tasks of shaping the future, which can also be realised in principle through the new medium of the Internet.

References

Bimber, B. 2000, 'Measuring the Gender Gap on the Internet', *Social Science Quarterly*, vol. 81, no. 3, pp. 868-876.

BMFSFJ & Statistisches Bundesamt (eds.) 2003, Wo *bleibt die Zeit? Die Zeitverwendung der Bevölkerung in Deutschland 2001/02*, http://www.bmfsfj.de/RedaktionBMFSFJ/Abteilung2/Pdf-Anlagen/wo-bleibt-zeit,property=pdf.pdf [24 January 2005].

Bohnsack, R. 1997, 'Orientierungsmuster: Ein Grundbegriff qualitativer Sozialforschung', in *Methodische Probleme der empirischen Erziehungswissenschaft*, ed. F. Schmidt, Schneider-Verlag, Hohengehren, Baltmannweiler.

Buchen, S. & Philipper, I. 2002, 'Die Bedeutung neuer Medien im Leben männlicher und weiblicher Jugendlicher unterschiedlicher Schulformen: Wie können biografische und generationsspezifische Bildungspotentiale durch veränderte Lernarrangements in der Schule genutzt werden?' *MedienPädagogik* 1/2002, http://www.medienpaed.com/02-1/buchen_philipper1.pdf [24 January 2005].

Carstensen, T. & Winker, G., 2005, 'Problemorientierte Suchstrategien und die Auffindbarkeit frauenpolitischer Inhalte im Internet', in *Virtuelle Räume – neue Öffentlichkeiten. Frauennetze im Internet*, eds. Ch. Schachtner & G. Winker, Campus, Frankfurt, New York.

DiMaggio, P. & Hargittai, E. 2001, 'From the "Digital Divide" to "Digital Inequality": Studying Internet Use as Penetration Increases' *Princeton University Center for Arts and Cultural Policy Studies, Working Paper Series*, no. 15, http://www.princeton.edu/~artspol/workpap/WP15%20-20DiMaggio%2BHargittai.pdf [24 January 2005].

Eimeren, B. von; Gerhard, H. & Frees, B. 2004, 'ARD/ZDF-Online-Studie 2004. Internetverbreitung in Deutschland: Potenzial vorerst ausgeschöpft?' *Media Perspektiven* 8/2004, pp. 350-370.

EOS Gallup Europe (ed.) 2002, *Flash Eurobarometer 135. Internet and the Public at Large*, http://europa.eu.int/comm/public_opinion/flash/fl135_en.pdf [24 January 2005].

Frauen geben Technik neue Impulse e.V (FTI), Initiative D21 & TNS Emnid (eds.) 2004, *Internetnutzung von Frauen und Männern in Deutschland 2003*, http://www.frauen-technik-impulse.de/var/storage/original/application/phppGFm7Z.pdf [24 January 2005].

Hargittai, E. 2002, 'Second-Level Digital Divide: Differences in People's Online Skills', *First Monday* 7(4), http://firstmonday.org/issues/issue7_4/hargittai [24 January 2005].

Hauptmanns, P. & Lander, B. 2001, 'Zur Problematik von Internet-Stichproben', in *Online-Marktforschung*, eds. A. Theobald, M. Dreyer & T. Starsetzki, Gabler, Wiesbaden.

Heimrath, R. & Goulding, A. 2001, 'Internet Perception and Use: a Gender Perspective', *Program, electronic library and information systems*, vol. 35, no. 2, April, pp. 119-134.

Howard, P. E. N., Rainie, L. & Jones, St. 2003: 'Days and Nights on the Internet', in *The Internet in Everyday Life*, eds. B. Wellman, & C. Haythornthwaite, Blackwell, Malden.

Mann, Ch. & Stewart, F. 2002, *Internet Communication and Qualitative Research*, 2nd edition, Sage, London.

Minks, K.-H. 2000, 'Studienmotivation und Studienbarrieren', *HIS Kurzinformation A8*, pp. 1-12.

Nielsen & NetRatings (eds.) 2002, *Digital Divide for Women Persists at Work*, http://www.nielsen-netratings.com/pr/pr_020313.pdf [24 January 2005].

Norris, P. 2001, *Digital Divide. Civic Engagement, Information Poverty, and the Internet Worldwide*. University Press, Cambridge.

Ono, H. & Zavodny, M. 2003, 'Gender and the Internet', *Social Science Quarterly*, vol. 84, no. 1, pp. 111-120.

Pew Internet & American Life Project 2003, *America's Online Pursuits, The changing picture of who's online and what they do*, http://www.pewinternet.org/pdfs/PIP_Online_Pursuits_Final.PDF [24 January 2005].

Schachtner, Ch. & Winker, G. (eds.) 2005, *Virtuelle Räume - Neue Öffentlichkeiten. Frauenpolitik im Internet*, Campus, Frankfurt/New York.

Schäffer, B. 2003, *Generationen – Medien – Bildung*, Leske+Budrich, Opladen.

Singh, S. 2001, 'Gender and the Use of the Internet at Home', *New Media & Society*, vol. 3 (4), pp. 395-416.

Stegbauer, Ch. 2001, *Grenzen virtueller Gemeinschaft. Strukturen internetbasierter Kommunikationsforen*. Westdeutscher Verlag, Opladen.

Taube, W. & Winker, G. 2005, 'Virtuelle Nachbarschaften zur Unterstützung subalterner Gegenöffentlichkeiten', in Schachtner Ch. & Winker G., eds., *Virtuelle Räume - Neue Öffentlichkeiten. Frauenpolitik im Internet*, Campus, Frankfurt, New York.

Tuten, T. L., Urban, D. J. & Bosnjak, M. 2002, 'Internet Surveys and Data Quality: A Review', in, Batinic B., Reips U.-D & Bosniak M. eds., *Online Social Sciences*, Hogrefe & Huber Publishers, Seattle.

Vogel, U. & Hinz, Ch. 2000, *Zur Steigerung der Attraktivität des Ingenieurstudiums*, Kleine, Bielefeld.

Wajcman, J. 1991, *Feminism Confronts Technology*, Pennsylvania State Univ. Press.

Winker, G. 2004, Fokus Bürgerin. Zur genderbewussten Gestaltung öffentlicher Räume in kommunalen E-Government-Portalen, in *Kursbuch Internet und Politik 2003*, eds. A. Siedschlag & A. Bilgeri, VS Verlag für Sozialwissenschaften, Wiesbaden.

Winker, G. & Preiß, G. 2000, Unterstützung des Frauen-Alltags per Mausklick? Zum Potenzial elektronischer Stadtinformationssysteme, *Zeitschrift für Frauenforschung und Geschlechterstudien*, Heft 1+2, pp. 49-80, http://www.tu-harburg.de/agentec/winker/publikationen/stadtinfo.pdf [24 January 2005].

Yates, S. J. & Littleton, K. 2001, 'Understanding Computer Game Cultures. A Situated Approach', in Green E. & Adam A. eds. 2001, *Virtual Gender*, Routledge, London.

Notes

I would like to thank Katy Derbyshire, who translated this text.

1 This evaluation is not published. Other findings of the teleworking study are included in ed. G. Winker 2001, Telearbeit und Lebensqualität. Zur Vereinbarkeit von Beruf und Familie, Frankfurt/New York, Campus.

Education:
Context and Content

Rosemary O. Agbonlahor

Christina Björkman

Hilde Corneliussen

Debbie Ellen,
Clem Herman

Sigrid Schmitz,
Ruth Meßmer

16 Gender Differentials in the Adoption and Use of Information and Communications Technologies by Lecturers in Nigerian Universities

Rosemary O. Agbonlahor

Africa Regional Centre for Information Science, Ibadan, Nigeria

Abstract

Information and communications technologies (ICT) are gradually becoming pervasive in Nigerian universities and there is a need to consider gender issues early in the diffusion process so as to help female academics maximise the potential of ICT to facilitate their job functions and empower them as key players in the diffusion process. This paper is based on a study of gender differentials in the adoption and use of ICT in Nigerian universities. The study found that there were no significant differences in the average length of time for which male and female academics had been teaching at the university level, average number of years for which they had used computers, their frequency of using computers, stages of technology adoption, and levels of access to computers. Significant differences were however observed in the average number of computer applications used by male and female academics with male academics using an average of 4.3 applications and females using an average of 3.9. Female academics also tended to use computers for tasks that did not require great technical skills such as word processing, emailing and searching library CD-ROMs. They were also less enthusiastic about IT use, and showed higher levels of computer anxiety and computer avoidance than male academics. The only attitudinal factor which emerged as a significant predictor of the frequency (or regularity) of use of computers by female academics was perceived ease-of-use. The greatest inhibitors to use of IT reported by female academics were lack of university commitment to providing computers for staff and volume of workload.

The paper suggests that if female academics perceive information technology as easy to use, they would be likely to use IT more regularly and this could in turn lead to higher enthusiasm and lower levels of anxiety about, and avoidance of IT. Therefore activities geared at increasing effective use of ICT by female academics should aim at reducing the perceived complexity of computers and other ICT. Measures should also be put in place to reduce academic workloads and improve access to ICT by female academics. The paper concludes by suggesting areas for further research.

1. Introduction

Rapid advances in information and communication technologies (ICT) are affecting the way university education is delivered and research conducted. ICT is currently being used effectively in higher education for information access and delivery in libraries, for research and development, for communication, and for teaching and learning (Jacobsen 1998). Many universities offer courses on-line via telecommunications and computer networks and there is a trend towards distance education. Furthermore, with national boundaries playing a lesser role in the information age, graduates are increasingly expected to compete for jobs in a global marketplace and universities are expected to prepare them for this market. This is probably one of the reasons behind the increased demand for IT-based courses in many developing countries' universities, including Nigeria. It is thus becoming obvious that to remain relevant in the information age, developing countries' universities need to take advantage of the opportunities offered by modern ICT to enhance teaching, learning and research.

2. Background

There are varying arguments about the benefits of the adoption and use of ICT in universities. Some writers are of the opinion that information technology (IT) would enable academics to teach large numbers of students in a more effective manner thereby allowing them (academics) to concentrate their limited time on activities that IT cannot replace, such as mentoring and problem solving (Gell and Cochrane 1996; Capper et al. 2000). Others are of the opinion that with increasing globalisation ICT can enable teachers and students alike to have access to the best resources available in any field regardless of distance (Gell and Cochrane 1996).

Despite the much-vaunted benefits of IT use in education, it is pertinent to note that the technology itself is not enough, instead it is its use to exploit information in support of the university's mission that counts (Beller 1997). Holt and Crocker (2000) observe that though effective use of IT can result in considerable benefits to an organisation, successful use of IT depends not only on the technology itself but also on the levels of skills and expertise of the individuals using this technology. They also note that though the skills of an individual can be improved by proper training, the attitudes of a user towards the technology will affect his/her willingness to learn about the technology, the decision to use the technology, and the actual uses to which the technology is put.

For developing countries information technology affords university academics and researchers a unique opportunity to bridge the knowledge gap between them and their counterparts in developed nations. In fact, information technology is seen as crucial to the continued survival of universities and research institutes in developing countries (UNISIST Newsletter 1999).

2.1 ICT in Nigerian Universities

In Nigeria the evidence for the growing importance of ICT in modern university education is the increasing rate of acquisition of computers and other information technologies (including VSATs), for the use of staff and students. However, though much has been written and said about the value of ICT in teaching, learning and research, studies have shown that successful integration of technology into the university system depends not only on access and availability but also on the extent to which staff and students embrace these technologies (Horgan 1998). For Nigerian universities wishing to integrate ICT into their curriculum, their academic staff are a core user group who will play a vital role in the successful implementation of new information and communication technologies.

Studies of ICT use in Nigerian universities have typically focused on their use in university libraries (for example Oduwole 2000; Ogunleye 1997). Such studies have concentrated on determining factors that promote or hinder use of ICT at the organisational level and have tended to gloss over individual level factors. Studies that have focused on individual level use of ICT in Nigerian universities have concentrated mainly on IT adoption and use by students (for example Ajuwon 2003; Isokpehi et al. 2000). Such individual level studies typically do not disaggregate their findings by gender. The few existing gender-based studies are not detailed enough to enable one to reach definite conclusions about factors that affect gender use of ICT in Nigerian universities (for example, Idowu, Adagunodo, and Popoola 2003; Olorunda and Oyelude 2003). Writers such as Green (2003), and Hafkin and Taggart (2001) have noted that factors which affect the use or non-use of ICT by men may actually be different from those that affect use or non-use by women and that it is important to study gender differentials in ICT adoption and use because technology is not gender neutral. There is thus currently a dearth of knowledge regarding gender differentials in ICT adoption and use in Nigerian universities.

2.2 Gender and ICT

Gurumurthy (2004) observes that the dramatic positive changes brought in by ICT have not touched all of humanity. She notes that existing power relations in society determine the enjoyment of benefits from ICT hence these technologies are not gender neutral. Hafkin and Taggart (2001) express special concern for women in developing countries. They stress that it is imperative for women in developing countries to understand the significance of ICT and to use them or they will become marginalized from the mainstream of their countries and of the world. They are also of the opinion that gender issues should be considered early in the process of the introduction of information technology in developing countries so that gender concerns can be incorporated from the beginning and not as a corrective afterwards. In line with this, The Commonwealth of Learning (2000) observes that if women are disadvantaged in accessing and using new technologies and therefore do not have the experience and confidence, they may be restricted in the types of positions for which they are employed.

Already, there are growing concerns about the low participation of women in information technology related careers (Green 2003; Idowu, Alu and Popoola 2003) and studies have shown that even when women use ICT, they are mostly used for tasks which do not require high technical skills such as data entry and word processing (Hafkin and Taggart 2001). Factors that have been cited as affecting female enrolment in IT courses and their use of computers include socialization and cultural practices, importance of role models, access to computers, experience with computers, ability and perceived ability and anxiety (Idowu, Alu and Popoola 2003; Olorunda and Oyelude, 2003).

In spite of the foregoing observations, not many empirical studies have been carried out to investigate the gender dimension of access to and use of ICT in developing countries, especially in Africa. This paper is an attempt to bridge the knowledge gap and presents some of the results from my ongoing PhD research. It reports on gender differences in the levels of information technology adoption and use by academics in Nigerian universities, factors which influence IT adoption and characteristics of IT use by lecturers, with a view to generating information that will help define the current status of IT adoption by male and female academics in Nigerian universities. The next section describes the population of the study and the sampling procedure as well as the data collection method employed in the study.

3. Methodology

3.1 Profile of the study population

The first university in Nigeria – the University of Ibadan (formerly the University College, Ibadan) was established in Ibadan in the Southwestern part of Nigeria in 1948, and the second at Nsukka in the Eastern part of the country in 1960. From 1960 till now Federal and State governments and other organizations in Nigeria have established over 40 universities geographically dispersed all over the country. The population for this study comprised academic staff (lecturers) in all Federal and state universities in Nigeria. The Nigerian Universities Commission (NUC)'s statistics for the year 2002 gives the number as 5799 (comprising 4850 males and 949 females, a ratio of approximately 5 male academics to 1 female academic).

3.2 Sampling

A survey design that employed a questionnaire for data collection was used in the study.

One thousand lecturers selected from ten universities in Nigeria were sampled using a proportionate sampling method. Also, lecturers were proportionally sampled by faculty (or college) within each university so as to ensure proportional representation of lecturers from all faculties (or colleges).

Efforts were made during the process of questionnaire administration to ensure proportional representation of male and female academics and that all cadres of lecturers, from Graduate Assistant to Professor, were sampled. In addition to the questionnaire, short personal interviews with lecturers at the universities yielded further information on the status of IT use and factors that affected their use of IT in academic work.

3.3 Data collection

Of the 1000 copies of questionnaire distributed, a total of 760 were returned out of which 42 were found unusable, leaving a total of 718 usable questionnaires. Table 1 shows the distribution of usable questionnaires by university, while Table 2 shows the distribution by faculties and gender.

University	Copies of Questionnaire distributed	Usable questionnaires returned	Response rate (%)
Ahmadu Bello University, Zaria	120	107	89
Obafemi Awolowo University, Ile-Ife	155	135	87.1
University of Nigeria, Nsukka	150	122	81.3
University of Jos	90	34	37.8
University of Port Harcourt	68	44	64.7
University of Agriculture, Abeokuta	48	48	100
Delta State University, Abraka	39	25	64.1
University of Lagos	105	58	52.3
University of Ilorin	70	49	70
University of Ibadan	155	96	61.9
Total	1000	718	71.8

Table 1: Questionnaire distribution and response rate

Data from the questionnaire were analysed using the Statistical Software for the Social Sciences (SPSS).

Faculty	Gender		Total
	Male	Female	
Arts	84 (12.0%)	18 (2.6%)	102 (14.6%)
Social and Administrative Sciences/Law	93 (13.3%)	28 (4.0%)	121 (17.3%)
Medical Sciences	52 (7.4%)	25 (3.6%)	77 (11.0%)
Pure Sciences	90 (12.9%)	34 (4.9%)	124 (17.7%)
Education	84 (12.0%)	39 (5.6%)	123 (17.6%)
Engineering/Technology	50 (7.2%)	8 (1.1%)	58 (8.3%)
Applied Sciences	76 (10.9%)	18 (2.6%)	94 (13.4%)
Total*	529 (75.7%)	170 (24.3%)	699 (100.0%)
* Some respondents did not answer this and a number of other questions so responses do not always add up to 718			

Table 2: Distribution of Respondents by Faculty and Gender

4. RESULTS

4.1 Demographic profile of respondents

Five hundred and twenty-nine respondents (75.7%) were males and 170 (24.3%) were females. Respondents' ages ranged from 25 to over 55 years and the length of time for which they had been teaching in the university system ranged from less than one year to over 30 years with a mean of 10.80 years for male respondents and 10.38 years for female respondents (this difference was not statistically significant t = 0.666, p >0.05).

4.2 Use of computers

Six hundred and forty-five respondents (92.5%) reported that they used computers. Respondents had been using computers for periods ranging from less than a year to over 30 years, with a mean of 5.5 years and a median of 4.0 years. The bulk of the respondents (88.5%) however, had been using computers for ten years and less. There were no significant differences in the average number of years for which male and female respondents had been using computers (t = 1.908, p > 0.05).

Two hundred and ninety-eight respondents (41.5%) used computers daily, 26.2% every 2-3 days, 10.0% weekly, 4.0% once a month and 9.5% 'only when needed' (infrequently). Some respondents who reported that they did not use computers also reported that they used it only when needed. Further probing revealed that such respondents employed people to perform computer-related tasks on their behalf, usually for a fee.

There was no significant relationship between frequency of computer use and gender of respondents (Mann-Whitney U 40322.00, p > 0.05). Frequency of computer use was however not independent of respondents' faculties (Kruskal-Wallis H test: Chi-square = 21.025, p < 0.05). Exploring the data further revealed that the differences in frequency of use of computers were significant only for male lecturers in the different faculties (Chi-square = 21.251, p < 0.05). Between faculties, male respondents in engineering/technology, medical sciences and social sciences faculties ranked higher in frequency of computer use than male respondents from other faculties. This implies that male academics in the former three faculties used IT more often than male academics in other faculties. There were no significant differences in the frequency of use of computers by female academics in the different faculties (chi-square = 2.81, p > 0.05).

The most common use of computers was for Word processing (81.4%), followed by email (81.3%) and Web browsing (74.8%), the least used applications were searching library CD-ROMs (31.3%), desktop publishing (25.3%), and database management (19.5%). Aside from word processing, email, and searching library CD-ROMs, there were noticeably higher percentages of male than female academics who used computers for other tasks (Table 3).

Computer Applications	Gender				Total	
	Male		Female			
	Frequency	Percent	Frequency	Percent	Frequency	Percent
Word processing	431	81.50%	138	81.20%	569	81.40%
Spreadsheets	211	39.90%	52	30.60%	263	37.60%
Presentations	179	33.80%	44	25.90%	223	31.90%
Statistical analysis	197	37.20%	52	30.60%	249	35.60%
Desktop publishing	143	27.00%	34	20.00%	177	25.30%
Database management	108	20.40%	28	16.50%	136	19.50%
Library CD-ROM searching	165	31.20%	54	31.80%	219	31.30%
Email	432	81.70%	136	80.00%	568	81.30%
Web browsing	402	76.00%	121	71.20%	523	74.80%
Other (GIS, programming languages, games, etc)	25	4.70%	5	2.90%	30	4.30%

Table 3: Percentages of male and female lecturers using different computer applications

The number of computer applications used by respondents ranged from one to over ten, with a mean of 4.2 and a median of four applications. Significant differences were observed in the average number of computer applications used by male and female academics ($t = 2.115$, $p < 0.05$) with males using an average of 4.3 computer applications and females using an average of 3.9 applications.

4.3 Use of the Internet

Only 4.7% of the academics in this study reported that they did not use the Internet. Repondents were asked how often they used the Internet and what they used the Internet for. The two major Internet facilities used were e-mail and the World Wide Web (WWW). There were no significant differences in frequency of use of e-mail (Mann-Whitney $U = 32808.00$, $p > 0.05$) or the WWW (Mann-Whitney $U = 32808.00$, $p > 0.05$) by gender. Table 5 presents a summary of the lecturers' use of the Internet broken down by gender.

From Table 5, it can be observed that the bulk of Internet use by the academics in this survey was for personal and professional communication (66.0% and 65.8%, respectively). Higher proportions of female than male academics used the Internet for personal communication, locating information on conferences and workshops, and job searches/posting resumes. On the other hand, the percentage of male academics that used the Internet for professional communication and for communicating with students was higher than that for female academics. The proportion of academics that used the Internet for other tasks was comparable for both genders.

Internet use	Gender				Total	
	Male		Female			
	Frequency	Percent	Frequency	Percent	Frequency	Percent
Professional communication	351	66.40%	110	64.70%	461	66.00%
Job searching/ posting resumes	136	25.70%	62	36.50%	198	28.30%
Downloading software	215	40.60%	68	40.00%	283	40.50%
Personal communication	343	64.80%	117	68.80%	460	65.80%
Locating information on conferences/workshops	279	52.70%	101	59.40%	380	54.40%
Communicating with students	92	17.40%	23	13.50%	115	16.50%
Getting materials for lecture notes/research	215	40.60%	68	40.00%	198	28.30%

Table 4: Use of the Internet by gender

4.4 Access to IT

When asked where they used computers, respondents reported a variety of places. Over half of the respondents (54.9%) reported that they used computers in their offices, 50.1% used computers at home, 46.1% used computers in a cyber café or commercial computer centre, 8.4% used computers in the house of a friend, neighbour or colleague, while 9.7% used computers in the office of a friend, neighbour or colleague. Broken down by gender, the data indicated that male lecturers used computers more in their offices while a greater proportion of females used computers at home (Table 5). Aside from their offices, male lecturers also used computers in places such as cybercafés, friends/colleagues homes and offices more than female lecturers.

Access	Gender		Total
	Male	Female	
Computer use in office	300 (56.70)	84 (49.40%)	384 (54.90%)
Computer use at home	249 (47.10%)	101 (59.40%)	350 (50.10%)
Computer use in cyber café/commercial computer centre	246 (46.50%)	76 (44.70%)	322 (46.10%)
Computer use in friend/colleague's house	49 (9.30%)	10 (5.90%)	59 (8.40%)
Computer use in friend/colleague's office	58 (11.00%)	10 (5.90%)	68 (9.70%)
Do not use computers	38 (7.20)	12 (7.10)	50 (7.20%)

Table 5: Access to computers by gender

The data on access to computers was used to create an index of IT access as follows: weights of 1 each was attached to access from home and office while a weight of 0.5 each was attached to access from a cyber café, commercial computer centre, a friend/colleague's home or office. An index of the level of access to computers for each respondent was computed by adding up the weights for each reported access point. The mean index of access was 1.7 with a median of 2.0 and a mode of 1.0. There was no significant difference in average level of access to IT by male and female academics (t = -445, p > 0.05). This implies that overall level of access to IT by male and female academics in this study did not differ significantly even though each gender appeared to have preferences as to where they used IT.

4.5 Attitudes towards IT

Lecturers' attitudes towards IT were measured using seven scale instruments, namely; Enjoyment, Enthusiasm, Anxiety, and Avoidance, Perceived Usefulness, and Perceived Ease of Use, Use of computers in education. Each scale instrument contained five-point Likert-type questions with the value 5 assigned to 'strongly agree', 4 to 'agree' 3 to 'undecided' 2 to 'disagree' and 1 to 'strongly disagree'. Scale items that were negatively worded were reverse coded. Item scores on a scale were added up to generate a respondent's attitude score on that scale. Thus on the Enjoyment, Enthusiasm and Avoidance scales which had three items each, respondents could score a maximum of 15 points on each scale, while on the Anxiety, Perceived Usefulness, Perceived Ease of Use, and Use of IT in Education scales which had four items each, respondents could score a maximum of 20 point on each scale. Blank responses were coded as missing and excluded from the summation of individual scores. Table 7 presents the mean and median values of respondents' scores on the attitude scales.

Respondents' Scale scores							
	Enthusiasm Score	Enjoyment score	Anxiety score*	Avoidance Score*	Perceived Usefulness	Ease of Use	Computers in Education
N	713	715	712	711	715	703	716
Mean	12.79	12.67	15.44	12.58	16.26	13.56	15.53
Median	14.00	13.00	16.00	14.00	17.00	14.00	16.00
Minimum	1	1	1	1	1	1	1
Maximum	15	15	20	15	20	20	20

* Due to reverse coding, higher scores on these scales translate to lower anxiety and avoidance

Table 6: Mean and median of respondents' scores on attitude scales

From table 6 it can be observed that the academics in this survey generally had positive attitudes towards IT and the use of IT in higher education because their average score on each scale is closer to the maximum scale score than the minimum score.

4.6 Gender differences in attitudes towards IT

Table 7 shows the mean and median values of respondents' scores on the attitude scales broken down by gender. As can be observed, female academics had lower median scores on the enthusiasm, avoidance, anxiety and perceived usefulness scales.

Attitude Scores						
	Males			Females		
	N	Mean	Median	N	Mean	Median
Enthusiasm Score	526	12.91	14	168	12.38	13
Enjoyment score	527	12.76	13	169	12.44	13
Anxiety score	525	15.62	16	168	14.88	15
Avoidance Score	523	12.78	14	169	12.09	13
Perceived Usefulness	527	16.43	17	169	15.78	16
Ease of Use	516	13.54	14	168	13.54	14
Computers in Education	528	15.63	16	169	15.24	16

Table 7: mean and median values of respondents' scores on the attitude scales by gender

When tested for significance (Mann-Whitney U test) the observed differences were significant only for the enthusiasm (Mann-Whitney U=37864.500, p < 0.05), anxiety (Mann-Whitney U=38215.500, p < 0.05) and avoidance (Mann-Whitney U=38783.500, p <0.05) scales. On these three scales, male respondents ranked significantly higher than female respondents implying that female academics were less enthusiastic, more anxious and avoided using computers more than male academics. There were no significant differences in scores between male and female respondents on the enjoyment, perceived usefulness, perceived ease of use, and use of computers in education scales (p>0.05 in each case).

Mann-Whitney U Test Statistics							
	Enthusiasm Score	Enjoyment score	Anxiety score	Avoidance Score	Perceived Usefulness	Ease of Use	Computers in Education
Mann-Whitney U	37864.500	41490.000	38215.500	38783.000	40208.500	42693.000	41275.500
Sig. (2-tailed)	.004*	.172	.009*	.013*	.055	.768	.140
Grouping Variable: gender *: Significant difference in scores.							

Table 8: Test for gender differences in attitude towards IT

4.7 Relationship between access to, and attitudes towards IT

The relationship between respondents' level of access to IT and their attitudes towards IT was tested by correlating their scores on the seven attitude scales with their index of access. For male respondents, access to IT correlated significantly with their scores on all seven scales. However, level of access to IT for female respondents correlated significantly only with enthusiasm, anxiety, avoidance and the use of computers in education. This possibly implies that for female academics, improving levels of access to IT could lead to corresponding increase in enthusiasm for IT use, less computer anxiety and avoidance, as well as more positive perception of the importance of ICT in education.

	Correlations					
	Males			Females		
	Level of access to IT			Level of access to IT		
	N	Pearson Correlation	Sig. (2-tailed)	N	Pearson Correlation	Sig. (2-tailed)
Enthusiasm Score	486	.129(**)	0.005	151	.209(*)	0.010
Enjoyment score	487	.206(**)	0.000	152	0.14	0.086
Anxiety score	487	.176(**)	0.000	151	.179(*)	0.028
Avoidance Score	483	.201(**)	0.000	152	.182(*)	0.025
Perceived Usefulness	487	.231(**)	0.000	152	0.064	0.432
Perceived Ease of Use	478	.148(**)	0.001	151	0.066	0.423
Use of Computers in Education	487	.166(**)	0.000	152	.189(*)	0.020
** Correlation is significant at the 0.01 level (2-tailed).						
* Correlation is significant at the 0.05 level (2-tailed).						

Table 9: Correlations: Levels of access to, and attitudes towards IT

4.8 Attitudes towards IT and frequency of IT use

A regression analysis was carried out to find out which of the attitude variables significantly influenced the frequency of IT use by male and female academics. The results revealed that influential attitudes were different for both genders. For female academics, the only attitudinal variable that significantly influenced frequency of IT use was ease of use (Table 10).

Variable	B	SE B	Beta	t	Sig. t
Enthusiasm Score	5.176E-03	.069	.008	.075	.940
Anxiety score	6.061E-02	.048	.139	1.266	.208
Avoidance Score	-2.359E-02	.049	-.045	-.478	.634
Perceived Usefulness	3.346E-02	.048	.081	.693	.489
Ease of Use*	.200	.050	.397	3.982	.000
Computers in Education	-5.266E-02	.046	-.109	-1.153	.251
(Constant)*	1.583	.666		2.378	.019
*Significant predictor					
[R2 = 0.238; Adj R2 = 0.202; F = 6.571; Sig. F = 0.000]					

Table 10: Regression analysis: Attitudes with frequency of IT use for female respondents

Attitudes that significantly influenced frequency of use of computers by male respondents were anxiety, perceived usefulness, perceived ease of use and use of computers in education (Table 11).

Variable	B	SE B	Beta	t	Sig. t
Enthusiasm Score	1.457E-02	.034	.024	.434	.664
Anxiety score*	6.195E-02	.026	.135	2.388	.017
Avoidance Score	-1.727E-02	.029	-.032	-.589	.556
Perceived Usefulness*	8.085E-02	.028	.169	2.921	.004
Ease of Use*	8.457E-02	.028	.149	3.070	.002
Computers in Education*	-5.900E-02	.027	-.111	-2.153	.032
(Constant)*	2.280	.468		4.872	.000
*Significant predictor [R2 = 0.096; Adj R2 = 0.085; F = 8.228; Sig. F = 0.000]					

Table 11: Regression analysis: Attitudes with frequency of IT use for male respondents

4.9 Hindrances to IT use

Respondents were asked to indicate the extent to which a range of factors inhibited their use of IT and their responses were ranked using the Friedman test as shown in Table 12. For female respondents, the most significant inhibitors were 'My University is not very committed to providing computers for academic staff' (mean rank = 10.31) and

Friedman Test		
Hindrances to IT use	Mean Rank: Females	Mean Rank: Males
Nearest cybercafÈ (or other access point to the Internet) is too far away.	8.47	7.53
High cost of acquiring computer systems.	8.76	10.74
High cost of accessing/browsing the Internet.	8.42	9.56
High cost of computer training programmes.	9.00	9.95
Lack of time to learn how to use computers.	9.00	9.29
Few people in my department or faculty use IT.	8.55	8.48
Lack of technical person in the department/faculty to help solve computer problems.	8.86	8.90
No knowledgeable person to consult about the use of computers in my discipline.	9.29	8.02
My university is not very committed to providing computers for academic staff.	10.31	10.45
I tried using a computer sometime ago and lost valuable data.	8.33	7.41
Lack of access to computers to practice with.	9.38	8.34
My previous experience with computers was quite frustrating.	7.87	7.22
One hears a lot of stories about dangerous computer viruses.	8.48	8.33
Lack of funds to purchase new software.	9.89	10.59
Cost of maintaining computers is too high.	9.29	9.93
Volume of my workload as an academic staff.	10.20	9.95
Having to share access to the computer(s) in my department/faculty with students.	8.89	8.32
	N = 72; Chi-Square = 30.458, sig = 0.016	N = 246; Chi-Square = 282.510, sig = 0.000

Table 12: Hindrances to IT use

'volume of my workload as an academic staff' (mean rank = 10.20). On the other hand, the most significant inhibitors for male respondents were 'High cost of acquiring computer systems' (mean rank = 10.74) and 'Lack of funds to purchase new software' (mean rank = 10.59). Factors that ranked least as hindrances to IT use were the same for male and female respondents. These were 'my previous experience with computers was quite frustrating' (mean rank = 7.22 and mean rank = 7.87 for males and females respectively), and 'I tried using a computer sometime ago and lost valuable data' (mean rank = 7.41 and mean rank = 8.33, respectively). The academics in this study seem to consider financial and infrastructural constraints as being of much greater hindrance than any previous negative experience with IT use although financial concerns seem to be of greater importance to male academics.

4.10 Sources of information about IT use in teaching and research

Respondents were asked to rate the importance of a number of channels as sources of information about applications of IT to teaching and research in their disciplines and their responses were ranked using the Friedman nonparametric test. Not surprisingly, for both male and female respondents, the most important source of information was the Internet (mean rank = 7.15). This was followed by academic conferences (mean rank = 6.73) and research journals (mean rank = 6.26). The least important sources were Heads of Departments/Deans of Faculties (mean rank = 4.29) and University bulletins and newsletters (mean rank = 4.01).

5. Discussion

Female academics are amongst the highest educated women in any society, especially African ones. It should therefore be expected that they will be at the vanguard of information technology use in any African society and that factors which affect their use of ICT should not be too radically different from those which affect use of ICT by male academics. This study has found the converse to be the case. Even though there were no significant differences in the length of time for which males and female academics had been teaching at the university level, the average number of years for which they had used computers, their frequency of using computers and levels of access to computers, significant differences were observed in the average numbers of computer applications used by male and female respondents with male respondents using computers for significantly higher number of tasks than female respondents.

In addition, the female academics in this study tended to use computer applications that did not require great technical skills such as word processing and searching library CD-ROMs. They were also less enthusiastic about IT use, showed higher levels of computer anxiety and higher levels of computer avoidance than male academics. The attitudes of female academics towards IT appear to be affected by such issues as levels of access to computers and time to use computers as reflected in the fact that the two major inhibitors to ICT use they reported were the fact that their universities were not committed to providing computers to staff, and the volume of their workloads as academics. Interestingly, the only attitudinal factor that emerged as a significant predictor of the frequency (or regularity) of use of computers by female academics was perceived ease-of-use. This could be another factor accounting for the low number of tasks (and for the types of tasks) for which computers were used. In other words if female academics perceive IT as easy to use, they would be likely to use IT more regularly and for a greater number of tasks. This could in turn lead to higher enthusiasm and lower levels of anxiety about and avoidance of IT.

Activities geared at increasing effective use of ICT by female academics should therefore aim at reducing the perceived complexity of computers, for example by practical hands on use in real life situations rather than through formal technical lectures. Mentoring by female academics that have successfully adopted IT in their work can also help to create more positive perceptions about the ease of use of IT. Mentors do not necessarily have to be in the same discipline as those being mentored since results from this study indicate that discipline did not have a significant effect on regular use of IT by female academics. There should also be measures aimed at reducing the volume of workload of female academics so as to free up time for them to learn to use the technology. Paradoxically, information technology can help in this area. Providing access to computers and the Internet directly from their offices and homes can also help to maximise the use of available time to use/learn to use the technology.

Both male and female academics in this study rated the Internet as of greatest importance as a source of information about the applications of information technology to teaching and research in their disciplines. This has a number of implications. First is the need for affordable and accessible Internet provision for university academics. A number of universities in the study had acquired VSATs and some were in the process of installing campus-wide networks for Internet access by the university community. Another implication of this is the need to ensure that academics are equipped with the skills to effectively search, retrieve and evaluate materials from the Internet. Even though peers and colleagues did not rank very high as sources of information they can serve as role models of effective Internet use and help train peers, alongside any formal training programs that might be organised by the university.

The study also indicated that male lecturers accessed IT from a variety of places while the majority of females tended to access IT from their homes or offices with access from home being more predominant. This may be because the effort to balance domestic and professional activities leaves many women academics very little time to try to use IT outside their homes or offices. It could also be that the women do not feel comfortable using computers in places such as cybercafés or offices of colleagues (especially male ones) due to social and cultural expectations of acceptable behaviour. In any case, this is an area that requires further investigation.

6. Conclusion

This study has shown that factors that affect the adoption and use of ICT in Nigerian universities differ for male and female academics. Therefore in order to achieve effective integration of ICT into the Nigerian university system, policy makers and university administration will need to consider gender issues as they plan for the integration of modern ICT into university education.

This paper has reported on Nigerian universities. Factors that affect gender use of IT in Nigerian universities may be different from those that affect use in other African universities, there is therefore need for further research. A number of issues, such as ownership of computers, marital status, educational backgrounds of respondents, and cultural norms have not been explored here. These are also areas that could benefit from further exploration.

References

Ajuwon, G.A. 2003, 'Computer and Internet use by first year clinical and nursing students in a Nigerian university teaching hospital', BMC Medical Informatics and Decision Making, Vol. 3. No. 10, http://www.biocentral.com/1472-6947/3/10 [17 February 2004].

Beller, M. 1997, 'Integrating technology into distance teaching at the Open University of Israel', ALN Magazine Vol. 1, No. 1, http://www.aln.org/alnweb/magazine/issue1/beller.htm#1 [3 June 2002]

Capper, P. et al. 2000, 'Technology and the coming transformation of schools, teachers and teacher education' in Tomorrow's Teachers: International Critical Perspectives on Teacher Education, eds. A. Scott and J. Freeman-Moir, Canterbury University Press, Christchurch, http://www.webresearch.co.nz/docs_public/TommorrowSchools.pdf [27 January 2005].

Gell, M. & Cochrane, P. 1996, 'Learning and Education in an Information Society', in Information and Communication Technologies: Visions and Realities, ed. W. H. Dulton, Oxford University Press, Oxford, pp. 249-263.

Green, L. 2003, 'Gender-based issues and trends in ICT applications in education in Asia and the Pacific', in Meta-survey on the use of Technologies in Education in Asia and the Pacific 2003-2004, ed. G. Farrell & C. Wachholz, UNESCO, Paris, pp. 29-39.

Gurumurthy, A. 2004, 'Gender and ICT overview report', Institute for Development Studies, University of Sussex, Brighton, England, http:// www.bridge.ids.ac.uk/reports/cep-ICT-or.pdf [5 January 2005].

Hafkin, N. & Taggart, N. 2001, Gender, Information Technology and Developing Countries: an Analytic Study, for the Office of Women in Development Bureau for Global Programs, Field Support and Research, United States Agency for International Development (USAID)', LearnLink Project, AED, Washington

Holt, T.D. & Crocker, M. 2000, 'Prior negative experiences: their impact on computer training outcomes', Computers and Education, Vol. 25, pp. 295- 308.

Horgan, B.H. 1998, 'Transforming higher education using information technology: first steps', The Technology Source, http://www.microsoft.com/education/hed/news/january/1ststeps.htm [21 March 1999].

Idowu, P.A., Adagunodo, E.R. & Popoola, B.I. 2003,' Computer literacy level and gender differences among Nigerian university staff', *The African Symposium*, Vol. 3, no. 3, http://www2.ncsu.edu/ncsu/aern/comlit.pdf [17 February 2004].

Idowu, P.A., Alu, A.O. & Popoola, B.I. 2003, 'Nigerian women in information technology and computer science education', *The African Symposium*, Vol. 3, no. 3, http://www2.ncsu.edu/ncsu/aern/infotek.html [17 February 2004].

Isokpehi, R.D. et al. 2000, 'Information technology literacy among Nigerian microbiology students and professionals', *World Journal of Microbiology and Biotechnology*, Vol. 16, pp. 423-424.

Jacobsen, D.M. 1998, *Adoption patterns of faculty who integrate computer technology for teaching and learning in higher education*, Paper presented at the ED-MEDIA AND ED-TELECOM 98: World Conference on Educational Multimedia and Hypermedia, and World Conference on Educational Telecommunications, Freiburg, Germany, June 20-25, 1998.

Oduwole, A.A. 2000 'A study of the use of CD-ROM databases in Nigerian academic libraries', Brief Communication, *Journal of Information Science*, Vol. 26, no. 5, pp. 364-369.

Ogunleye, G.O. 1997, 'Automating the Federal University libraries: a state of the art', *Africa Journal of Library, Archives and Information Science*, Vol. 7, no. 1, pp. 71-89.

Olorunda, O. O. & Oyelude, A. A. 2003, *Professional women's information needs in developing countries: ICT as a catalyst*, Paper presented at the World Library and Information Congress: 69th IFLA General Conference and Council, 31 July 2003, http://www.ifla.org/IV/ifla69/papers/600-Olorunda_Oyelude.pdf [14 January 2005].

The Commonwealth of Learning 2000, 'Identifying Barriers Encountered by Women in the Use of Information and Communications Technologies for Open and Distance Learning in Africa', Unpublished manuscript, http://www.col.org/wdd/BarriersICT_Africa_papers.pdf [14 January 2005].

UNISIST 1999, 'Electronic Theses', *UNISIST Newsletter*, Vol. 27, no. 2, p. 23.

17 Invitation to Dialogue

Feminist research meets computer science

Christina Björkman

Blekinge Institute of Technology, Uppsala, Sweden

Abstract

In this paper I discuss how feminist research focused on epistemological issues can be used within computer science (CS). I approach and explore epistemological questions in computer science through a number of themes, which I believe are important to the issues of 'what' knowledge is produced as well as 'how' it is produced and how knowledge is perceived in CS. I discuss for example paradigms and metaphors in computer science, the role of abstractions and the concept of naturalisation. In order to illustrate epistemological views in CS and how these can be questioned from the viewpoints of feminist epistemology, I also do a close reading and commenting of a recent book within the philosophy of computing.

1. Introduction

Can feminist research be used in computer science[1]? And if so, can it be used not only for studying and criticising CS, but also for transformation so contributing to the development of the discipline? In this article I want to invite the reader to a dialogue between feminist research and computer science. My interest and goal concerns how to broaden the concepts and approaches to knowledge in CS, with the main issue being: can CS cherish epistemological pluralism, i.e. different ways of knowing and learning?

Feminist/gender research concerning computer science has to a large extent focused on issues of gender in relation to computer science, for example the lack of women within computing, and gender equality aspects (see for example the overview and discussion in Björkman 2002). In these studies, CS is often seen as firmly defined, and the underlying perceptions of development and knowledge are seldom brought into focus. In this paper, I want to give some examples of how feminist research can be a resource within CS for discussions concerning the discipline itself and its practices.

My approach is threefold: I highlight some feminist research that has been done within CS, which can serve as inspiration as well as foundations for future work. I also point to issues within CS that I consider relevant to study further, by asking questions that I see as important to pursue. In order to highlight both some strongly prevalent views of knowledge in computer science, and to show how feminist epistemologies can interrogate these views and offer alternatives, I end the paper with a close reading of some texts from a recent collection on the philosophy of science in CS.

2.Theoretical starting points

2.1 Feminist epistemologies

Feminist research represents many theoretical and methodological approaches, and the meaning and focus of the research is different within different disciplines. I will here discuss some of the epistemological ideas and concepts that I use as starting points[2].

Sandra Harding, in her ground-breaking book 'The Science Question in Feminism' (Harding 1986), emphasizes the importance of epistemology, or as she phrases it, 'concepts of knowers, the world to be known, and the process of knowing' (Harding 1986, p. 140). It is particularly important here to note that she does not primarily talk about 'knowledge' as a noun, but of the activity of knowing, and of knowing subjects. She points out (Harding 1987) that methodology and epistemology are intertwined with what we do and how we do it, thus underlying all research and knowledge production.

The feminist epistemologies I build my work on do not accept the (still strongly prevalent) ideas of science and the scientist as neutral and objective. Sandra Harding eloquently expresses this:

> ...observations are theory-laden, theories are paradigm-laden, and paradigms are culture-laden: hence there are and can be no such things as value-neutral, objective facts. (Harding 1986, p.102)

Feminist epistemologies are thus critical of objectivity paradigms, and of the neutral and objective observer, what Donna Haraway terms 'the God-trick of seeing everything from nowhere' (Haraway 1991, p. 189). Instead, Donna Haraway develops the concept of 'situated knowledge':

> I am arguing for politics and epistemologies of location, positioning, and situating, where partiality and not universality is the condition of being heard to make rational knowledge claims. These are claims on people's lives; the view from a body, always a complex, contradictory, structuring and structured body, versus the view from above, from nowhere, from simplicity. (Haraway 1991, p. 195)

'Situated knowledge' is a far-reaching concept, which I understand and use as implying an epistemological standpoint. Thus, 'situatedness' refers to conscious epistemological positioning. It is not simply a matter of an individual place or state, it is part of practice and knowledge production, and it means actively taking a stand. And there is no such thing as an innocent position.

The feminist epistemologies that I talk of here attempt to refuse the choice and dichotomy between on the one hand universalism and on the other relativism. Instead, Donna Haraway puts forward a feminist concept of objectivity:

> I would like a doctrine of embodied objectivity that accommodates paradoxical and critical feminist science projects: feminist objectivity means quite simply situated knowledges. (Haraway 1991, p. 188)

Thus, her alternative to relativism and universalism is partial, locatable, situated knowledge.

2.2 Knowledge

The common definition of knowledge in (analytical) philosophy is in the form of: 'S knows that P'. However, this is only a definition of one type of knowledge, often called propositional knowledge (or sometimes simply theoretical knowledge). This has come to be seen as the only important form of knowledge, at least within western science (e.g. Turkle and Papert 1990). What about the knowing subject in this definition? S is not defined here, and thus takes on the form of a universal, disembodied knower, having a view from nowhere in particular. This is also the knowledge of the mind, building on the dualisms between mind and body, culture and nature, man and woman etc. Abstract and theoretical thinking and knowing ('knowing that') is seen as superior while bodily knowing and practical thinking, ('knowing how') is seen as inferior. In this view, the body is seen as a hindrance for the 'pure' intelligence of the mind, thinking and reasoning are presented as fundamentally mental. Skills and tacit knowledge, on the contrary, are seen as a lower form of knowledge compared to that of the mind. To put it bluntly: knowledge that is not propositional is not considered knowledge. These different types of knowledge have traditionally been connected to men and women respectively; and the 'true' knower has been a man (Adam 1998).

Some feminist thinking, as a contrast to the view above, wants to call attention to other kinds of knowledge, such as those derived from practical experiences of the world. This includes the body as an inseparable part of knowledge, and not only the mind. Thus, feminist epistemologies acknowledge (embodied) experience as a valid basis for knowledge, and argue for a unity of knowledges, to borrow Hilary Rose's expression of 'hand, heart and brain'.

3. Feminist Research Meets Computer Science

Both feminist research and CS are competence areas, but they also bring with them modes of thinking about the world. My belief is that feminist epistemological thinking has the potential to enrich computer science, as do Norwegian informaticians[3] Tone Bratteteig and Guri Verne, who see 'epistemological inquiries to establish alternative understandings of knowledge' as being the most challenging and having the greatest potential for contributing to change in CS (Bratteteig and Verne 1997, p. 60).

> We do not accept the dichotomy between feminism and technology. The challenge is to learn to live with, and possibly harvest from, the contradictions and alleged paradoxes that arise. (Bratteteig and Verne 1997, p.70)

Knowledge and knowledge processes within science are of particular interest for a feminist analysis. In the sections below, I approach knowledge issues in computer science through a number of themes that I find to be of particular interest to focus upon, and I do this by asking questions. These are generally not questions that look for immediate answers; they should rather be seen as comments from a feminist position. Asking questions is a way of starting a reflective process as well as a way to communicate. These questions are meant to take us into respectful, shared conversations; the invitation is to dialogues where feminist researchers and computer scientists together look for potential answers.

3.1 What knowledge? Whose knowledge?

Questions about knowledge are particularly important in the field of Artificial Intelligence and so called expert systems. Alison Adam has contributed extensively to the critique of AI from a feminist perspective, for example in Adam (1994, 1995, 1998). She claims that using knowledge and experiences from feminist epistemology it is possible to get more radical insights into epistemological issues in AI than by using more traditional approaches (Adam 1994). Most critiques of AI de-emphasises the cultural production of AI thus being, as Alison Adam sees them, 'epistemologically conservative' (Adam 1998, p. 50).

Traditional criticism of AI concentrates on whether it can create true intelligence, while feminist critique looks to the cultural settings of AI – whose knowledge and what knowledge are represented. What world-view comes with the concretisation of knowledge in an expert system? Alison Adam is worried about 'the taken for granted nature of the expert and expert knowledge' (Adam 1998, p. 42). For example, it poses big difficulties to represent skills knowledge ('knowing how') and common sense in AI-systems which means that only some types of knowledge will be represented in the systems.

Issues concerning knowledge are by no means limited to the area of AI. An equally important question to 'whose knowledge is represented in an AI system' is the question 'whose knowledge is built into objects in object-oriented design?'. Cecile Crutzen and Jack Gerrissen have made a feminist analysis of the object oriented paradigm[4] (OO) (Crutzen and Gerrissen 2000). They make a case for making visible what is hidden:

OBJECTS should stop acting behind their surface, even if this would render our self-created OBJECTS unpredictable or unreliable (Crutzen and Gerrissen 2000, p. 134)

Crutzen and Gerrissen argue that object orientation is based on the idea of objectivity and neutrality of representation, as well as the idea that everything and everybody can be represented in terms of objects.

It is interesting to compare this analysis of OO with the views expressed by Sherry Turkle and Seymour Papert ten years earlier (Turkle and Papert 1990), where they see OO as potentially revolutionising programming methods and also challenging traditional ways of thinking and knowing.

Many other questions regarding knowledge are important to ask in the context of computer science, such as the crucial question: 'What does it mean to know CS and how could it be different?' As a member of the community of computer scientists I also want to ask: 'can we extend our view of knowledge within CS?' I see these questions as important for many reasons. For one thing, they relate to the learning of programming, which is one of the fundamentals of CS education[5]. These questions can also be important with regard to the under-representation of women within computing (Alsbjer 2001, Björkman 2002, Turkle and Papert 1990). A broadening of the meaning of 'knowing CS' could potentially accommodate greater diversity in the practices of CS as well as among its practitioners.

3.2 Paradigms[6] and metaphors in computer science

CS is often seen as growing out of and combining other disciplines: mathematics, natural science and engineering. Tensions between these roots exist within the discipline, they do in some sense compete with each other and to study their influence on knowledge production is important. Frances Grundy has raised questions concerning the 'fundamental nature' of CS, and has challenged these three major paradigms from feminist viewpoints (Grundy 1998, 2000a, 2000b).

The three important paradigms identified in Denning, Comer and Gries (1989), 'theory, abstraction and design' are in the ACM and IEEE-CS Computing Curricula (2001) complemented with the concept of 'professional practice'. This addition of practice can mark a potential change in the view of CS, having effects in education, as well as for the question 'What does it mean to know CS?'

New paradigms or metaphors for computing surface; the most important one today seems to be interactivity or interactionism. This concept has been discussed by a number of researchers. To take some examples: Lynn Andrea Stein talks about a new computational metaphor: 'computation as interaction' (Stein 1999) and Peter Wegner writes about 'why interaction is more powerful than algorithms' (Wegner 1997). From feminist perspectives Frances Grundy discusses a new conception of computing that she terms 'interactionism' (Grundy 2001), and Heidi Schelhowe sees interaction as a successful approach to development of software (Schelhowe 2004). Metaphors create images that are of importance in the knowledge processes, different metaphors call for different ways of thinking. Can new and different metaphors or paradigms also support other ways of knowing?

Paradigms or metaphors will take on a significant role in education. A rethinking of these could likely have significant impacts on what we teach and how we teach. I see the teaching of programming as being of particular importance. My feminist comments here are: What are the paradigms and views of knowledge, CS and programming behind programming courses? Is this visible in the courses or not recognised but taken for granted? If and how a different paradigm or metaphor can promote learning of programming is a question that ought to be of great interest to the whole computer science community.

3.3 Abstractions, formalisations and representations

In computer science abstractions, formalisations and representations are important. However, there is little discussion about the role of these and how they are used.

Representations, categorisations and thus simplifications are necessary but it is also important to look at how they are chosen. How is knowledge represented within software? I suggest that exploring the concept of situated knowledge could be useful: How can knowing situated in social and cultural contexts be represented so that its situated nature does not disappear into universalising and de-contextualising?

Another important issue for research is the role of abstraction in CS. Abstraction is held to enable methods to be value-free. Computer science focuses on understanding the world via a rationality based in the abstract (Stepulevage and Plumeridge 1998). However, the products of CS are very concrete. Why is abstract, formal and logical thinking and knowing seen as superior within CS? This question is connected to the issue of how CS relates to mathematics. I argue that, even though mathematics is important, CS is in many (maybe most) aspects not a mathematical discipline. In contrast, CS could be viewed as concrete science where important aspects are materiality and social practices (Clegg 2001).

Problems can arise when extending abstractions, formalisations and de-contextualisations too far out of their right environments, and applying them in other areas which do not readily lend themselves to these kinds of descriptions, e g. systems design. I believe that the use of (necessary) abstractions could easily lead to abstracting away also ideas, values and meaning. Thus abstractions, maybe without being noticed, diffuse into areas where they might not belong and make us forget to realise complexities and social and cultural circumstances.

Computer science does require a certain amount of abstract thinking. However, there is no doubt also need (and space!) for what Thelma Estrin calls 'concrete thinking,' by which she means practical involvement (Estrin 1996) and not least concrete learning. This could introduce new ideas for gaining knowledge that may make CS more relevant to a more diverse group of people. Knowledge about, and acceptance of, different types of knowledge construction (e.g. Alsbjer 2001) is essential in order to extend the view of knowledge within CS.

3.4 Naturalisation

Closely related to representations is the concept of 'naturalisation'[7]. In the process of naturalisation, something (an artefact, an idea, a concept etc) is stripped of its origins, context and consequences and is seen as given, as self-evident.

An example of naturalisation within computing is the computer itself. This becomes very clear in meetings with undergraduate students. To most of them 'computer' does not only mean an artefact, but also a very special artefact – the PC of today! They (and probably most of us) take the construction of the PC for given; not only in the way it appears but most of all in the von Neumann-model it builds on, and in the digital technology used. The historical contingency of the way that today's computer is constructed has disappeared. However, there is nothing 'natural' or given with the construction of the present-day computer, not even the digital technology used. For example, Heike Stach (Stach 1997), shows how von Neumann, in his design of the model, was greatly influenced by ideas within neurophysiology and psychology (behaviourism) of the time, and not the least by the emerging cybernetics and its ideas of self-regulation and control. He came to formulate his design in terms of the prevailing beliefs of that time concerning how the human brain works. Quite soon, however, the brain came to be thought of in terms of the computer. So – the computer is a brain, and the brain is a computer! The computer is thus an obvious case of naturalisation, where the choices that were made 60 years ago, and the reasons for these choices are, if not forgotten, at least never brought to the fore. A feminist question/comment to this is: What does this naturalisation mean not only for our understanding of the computer but also for our applications which are, at the deepest level (machine organisation), completely dependent on this model?

What consequences can naturalisation have? For one thing, it is easy to see how everything, from hardware to software tend to be taken as 'natural', as something given, once they have existed for some time. This means that the reasons why things are constructed in a certain way are forgotten and hence there is likely to be a tendency not to question whether this was actually 'the best way' to do something thus contributing to technical inertia. Designers, machines and software are made invisible, thus hiding the choices that have been made during the processes.

Christina Mörtberg (1997) points to how this not only affects artefacts but the making of these as well. Actions and processes are reduced to structures and things and technology becomes a naturalised object:

> In the processes, doings and actings are transformed, through collective oblivion, into 'taken-for-granted-ness', which entails that verbs become substantives, with reification as result. (Mörtberg 1997, p. 147, my translation)

Feminist analysis can contribute to de-naturalisations of the objects created, for example software, in order to understand what intentions and choices are built into the technology and can help bring back the active and process nature of technology creation. This will mean that the objects and the processes will become *situated* in the context where they were created, and this situating brings with it valuable knowledge about the different circumstances surrounding the creation.

3.5 Technology as culturally situated

All processes that produce knowledge are situated, socially, culturally and historically. Sandra Harding discusses this:

> Most engineers would argue that their technologies are not social at all in any meaningful sense of the term [...]. By excluding from their definition of a

229

"technology" not only its social applications and meanings, but also the knowledge of how to make it, use it and maintain it, they can perpetuate the illusion that technologies are not cultural at all. (Harding 1996, pp. 283-284)

To exclude social and cultural aspects from knowledge and artefacts relates to attempts at universalising, a process that Donna Haraway, along with naturalising, sees as connected to the 'view from nowhere', the disembodied knowledge. I find it hard to claim universal validity of products of computer science. Software is tightly interwoven with cultural and other pre-understandings of western culture (as mostly interpreted by Microsoft!). Just to mention one example, Introna and Nissenbaum (2000) have shown how the design of search engines is laden with value choices.

It is necessary to become aware of, even emphasize, that technology is both created by and creates cultures. Furthermore the cultures of science cannot be separated from the production of knowledge, they are closely intertwined.

4. Examples of Epistemological Views in CS with Feminist Comments

In order to highlight both some strongly prevalent views of knowledge in computer science, and to show how feminist epistemologies can interrogate these views and offer alternatives, I have chosen to do a close reading of a recent collection regarding the philosophy of science in CS: 'The Blackwell Guide to the Philosophy of Computing and Information', edited by Luciano Floridi (2004, below simply called GPCI[8]). This volume 'seeks to provide a critical survey of the fundamental themes, problems, arguments, theories and methodologies' (p. XII) in the philosophy of information. In this collection, many prominent scholars within CS as well as within related areas write about different aspects of the 'nature' of computing and information which thus give a picture (although of course not the whole or only picture) of CS.

The overall feeling I get when I read the GPCI, is that most of the authors (though not all, see below) assume a 'traditional' view of 'science – as – usual', supporting objectivism, realism and empiricism. These aspects are held out as foundational for computer science. For example, there is an almost total absence of the embodied subject. However, with a different epistemological point of departure, the picture can look very different. I argue that in this context, it is very appropriate to pose questions such as 'Whose knowledge?' and 'What knowledge?' as I will show examples of below.

I will also point to how quite different views of computing can be seen dependent on the position and background of the author. In GPCI, the authors who are closer to 'pure' computer science tend to lean towards a preference for the abstract, logical and formal, while those that discuss the broader aspects of information technology or the use of computers talk about embodiment, interaction, interpretation and hermeneutics. The views of these different authors reflect different philosophical traditions and different epistemologies.

4.1 Information, knowledge and truth

Information is a basic concept in the GPCI. A common definition of information, for example used by the editor and chief proponent of the new Philosophy of Information, Luciano Floridi, is that information is considered to have 'objective semantic content'. He defines objective as 'mind-independent or external, and informee-independent' (p. 42). This means that information exists independently of its encoding and transmission. This view tends to prioritise a view of information as 'object', rather than as process. Primarily, the informee-independence can be interpreted as 'independent of a particular receiver', or assuming a 'standard receiver', in which case the obvious feminist question becomes: who is this standard observer? However, Floridi also argues that an instance of information 'can have a semantics independently of any informee' (p. 45), or, in other words, information does not require an informed subject. Can information really be said to exist if there is no receiver, and if no communication is going on? Is information just lying around, waiting to be exposed? In a different view, it can be argued that information in itself always involves interpretation (see e.g. below on the chapter by Carl Mitcham). Floridi also points out that information requires that data is both well-formed and meaningful. But can data be meaningful without an informed subject? Or, is it meaningful for any receiver, independently of who this is?

I oppose this view of information. Instead, I take the position that information is (at least to a non-trivial extent) dependent on the position and situation of the informed subject and dependent upon his or hers (situated) interpretation. This means a view that focuses on the subject and the process instead of on the object. I agree that data can exist 'in itself' but I think this is doubtful when it comes to information.

Floridi argues in favour of a centralised approach to information, a view of information that has 'a core notion with theoretical priority' (p. 41). At the same time he makes a strong attack on what he terms 'decentralised or multicentred approaches' to information (p. 41[9]), according to which there is no key concept of information. Words like 'core notion' and 'priority' suggests a hierarchical and I would say also possibly authoritarian view. Floridi presupposes factual information, i.e. information about 'reality' – but what reality and whose reality does he talk about?

Carl Mitcham provides a different view of information in the chapter on 'Philosophy of Information Technology'. He sees information as much more related to humans and human activities such as language while in many other chapters information is strongly connected to computing and data processing.

Mitcham puts information and information technology into its historical context. He provides an in-depth interpretation of Martin Heidegger on IT. This view emphasises the processes of interpretation of information and the necessity of a more holistic perspective: 'all information technology is part of a larger life-world and cannot be understood apart from such an implicit whole.' (p. 333) Heidegger claims that information technology not only reveals, at the same time it conceals. This thinking casts another light on the use of formalisms and de-contextualising and one feminist question becomes: what is concealed and hidden from view, for example in software?

According to Fred Adams in the chapter on Knowledge, only two types of knowledge count: empirical and logical-mathematical. He furthermore claims that: 'It is uncontroversial that knowledge requires truth and belief.' (p. 228). The standard definition of knowledge in mainstream (analytical) philosophy is 'knowledge = true justifiable belief' but it is *not* uncontroversial when read from a feminist view, mostly because it contains that very tricky little word 'true'! Even if the term is used as meaning something limited and even contingent, it is problematic since it brings with it connotations of grand theories and universal, objective truth beyond the subject. But 'truth' is a carrier of values; it automatically carries with it the value of accepting something as true.

4.2 Abstractions

The computer scientist's world is a world of nothing but abstractions (Colburn, p. 322)

Taken out of its context, this is a stunning, and quite fearsome statement. However, it becomes clear in the rest of the chapter (Timothy Colburn: Methodology of Computer Science), that Colburn discusses the abstraction of the physical machine, of 'the mundane and tedious level of bits and processors' (p. 322) that computer scientists learn to abstract away from. This means some kind of 'bottom-up' abstraction in contrast to the 'top-down' abstraction involved in translating real-world problems to be solved into program systems. The kind of abstraction Colburn talks about is of course very important. However there is the question concerning where, at what level, shall these abstractions meet? At the level of design? Or at the implementation level? Somewhere a computer scientist must in the end consider the limitations of the machine and system software she/he has at hand, the machine cannot be completely abstracted away.

To Colburn abstractions are fundamental. He argues that 'software developers need to become conversant in the analytical tools of philosophers', such as logics, classifications, hierarchies 'and other convenient abstractions.' (p. 325). This again, reveals a view that prioritises the abstract, disembodied knowledge. I want to argue that that is *not* what software developers primarily need today, instead they need the competencies connected with the domains of use, for example to understand and account for complexity and heterogeneity among users.

Through many chapters of the book runs this thread of computer science as abstract, formal, logical and objective and its (supposedly strong) connection to mathematics. Is the world understandable and describable in formal terms? My position is that it is not. Whose world is captured in the formal methods/models? I believe a fundamental question becomes: what is computing mostly about: formal systems and abstractions or 'thinking things', i.e. people? The answer to this question will depend to a great deal on the view one takes not only of computer science, but also of technology on the whole and of course of one's epistemology.

Colburn (p. 319) gives an interesting example regarding two fundamentally different views on programs: one that sees computer programs as mathematical expressions and another that sees them from the perspective of functionality. These examples signal contrasting interpretations as to how computer programs ought to be designed, built and used. Which of these views dominates within different computer science communities? This is likely to depend on the particular context and history of the community in question. I believe that the formal view (mathematical expressions) used to be the strongest but is losing ground to the more use- and functionality oriented view. This can potentially mean an important twist in the view of what computer science is about.

4.3 The (dis?)embodied subject

In a section above, I discussed some feminist critique of AI. This critique can be applied to the view held out by Barry Smith in the chapter on Ontology. According to Smith, AI should concentrate on the task of 'formalizing the ontological features of the world itself, as this is encountered by adults engaged in the serious business of living.' (p. 160). But who are these adults? The AI researchers themselves? The idea that the experiences of a human being are independent of which human being is selected is seductive and very dangerous. Feminist scholars have shown that this 'archetype' for a human being is most often a white, western, even middle-class man and how well does he represent humanity?

This can be contrasted with the views expressed by Charles Ess in the chapter on Computer-mediated Communication and Human-Computer Interaction. He discusses the work of Terry Winograd and Fernando Flores[10]. They have explored how tacit, non-articulated understandings are built into computer technology. A design of a tool includes certain assumptions including world-views and 'tools thus embody and embed these assumptions while excluding others.' (p. 78). This is what Winograd and Flores express as 'in designing tools we are designing ways of being.' (quoted on p. 78). They see much of the world-view underlying design of computer artefacts as 'rationalistic' and instead want to highlight social interaction.

5. Concluding Remarks

As I wrote in the introduction, this article is full of questions. The questions have implications for practice, such as what we convey to students. What (implicit) assumptions and commonly accepted views underlie the knowledge processes in CS, e.g. (teaching of) programming? As for curricula and syllabi, what assumptions about knowledge and the subject do they presuppose? I believe that reflection around issues of knowledge is important for every discipline, especially for teaching and for meeting potentially new groups of students. Can we, as computer scientists, by becoming aware of our own views of knowledge (and hopefully also challenge these) become aware of, respect and accommodate, greater diversity amongst students and their backgrounds, interests, motives and understandings? Can we thus, in the long run, change our discipline into one that is more attractive to a broader range of students, for example women? I believe that this can be one contribution to the large task outlined by Maria Klawe that I deem to be of great importance for computer science to pursue (Klawe 2001, p. 68):

> We need non-nerds in computer science, so let's figure out the proper approaches to integrate their talents and perspectives into our field.

I strongly believe that one of the most important things for feminist research in technology in general as well as within computing is to work on broadening the concepts and understandings of technology. There is nothing inevitable about how computing is constructed, thus it can be re-visioned and re-conceptualised. I want to conclude by quoting Christina Mörtberg (Mörtberg 2003, pp. 57, 66-68):

> Feminism is a resource that can be used to formulate alternative goals, visions and dreams about our existence [...] Feminist research may contribute to re-configure, re-formulate or to give technoscience [...] other directions.

References

Adam, A. 1994, 'Who knows how? Who knows that? Feminist epistemology and artificial intelligence', in Adam A., Green E., Emms J. & Owen J. eds *Women, Work, and Computerization: Breaking Old Boundaries - Building New Forms*, North-Holland, Amsterdam

Adam, A. 1995, 'Artificial Intelligence and women's knowledge: what can feminist epistemologies tell us?' in *Women's Studies International Forum*, vol 18, no 4, pp. 407-415

Adam, A. 1998, *Artificial Knowing: Gender and the Thinking Machine*, Routledge, London & New York

Alsbjer, M. 2001, *Att hitta ingångar i formandet av programmeringskunskap [To find entrances in gaining programming knowledge]*, BSc thesis, Blekinge Institute of Technology, Karlskrona, http://www.bth.se/fou/cuppsats.nsf/all/038630f4efec13e5c1256a6a006be4a0/$file/kandarb MA.pdf [29 September 2004]

Björkman, C. 2002, *Challenging Canon: the Gender Question in Computer Science*, Licentiate thesis 04/02, Blekinge Institute of Technology, Karlskrona, http://www.bth.se/tks/teknovet.nsf/(WebFiles)/E6B9EC47A40B955BC1256F42003F5D72/$F ILE/Christinas%20lic.pdf [28 January 2005]

Bratteteig, T. & Verne, G. 1997, 'Feminist or merely critical?' in *Technology and Democracy: Gender, Technology and Politics in transition?*, eds I. Moser & G.H. Aas, Centre for Technology and Culture, University of Oslo, Oslo

Clegg, S. 2001, Theorising the machine: gender, education and computing, *Gender and Education*, vol 13, no 3, pp. 307-324

Colburn, T. (2004), 'Methodology of Computer Science' in *The Blackwell Guide to the Philosophy of Computing and Information*, ed L Floridi, Blackwell Publishing, Malden, Oxford, Carlton.

Computing Curricula 2001, *Computer Science Volume* 2001, http://www.sigcse.org/cc2001/ [29 September 2004]

Crutzen, C. & Gerrissen, J. 2000, Doubting the OBJECT World, in Women, Work and Computerization: *Charting a course to the future*, eds E. Balka & R. Smith, Kluwer Academic Publishers, Boston

Denning, P. Comer, D. & Gries, D. 1989, 'Computing as a discipline' in *Communications of the ACM*, vol 32, no 1 pp. 9-23

Estrin, T. 1996, 'Women's studies and computer science: their intersection' in *IEEE Annals of the history of computing*, vol 18, no 3, pp. 43-46

Floridi, L. (ed.) 2004, *The Blackwell Guide to the Philosophy of Computing and Information*, Blackwell Publishing, Malden, Oxford, Carlton

Grundy, F. 1998, 'Computer engineering: engineering what?' in *AISB Quarterly*, no 100, pp. 24-31

Grundy, F. 2000a, 'Mathematics in computing: a help or hindrance for women?', On CD-ROM from *Charting a course to the future. Proceedings of the 7th International IFIP [[TC9/WG9.1] Women, Work and Computerization Conference*, Vancouver, Canada

Grundy, Frances, 2000b: 'Where is the science in computer science?', on CD-ROM from *Charting a course to the future. Proceedings of the 7th International IFIP [[TC9/WG9.1] Women, Work and Computerization Conference*, Vancouver, Canada.

Grundy, F. 2001, 'A new conception of computing: interactionism replaces objectivism', paper presented at *GASAT 10 Conference*, Copenhagen, http://www.keele.ac.uk/depts/cs/staff/a.f.grundy/home/interact.htm. [1 May 2004]

Haraway, D. 1991, *Simians, Cyborgs and Women:The Reinvention of Nature*, Free Association Books, London

Harding, S. 1986, *The Science Question in Feminism*, Cornell University Press, Ithaca

Harding, S. 1987, *Feminism and Methodology*, Indiana University Press, Bloomington

Harding, S. 1996, 'Multicultural and global feminist philosophies of science: resources and challenges' in *Feminism, Science and the Philosophy of science*, eds. L. H. Nelson & J. Nelson, Kluwer Academic Publishers, Dordrecht

Introna, L. D. & Nissenbaum, H. 2000, 'Shaping the web: why the politics of search engines matter', *The Information Society* vol 16, no 3, pp. 169-185

Klawe, M. 2001, 'Refreshing the nerds', *Communications of the ACM*, vol 44, no 7, pp. 67-68

Mörtberg, C. 1997, *"Det beror på att man är kvinna"..., Gränsvandrerskor formas och formar informationsteknologi ["It's because one is a woman...", Transgressors are shaped and shape Information Technology]*, Ph.D dissertation 1997:12, Luleå University of Technology, Luleå

Mörtberg, C. 1999, 'Technoscientific challenges in feminism', *NORA (Nordic Journal of Women's Studies)*, Vol 7, no 1, pp. 47-62

Mörtberg, C. 2003, 'In dreams begins responsibility – feminist alternatives to technoscience' in *How do we make a difference?*, eds. C. Mörtberg, P. Elovaara & A. Lundgren, Luleå University of Technology, Luleå

Schelhowe, H. 2004, 'Computing science and software development: paradigms of mathematics, engineering, interaction', paper presented at *Symposium Gender and ICT: Strategies of inclusion*, 20th January, Brussels

Stach, H. 1997, 'The construction of the von Neumann concept as constituent for technical and organic computers', in *Women, Work and Computerization. Spinning a Web from Past to Future*, eds. F. Grundy, D. Köhler, V. Oechtering & U. Petersen, Springer-Verlag, Berlin

Stein, L. A. 1999, 'Challenging the computational metaphor: implications for how we think', *Cybernetics and Systems*, vol 30, pp. 473-507

Stepulevage, L. & Plumeridge, S. 1998, 'Women taking positions within CS', *Gender and Education*, vol 10, no 3, pp. 313-326

Trojer, L. 2002: *Genusforskning inom teknikvetenskap - en drivbänk för forskningsförändring [Gender research within Technoscience – a Hotbed for Research Transformation]*, Swedish National Agency for Higher Education, Stockholm

Turkle, S. & Papert, S. 1990, 'Epistemological pluralism: styles and voices within the computer culture', *Signs: Journal of Women in Culture and Society*, Vol 16, no 11

Wegner, P. 1997, Why Interaction is more powerful than algorithms,, *Communications of the ACM*, vol 40, no 5, pp. 80-91

Notes

1 I use the term 'computer science' (CS) in a broad sense, including software engineering and most parts of computer engineering. In all relevant aspects, I use this term as synonymous to the word 'computing'. I use CS to emphasise the discipline aspect, an aspect that is not always clear from the word 'computing'.

2 Lena Trojer gives a thorough account of feminist/gender research within science and technology in Trojer (2002). Christina Mörtberg has also developed and discussed these issues (e.g. Mörtberg 1999).

3 *Informatics is the term for computer science departments in universities in Norway, indicating that the discipline is defined more broadly than in traditional computer science departments.* (Bratteteig & Verne 1997, p. 59)

4 Note that what they criticise is the paradigm of object-orientation at a fairly high level, for example for making analysis of 'human worlds', *not* the low level object-oriented programming, used for 'realisation of software'.

5 Maria Alsbjer has shown how feminist theories of knowledge can be useful in studying the processes involved in learning to program (Alsbjer 2001).

6 I use the word 'paradigm' here in the loose sense that it is often used within CS, where it is often talked about for example different programming paradigms.

7 *By naturalization I mean stripping away the contingencies of an object's creation and its situated nature* (Star, S. L. 1994, 'Misplaced concretism and concrete situations: feminism, method and Information Technology' in *Gender-Nature-Culture Feminist Research Network Working paper No 11*, Odense University, Odense).

8 If nothing else is said, the references below are to pages in GPCI.

9 *Thus, philosophers like Baudrillard, Foucault, Lyotard, McLuhan, Rorty and Derrida, are united by what they dismiss, if not challenge: the predominance of the factual* (p. 41).

10 Winograd, T. & Flores, F. 1986, *Understanding Computers and Cognition: A New Foundation for Design*, Addison-Wesley, Reading, MA.

18 Women's Pleasure in Computing

Hilde Corneliussen

Department of Humanistic Informatics, University of Bergen, Norway

Abstract

Enthusiasm over technology is found among men. Or, at least, that is the impression we get from the main body of earlier research, which leaves us with an understanding of men as computer enthusiasts, while women are more reluctant and 'rational' in their relation to the computer. In this paper I will argue that women do in fact enjoy working with computers. The empirical material is from a study of a group of students taking a computer course. We will meet women who enjoy working with computers, and explore how they express their pleasure in relation to the computer. Contrary to earlier claims that 'computing is incompatible with being a girl', we will find that many of the 21 women in this study are not afraid to articulate their pleasure in computing.

1. Enthusiasm about Technology is Found among Men

Studies of women's experiences with computers have often focused on problems women encounter being a minority in a male dominated arena, or on how women negotiate being *both* a woman *and* having a close relationship to computers (Corneliussen 2002a; Mörtberg 1997; Levold 2001; Nordli 2003; Kvaløy 1999; Lagesen Berg 2000; Langsether 2001). It has been reported that women are not particularly interested in the computer itself. They are not interested in the technical aspects of computers or technical subjects, often regarded as the most important subjects in computer education. Women rather see the computer as a tool, and find its usefulness and its social aspects interesting (Håpnes 1992). And women use the computer primarily for communication and obtaining information from the Internet, or for writing (Håpnes & Rasmussen 2003). Studies of women's relationships with the computer leave us with an impression that women use the computer because they find it useful or necessary, not because they want to or because they like it (Aune 1996). Studies of men however, have directed attention towards men's fascination with the technology and their absorption in computers (Turkle 1984). One such male figure is the hacker, and one of the most famous descriptions of the hacker life style comes from Weizenbaum's description of the 'compulsive programmers' from 1976, as

> bright young men of dishevelled appearance, often with sunken glowing eyes [...] oblivious to their bodies and to the world in which they move. They exist, at least when so engaged, only through and for computers (Weizenbaum 1976).

This image has not changed much since 1976 (cf. Nordli 2003), and the hacker figure has come to represent a typical male relationship with the computer. In this way, men are not only perceived as skilled computer users, but also fascinated by and enthusiastic towards the technology, in contrast to women (cf. Sørensen 2002). It seems that enthusiasm about technology is mainly found among men and, while male enthusiasts have been an interesting topic to researchers, women's feelings for the technology is rarely discussed and, if so, mostly connected to dislikes, anxiety or reticence (Turkle 1988). But is it true that women are not enthusiastic about computers? The aim of this paper is to look for women's positive experiences with computers. Through a study of 21 female computer students we will explore how they express joy and pleasure about computing.

1.1 Men's pleasure – a barrier for women?

Over the last decades, the gender gap within computing has caused worries and has given rise to attempts to explain why women do not seem to *want* to enter the field of computing. It has been claimed that technology is linked to masculinity, that it is 'embedded' in a masculine culture, and that it acts as a signal of masculinity, and is thus perceived as incompatible with femininity (Turkle 1988; Wajcman 1991; Grint & Gill 1995; Håpnes & Rasmussen 2003). The association between masculinity and technology has been one explanation of women's absence from computing. Men's relationship to technology has often been referred to in terms of 'intimacy' and 'love' (Turkle 1984; Hacker 1989), and the special pleasure in technology found among men has also been identified as a barrier for women.

In their study of 'men's love affair with technology', Faulkner and Kleif claim that '[e]ngineering may be one of the most pleasurable of occupations' (Faulkner & Kleif 2003, pp. 296-297). They found that men express a greater pleasure in technology than women do. Men's satisfaction is explained by technology as a logical and rule driven system that they feel they can control, in contrast to the impossibility of controlling unpredictable human beings. Turkle claims that while women tend to be focused on people, men are more focused on objects, and these men 'come to define themselves in terms of competence, skill, in terms of the things they can control' (Turkle 1988, p. 44). Faulkner and Kleif argue that men's pleasure in technology reproduces male dominance within engineering, partly because the (assumed) male focus on technology stands out as incompatible with women's (assumed) interest in people. Men's intimacy with technology has been described as 'sensual absorption, spiritual connection, emotional comfort, and aesthetic, even erotic, pleasures' (Faulkner & Kleif 2003, p. 297, cf. Hacker 1989). Men's pleasure becomes a signal that computing is a special masculine field, and in order to 'preserve' their femininity, girls and women reject the intimacy with the computer (Håpnes & Rasmussen 2003; Turkle 1988). The negative effect of men's pleasure has also been reported among women who have chosen to study computing. Margolis and Fisher found in their study at Carnegie Mellon

University that women started their career as students in computer science with both interest and pleasure in working with computers. However, women experienced that the male students appeared to have more knowledge than them, and interpreted this as being 'more interested'. This made some of the women conclude that they 'were just not interested *enough*', and they lost their motivation to continue with computer education (Margolis & Fisher 2002). It seems that men's and boys' fascination for the technology makes women refrain from portraying their own relationship with the computer in terms of interest or pleasure (Aune 1996).

Even though very few studies have focused more directly on women's pleasure, there are two examples from Norway. The first example is a quantitative study of motivation among students at a computer course at the Norwegian University of Science and Technology (NTNU) in the latter part of the 1990s. Here it was found that both men and women enjoyed the course when they felt that they could master the assignments and the technical demands (Berg & Kvaløy 1998). It is perhaps no surprise that mastering increases the comfort and feeling of wellbeing, and this is also the case for the women we will meet shortly. The second study explores female computer enthusiasts (Nordli 2003). Nordli, who wanted to find *female hackers*, did not find any women who agreed to call themselves hackers, but she did find female computer enthusiasts. She found 'professionals', 'IRC-babes' and 'geek-grrls', women who more or less dedicated their lives to working and playing with computers. Nordli's study demonstrates that female computer enthusiasts do indeed exist, but it also demonstrates how these women have to negotiate the dominant expectation that women do not have computer interest or skills. Some of the women who participated in a group of computer enthusiasts even used this expectation themselves, worrying that new women entering the group were 'stereotypical' girls who were not really interested in computers, and therefore could undermine their own position in the group (Nordli 2003). In other words, they did not expect to find other women with the same intense relation to the computer that they experienced themselves.

1.2 Background and empirical material

The women we will meet here were neither 'professionals', 'geek-grrls' nor 'IRC-babes'. They were students in a first term computer course at the Department of Humanistic Informatics at the University of Bergen, Norway. All of them had used a computer before, but most of them described themselves as inexperienced. Their motivation for attending the course varied, from being curious, to not wanting to be an 'illiterate' anymore, to feeling that they needed computer knowledge. One started because her girlfriend had started, while others took the course while waiting for admission to other courses. They did not spend all their leisure time working or playing with computers, and they did not plan a career within computing.

These women were part of the fieldwork I did during my Ph.D. in the period 1998-2002.[1] In this project, I followed 7 male and 21 female students through the first term of a computer course. The empirical material is based on weekly email communication and observations of the informants in the computer lab during a period of three months, as well as interviews at the end of the term. The informants were asked questions about their past and present experience with computers, as well as their perception and experience with gender being associated with computers.

In my Ph.D. thesis (Corneliussen 2002a) I discuss how expectations towards men's and women's relations to computers create certain gendered positions, and how the male and female students relate to these positions when they create their own relationships with computers. All the informants supported one particular understanding of gender and computing, a dominating or hegemonic discourse of computing, which describes some basic expectations towards men's and women's relationships with the computer. Men are expected to have more interest, experience and knowledge about computers than women. Men are expected to be fascinated by the technology, and they are associated with computer games, programming and technical tasks, while women are associated with tasks like communication, information and writing. The study demonstrates in many ways that women are 'the others' in relation to the masculine associations of computer technology. What puzzled me was that, contrary to what we could expect, the women expressed great pleasure in their relationships with computers. And besides: how could 'the others' (women) express so much pleasure in relation to something that was not 'theirs'?

2. Women's Pleasure in Computing

Most of the women expressed pleasure about a wide range of computer activities, and some were thrilled that they had the courage to attend a computer course. The pleasure they expressed is perhaps not surprising, since they all had chosen to attend a computer course. Still, it is not an obvious reaction, and there were a few women who expressed more dissatisfaction than pleasure. But these are the exceptions rather than the rule among the 21 women. Shouts of joy were more or less daily observable in the computer lab, and the sounds gave clear evidence of pleasure in working with computers: 'It was very fun when the code passed through and I managed exactly the things I had worked with for a long time... Oh yes, many cheers of joy in the computer lab then...' [Ingunn]. As already mentioned, the connection between mastery and pleasure was also evident among these students, and there were no obvious gendered differences in this respect. However, the cheers of joy were much more apparent among the women than among the men. It was mostly women who drew attention to themselves in the computer lab with their laughter, or they made the whole class gather around them, showing them some funny things they had made on the computer. In the following, we will explore how the women articulated their pleasure in computing, first by looking at what it meant to be a woman in a computer course. Second, we will explore what it meant to *these* women to attend the course, before we turn to the activities the women found especially pleasurable.

2.1 The unexpected female computer students

Women are not expected to be found in large numbers on a computer course, and many of the women were surprised to find a majority of female students in Humanistic Informatics.[2] They saw it as an evidence of a 'women want, women can' attitude among women, and claimed that it improved their self-confidence. The female lecturers were also seen as positive role models: 'I think that it is very positive that there are female lecturers. It gives inspiration and it helps the self-esteem. When a lie is repeated time after time, you believe it ('Girls are lousy with computers')' [Marte]. The presence of women helped to repudiate the 'lie'. It also affected their perception of computing: 'Earlier I had the perception that the computer culture was masculine, but I have changed my opinion on this, perhaps because of the big majority of women in this course' [Turid]. The fact that female students were in the majority was an important factor in enabling the women not to see themselves as 'misplaced': 'the girls encourage each other, you see that the choice [of education] is not quite as strange for a girl, rather the opposite; here, the boys are in a clear minority' [Bente]. It seems that the female majority had a positive effect on the women's well-being as computer students.

Even though being a female computer student was not an expected position, this was not necessarily seen as negative, and some of the women even thought that they had certain advantages *because* they were women: '[T]he expectations towards a girl who is doing things with a computer is not as big as those towards boys. [...] the surroundings get more impressed if a girl manages something in the computer field' [Kathrine]. They felt that they got more positive attention than boys and men working with computers. However, this clearly is double edged; on the one hand it is a well-meaning and positive encouragement while, on the other hand, it points to the low expectations people generally have of them.

2.2 What does it mean to attend a computer course?

The female majority might have made it easier for these women, but, what did it actually mean to them to be a computer student? 'It means incredible much for me to have started on a course like this, since I lacked all the basic knowledge, I didn't know anything! Now I can do thousands of things that I couldn't do before' [Mette]. Mette felt that she was 'finally doing something useful', and after only a few weeks, she felt more confident and had learnt a lot. However, this surprised her: 'This term is the best term I have had at the university. It exceeded all my expectations, [I] thought it would be more "incomprehensible", if you see what I mean, but it was actually possible for me to absorb the knowledge, in spite of a lousy starting point' [Mette]. Even though the computer was not new to Mette, she described her starting point as 'lousy', and she was surprised, not only that she actually managed to learn something, but also about her new and intimate relation to the computer, and she claimed that 'it has become a tool that I am addicted to! You would never believe this about me!' [Mette]

Lillian also was surprised by her new knowledge. She was one of the discontented women, striving hard to learn. She claimed that it is natural that women understand less about the computer than men, and she used gender to explain her own relationship to computing: 'I don't understand any of that [computer programming], because I'm a woman!' [Lillian]. However, she did learn something on the course. She told about how her husband, who 'didn't have a clue' about computers, kept 'messing things up' – in the way she used to do. But now she could fix it, and illustrated her pleasure by exclaiming happily: 'I know something, I know something' [Lillian]. She was excited, not about any special things she had learnt, but about how she actually *had* learnt something about computers.

Another woman fulfilled a dream by attending the course: 'I have always wanted to learn a little bit more about the computer. I have sort of seen that as very unattainable, but when I got in here [on the course] it became attainable' [Tone]. Tone was quite new to the computer and she worked hard to understand it. Yet, she maintained her positive attitude and was almost grateful because she finally learnt more about computers.

Several of the women compared computer knowledge to literacy: 'To me it was a conscious decision to enrol in a computer class. I did not want to continue being the illiterate that I felt like' [Marte]. Being literate is not only a matter of being able to read or write – or in this case, being able to use the computer, but it can also act as a symbol for being able to participate in society. To Marte, the computer course meant that she was about to acquire skills that appear to be necessary in our society. Another woman pointed to how her new computer skills affected her social position in another way: 'We haven't had much practical work with hardware, but a little theory, and now I feel that I am more prepared when men talk about RAM and processors etc. I am really happy that I took this course' [Anne]. Also Anne claimed that she had become better 'socially equipped'; she had become able to participate in the men's discussions about hardware. While Anne expressed her pleasure in relation to a male community, Helga expressed her pleasure in relation to other women: 'I have advantages because I'm considered to be "fresh thinking" and courageous in choosing subject [...] a subject where you sort of depart from women's traditional areas, and at the same time go into one of the most important areas of the future' [Helga]. Helga felt that she benefited from being an 'untraditional' woman by attending a computer course. To move outside fields that women traditionally have been engaged in is part of the post-modern project, according to Annfelt, and by doing so, women signal that they are 'post-traditional actors' who have internalised the message about an expanded 'room of manoeuvre' for women (Annfelt 1999). Helga had made an effort both to learn and to like working with computers before, but she had not been 'turned on':

> I started at the bottom when it comes to computer knowledge – but I feel that with every new day I master new things [...] It feels like a new world has opened up to me ... and every day I think 'How on earth is it possible to cope without knowing what I know today!??' It has to be a feeling close to something like going from being illiterate to being able to read... [Helga]

Even though Helga had used a computer – and attended courses in order to get herself 'updated', she described her starting point at the beginning of the term as 'at the bottom'. Also she compared computer knowledge to literacy and described how it felt like entering a new world filled with indispensable knowledge, and she exclaimed:

I think that I have become addicted to the computer!!! Earlier I did not think it was either appealing or attractive – but now I can hardly manage a day without it... I use it as a tool both for learning and in daily life. It has become an important source of pleasure... [I] feel very different about it now, after having learnt how it works. It is not something distant and difficult, but a useful tool – and not the least a thing that I can manipulate and use as I want to. I am addicted – but I have the power over it – not the reverse... [Helga]

Helga experienced a 'revolution' in relation to the computer, and it had become a fascinating tool for both work and pleasure. Contrary to what we have seen in other studies (Turkle 1988; Håpnes & Rasmussen 2003), she had no reservations about calling herself 'addicted'. Also other women had experienced a 'revolution' in relation to the computer. Like Åse, who did not really like computers:

I have got a much better relation to the computer now. It has in fact come so far that I miss it after one day of absence. Before, I hated everything that had to do with computers. Couldn't understand that anyone would sit down in front of the machine voluntarily. I think different now. I have in fact become fond of the machine. [Åse]

Åse started on the course because her girlfriend had started and, although she was sceptical in the start, she had '*in fact*' – as if it was highly unlikely – become fond of the computer.

Sara had her revolutionary turning point a couple of years before she started on the computer course. Before this point, she saw computers as 'nonsense and rubbish' and she strongly rejected that she would ever use a computer. Her first contact with a computer changed this completely:

I had my first meeting with computers when I attended [another course in the late 90s]. A friend of mine introduced me to a small Mac which I borrowed. I used it writing assignments at the course. I fell in love with the machine and dreamt about it at night and looked forward to the next session. Even today I miss the printer's beautiful melody and its rhythm when it fetched a paper and printed on it. [Sara]

In spite of her previous negative attitude, Sara experienced the first meeting with a computer as so intense that she described it as a love story. Her fascination seems to have been directed towards the beauty of the technology itself. One of her motivations for attending the computer course was that she wanted to learn more about how to use a computer in a creative way, and she had fantasies about how she could use the computer, especially programming, as a creative tool. She described her experience with the computer almost as a voyage of discovery and compared it to a craft: 'It has resemblances to a craft, right – the medium itself wants something – you don't have complete freedom, but you can do something with it if you know how to do it' [Sara]. In Sara's articulations, the computer had become something more than 'technique and logic'. She both enjoyed the intimate relation to the machine as well as the creative aspect, just as it has been found among hackers and other male computer enthusiasts (Turkle 1988; Aune 1996; Håpnes 1996; Hacker 1989; Faulkner & Kleif 2003). However, contrary to the pleasure found among male enthusiasts, it was not the controllable and predictable aspects of the technology that fascinated Sara, but rather the unpredictable – the things she did not yet know, which could, because they were still unknown, hide inconceivable possibilities.

As we can see, women express in various ways how joining a computer course meant a lot to them. According to the hegemonic discourse, women are neither expected to be interested, nor have experience or computer skills, and many of them were surprised that they could manage it and that they actually found it interesting. However, when they reached this stage, they were totally absorbed and 'addicted'.

The women in this study expressed pleasure, gratitude and pride because they had attended a computer course. But what is it about the computer that these women like? In the next section we will explore which activities they described as their favourite activities.

2.3 What *do* women actually like?

Girls like to use the Internet for communication and information and, according to earlier research, they like to use the computer to write text (cf. Håpnes & Rasmussen 2003). Also the informants, both men and women, described these things as typical activities for girls and women. None of the informants, however, claimed that they enjoyed using the computer for writing, but a few of the women pointed to the Internet as interesting: 'It's fun to see the advantages of using the computer as communication – news groups and chatting – this is new to me!' [Helga]. Interest in the Internet was also expressed by the men in this study, and it is not possible to see a particular gender difference here. There are however other aspects and activities that the women described as exciting and interesting. A few of them told how they had been hooked on computer games and used games as relaxation in between other activities [Lise, Turid]. Women do play computer games and they enjoy it (cf. Nordli 2003). However, to some women it seems important to express their pleasure as moderate compared to men's pleasure (Håpnes & Rasmussen 2003). I asked the women in one of the interview groups what they did in order to have fun with the computer. One of them started to laugh, as if I had said something unthinkable, and suggested that perhaps boys might have fun with the computer. We continued talking about computer games, and the three women agreed that games were fun, but they were also a 'boy-thing'. The three women admitted using games and that they found it pleasurable, but they also emphasised that they did not spend as much time or money as boys playing games. They made it a 'typical girl' thing to have a moderate experience of pleasure as a contrast to boys.[3] It seems that they relate to the hegemonic discourse and the different pleasures it makes 'available' to men and women; these women might play, but they described themselves as less fascinated than men.

Not all of the women played games, but they found pleasure in things they worked with on the computer course, including activities associated with men in the hegemonic discourse. To some of the women it was precisely this new and unfamiliar knowledge which seemed most attractive:

> The fun part is when you manage something which earlier seemed to be 'totally inconceivable', like the HTML code and programming. You wait in excitement when you save it and check if you get it right, have to work for a long time to manage, until you get tired sick, but you sort of can't give up, and when you manage it, it is only joy and happiness [...] There are perhaps more downs than ups, but the positive moments count twice as much!!! [Mette]

To Mette, programming had appeared as 'totally inconceivable' before, and she emphasised that the positive experiences overshadowed the toil. Kathrine also described her pleasure in finally managing something: '[...] on that programming assignment, when you sort of understood more and then it was like 'hallelujah' [...] I wouldn't have believed I could make it, but .. I could' [Kathrine]. As already mentioned, pleasure and mastery go hand in hand, and many of the cheers of joy in the computer lab were undoubtedly connected to these moments, and many of the women said this in relation to things they had not expected to master.

Many of the women also expressed a special pleasure when they talked about having knowledge that *others* did not expect them to have. Programming was described as one of the activities most exclusively associated with men:

> Maybe that is why I want to work with programming, because it is so masculine [...] I feel sort of as if I were in a world that's a little bit forbidden. [...] Very few expect that a woman can do programming. That is probably why I find it especially exciting. [...] I think there is some kind of status symbol connected to it. [Bente]

Bente was fascinated by the forbidden world of programming – the world where women do not have an obvious position, and she also suggested that she gained authority from having knowledge in a male dominated field. Another woman told how she enjoyed having the skills that impressed her girlfriends: 'I think it is much cooler to come and fix the computer [compared to programming]. A girlfriend of mine was pretty impressed yesterday when I defragmented her hard drive' [Marte]. The person fixing a computer is normally a man, according to Marte, and she enjoyed having acquired these skills herself, because she could both surprise and impress others.

It has been claimed that technology is something men more or less can 'put on' to activate the signal of masculinity (Lie 2003, p. 259). It has also been claimed that technology can not do the same for women: 'Women's identity is not enhanced by their use of machines' (Wajcman 1991, p. 89). The women in this study do not seem to have acquired masculinity through their engagement with technology. It is however clear that the computer did affect these women's identities, by providing them with 'status', or changing them into 'non-traditional' and 'fresh thinking' women.

3. Conclusion

If we see the women's expressions of pleasure in relation to the hegemonic discourse, we can first of all see that they crossed a gendered border by being engaged with computers. According to the discourse, they are 'the others', about to find their way into the new, exciting and 'forbidden' field of computing. Second, the women were surprised that they actually had acquired knowledge that they neither thought they would enjoy nor be able to master. Third, it seems like the women felt that they gained access to some of the status that they associated with computing as a masculine field – especially the most 'exclusive' masculine areas, like programming and the technical part of the computer. And last, it seems like the women used their new knowledge and its status to both surprise and impress others.

Their pleasure can be seen as a result of a dissolved discursive understanding; computers are not incomprehensible or boring for women but, on the contrary, both fun and interesting. They discovered that they *could* manage and they *could* learn. And when they finally realised this, they enjoyed working with computers, almost as if they were 'starved' of computer knowledge. Cynthia Cockburn has documented how men's exclusion of women through monopolisation of technical know-how has been a strategy to preserve the male dominance in technological contexts (Cockburn 1988 (1985)). In relation to computers during the period of this study, it is not men's (intentional) monopolising which excludes women, but rather a hegemonic discourse that women have internalised, which gives guidelines for understanding gender and computers. If we had also met the male informants from this group of students, we would have seen that the women's articulations about pleasure were much more expressive than the articulations found among the men. We would also have seen that the men did not articulate pleasure about having 'discovered' that the computer, after all, is interesting. Also the men expressed the joy of having knowledge in a masculine field, not as a 'forbidden' field, but rather as a more original masculine field that they seemed to feel that they should have been familiar with in the first place.

Gender is not the only factor affecting individuals' articulations of pleasure, but it clearly influenced how these men and women expressed their pleasure in computing. The reported incompatibility between women and technology might have had the result that girls' and women's pleasure in technology is underrepresented. Women might enjoy playing with computers, but some women moderate their pleasure compared to men's pleasure when they talk about their own relationship with the computer. However, as we have seen, this is clearly changing, and a number of women in this study were not afraid to articulate their pleasure, joy and addiction, or even love of the computer. When we look at how the women expressed their pleasures in relation to the computer, we do not see an image of reticent women, as we could expect from earlier research. It is evident that, even though very few women participate in men's technological communities, as Faulkner and Kleif claim (Faulkner & Kleif 2003), there is no reason to underestimate women's fascination and pleasure in learning more about computers.

The fact that women do enjoy working with computers – *and* express it – could mean that the 'gendered code' of computers is about to change (Annfelt 1999, p. 370). However, one of the things that does not seem to change very fast is the *perception* about women's relations to computers. In some of the latest initiatives to recruit women to computer education in Norway it has been emphasised that 'computing is about communication' – a skill especially associated with women (Lagesen 2003). We have met women with different motivations for attending a computer course, and for quite a few of them it seems to have been more of a coincidence than a deliberate plan to end up with an intimate relationship with the computer. And perhaps one of the informants is right in saying: 'I think that some [women] have to be tempted to discover that it can be fun working with [computers]' [Lise]. However, by inviting women into computer education because they are expected to be good at 'something else' (communication) confirms the discursive description of women as 'not really interested in computers' (cf. Nordli 2003; Corneliussen 2003a). One of the challenges we face today is that the stories about pleasure in computing do not seem to 'stick' to women; there are not many 'cultural stories' about women's pleasure in computing readily available for women to identify with. The women we have met here might not represent women in general, but they do however portray *real* stories about women's pleasure in computing – stories that hopefully can be available as cultural stories to future female computer enthusiasts. We have seen here that women enjoy working with computers, and they are not afraid to express this. For the future, why not invite women to computer education by telling them that 'you might even fall in love with the technology!'

References

Annfelt, T. 1999, *Kjønn i utdanning. Hegemoniske posisjoner og forhandlinger om yrkesidentitet i medisin- og faglærerutdanning*, NTNU, Senter for kvinneforskning 2/99, Trondheim.

Aune, M. 1996, 'The Computer in Everyday Life. Patterns of Domestication of a New Technology', in M. Lie & K. H. Sørensen (eds), *Making Technology Our Own?*, Scandinavian University Press, pp. 91-120.

Berg, V. L. & Kvaløy, K. 1998, *En kvantitativ undersøkelse av trivsel og studiemotivasjon blant førsteårsstudentene ved linjen for datateknikk, NTNU, samt en evaluering av fagmodulen "Kjenn ditt fag"*, Norges teknisk-naturvitenskapelige universitet, Fakultet for fysikk, informatikk, og matematikk. Institutt for datateknikk og informasjonsvitenskap, Trondheim, 8.

Cockburn, C. 1988 1985, *Machinery of Dominance. Women, Men, and Technical Know-how*, Northeastern University Press, Boston.

Corneliussen, H. 2002a, *Diskursens makt - individets frihet: Kjønnede posisjoner i diskursen om data (The power of discourse - the freedom of individuals: Gendered positions in the discourse of computing)*, Dr. art. thesis, Dep. of humanistic informatics, University of Bergen.

Corneliussen, H. 2002b, 'The multi-dimensional stories of the gendered users of ICT', in A. Morrison, (ed.) *Researching ICTs in context*, vol. 3/2002, InterMedia Report, Oslo, pp. 161-184.

Corneliussen, H. 2003a, 'Konstruksjoner av kjønn ved høyere IKT-utdanning i Norge', *Kvinneforskning*, vol. 27, no. 3, pp. 31-50.

Corneliussen, H. 2003b, 'Male positioning strategies in relation to computing', in M. Lie (ed.), *He, She and IT Revisited. New Perspectives on Gender in the Information Society*, Gyldendal Akademisk, pp. 103-134.

Corneliussen, H. 2004, "I don't understand computer programming, because I'm a woman!' Negotiating gendered positions in a Norwegian discourse of computing', in K. Morgan, C. A. Brebbia, J. Sanchez & A. Voiskounsky (eds), *Human Perspectives in the Internet Society - Culture, Psychology and Gender*, WIT Press, Southampton, Boston, pp. 173-182.

Faulkner, W. & Kleif, T. 2003, "I'm No Athlete [but] I Can Make This Thing Dance!' - Men's Pleasures in Technology', *Science, Technology, & Human Values*, vol. 28, no. 2, Spring 2003, pp. 296-325.

Grint, K. & Gill, R. 1995, 'The Gender-Technology Relation: Contemporary Theory and Research', in K. Grint & R. Gill (eds), *The Gender-Technology Relation*, Taylor & Francis, London, pp. 1-28.

Hacker, S. 1989, *Pleasure, power, and technology. Some tales of gender, engineering, and the cooperative workplace*, Unwin Hyman, Boston.

Håpnes, T. 1992, 'Hvordan forstå mannsdominansen i datafaget? En dekonstruksjon av fag- og kjønnskultur', in T. Annfelt & G. Imsen (eds), *Utdanningskultur og kjønn*, NTNU, Senter for teknologi og samfunn 3/92, Trondheim, pp. 155-183.

Håpnes, T. 1996, 'Not in Their Machines. How Hackers Transform Computers into Subcultural Artefacts', in M. Lie & K. H. Sørensen (eds), *Making Technology Our Own?*, Scandinavian University Press, pp. 121-150.

Håpnes, T. & Rasmussen, B. 2003, 'Gendering technology. Young girls negotiating ICT and gender', in M. Lie (ed.), *He, She and IT Revisited. New Perspectives on Gender in the Information Society*, Gyldendal Akademisk, pp. 173-197.

Kvaløy, K. 1999, *Fortellinger om moderne flinke lekne ungdomsjenters forhold til datategnologi. En kvalitativ studie av datateknologiens roll i ungdomsjenters dannelse av kjønnsidentitet*, NTNU, Senter for kvinneforskning 3/99, Trondheim.

Lagesen Berg, V. A. 2000, *Firkanter og rundinger. Kjønnskonstruksjoner blant kvinnelige dataingeniørstudenter ved NTNU*, NTNU, Senter for kvinneforskning 3/00, Trondheim.

Lagesen, V. A. 2003, 'Advertising computer science to women (or was it the other way around?)', in M. Lie (ed.), *He, She and IT Revisited. New Perspectives on Gender in the Information Society*, Gyldendal Akademisk, Oslo, pp. 69-102.

Langsether, H. 2001, *Behov og barrierer for jenter på informatikkstudiet*, Senter for kvinne- og kjønnsforskning, NTNU, Trondheim.

Levold, N. 2001, "Doing gender' in Academia. The domestication of an information-technological researcher-position', in H. Glimell & O. Juhlin (eds), *The Social Production of Technology. On everyday life with things*, BAS Publisher, Gothenburg, pp. 133-158.

Lie, M. 2003, 'The new Amazons. Gender symbolism on the Net', in M. Lie, (ed.) *He, She and IT Revisited. New Perspectives on Gender in the Information Society*, Gyldendal Akademisk,

Oslo.

Margolis, J. & Fisher, A. 2002, *Unlocking the clubhouse. Women in computing*, MIT Press, Cambridge, Mass.

Mörtberg, C. 1997, *"Det beror på att man är kvinna..." Gränsvandrerskor formas och formar informationsteknologi*, Luleå tekniska Universitet.

Nordli, H. 2003, *The Net is Not Enough. Searching for the female hacker*, dr.polit.-avhandling, Institutt for sosiologi og statsvitenskap, NTNU, Trondheim.

Sørensen, K. H. 2002, 'Kommunikasjon.no', *Kvinneforskning*, vol. 2002, no. 2, pp. 5-9.

Turkle, S. 1984, *The second self. Computers and the human spirit*, Simon and Schuster, New York.

Turkle, S. 1988, 'Computational Reticence. Why Women Fear the Intimate Machine', in C. Kramarae (ed.), *Technology and women's voices. Keeping in touch*, Routledge & Kegan Paul, New York, pp. 41-61.

Wajcman, J. 1991, *Feminism confronts technology*, Polity Press, Cambridge.

Weizenbaum, J. 1976, *Computer power and human reason. From judgment to calculation*, Freeman, San Francisco.

Notes

1 The empirical material discussed here has its origin in the Ph.D.project; (Corneliussen 2002a). See also Corneliussen (2004) for an overview of the analysis of the informants' positioning strategies, Corneliussen (2002b; 2002a) for a discussion about theory and method, and Corneliussen (2003b) for a discussion about the male informants.

2 There have been between 60 and 70% female students in undergraduate courses at Department of Humanistic Informatics since the last part of the 1990s.

3 Håpnes and Rasmussen have reported a similar incident from an interview with two school girls, where one of them tells that she enjoys playing computer games. The other girl is more sceptical and refers to games as a thing for boys. The game-playing girl immediately moderates her story, claiming that she does not play *that* often (as boys do), and not for *that* long, and not alone (Håpnes & Rasmussen 2003). This illustrates that girls might have fun with computers, but in this case it was out of line with the unwritten rules for being a young girl.

19 Women's training revisited: developing new learning pathways for women IT technicians using a holistic approach

Debbie Ellen, Clem Herman

Department of Information and Communication Technologies,
The Open University

Abstract

While there have been many initiatives which have attempted to improve the numbers of professional women in computing, there has been little focus so far on women who work as IT technicians. This paper reports on a study of the lives and careers of a group of women working either in the IT industry or in other sectors as IT technicians. The women were participants in a supported training programme that formed one strand of the JIVE[1] project, a UK wide initiative that was set up to tackle gender segregation in the engineering, construction and technology sectors. The paper begins with a review of a number of strategies that have been used to try and tackle the issues facing women in IT, highlighting the role and approach of women's vocational training centres. Then, using qualitative data from two sets of interviews we explore barriers facing women in technical IT occupations including gender stereotyping and difficulty in gaining qualifications. We then examine the impact of the training programme, exploring the role of a women only learning environment and accompanying support measures, in tackling gender segregation in this sector.

1. Introduction

For many years those of us working around gender and ICT have pondered over the question of why are there so few female computer scientists (Spertus 1991). While the focus on the recruitment, education and careers of computer science students, graduates and professionals has been important in trying to tackle the perpetuation of male dominance in this field, this paper addresses the training and careers of IT technicians who face many of the same issues as those at higher professional levels, but who as yet have received very little attention within the academic literature. Indeed it may be from the experiences of women working as IT technicians, in jobs that suggest a greater fluidity in terms of gender boundaries, that we can gain valuable insight into the broader challenges for women in ICT.

The JIVE project was set up in 2002 in order to tackle gender segregation in a range of occupations in the UK, with an emphasis on vocational training in engineering, construction and technology. One strand of this was designed to offer professional skills development and qualifications to women who were already working as IT technicians or who were aspiring to move into these types of jobs. These jobs included user support roles, network administrators, and those doing help desk support. Twenty women took part in a research study that looked at their careers, aspirations, and attitudes to technology[2]. This paper will draw on qualitative material gathered during two interviews as well as observations and interviews with the training providers. Beginning with a review of existing strategies that have been implemented to support women into computing and ICT employment, we will then use results from qualitative interview data to examine how a supported training programme has been used to enhance the career progression of a group of women IT technicians.

2. Reviewing the problem – why are there so few women in ICT?

A number of factors have been offered as an explanation for the low number of women in computing – ranging from gender stereotyping, masculine work culture, gendered use of language, to the lack of appeal to girls and young women (Spertus 1991; Applewhite 2002). While studies have concentrated mainly on women in computer science education or in professional occupations, these issues are equally relevant to women working at technician level both within the IT industry and as IT technicians in other industries[3].

Image and identity continue to pose a barrier to women's entry into ICT at all levels but particularly in technical areas. Historically low numbers of women have been attracted to these occupations because they are seen as a male domain. During teenage years, at a crucial time in the formation of career aspirations, recreational use of computers is still a predominantly male pastime (Cassell & Jenkins 1998) and early interest in computing as a hobby has been shown to be a strong indicator for entry into a later computer science career (Margolis & Fisher 2002).

3. Strategies for change

There have been numerous initiatives and interventions aimed at redressing the gender balance in these areas, which can be categorised as follows:

- **Equal Opportunities** – this is based on the view that women have missed out on the chance to gain skills in ICT or other occupations that are dominated by men and so special schemes are required to offer catch up training that will equalise opportunities for women (Henwood 1995; Sørensen 2004).

- **Critical Mass** – based on getting enough women 'into' ICT education or jobs to bring about change. Sometimes referred to as the 'add-more-women' approach (Grundy 1996) this attempts to tackle the problem by increasing the total numbers of women in the hope that this will bring about change to cultural norms.

- **Plugging the Leaks** – while the numbers of women entering ICT are already low, a worrying trend is the number of women who leave the industry – these efforts are focused on encouraging women to stay - stopping the 'leaky pipeline', for example by offering recruitment and retention strategies for employers. This is often achieved by stressing the 'business case' that diversity within the workplace is good for business and women can offer unique skills and ways of working that will be profitable. (EqualiTEC 2004)

- **Mentoring and networking** – recognising that informal networking is an important strategy for career development that women often do not have access to, the creation of women's networks and mentoring schemes offer positive role models and a 'helping hand' up the career ladder. Some informal networks such as the email list Systers have been in existence for many years (Systers 2004) while structured mentoring has been more recent (and indeed forms an important strand within the JIVE project as a whole).

- **Cultural Change** – this approach moves away from a focus on the individual women and looks to bring about change at an institutional level in order to make the climate for women less 'chilly'. So the focus is on working with employers whether they are in industry or in education. Taking a top down approach and a view, the main focus is at policy level to remove barriers to women and alter work culture. This is one of the strategies employed by the JIVE project.

- **The Makeover** – many initiatives have focused on what we might call the image problem. Girls and women are not attracted to working in IT because of its association with 'geeky' men. Strategies such as challenging the image of occupations, stressing the human interaction involved, altering the name of courses are all aimed at making ICT occupations appear more suitable and appealing for women and girls. Computer Clubs for Girls, for instance, offers activities such as designing magazine covers, creating animations and recording music aimed at portraying ICT as relevant and fun (e-Skills 2003).

- **Changing the Conversation** - women friendly approaches to computer science have included looking at the curriculum and content – asking how the syllabus and content of the discipline can be changed (Margolis & Fisher 2002).

4. Women's training centres

While a large number of organisations have used a range of strategies to address the problem over the past twenty years, some of the most enduring and innovative of these have been women's training centres. A number of centres were set up in the 1980s in the UK primarily in order to offer a range of non traditional skills and although almost all were independent voluntary sector organisations, they broadly followed a similar agenda. Their philosophy nearly always originated from and used feminist pedagogical approaches, designed both for the personal empowerment of individual women (by enabling them with skills that were traditionally seen as male) but also with the political agenda of altering the gender segregation in the labour market. Sadly many of these have increasingly come under financial pressure and have been forced to close in recent years. However there are still a number in existence of which two (Oxford Women's Training Scheme and Cardiff Women's Workshop) have been participants in the JIVE project and have delivered the training programmes discussed in this study.

Women-only learning offers the chance to be free of usual gendered constraints – a site of resistance where gendered performances are subverted (Butler 1999) away from the 'male gaze' that can act as inhibitory force. In mixed gender training situations 'men tend to dominate not by design but through custom' (Coats 1994, p.44). Women-only space can allow women to have their voices heard without feeling intimidated.

One of the key tasks of women's training centres has been to build confidence. Many of these schemes and centres have been aimed particularly at women with social disadvantage (often funding driven when certain eligibility criteria are specifically stipulated). For many women their entry into training can coincide with significant life events. For example returning to work after childcare break; unemployment; divorce or separation often with low self esteem and lack of confidence; undervaluing of their prior experience and feeling that their knowledge and skills are out of date. The underlying ethos behind much of the training delivery is to support women who are vulnerable and lacking in confidence, both with practical measures such as travel and childcare costs, timing of classes during school hours, but also with personal development programmes (McGivney 1998).

The Women's Training Network (WTN) set up in 1984 to support and co-ordinate efforts of UK women's training centres offers the following key features for its programmes:

> "Community-based training for women to enter and progress in non-traditional, new and technical skills, e.g. information and communication technologies, media, construction, engineering, entrepreneurship.

> Learning delivery and environments to ensure accessibility of technology, tools and equipment to women.

> Teaching methods that recognise and value transferable skills from women's

traditional fields of work and learning.

Provision of childcare and essential support costs.

Integrated outreach, learning and skills delivery, work experience, personal development and progression support.

Targeted recruitment and participant support methods based on analysis of structural causes and impacts of inequality and under-representation.

Learning/action planning and individual personal tutoring. Integrated progression planning.

Positive role models of women in non-traditional roles " (WTN 2004)

In terms of content, while there has been a wide range and variety of learning provision offered under the umbrella of women's education and training, certain characteristics seem to be commonly understood to belong to a women-centred curriculum. Women's own experiences are incorporated but also contextualised within a wider social framework. Group support and collaborative work are often used to encourage participation and the curriculum itself is continually reviewed and developed. For women's education to be successful:

> *"... it is necessary to consider the whole curriculum and not just the content of what is provided or the methodology of how it is taught, but to look also at the values and ideologies which inform its design, the structures within which it is delivered, the evaluation and development which redefines and redesigns its ongoing practice"* (Coats 1994, p.62)

5. The JIVE project

The characteristics of good practice in women's training have by no means been limited to women in non-traditional skill areas. Indeed many of these methods have been used widely in more generic adult education contexts. However, the JIVE project has been one of the first attempts to formally transfer such expertise into the mainstream. By developing a partnership which includes two women's training centres as well as the WTN, the JIVE project has aimed to spread good practice from women's training more widely, taking a holistic approach that recognises the need for simultaneous intervention with a range of actors. Thus the JIVE project as a whole has involved work with careers advisors, educators, employers and policy makers as well as women and girls who are in work or undergoing training in gender segregated occupations.

One of the target areas for intervention was identified as women who were working in IT as technicians or network administrators but whose career progression appeared to be hampered by lack of qualifications. The two training centres in the partnership would offer a package of supported training using the best practice from their previous work in training women that would enable women to gain Microsoft Certified Systems Engineer (MCSE) certification. While the MCSE is recognised as the key qualification for people working in Windows network administration, training had for many years only been available through private training centres, at prices often prohibitive to individual learners (typically charging £1500 per course, with up to seven courses needed to achieve the full qualification). Not surprisingly, there are few women with this qualification – Microsoft have estimated that women constitute only 5% of those with even the first level of certification towards the MCSE[4].

The JIVE project identified that women IT technicians might be able to improve their career prospects by gaining MCSE certification and that by providing this within the context of the women's training centre model, they would be more likely to succeed in achieving this. Women in the study are still participating in MCSE training courses at the time of writing although the project will end in June 2005. As this paper was being finalised (April 2005) ten of the women in our study had taken and passed their first exam. Of these, three women had passed two or three exams and another four women had achieved full MCSE status. So, for the women in the study this has generally been a success. While the long term outcomes are still unknown as the programme has not yet finished, it is possible at this stage to reflect on the methodology employed and to consider how this might be taken forward as a model for others to follow.

6. Data collection

Twenty women were selected by the training providers to take part in a supported programme of training aimed at leading to their achievement of MCSE certification. Two interviews were carried out with each of the women - one at the start of the training period and the other approximately a year later, after they had completed a number of MCSE courses. In addition to the interviews with participants, data was also collected about the two training environments where the MCSE training took place. These included interviews with staff involved in recruitment and support of trainees as well as observation of the learning and teaching environment. Observations were also carried out at two mainstream Further Education colleges where similar courses were being delivered to mixed gender groups. Similar to the two women's training centres in the study, these institutions had both been registered as Microsoft Academies under a scheme introduced by Microsoft to enable MCSE training to take place within further education establishments. (Microsoft 2004)

7. Results

Due to the small scale of the study and the wide variation in personal circumstances of the women in the study, in presenting the following results we are not attempting to generalise from this research. Rather we explore themes that emerged during analysis which are illustrated by quotations from one or two women. Where appropriate we have given an indication of the number of women whose interviews included mention of a particular issue.

7.1 Gender norms

Women in our study were generally aware that their choice of career did not conform to gender norms and five women, when recounting their early experiences of technology, identified their interest in technology as transgressing gender boundaries in some way. For example one woman recalled:

> "I think I was not a typical woman right from the start if that's what you're after. I liked fixing things, I would just get hold of a screwdriver and see if I can fix something at home you know, pretty much just trained like that." (P20[5] 49 year old Community Education Team Leader)

This gender non-conformity was emphasised by the fact that their entry into IT technician occupations was neither obvious nor straightforward. For nearly all of the women in this study their routes into current working roles were winding and convoluted taking in a range of jobs and occupations before finding employment in IT. In fact only one woman had taken what could be considered to be the expected direct route from school via a modern apprenticeship into her technician role. For six of the women their current jobs had evolved from more traditionally female administrative posts to include responsibility for technical maintenance and support. (Herman & Ellen 2004).

7.2 Work culture

As we saw earlier one of the reasons for developing the JIVE training was a concern that women IT technicians faced barriers to career progression. One barrier continues to be the predominance of a male culture that can be hostile to women and perpetuate gender stereotyping in the workplace. For example, one woman in our study who had worked in the industry for a long time said:

> "I've been in networking for 20 years and I know what it's like to be a woman in a male dominated environment. [...]I was taken for a tea lady, with me being the only woman you know, they kept coming to me these guys and saying when is tea being served... so it's pretty shocking." (P20 49 year old Community Education Team Leader)

Six of the women experienced a lack of credibility with men who they encountered at work who could not believe they had the appropriate level of technical competence to do their work:

> "people have these pre-defined ideas about what people can do and they see a chap in a suit and he starts talking about all this jargon and whatnot, they think he must be pretty clever. If a woman went and did the same thing, she wouldn't have that same status." (P18 38 year old school IT technician)

7.3 Qualifications

One strategy to deal with these kinds of attitudes is to gain qualifications. The fact that there are no formal entry qualifications to working as an IT technician has been of benefit to women in this study – their routes into the jobs they currently do have been varied and do not follow a uniform pattern (Herman & Ellen 2004). Yet even once they are working competently in these occupations, an absence of formal qualifications can compound feelings of under confidence.

Seven of the women cited the importance of qualifications for their perceived status value and as a route to recognition and respect by male colleagues. Their need for certification was sometimes related to gender discrimination, feeling obliged to prove their skills and worth by paper qualifications to counteract discriminatory attitudes.

"If you're in an IT situation you're dealing with men [...] if they know you're an MCSE they will actually stop and look again because they do know, it's a good qualification. They might start talking to you then and think oh she does actually know what she's talking about". (P28 38 year old Technical Director of IT Company)

Achievement of qualifications could also alter attitudes from male colleagues, changing the way they perceived the women they work with.

"Well, being female and being black, sometimes I go into a workplace and the first thing they want to know "are you qualified to do this?" And I said "well I'm sure I wouldn't be sent here if I were not qualified". And they say "we want to know what sort of qualifications you've got". And, off the top of my head, I just tell them a few of them and they go "oh, alright then". (P6 46 year old ICT trainer)

7.5 Access to training

Although achieving qualifications can help to offset discriminatory attitudes, gaining access to training that leads to these qualifications can be difficult. While women predominate in basic level ICT training, higher level ICT training and education whether by private agencies or within the further or higher education sectors is more often taken up by men.

While over half of the women reported they had been on work related training courses, in all but two cases these had not led to qualifications. Although some of the women had considered taking MCSE training in the past it had not been affordable. Indeed one of the main reasons cited for taking part in the JIVE training programme was that the training would be free. Only two of their employers had ever paid for this kind of training in the past. One employer remarked:

"We would not normally support MCSE training because it is expensive and goes out of date so quickly because it is tied to specific versions of software. We are very grateful for the free course, and [the employee] has benefited from it." (Public sector employer)

Indeed all but one of the employers were extremely supportive of their employees attending the training, allowing them considerable time off to attend the training courses. The involvement of employers was positively encouraged by the training providers in the hope that this would help make an impact in the workplace and on the prospective career development of the women themselves.

7.5 Curriculum and Content

One issue which this study raised was whether the delivery of vendor specific qualifications such as the MCSE, which have a rigid and prescribed teaching and learning strategy, can be reconciled with the ethos and traditional values of women's education and training as outlined above. All courses follow a clearly defined syllabus that is strictly controlled with the specific target of passing a set of exams. The design of the curriculum in this case was clearly out of the control of the training providers as all materials were designed and created by the vendor and informed by their own values and ideologies. These materials included PowerPoint slides for use by the trainer, student manuals, and CD ROMs with practical assignment materials (known as 'labs'). The primary purpose of the training was to acquire skills in the operation of a specific software package, and the curriculum and materials were identical to those used in other similar courses elsewhere. Within the syllabus there is no time for reflection on own learning – review questions are already prepared rather than being stimulated by the needs of learners. Therefore there was little opportunity for the type of reflection and group learning that we have seen typifies women's education.

7.6 Support measures

Despite the fixed curriculum and content delivery, in terms of the total support package the training drew on many of the positive features of the women's training centre approach. By offering a range of additional support measures, it was felt that the women would be more likely to succeed in gaining qualifications and improving their career prospects. Empowerment, a requirement of the Equal funding (Employment Support Unit 2001) and a cornerstone of the philosophy of both training organisations involved, played an important part in both the recruitment strategy and the subsequent support offered to the trainees. While all the participants in this study were already competent ICT users, the process of improving their technical skills can still be seen as personally and professionally empowering.

One of the key features that women identified as differentiating this training course from others in which they had participated, was the importance of being supported through the whole process. With up to eight courses, each lasting three to five days, there was the need for participants to make a strong commitment to the learning process in order to succeed. Support from the trainer and other centre staff, coupled with the peer support provided by other women following the same courses throughout the programme, enabled the development of a strong and consistent learning group. This approach seems to have been important to the women and increased motivation and commitment.

> "That's been different because you feel like you are sort of together going through it and I mean it is a unique situation because you don't usually go on a course that lasts two years with the same people all the time." (P24 31 year old IT Help Desk Manager)

Specific support measures offered to the women in this study included a range of features outside of the taught sessions. While other learning providers might well offer some of these, the total support package was clearly valued and frequently commented on by the women in the study. Features included:

- all course and exam fees paid for
- revision/coaching sessions prior to the exams
- staff offered 'moral support' through tutorials
- free access to 'Transcender' revision software (commercial product used to practice exam questions)
- making available a practice network for students without access at their workplace
- travel expenses, meals, accommodation for those lived too far for daily travel to the centre.

7.7 Women-only environment

The training was delivered in a women-only environment. Not only were all the trainees and the trainer female but the training centres themselves had only women staff and students, something which was new to a number of the participants. While a couple of women expressed initial ambivalence when asked about their reactions to the women-only environment, other than that there was a positive response. Some contrasted the atmosphere of the course favourably to mixed gender ICT training courses that they had previously attended using words like 'relaxed', 'friendly', 'fun', 'supportive', 'less competitive', 'enjoyable' etc. Women-only space seemed to enable fuller participation. Several described how men dominated other training courses and made them feel intimidated. They perceived the women-only group to be more co-operative and less aggressive.

> "it's nice to be there with a group of women because of courses that I've done in the past, or sort of training within work, [...] internal training, you tend to always get the one cocky guy and you don't have that really." (P39 25 year old IT Support Technician)

One woman described how she felt freer to express herself in a non-competitive training environment, finding it easier to participate and not feel foolish or shy.

> [men on training courses are] " too outspoken, too competitive, too know-it-all and they don't really let you take part and they don't share. So, yes, for me I think it is

great to be in a female environment here. It is more relaxed and people help each other. Working with men is bad enough, but in a course, if you are a little bit insecure or you miss information, you don't get the chance to assert yourself unless you are really a pain. I'm not. Not because I think 'oh, what are they going to think of me if I don't know this' but, basically, because I just feel it's too much effort to compete with them and I just can't be bothered to compete." (P40 58 year old Computing Support Officer)

One woman talked about how she behaved differently herself in a mixed gender environment:

"comparing it to courses where men have been involved… sometimes, I think it's my personality as well, they tend to take over and I sort of sit there like the shy violet at the back and not say anything" (P42 38 year old School IT technician)

However another who had more experience of mixed training had developed her own coping strategies:

"I've done two courses already that were mixed where I was the only woman and I think I've come to expect that really, working in IT, there aren't that many women that I've come across, certainly when I was working at the high school I was one of very few women working in IT at schools. And I also don't let it phase me really, I think I'm probably - strong enough is probably the wrong word to use but strong enough to not bother about what they're thinking or what they're saying or what they're doing." (P23 34 year old IT Support and Training Officer)

7.8 Role models and networking

While not always the case, women's training centres usually aim to have a woman tutor, often with the purpose of providing a positive role model for the trainees. In this case the trainer proved a strong inspiration to women who lacked visible female role models in their working lives:

"she is so able and she has done so much which she tells us about […] her career before she became a Microsoft trainer. It just makes you think yeah, I could do that as well." (P23 34 year old IT Support and Training Officer)

"you are much more inspired, you can see that if she could do it, why can't you, we can do it … [we get] inspiration from a woman tutor who might have got MCSE herself or perhaps MSc herself in ICT and teaching for years and you can see her career prospects were so high you get inspiration and she could become a role model for you" (P22 40 year old ICT Development Worker)

Others felt they were able to participate in a way they could not have otherwise have done if the tutor had been male:

"I feel sort of free to say anything I want to her because I know you know, if I want to ask her a question on anything I could, just come out and say it […] whereas well I wouldn't dare ask a man." (P27 46 year old IT trainer)

Studying with other women in the same occupation as themselves was a new experience for many of the women, something that validated their own situation and offered them support from others with similar experiences. The training providers tried to develop a culture of networking between the women in order to share concerns and support each other in their career development. This was important in validating their own career choices, for example one woman commented on how important it was for her to meet others in the same situation:

> *"it's strange feeling that there are women out there who are doing all this job, except maybe they haven't got qualification, [...] generally ICT was very male dominated, [...], this is saying you can do it as well. You feel [...] you're not in the wrong job"* (P41 44 year old PC Support Analyst)

Outside of the formal training there were a number of ways in which the women were encouraged to support each other - networking/social events were organised with the aim of strengthening links and sharing experiences and expertise. There was also an expectation that women who participated in the training would begin to generate some kind of critical mass of women within this area of work and provide informal mentoring to those who came after them. The training centres organised social networking events so that women could share experiences and build contacts within their own group and with women who would follow them on the programme.

> *"I think it was quite free form, it's just being someone for the next courses to talk to. Pick our brains on how we found the courses and the exam and how we find the industry - some people are already in the industry and others are wanting to qualify in what they will be doing. For those wanting to get in the industry the people already in there are a source of information and contacts."* (P28 38 year old Technical Director of IT Company)

8. Conclusions

As the training courses have not yet been completed at the time of writing, it is too early to assess the impact of the training on the career progression of those women who participated in the programme, and a follow up study is planned in order to explore this further.

This study has suggested how approaches developed within women's training centres can successfully be adapted for the delivery of vendor specific qualifications. Given the low numbers of MCSE qualified women IT technicians in the UK even a small scale scheme of this nature can begin to bring about cultural change within the sector and offer an insight into how barriers can be overcome in other areas of the IT industry. A comprehensive support package based on established good practice in women's training can make a difference, offering encouragement and motivation as well as overcoming practical barriers.

Within IT technical occupations, the workplace culture is still predominantly male and at times even hostile to women. We have seen how for some women this can be compounded by a lack of status and respect in the eyes of male colleagues. Gaining qualifications can go some way to countering this problem by building confidence and legitimising and validating women's skills. The JIVE project successfully merged the good practice approaches of women only training with a vendor specific training programme leading to an industry standard qualification. This has provided an important example of how culture and practice can be challenged and changed within the workplace by enabling women to become more confident and visible in their roles as IT technicians.

Bringing about change for women in computing at all levels requires a concerted effort by a range of actors: employers as well as training and education providers, practitioners as well as policy makers. Indeed if we reflect on our original range of strategies that have been employed over the past 20 years, it seems clear that a multi faceted approach is required. Achieving a critical mass of women IT technicians will not be enough unless employers adopt family friendly working practices in order to retain their employees, and unless there are wider media and cultural changes. Yet the role of women IT technicians who have crossed over and blurred boundaries between traditionally gender segregated sectors, offers a hopeful sign that the picture may not be as uniformly bleak as we sometimes imagine and that change could come about in surprising places.

References

Applewhite, A. 2002, Why So Few Women? *IEEE Spectrum*, May 2002, pp. 65-66.

Butler, J. 1999, *Gender Trouble: Feminism and the subversion of identity*, Routledge, London & NY.

Cassell, J. & Jenkins, H. (eds), 1998, *From Barbie to Mortal Kombat: Gender and Computer Games*, MIT Press, Cambridge, MA.

Coats, M. 1994, *Women's Education*, SRHE and OUP, Buckingham.

Employment Support Unit 2001, *Towards an empowerment approach: a guide for projects*, ESU, Birmingham. [Online] Available: http://www.employment.ecotec.co.uk/download/Empowe1.doc [30 January 2005].

EqualiTEC: For Women: 2004 *For Companies* [Online] Available: http://www.equalitec.org.uk/forcompanies/index.cfm [30 January 2005].

e-Skills 2003, *Computer Clubs for Girls Brochure*. [Online] Available: http://www.e-skills.com/docs/it/cc4g_brochure_inside.pdf [30 January 2005].

Grundy, F. 1996, *Women and Computers*, Intellect, Exeter UK.

Henwood, F. 1995 'Establishing Gender Perspectives on Information Technology: Problems Issues and Opportunities,' in K.Grint & R.Gill (eds) *The Gender Technology Relation: Contemporary Theory and Research*, Taylor and Francis, London.

Herman, C. & Ellen, D. 2004 *"I would say I've fallen into IT": Career paths of women network technicians participating in the JIVE project*, Paper presented at the Gender and ICT

Symposium, Brussels 20 January 2004. [Online] Available:
http://www.ua.ac.be/main.asp?c=*GENDERICT&n=17444&ct=012369&e=o30174 [30
January 2005].

Margolis, J. & Fisher, A. 2002, *Unlocking the Clubhouse: women in computing*, MIT Press,
Cambridge MA.

McGivney, V. 1998 'Dancing into the future: Developments in Adult Education', in Benn, R.,
Elliott J., & Whaley P. (eds), *Educating Rita and her sisters: Women and continuing
education*, NIACE, Leicester.

Microsoft, 2004, *Microsoft ICT Academy ICT Programme* [Online] Available:
http://www.microsoft.com/uk/education/skills-dev/it-academy/programme/ [30 January 2005].

Sørensen, K.H. 2004, *Gender and Inclusion Strategies for the Information Society*, Public
version of Deliverable 7 from SIGIS project [Online] Available:
http://www.rcss.ed.ac.uk/sigis/public/displaydoc/full/D07_EC file: SIGIS_D07_EC.pdf [30
January 2005].

Spertus, E. 1991 *Why are there so few female computer scientists?* AI Technical Report 1315,
MIT, Artificial Intelligence Laboratory. [Online] Available:
http://www.mills.edu/ACAD_INFO/MCS/SPERTUS/Gender/why.html [30 January 2005.].

Systers, 2004 Systers Online Community website *About Systers* [Online] Available:
http://athena.systers.org/about.html [30 January 2005].

Women's Training Network, 2004, Women's Training Network website *About WTN*. [Online]
Available: http://www.wtn.org.uk/about.htm [30 January 2005].

Notes

1 JIVE is an abbreviation of Joint Interventions which stresses the holistic nature of the project
and the importance of partnership working.

2 For details of the range of job titles of the women who were interiewed for this study see
Herman and Ellen (2004).

3 The term IT technician is difficult to define as it can incorporate a wide range of roles. For an
idea of the types of occupations which are included under this heading see SOC codes 3131
IT operations techicians and 3132 IT user support technicians.

4 During the research study we discovered that Microsoft did not collect diversity data
including a gender breakdown amongst MCSEs. Consequently, it is not possible to accurately
pinpoint the number of women holding MCSE certification. However, in a survey of those
with MCP (Microsoft Certified Professional) status in November 2004, Microsoft reported that
only 5% of the 289 respondents in the UK were women. MCP status is the lowest level of
certification offered by Microsoft. As a result of our dialogue with Microsoft the corporation
has indicated that they will start collecting diversity data.

5 The Pxx numbers associated with quotations are identifiers using Atlas/ti data analysis
software and represent one person's interview. As we interviewed women twice a single
respondent is associated to two Pxx numbers.

20 Learning in Groups: Gender Impacts in E-Learning

Sigrid Schmitz, Ruth Meßmer

Kompetenzforum [gin], Institut für Informatik und Gesellschaft, Universität Freiburg, Germany[1]

Abstract

E-learning currently offers a wide range of technical support for virtual or partially virtual learning scenarios. Until now tools for individual learning have been more common than facilities for group working, although research provides us with obvious indications that many learners and especially a lot of women prefer to work together. In this paper, we want to examine the state of research in the field of collaborative learning and discuss implications for a gender-balanced and diversity-sensitive modelling of e-learning. Referring to the *concept of constructive realism*, we have to take the diversity of users into account and, at the same time, pay regard to group-specific aspects in order to figure out which facilities can benefit collaborative learning of women and men. In a comparison of common e-learning platforms in Germany we discuss to what extent current e-learning technology could support gender sensitive demands and how further development could adapt to gender-oriented concepts.

1. Constructive realism as a basis for working in the field of gender, group working and e-learning

Approaches to gender and e-learning deal with the crucial questions whether men and women profit equally from the opportunities offered by e-learning and which impediments have to be surmounted in order to accomplish equal benefits for all groups of users.

Referring to the keyword *co-construction of gender and technology* (e.g. van Oost 2004, p. 7), current gender studies examine how gender is permanently being re-constructed and tied into the complex network of Human Computer Interaction (HCI). Although they are constructions aspects of gender are not out of the reach of analyses, they are real and measurable. Women and men do show group-specific tendencies in the use of e-learning facilities. However, there are some pitfalls which have to be paid regard to if we talk about gender differences concerning access to computers, use of computers, learning styles, or strategies of communication. Such a division into separate (dichotomous) male and female patterns of behaviour is not only too simple and falsifying, it is nothing short of stabilizing the existing prejudices and the trenches of the postulated 'Digital Divide'. More detailed analyses on gender and ICT prove that gender differences are frequently reconstructed in a stereotyped way by conclusions that are often not drawn with much deliberation (see Rommes & Faulkner 2004).

Consequently focussing on gender aspects in collaborative work in e-learning requires keeping both aspects in mind: an analysis of still existing gendered structures and how limitations can be diminished on the one hand; concentration not on fixed differences but on the diversity and flexibility of perception and performance in the field of gender and technology on the other hand. This is not an easy task and it can only be solved by referring to a theoretical background that tries to close the gap between difference and construction of gender in ICT.

Constructive realism (Berszinski et al. 2002; Meßmer & Schmitz 2004) means that strategies of behaviour concerning the use of technology performed by men or women are neither inherent, fixed personal features, nor determinants of biology. They are multiple, dynamic, and flexible. Various factors such as age, ethnicity, class, education, social and economic aspects are responsible for the shaping of these strategies of behaviour. They are being developed, however, in a society where gender is present in every sphere and where it is engraved even in technology. Living in a gender stereotyped world and interacting with gendered technology leads to gendered cultural and social experiences and constitutes diverse and gendered strategies in learning as well as in dealing with new media. Feminist scientists (e.g. Cockburn 1988, Wajcman 1991) detected how the symbolic conjunction between technology and masculinity influences and forms scientific work, methods and artefacts. New technology "has been built into the pre-existing relations of sex, class and race" (Wajcman 1991, p. 52). Ruth Woodfield showed that "women's underrepresentation within computing is largely a result of the field's cultural development" (Woodfield 2000, p. 24). Consequently, the affiliation to a gender group in a particular cultural context is characterized by similar experiences which might be constructed but which are nonetheless always real within one's own experience and have impact on the shaping of individual strategies.

According to our theoretical background the recognition and integration of gender aspects in the development of e-learning technology requires us to concentrate on two facets simultaneously: the sensitivity to realize gender effects and the openness of systems to permit a variety of strategies (diversity) in the interaction between the users and the ICT products beyond gender stereotypes.

Our attempts to promote the access of women to e-learning technology started a couple of years ago based on analyses on the concurrence of societal, cultural, economic, and political aspects that form the basis of the still limited participation of women in information technology (Schinzel 2002; Schinzel & Ruiz Ben 2002). A first step was to categorize the multiple facets that relate to each other in the *interaction network of gender and e-learning* (for detail, see Meßmer & Schmitz 2004). It comprises learners who differ regarding their experience, their computer literacy and their access to technical and economic resources as well as their family and work situation, their cognitive, learning and communication styles, their motivation, interests, opinions and values with regard to e-learning facilities. The network also includes 'learning scenarios'. Beside discipline-specific didactic settings, methods and cultures, learning scenarios are particularly defined by the underlying learning theories like behaviourist, cognitivist or constructivist theories. Learning systems based on behaviourist theories consider behaviour and knowledge as results of reinforcing factors. For that reason, training and testing are very important. Exponents of cognitivism regard knowledge as a process of understanding and digesting information. Consequently cognitivist learning programmes offer complex situations, problem-oriented mediation of knowledge and they illustrate relations and contexts. Communication and cooperation between learners and an active creation of knowledge are essential for the learning process in constructivist theories of learning (Thissen 1999). As a consequence synchronous and asynchronous communication tools are applied in order to make online collaboration possible. Another aspect of the network is the technical shaping of e-learning systems which varies concerning their functions, design, usability, and technical requirements for usage. The presentation of contents also comprises a variety of discipline-specific languages, of metaphors, pictures or the arrangement of topics (e.g. hierarchical or cross-linked).

All these facets and their mutual interactions have to be taken seriously into account for constructing e-learning technology. With modifiable and modular systems, we encourage variable access for users with different levels of computer literacy (Meßmer et al. 2003; Meßmer & Schmitz 2004; Schmitz 2004). These approaches to a construction of groupware tools that are balanced for gender and diversity offer access through an interactive space where lecturers and students can decide which technical support they need for their learning scenario. They arrange only those functions which they need on a learning interface which is organized in an intuitive way in order to render easy access possible. According to the requirements of diverse levels of computer literacy, the modular arrangement offers expanding options. The learners and the teachers are able to control the increase of complexity to match their growing technical skills and in order to extend didactic demands.

In this paper, we want to focus on another facet of the network as a starting point and concentrate on the gender impact on group working in e-learning. Although the possibility of collaborative working and learning independent of time or location is being highlighted as one of the benefits of e-learning, a detailed analysis of what female and male students really want in order to promote their learning progress still remains on a more or less general level.

In the following chapters, we want to outline some approaches to the support of group working and collaborative learning with respect to gender aspects. Is group working equally important for women and men? What is needed for successful and effective group working and which research questions are still to be answered? Which demands on e-learning products can be derived from these analyses and how have these demands been realized in e-learning systems so far?

2. Group working

2.1 The state of the debate on group working in e-learning[2]

The current e-learning market serves mainly individual learners. An evaluation of 100 multimedia projects in German universities showed that individual learning strikingly prevails over online group working (Rinn 2004). In 2000, 25% of German students used the internet to download information, scripts and tests, while only 3% participated in virtual courses (Middendorff 2002). Mioduser et al. (2000) evaluated 436 educational web sites in the USA focusing on mathematics, science, and technology. None of them supported working groups or learning communities. Not more than 13% of the sites permitted interaction with other users, only a small number of sites included feedback features, on 65% of the sites, e-mail was the only communication facility at the user's disposal. The question whether working individually or in groups turns out to be the more effective learning strategy depends on many factors such as the learning targets (see Kerres 2004), the learner's situation, his or her learning preferences, etc. But there are arguments in favour of fostering group working. Empirical studies show that, under certain circumstances, learning in small groups can have more positive effects on achievements and outcomes than individual learning (e.g. Lou, Abrami & d'Apollonia 2001; Schulmeister 2001; Kerres 2004). Contrary to instructivist models based on the imparting of knowledge from teacher to student, the constructivist model emphasizes the role of 'exploring/explorative learning'. The aim is to present multiple perspectives and various approaches to a topic in order to enable students to choose an individual access to the subject-matter and to bring about an active and explorative discussion of contents. Such an approach not only stimulates the complex acquisition of knowledge, it also combines aspects of communication with those of cooperation between students (and teachers). Different points of view and complex contents can be acquired more effectively in discussions. Consequently there is an intensive discussion about the aspects of communication and cooperation in combination with virtual teaching, about how constructivist learning theories can be integrated (e.g. Thissen 1999; Schulmeister 2001), and about how the modelling of role distribution can promote performance in situated learning scenarios (e.g. Allert, Richter & Nejdl 2004).

There may be as many learning styles and preferences as there are learners. However gender research in the field of e-learning shows one outstanding aspect despite the wide range of diversity. That is the preference of many women to work together in order to solve learning tasks.

2.2 Gender aspects in group working and collaborative learning

The indication that women and girls tend to prefer working collaboratively in e-learning scenarios to a greater extent than men and boys and that they articulate preferences for interactive problem solving and discerning thinking skills was substantiated by several earlier researches (e.g. Blum 1998; Martin 1998) and goes along with results from analyses of face-to-face learning situations (Pusch 1984; Opermann & Weber 1995). Recent research in different countries comes to similar results in groups with different age and education levels. Interviews with German university students who worked with an e-learning tool in an economics course showed that 44% of the female and only 24% of the male students wanted the tool to be server-based in order to make working in groups possible. Only 12% of the female students but 43% of the male students explicitly did not want to work in groups (Frank et al. 2002). In a study conducted by the American Association of University Women girls reported a preference for interacting with others in computer supported working and were more engaged by software that provided opportunities for collaboration (AAUW 2000). Leong and Hawamdeh (1999) analysed the attitudes of 11-year-old students in Singapore and found that the girls did not only prefer to learn in groups, but that they also learned better this way, whereas boys learned better on their own and preferred this way of learning. Agosto (2001) stated a preference for collaboration referring to 14- and 15-year-old females in educational settings but not for leisure pursuits, such as reading e-mails and playing computer games, which they preferred to do alone. Savard and co-workers (1995) did not find many gender differences concerning attitudes and achievements of students regarding the question of working cooperatively or on their own. But female students working with partners were more interested in exchanging ideas and had a more positive opinion of their own performance compared to those who worked individually.

Some women evaluate the quality of teaching according to its facilitation of group working. Sullivan's 2001 study (cited in Rajagopal 2003) found that women experienced teaching-learning situations more positively when peer interaction occurred. A survey of Burdett yielded that the female style of decision-making attaches importance not only to the decision reached itself but also to the question of whether everyone has had the opportunity of contributing openly and fairly to the process of decision making (Burdett 2000). Furthermore, community building seems to prevent women especially from resigning from e-learning courses (Wiesner 2001).

Research shows the preference of female learners to work together in corresponding e-learning scenarios. It fosters their motivation, makes their learning more effective and is important for a better rating of their performance and for a more positive evaluation of the teaching quality. According to Coy and colleagues (2001), Rajagopal and Bojin described that "...female, rather than male students seem to be interested in technology for the reason that it helps them experience a different structure of learning — cooperative and dialogic — process and thereby enhance their learning of course materials." (Rajagopal & Bojin 2003).

However, despite these gender trends it should not be dismissed that the data also show a great number of men who consider group learning important. In the German

Virtual University of Hagen, which only offers distant learning courses, 68% of the students explained that working in student groups was important for them (Mittrach 1999). As 76% of the university's students are male, this survey shows that regardless of gender, group working may be one facility that promotes success in e-learning for many students the number of whom is not to be underestimated.

2.3 Group working in detail: from gender aspects to demands on technical support

It is important to have a closer look at aspects of group working in order to outline the demands on technical support, especially with regard to a gender-balanced and diversity-sensitive background. What do students experience when they work and learn with others in virtual environments? Learners can interact on different levels with each other. Teufel and co-workers (1995) classified three levels of group working relating to each other: communication, coordination and collaboration. In this context, coordination means communication between members of a working group to adjust responsibilities and tasks. Collaboration means communication in order to discuss and decide on group goals. Kraut et al. (1988) analysed elementary preconditions for cooperation between scientists. According to them, effective cooperation is based on efficient communication. That is, communication as often as required, be it on purpose or by chance and of good quality (free, simultaneous speaking with direct feed-back, combined availability of documents, and exchange of outlines). Communication should also be brought about with little expenditure of money and time (Mittrach 1999). Kraut et al. suggest that these results can be assigned from scientists to team-workers in general.

Starting with the elementary aspect of communication, the controversial discussion about gender aspects in online communication has to be outlined first. Herring's survey on postings in academic mailing lists named two general communication styles which she assigned to males and females (Herring 1996, 2000). According to her, the male style is more aggressive and competitive with put-downs and strong, often contentious assertions, lengthy and frequent postings, self-promotion, and sarcasm. She characterized the female style, in contrast, by the two typically co-occurring aspects of supportiveness and attenuation. Subsequent surveys, however, showed that these styles are not as gender-stereotyped as Herring proposed and they do not appear in every context. The male-female ratio in groups, the group size and the level of professionalism influence styles of communication. In huge anonymous groups people tend to resort to gender stereotypes, whereas personal contacts attenuate or avert gender effects (detailed review, Meßmer & Schmitz 2004). Accordingly, Pohl (1997) found no gendered communication styles in mixed-sex e-mail communication of students. Not surprisingly, more women reported a tendency for bilateral e-mail contacts (Lehmann 1996; Shade 1996, Kirkup 1999) or semi-public communication, such as private mailing lists or chat channels (Tangens 1996).

Some surveys show that women can also profit from virtual communication. For example, it enhances the frequency and length of women's contributions to discussions compared to face-to-face communication (Zorn 2001). Furthermore anonymity in online communication can have positive effects. In small groups, women often experience anonymity as helpful. It enhances their participation in discussions in chats (Müller 2001), which underlines that the behaviour of men and women is not altogether different but that it is flexible and depends on the specific contexts. Burdett (2000) compared the participation of women in an anonymous electronic meeting system (EMS) to that in f2f-meetings and found that only 10% of the women in EMS noted personal or aggressive comments compared to 18% in f2f-meetings. Up to 60-80% reported that they experienced no repression in EMS. In a lecture-accompanying mailing list, 81% of the female and only 19% of the male students chose nicknames (Jaffe et al. 1995). This outstanding percentage of women emphasizes the positive aspects of anonymity for women as well.

We can draw some preliminary conclusions on how communication in e-learning can be improved considering gender and diversity aspects. There are some indications for gendered strategies insofar as women concentrate more on the use of e-mail and communication in small groups. The technical system should facilitate non-public communication. Additionally, the moderation of a chat or a forum by teachers, tutors or by students themselves can help to enhance discussions on a more professional level and so help to avoid repressions. If wished, the system should permit anonymity in communication and co-operation. Presumably, the most important aspect is to clarify preferences for different ways of communication at the beginning of the learning situation and to agree on those e-learning facilities that are most suitable to meet the diversity of communication demands.

Regarding collaborative working in learning situations in higher education, a second aspect of group working is of importance. Collaborative working on documents and producing presentations of the results of group working is a very frequent task in seminars or lectures at universities. The aim is that students discuss documents and texts and gain knowledge on the respective contents. In order to support collaborative learning, e-learning systems should offer certain functions and render these functions open for combination. Students should be able to discuss the text, make comments on it, clear up problematic passages and answer questions virtually. Synchronous or asynchronous text editing services are required for this kind of work. Moreover, students should be able to fix the conclusions and reports which they have created collaboratively in a collective document by electronic means that facilitate writing texts together. They should also be able to comment to each other and discuss their work during the process of the production of this document. These demands require the combination of text editors with communication functions such as forum, e-mail, or chat. Remmele & Walloschke (2004) found that female students especially considered the combination of communication and distribution of information very useful.

3. Technical implementations: gender and diversity-sensitive?

The following examination focuses on the question if and to what extent demands on collaborative work (facilitating discussion, editing and producing textual content and effective communication) have been realized in e-learning systems so far.

CSCL-systems offer more and better ways to collaborate but CSCL is mostly used in a particular community of teachers who are very interested in this kind of work. In practice, in many disciplines of higher education the common tools are still e-learning systems. For that reason it is important to evaluate which operations are permitted and which are restricted by these systems. Effective communication often depends on details. Of interest are not only the communication facilities, e.g. synchronous or asynchronous, that e-learning systems offer but also how the different functions are shaped. We analysed five e-learning platforms that are frequently used in educational settings at universities in Germany: WebCT (Web Course Tools, http://www.webct.com), BSCW (Basic Support for Cooperative Work, http://bscw.gmd.de), CLIX (Corporate Learning and Information Exchange, http://www.imc.de), Ilias (Integriertes Lern-, Informations- und Arbeitskooperationssystem, http://www.ilias.uni-koeln.de), and Hyperwave eLearning Suite (http://www.hyperwave.com/d/products/els.htlm).

Our first focus is set on how *communication facilities* in these e-learning platforms meet gender and diversity demands as outlined above.

In WebCT users can send information within the working group via messenger. It is possible to forward these mails automatically to an external e-mail-address. Topics can also be discussed in the forum. For synchronous communication, WebCT offers public and non-public chats and a whiteboard.

The main aim of BSCW is document management for groups. It also offers a forum but no chat. It is possible to write e-mails to group members via an address book. For synchronous group working, it is necessary to install an applet called „JMonitor". With this applet, users can see who is online, they can send e-mails, short internal messages or chat with each other.

CLIX affords a forum and a blackboard for asynchronous communication. Users can also write public or private messages into the CLIX-guestbook of a group member. The system also offers a chat. The user needs "moderator"-rights to open new chat channels.

Ilias is the biggest open source e-learning platform in Germany. It has a messenger, forums and a chat for which the user needs an additional java-plug-in. A very simple whiteboard is also available.

Hyperwave affords a messenger and a forum for asynchronous contacts. Synchronous contact via chat can be either public or non-public. Hyperwave eLearning Suite also offers an additional applet called Hyperwave eConferencing Suite, a module for audio- and videoconferencing and a whiteboard.

This short outline shows that e-mail communication, as it is preferred by women, can be used in all platforms. WebCT, Hyperwave and Clix offer asynchronous and synchronous communication channels on one single platform. This makes access and use easier for a diversity of learners and teachers with limited technical experience who are not used to installing additional programmes. In contrast, synchronous communication in BSCW and in Ilias is only possible via additional programmes the installation of which requires some technical competence (JMonitor in BSCW, Hyperwave eConferencing in Hyperwave or java plug-ins in Ilias) and so may deter users with limited computer literacy (women and men) from using these platforms. The possibility to use non-public chats for synchronous communication in WebCT and Hyperwave can meet the preferences of women. However, none of the platforms provides additional facilities for moderation in chat or forum by students or teachers to avoid gendered repressions.

The analysis of current research showed that *collaborative working and learning* do not only support women but also benefit all students for discussing different points of view on various topics and for developing discerning and deliberative evaluation of content. These demands for collaborative work generate the question of how communication services can be combined with synchronous or asynchronous text-editing and text-writing functions. In their "media synchronicity theory", Dennis and Valacich (1999) connected two types of cooperation processes (conveyance and convergence) with the synchronicity of media. According to them, cooperation processes, where information is distributed, afford a low level of synchronicity, whereas cooperation processes, where groups converge on shared meanings, need a high level of synchronicity. Groups which want to stick their results together and create a text will then need functions that permit synchronous work. This facilitation is especially important in order to meet the preferences of women for group working in e-learning.

Unfortunately, most e-learning platforms do not provide the use of communication services and text working functions at the same time. Hyperwave eLearning Suite is the only tool that offers the possibility to chat while the text annotation function is in use. Additionally, in the compared e-learning platforms creating texts collaboratively is only possible in an asynchronous way. Students create papers and have to upload them to the e-learning-tool. If someone wants to add or modify the text, it has to be downloaded and after being edited, uploaded again (BSCW, Ilias, Clix, WebCT, Hyperwave). This not only imposes limitations for students with limited technical competences (which may rather deter women), it also violates the principles of constructivist learning including active and explorative discussion of content. As women tend to appreciate dialogic and cooperative processes of learning, this constrains their preferred learning styles in e-learning. Only two out of the five examined systems offer annotation options for editing texts in a way that the other group members can read and respond to (BSCW and Hyperwave eLearning Suite).

If teachers want to apply e-learning technology in order to foster collaborative work they have to decide whether they use an e-learning platform and let the students work asynchronously or if they combine an e-learning tool with an editor of a groupware system, like REDUCE, FORCE, NTE, or NetEdit. These systems permit synchronous text writing but, unfortunately, for the most part they do not offer communication and annotation functions. In this case, students have to log-in into two different systems and remember two passwords. Again, this not only requires some sacrifice of time, it is also likely to deter students with limited computer literacy from virtual working. Experiences of the Virtual University Hagen showed that the students used the additional facilities of BSCW only very modestly. They stated that working in a second programme was too much effort for them since the exchange of data could be realized as easily via e-mail (Mittrach 1999). Considering gender-balanced and diversity-sensitive approaches, the combination of different systems turns out to be problematic. Whereas computer science students may be motivated by an extensive range of programmes, tools and systems according to their technical competences, for many other students and teachers of disciplines with a greater distance from information technology, these can easily prove to be deterrents (e.g. Claus, Otto & Schinzel 2004).

4. Impacts for further research and technical development

Meanwhile technical systems offer a number of services which facilitate communication and collaboration in manifold ways. Concerning the e-learning systems we compared, however, there are certain limits to a reasonable combination and especially to that of simultaneous use of tools for communication and text editing functions. In order to realize group working in seminars and lectures of higher education, several systems, e.g. e-learning platforms and CSCL-systems, would have to be applied simultaneously. The question is how collaborative work can be facilitated in e-learning without overtaxing learners and teachers by a huge and technically too demanding system or by more than one system of that kind.

We propose an approach that could help to involve the prospective users of the technology in decision-making processes. We refer to Cecile Crutzen's feminist approach that fosters the elimination of the exact division between software designers on the one hand, and software users on the other (Crutzen 2000). Crutzen (2004) demands the use of e-learning scenarios as discursive spaces, where teachers and students have to point out their particular needs (maybe ranging from the pure distribution of information to diverse and gendered individual learning styles) and have to negotiate the corresponding technical requirements. At an early point of time they should be permitted to discuss and decide which functions or services may be useful to meet their particular teaching and learning context and which kind of technical support they prefer for communication and group working on topics. Our concepts of

Modular Learning Management Systems (MoDUS, Modular User-oriented Systems, see Meßmer et al. 2003; Meßmer & Schmitz 2004) seems to meet these demands and will hopefully turn out to be a useful approach to account for gender and diversity aspects. The modular system is to offer the opportunity to keep a multitude of possible tools and services to hand in the background. But these functions are not fixed on one e-learning platform right from the beginning. Instead, users can decide for which of their learning or teaching demands they want to have support by technical services that do not overtax their technical competences. Based on these decisions they can choose to combine just the corresponding functions or services on their interface (Schmitz 2004).

The concept of a modular system bears the potential to enable the sensitivity to realize gender effects and the openness of systems to permit a variety of strategies (diversity) in the interaction between users and ICT products beyond gender stereotypes, which we pointed out at the beginning. At present we have begun to meet the demands on gender-balanced and diversity-sensitive e-learning that we derived from the current state of research in the construction of a Learning Management System. Male and female students and those with minor computer literacy will not have to get used to huge or different technical systems with an outstanding number of other functions they do not need. For example, it ought to be possible to combine only particular communication services with tools for synchronous text editing for a working group in a university seminar. If some students (female or male) prefer to communicate only by e-mail, communication facilities can be reduced for them. According to women's preference for dialogic group working processes, some student groups might decide to also take a chat that accompanies their text annotation service. In other cases, students (female or male) may prefer to have more facilities for individual work and they may decide to use asynchronous tools such as a forum in combination with file down- and uploads on their platform. Many other combinations according to the user's decisions are quite possible. This flexibility in the use of technical services indeed requires continuous discussion between learners and teachers to determine whether the selected options meet the altering demands in the process of the learning situation.

Gender research in ICT has currently outlined a number of strategies to improve the inclusion of women (for overview, Rommes et al. 2004). However, an examination of whether the respective changes of technological constructions are indeed effective remains in many cases yet to be done. It is now important to test and evaluate whether the derived demands and their implementation in technical services for collaborative work do foster access, motivation, and satisfaction of women in different e-learning scenarios. We plan to apply our modular system in teaching courses of „Computer Science and Society" and „Gender Studies in Computer Science and Natural Sciences" within the scope of our centre of competence [gin][3] and to evaluate them. Aspects of further research and of a technological progress which is sensitive to demands on gender and diversity will be derived from these evaluations.

References

Agosto, D. E. 2001, 'Propelling Young Women into the Cyber Age: Gender Considerations in the Evaluation of Web-Based Information', [Online], *School Library Media Research*, vol 4, Available: http://www.ala.org/ala/aasl/aaslpubsandjournals/slmrb/slmrcontents/volume42001/agosto.htm [4 October 2004].

Allert, H., Richter, C. & Nejdl, W. 2004, 'Situated Models and Metadata for Learning Management', *Journal of Universal Computer Science, Special Issue on 'Human Issues in Implementing eLearning Technology*, vol 10, no 1, pp. 4-13.

Berszinski, S., Nikoleyczik, K., Remmele, B., Ruiz Ben, E., Schinzel, B., Schmitz, S. & Stingl, B. 2002, 'Geschlecht (SexGender): Geschlechterforschung in der Informatik und an ihren Schnittstellen', *FIfF-Kommunikation*, vol 3, no 2, pp. 32-36.

Blum, K. D. 1998, 'Gender Differences in CMC-based Distance Education', [Online], *Feminista!*, vol 2, no 5, Available: http://www.feminista.com/archives/v2n5/blum.html [13 October 2004].

Burdett, J. 2000, 'Changing channels: Using the electronic meeting system to increase equity in decision making', [Online], *Information Technology, Learning, and Performance Journal*, vol 18, no 2, pp. 3-12, Available: http://www.nyu.edu/education/alt/beprogram/osrajournal/burdett.pdf [4 October 2004].

Claus, R., Otto, A. & Schinzel, B. 2004, 'Gender Mainstreaming im diversifizierten Feld einer Hochschule: Bedingungen – Akzeptanz – Strategien', *IIG_Berichte*, vol 1, no 4, Freiburg.

Cockburn, C. 1988, *Die Herrschaftsmaschine: Geschlechterverhältnisse und technisches Know-how*, Argument-Verlag, Berlin, Hamburg.

Coy, L., Velazquez, N. & Bussmann, S. 2001, 'A learning community of educational leaders', [Online], *Learning Technology Newsletter*, vol 3, no 4, Available: http://lttf.ieee.org/learn_tech/issues/october2001/index.html#14 [15 September 2002].

Crutzen, C. 2000, *Interactie, en wereld von verschillen. Een visie op informatica vanuit genderstudies*, Dissertation, Open Universiteit Nederland, Heerlen.

Crutzen, C. 2004, 'Questioning Gender, Questioning E-Learning' in *Grenzgänge: Genderforschung in Informatik und Naturwissenschaften*, eds S. Schmitz & B. Schinzel, Helmer Verlag, Königstein/Taunus, pp. 65-88.

Dennis, A. & Valacich, J. 1999, 'Rethinking Media Richness' in *Proceedings of the 32nd Hawaii International Conference of System Sciences (HICSS 32)*, eds R. Sprague et al., IEEE Computer Society, Los Alamitos, California.

Durndell, A. & Thomson, K. 1997, 'Gender and Computing: A decade of Change?', *Computers & Education*, vol 28, no 1, pp. 1-9.

Frank, C. , Kassanke, S. & Suhl, L. 2002, 'Meeting Students Expectations and Realizing Pedagogical Goals within the Development of a Virtual Learning Environment', *Proc. of the World Conference on E-Learning in Corp., Govt., Health., & Higher Ed.*, Phoenix, Arizona, USA, pp. 2790-2795.

Herring, S. 1996, 'Two variants of an electronic message schema' in *Computer-mediated communication: Linguistics, social and cross-cultural perspectives*, ed S. Herring, Benjamins, Amsterdam, pp. 81-106.

Herring, S. 2000, 'Gender Differences in CMC: Findings and Implications', [Online], *The CPSR Newsletter*, vol 18, no 1, Available: http://cpsr.org/publications/newsletters/issues/2000/Winter2000/herring.html [4 October 2004].

Jaffe, M., Young-Eum, L., Huang, L.N. & Oshagan, H. 1995, 'Gender, Pseudonyms, and CMC', [Online], *Masking Identities and Baring Souls. Interpersonal CMC: Socioemotional and Relation Communication*, Available: http://research.haifa.ac.il/~jmjaffe/genderpseudocmc/intercmc.html [4 October 2004].

Kerres, M., Nattland, A. & Nübel, I. 2004, 'Didaktische Konzeption von CSCL-Lernarrangements', [Online], in *CSCL-Kompendium*, eds J. Haake, G. Schwabe & M. Wessner, Oldenbourg, München, Available: http://www.kerres.de/publications/3-5-1-kerres-cscl4.pdf [29 October 2004].

Kirkup, G. 1999, 'A Computer of One's Own (With an internet connection!)', *Adults learning*, vol 10, no 8, pp. 23-26.

Kraut, R., Egido C. & Galegher, J. 1988, 'Patterns of contact and communication in scientific research collaboration', [Online], *Proceedings of the 1988 ACM conference on Computer-supported cooperative work*, ACM Press, pp. 1-12, Available: http://portal.acm.org/citation.cfm?id=62267 [25 October 2004].

Lehmann, B. 1996, 'Internet – reine Männersache?' in *Kursbuch Internet. Anschlüsse an Wirtschaft und Politik, Wissenschaft und Kultur*, eds S. Bollmann & C. Heibach, Berlin, pp. 332–354.

Leong, C. & Hawamdeh, S. 1999, 'Gender and learning attitudes in using web-based science lessons', [Online], *Information Research*, vol 5, no 1, pp. 1-14, Available: http://InformationR.net/ir/paper66.html [4 October 2004].

Lou, Y., Abrami, P.C., & d'Apollonia, S. 2001, 'Small group and individual learning with technology: A meta-analysis', *Review of Educational Research*, vol 71, pp. 449-521.

Martin, S. 1998, 'Internet use in the classroom: The impact of gender', *Social Science Computer Review*, vol 16, no 4, pp. 411-418.

Meßmer, R. & Schmitz, S. 2004, 'Gender demands on e-learning' in *Human Perspectives in the Internet Society: Culture, Psychology and Gender. Advances in Information and Communication Technologies*, eds K. Morgan, C. A. Brebbia, J. Sanchez, & A. Voiskuonsky, vol 4, WIT-Press, Wessex, pp. 245-254.

Meßmer, R., Kaiser, O., Taubmann, C., Schmitz, S., Heidtke, B. & Schinzel, B. 2003, 'ModUS – a Modular User-Oriented CSCL System in Line with Gender Research', *Proceedings of E-Learn 2003, World Conference on E-Learning in Corp., Govt., Health., & Higher Ed.*, Phoenix, Arizona, USA, pp. 2337-2340.

Middendorff, E. 2002, *Computernutzung und Neue Medien im Studium. Ergebnisse der 16. Sozialerhebung des Deutschen Studentenwerks*, ed Bundesministerium für Bildung und Forschung, Bonn.

Mioduser, D., Nachmias, R., Lahav, O. & Oren, A. 2000, 'Web-based learning environments: Current pedagogical and technological state', *Journal of Research on Computing in Education*, vol 33, no 1, pp. 55-76.

Mittrach, S. 1999, *Lehren und Lernen in der Virtuellen Universität. Konzepte, Erfahrungen, Evaluation*, Shaker, Aachen.

Müller, B. 2001, *Doing Gender im Chat: Auswirkungen von Geschlechtsanonymität auf das eigene Erleben und Verhalten sowie die Wahrnehmung anderer Personen*, Thesis, Heidelberg.

Opermann, K. & Weber, E. 1995, *Frauensprache - Männersprache*, Orell Füssli Verlag, Zürich.

Pohl, M. & Michaelson, G. 1997, '"I don't think that's an interesting dialogue": Computer-Mediated Communication and Gender' in *Women, Work and Computerization: Spinning a Web from Past to Future*, eds F. Grundy et al., Springer, Berlin, Heidelberg, New York, pp. 87-97.

Pusch, L. F. 1984, *Das Deutsche als Männersprache*, 1st edn, Suhrkamp Verlag, Frankfurt.

Rajagopal, I. & Bojin, N. 2003, 'A Gendered World: Students and Instructional Technologies', [Online], *First Monday*, vol 8, no 1, pp. 1–23, Available: http://firstmonday.org/issues/issue8_1/rajagopal/index.html [4 October 2004].

Remmele, B. & Walloschke T. 2004, 'Entwicklung hypermedialer Lernarrangement im Seminarbetrieb des Verbundprojektes RION' in *E-Learning im Hochschulverbund*, eds S. Schinzel et. al., DUV, Wiesbaden, pp. 57ff.

Rinn, U. & Bett, K. 2004, 'Revolutioniert das „E" die Lernszenarien an deutschen Hochschulen? Eine empirische Studie im Rahmen des Bundesförderprogramms „Neue Medien in der Bildung"' in *Campus 2004*, eds D. Carstensen & B. Barrios, Waxmann, Münster, pp. 428-437.

Rommes, E. & Faulkner, W. 2004, 'Chapter 7: Conclusion', in *Designing Inclusion. The development of ICT products to include women in the Information Society*, [Online],eds E. Rommes, I. von Slooten, E. van Oost & N. Oudshoorn, pp. 69-79, Available: www.sigis-ist.org [17. January 2005].

Rommes, E., von Slooten, I., van Oost E. & Oudshoorn, N. 2004, *Designing Inclusion. The development of ICT products to include women in the Information Society*, [Online], Available: www.sigis-ist.org [17 January 2005].

Savard, M., Mitchell, S. N., Abrami, P. C. & Corso, M. 1995, 'Learning together at a distance', *Canadian Journal of Educational Communication*, vol 24, no 2, pp. 117-131.

Schinzel, B. & Ruiz Ben, E. 2002, 'Gendersensitive Gestaltung von Lernmedien und Mediendidaktik: von den Ursachen für ihre Notwendigkeit zu konkreten Checklisten', [Online], in *Gender Mainstreaming in der beruflichen Bildung: Anforderungen an Medienpädagogik und Medienentwicklung*, Berlin, Available: http://www.gmd.de/PT-NMB/Gender/Dokumentation_Berufliche_Bildung.pdf [29 October 2004].

Schinzel, B. 2001, 'e-learning für alle: Gendersensitive Mediendidaktik', [Online], in *Gender und Neue Medien*, ed U. Ernst, Innsbruck, Available: http://fem.uibk.ac.at/nmtagung.html [29 October 2004].

Schmitz, S. 2004, 'E-Learning für alle? Wie lässt sich Diversität in Technik umsetzen?' in *Campus 2004. Kommen die digitalen Medien an den Hochschulen in die Jahre?*, eds D. Carstensen & B. Barrios, Waxmann, Münster, pp. 123-133.

Schulmeister, R. & Wessner, M. 2001, *Virtuelle Universität - virtuelles Lernen*, Oldenbourg, München.

Shade, L. R. 1996, 'The Gendered Mystique: Looking closer at Web Demographics', [Online], *CMC*, vol 1, Available: http://www.december.com/cmc/mag/1996/mar/shast3.html [11 April 1999].

Sullivan, P. 2001, 'Gender differences and the online classroom: Male and female college students evaluate their experiences', *Community College Journal of Research and Practice*, vol 25, no 10, pp. 805-818.

Tangens, R. 1996, 'Ist das Internet männlich? Über Androzentrismus im Netz' in *Kursbuch Internet. Anschlüsse an Wirtschaft und Politik, Wissenschaft und Kultur*, eds S. Bollmann & C. Heibach, Bollmann Verlag, Mannheim, pp. 355-379.

Teufel, S., Sauter, C., Mühlherr, T. & Bauknecht, K. 1995, *Computerunterstützung für die Gruppenarbeit*, Addison-Wesley, Bonn.

Thillosen, A. & Arnold, P. 2001, 'Entwicklung virtueller Studienmodelle im Rahmen des Bundesleitprojekts "Virtuelle Fachhochschule für Technik, Informatik und Wirtschaft": Evaluationsergebnisse' in *Virtueller Campus. Szenarien - Strategien – Studium*, eds E. Wagner & M. Kindt, Waxmann, Münster, München, Berlin, pp. 402-410.

Thissen, F. 1999, 'Lerntheorien und ihre Umsetzung in multimedialen Lernprogrammen: Analyse und Bewertung', [Online], in *BIBB Multimedia GUID Berufsbildung*, Berlin, Available: www.frank-thissen.de/Lernen.pdf [14 October 2004].

Van Oost, E. 2004, 'Chapter 1: Introduction' in *Designing Inclusion. The development of ICT products to include women in the Information Society*, [Online], eds E. Rommes, I. von Slooten, E. van Oost & N. Oudshoorn, pp. 5-11, Available: www.sigis-ist.org [17. January 2005].

Wajcman, J. 1991, *Feminism confront Technology*, Pennsylvania State University Press, University Park.

Wiesner, H. 2001, 'Virtuelles Lernen. Das Geschlecht läuft immer mit', [Online], *Tagung: Frauen und Technologien. Zum Einsatz neuer Medien in der Lehre*, Innsbruck, 7. / 8 Juni 2001, Available: http://fem.uibk.ac.at/nmtagung/a_aufsatz_wiesner.htm [23 October 2004].

Woodfield, R. 2000, *Women, work and computing*, Cambridge University Press, Cambridge.

Zorn, I. 1998, 'Internetbasiertes Lernen aus Sicht der Erwachsenen- und Frauenbildung', [Online], *Didactic Teaching Methods in Beginner's Internet Classes in Adult Education: A Gender-specific Approach*, Available: http://www.uni-jena.de/~x7zois/magarbei.htm [23 October 2004].

Zorn, I. 2001, 'Internetbasiertes Lernen: Vorschläge für eine frauenfreundliche didaktische Gestaltung' in *Internet-Based Teaching and Learning (IN-TELE) 99: Internet Communication 3*, eds W. Frindte, T. Köhler, P. Marquet & E. Nissen, Europäischer Verlag der Wissenschaften, Frankfurt/M., New York, Oxford, pp. 265-274.

Notes

1 We thank Patrick Pilarek for support in translation.

2 This is mainly an overview of the German e-learning market. We acknowledge the material from the Open University but came to it too late to include it in this paper.

3 Kompetenzforum „Genderforschung in Informatik und Naturwissenschaften [gin], http://gin. iig.uni-freiburg.de, supported by a grant from the Ministry of Science, Research, and the Arts of Baden-Württemberg (Az:24-729.18).

Employment

Alison Adam,
Marie Griffiths,
Claire Keogh,
Karenza Moore,
Helen Richardson,
Angela Tattersall

Frances S. Grodzinsky,
Andra Gumbus

Mayumi Hori,
Masakazu Ohashi

21 "You don't have to be male to work here, but it helps!" – gender and the IT labour market

Alison Adam, Marie Griffiths, Claire Keogh, Karenza Moore, Helen Richardson, Angela Tattersall

Centre for Gender Research in Information Systems, Information Systems Institute, University of Salford, UK

Abstract

This paper reports on the state of gender and the UK IT labour market following a year long research project funded by the European Social Fund. The WINWIT project – Women in North West IT – considered the situation for women in IT in the North West of England during 2004. An on-line questionnaire provided a snapshot picture but the main field work involved in-depth interviews with women in IT, those who had left the sector but were trying to return, those who had left vowing never to return and those women attempting to progress into higher status IT-related jobs. The data reveals women reporting a level of job satisfaction but also paints a picture of overt as well as indirect discrimination where women often distance themselves from their gender in an effort to blend in, hidden and overt pay discrimination and such an astounding level of fear and loathing towards them that it is remarkable that any women at all persevere with an IT career. We have theorised their responses against the well recognised relationship between masculinity and technology, particularly in terms of what are seen as technical skills and masculine identity.

1. Introduction

In this paper we consider the state of gender and the IT labour market. In particular, we report on the situation of women in IT in the North West of England and the key issues and themes raised by a series of in-depth interviews and an on-line questionnaire which were undertaken as part of field work conducted throughout 2004.

Given that there have been decades of equal opportunity and related policies as well as many government initiatives designed to address the gender imbalance in IT employment patterns, sex segregation in IT occupations and pay and progression disparity in the IT sector (including the latest initiative – a one million pound DTI funded gender and SET project), we could be forgiven for assuming that these initiatives have had a beneficial effect on the position and number of women in the IT workforce, and that even if we have not yet achieved gender equity, we can surely argue that there are positive moves in the right direction. Although we do not wish to make definitive claims about the success or failure of specific initiatives, our research, backed up by recent major surveys, paints a picture that remains far from rosy. Indeed a recent comparative survey of the IT workforce in Germany, Holland and the UK indicates that women are haemorrhaging out of the UK IT workforce (Platman and Taylor 2004). From a high point of 100,892 women in the UK IT workforce in 1999, Platman and Taylor (ibid., 8) report a drop to 53,759 by 2003. As the IT industry was moving into recession anyway, the number of men in the industry has also declined, but by nothing like as much; hence the figures for women are stark.

We are hesitant to attribute specific causes to this sharp drop. The picture is clearly complex. Nevertheless, we argue that the liberal approach encapsulated by equal opportunities policies and more recent managing diversity policies does little to ameliorate women's position in the IT industry. Indeed in some ways equal opportunities/managing diversity rhetoric may reinforce women's positions as it may make it seem like all the battles are won and nothing else needs to happen to ameliorate women's lot. Although we acknowledge the force of equal opportunities discourse, for reasons of space we concentrate, instead on the gender-technology relation and technical skills in the present paper. The results of our research suggest that women (still) have a fairly hard time in the IT industry. It could be argued that the sorts of experiences that our respondents report are typical of the cut and thrust of corporate life and that women in IT may be having experiences that are similar to women in other parts of working life. This means that it may be unreasonable to expect to separate the experiences of women and IT from women in work, in general. Despite this we argue that there are potentially special features of women's experiences in working in technological domains, especially new technologies such as information and communications technology, which are harsh and possibly harsher than elsewhere. This is because of the long running association of masculinity with technology, the association of technology with masculine skill and the cultures surrounding technological work, including a long hours culture where flexibility often means constant availability (Hoque and Noon, 2004). This culture serves to marginalize and undermine women and has, in many cases, changed little over the last twenty years. Quite literally, as one example demonstrates below, women may be excluded from masculine space in the IT industry. Therefore although we may be saddened by women's exodus from the UK IT industry, we are not really surprised by it.

First, we look at current employment patterns. Then we introduce our case data and address key issues of the nature of the IT sector, on being an 'it' as a female in IT and the related issue of confidence. We reveal overt and hidden discrimination in the IT sector and finally we discuss masculinity and issues of organisational culture. We conclude that good intentions are not enough and the time for polite requests for change is over. However beautiful the policy and however well intentioned, we suggest that without understanding and theorising gender and technology, such policies will fail to address fairness and equality in the IT labour market and the struggle goes on. The liberal agenda does not work. Now is the time for noise and agitation to let the silenced voices be heard.

2. The shape of the UK IT labour market – still 'pale, male and stale'

When it comes to calculating who is employed in the UK IT sector and when trying to make historical comparisons, the first obstacle is defining the sector itself and studies vary quite substantially in the number of IT workers quoted, suggesting there is quite a bit of variation in what is taken to be an IT job. The IT industry has experienced considerable expansion over the past twenty years. In spring 2003 in Britain, it was estimated that almost 900,000 people worked in ICT firms, and there were over 1 million ICT workers, filling ICT roles in any sector (e-Skills UK, 2003). This growth has resulted in talk of a 'skills shortage' requiring the 'maximisation' of the workforce to its full potential: 'You don't just need pale, male, stale guys in the boardroom but a diversity of views' (Stone 2004).

In spring 2003 the Equal Opportunities Commission estimated there to be 151,000 women working in ICT occupations compared with 834,000 men (clearly using a different, much wider job definition from that of Platman and Taylor (2004)) , whilst in the childcare sector, there were less than 10,000 men working in these occupations, compared with 297,000 women (EOC 2004). It is estimated that the overall proportion of women working in ICT occupations is 15% (EOC 2004).

In the UK, Office of National Statistics (ONS) statistics indicate that women accounted for 30% of IT operations technicians, but a mere 15% of ICT Managers and only 11% of IT strategy and planning professionals (EOC 2004). Although women are making inroads into technical and senior professions there remains a 'feminisation' of lower level jobs, with a female majority in operator and clerical roles and a female minority in technical and managerial roles (APC 2004).

3. Gender and technology

As we have suggest above, many of the negative aspects women find in their careers in the IT industry may be common to other areas of working life. However the strong relationship between masculinity and technology may present an added burden for them. Women's more general exclusion from technology may be accounted for in terms of the historical and socio-cultural construction of technology as a 'masculine domain' (Wajcman 1991, Woodfield 2000). Lohan (2001) argues for example that:

technology is a significant site of gender negotiations where both masculine and

*feminine identities are constructed and deconstructed...By interpreting their usage
in our lives, they become part of the gendered division of labour and, through social
relations; technologies become assigned gendered symbolic values' (2001:189).*

As so much of the rhetoric surrounding putative shortages in the IT industry involves the
concept of a shortage of skills it is important to note the strong link between the notion
of skill, in particular technical skill and how something becomes defined as a technical
skill, and masculinity. Indeed Wajcman (1991) and Cockburn (1985) identify technical
skill and masculinity as mutually constitutive. Cockburn (1985) argues that power
differences between the sexes and their relationship to technology were consolidated in
the development of capitalism and the move to manufacturing production outside the
home. Skilled working class men formed into trade unions from which women could be
excluded and hence this served to exclude them from gaining skills which could earn
them a living. As Grint and Gill (1995; 9) note:

*'It could be argued that there is a dialectical relationship between women and 'skill',
such that women are concentrated in jobs which are deemed unskilled, and,
conversely, that those occupations in which women constitute the majority of
workers come to be seen as relatively less skilled than those dominated by men.
"Skill" is not some objectively identifiable quality, but rather is an ideological
category, one over which women were (and continue to be) denied the rights of
contestation.'*

If it is the case that (technical) skill and masculinity are as intimately entwined as all
these authors suggest then it is small wonder that women who challenge these
masculine skills by gaining them themselves are subject to the levels of hostility we
have encountered in our research.

This and other qualitative research on gender and IT concentrates on the ways in
which gender divisions are actively created and sustained in *organisational* and
domestic life. This enables researchers to highlight the binding together of the two
spheres, and pays particular attention to women's accounts of their experiences of IT
organisational culture, a culture which is embedded in the wider socio-political context
of gender discrimination and the 'masculine domain' of technology. Through such work,
notions of 'masculine' and 'feminine' skills can be problematised, and the co-opting of
skills and attributes into 'masculinist' work-place cultures can be challenged (Woodfield
2000).

4. The WINWIT research project

How are these ideas on skills shortages in the IT industry, the relationship between
masculinity and technical skill and women's threat to masculinity when they acquire
these technical skills reflected in women's experiences in the contemporary IT industry?

Throughout 2004, we conducted in-depth interviews and developed an on-line
questionnaire as part of an ESF funded research project to consider women in the IT

labour market and fulfill an ESF commitment to find ways to overcome gender discrimination at work. All the women who took part in our interviews are represented in the quotes below. In terms of hypotheses, we tried to be as open as possible but our own prior involvement in research in this area had suggested a number of issues still existed for women working in the IT industry. We were hoping to find more optimistic signs of equality awareness but were surprised how little had apparently changed for women in the IT industry over the last twenty or so years. We found interview partners at networking events, through existing contacts, promotional events and the project website. Interviews were typically around ninety minutes long and respondents were asked about their motivation in choosing an IT career, their career plans, why they thought there was a shortage of women in the industry and other work/life balance issues. Some women saw little problem, particularly in respect to their own situation, even though we as researchers might have felt that they had had a fairly hard time. More often, women freely reported discriminatory practices.

By using empirical material drawn from encounters with women in the IT industry, we are able to theorise about *how*, directly and indirectly, women are being discouraged from entering the IT sector and from progressing up the ladder if they do choose IT as a profession. In addition we are able to suggest *why* this situation continues despite years of equal opportunities legislation and workplace initiatives to tackle the gender and technology 'problem'. Our critical research approach aims to fulfill the tasks set by Alvesson and Deetz (2000) to provide insight and critique on the issue of gender and the IT labour market and also to challenge the status quo and let voices often silenced be heard. Our interviews with individual women in the IT industry enabled us to explore in more depth concerns raised by past and contemporary academic work, such as that of Morgan et al (2004) on the existence of 'Old Boy's Networks' in the IT industry – we were better able to understand the organisational and socio-cultural context in which these women's experiences are embedded. With such an understanding comes the possibility of change (Kvasny et al 2004, forthcoming), fulfilling the third task set of research taking a critical approach – that of transformative re-definition (Alvesson and Deetz 2000). Equal opportunities legislation and managing diversity discourse and practice continue to structure the way that women's under-representation in the IT field is understood. Yet concentrating on accounts of women's experiences, particularly their reports of continued gender discrimination in the IT workplace, should alert us to the possibility that equal opportunities legislation and managing diversity initiatives only goes so far – indeed not very far at all - in tackling the difficulties women face. The debate as to whether women are 'choosing' not to enter IT careers, or whether they are being actively excluded, becomes framed in different terms of reference when we examine the stories told by women in the field.

5. Key Issues

In the next sections we highlight some of the main themes and issues that emerge from the state of the UK IT labour market and gender discrimination and inequality as demonstrated by our research. Names have been changed to ensure anonymity and the profile of the women we quote are as follows: Tess is a board room member of a large multinational corporation; Ursula has established her career in IT and is progressing up the hierarchy in a public sector organisation; Vanessa has left IT following redundancy but is trying to find a way back in; Wilma works for the public sector at middle management level; Xena is mid-career in the private sector; Yvonne is in technical sales as a senior manager in the private sector and Zoe is a new entrant in the private sector.

5.1 On what constitutes 'working in IT'

Our interviewees and questionnaire respondents expressed job satisfaction particularly with the opportunity to combine technical skills and knowledge with 'people' and communication skills. However, it is notable that these often highly technically skilled women play down their technical knowledge when talking about their work in general terms, preferring to think of their role as using technology to manage and/or help people. The strength of feeling of 'we can but we won't' (Siann 1997) in terms of take-up of IT study and career paths is replicated in our investigations. A striking initial feature is the vehemence of women saying 'I'm not in IT but...' – 'I'm in sales', 'I'm in the people part of the organisation', 'I'm a manager' – overwhelmingly 'I'm not in IT'. Partly these responses reflect the changing nature of IT in the workplace and IT-related occupations. It is progressively more difficult to speak of a distinct 'IT industry' or sector in the UK. This is because of the rise of occupations involved in design and creative technology where IT is an integral element, and also because IT is embedded in business processes and management generally. Therefore 'IT' as we historically have known it – programming, systems analysis and design, tool development and evaluation and so on – is an increasingly diffuse sector. This view of not belonging directly to the IT sector, but to a wider work group which uses IT is reflected in Platman's and Taylor's (2004) research where they argue that many women are involved in wider employment rather than the IT industry itself, which, in any case, becomes harder and harder to define as a separate function as IT permeates through many more jobs and sectors. Taking this on board, we argue that a further reason for women failing to identify themselves as IT professionals lies in their ambivalence in identifying themselves in term of technical skills, a theme which is developed in the following sections.

5.2 On being an 'it' in IT

The situation and in fact 'problem' of being a woman and issues of self and identity at work in male dominated IT workplaces was revealed again and again. As Tess put it:

'I have almost forgot that I'm a female in this business, I'm not denigrating being a woman in any way but I've almost had to push aside being a female and get on with

the job like any man would do. '

Xena spoke of how certain characteristics which she perceived to be 'masculine' do not come 'naturally' to her:

'I think I've come to realise that more and more recently as I get round more clients is that it's all about confidence especially around men, sometimes I tend to take a back seat especially in my environment you have to see yourself. I think you almost have to have more arrogance. That doesn't come naturally to me.'

Woodfield (2000) shows that belonging to a gender group is obligatory and that individuals can no more be a gender-less than an ageless self. Indeed 'social categories provide individuals with both a social location and a value relative to other socially categorised individuals (2000:148)' Yet 'women who choose perform outside their gendered scripts' (Davies and Thomas 2000: 1134), in this case working as a minority in an occupation regarded as 'masculine' as well as in roles – as managers – where women are not commonplace, are perceived as having masculine characteristics. Liff (2001) reports that male interviewees perceived women that had attained managerial positions had 'lost their femininity' and the terms 'cut-throat, thrusting and ruthless' had also been used to describe female senior mangers, Displays of 'femininity' in the IT workplace were deemed problematic by some of the women contributing to our fieldwork. Vanessa recounted how in the early stages of her career she 'downplayed' her femininity, becoming a genderless 'it' in an attempt to make herself less visible, until she came to a point in her career at which she thought she would be recognised for her talents alone. She became more pro-active in relation to her gender status, although her pro-activeness led to jokes and comments about her sexuality. She recounts how:

'When I first started work (as a vendor), before I started at Company X the dress code was still very formal. Then when I came back to work for Company X as an employee they changed the rules and all of a sudden it became smart casual, and very soon I would only be wearing chinos and polo shirts because I really shouldn't be standing out. That took me a year and to the guys OK I was Vanessa, I was a woman but I was an 'it'. I was not a woman, I was not a man I was a person...I dressed like I dressed (chinos and polo shirt) for a year until I attended one of the (WITI) meetings on personal impact and how you should build your own confidence and I said "I'm too scared to show myself because I work in an all-male environment". Every time I mentioned I was going to a (WITI) meeting they always said "Oh you're going to one of your lesbian meetings" at work.'

Tess takes this discussion further:

'I don't know about my femininity but I have become more focused and self driven than quite a lot of men. I suppose I had a weird sort of compliment from my last manager who said to me "you know Tess you've got more balls than most men" which I took to be quite a compliment.'

The IT industry spokespeople often identify feminine characteristics that would be of benefit to the work involved. Wilma in fact identified some of these:

'I'm a woman and I've got more people skills - patience - I'm better at listening and questioning - I don't make assumptions as quickly - I don't rule things out.'

However, as Woodfield (2000) points out - women and traits associated with femininity are automatically significantly undervalued. We discuss this in relation to skills later in the paper. Vanessa noticed this when she finally decided to ditch her polo shirts and chinos:

'I wore a v necked shirt and they could physically see what was there and my guys really had trouble accepting that. I've had partners that come around and said oh and when you have got a minute could you rebook my hotel for me because they would automatically assume that I was part of the administration or a support person.'

The discomfort that these women felt with their gender roles in an IT is palpable. So strongly masculine is the world of technological skills within which these women move that the only way they were able to achieve a level of comfort was by denying their own gender and becoming an 'it.' Once again we could argue that the ambivalence these women felt about being women in a man's world could apply to other areas of life in the organisation. However we argue that technology and technological skill, and especially IT skill, is so strongly associated with masculinity, it is extremely hard for women to 'get comfortable', to feel at ease, to feel that they belong in such a working environment. One respondent reported that she felt that all the 'feminine' diplomacy she displayed was never enough and several reported that they were discouraged from displaying their technical skills. Many of our respondents appeared to be stuck in a no-win situation created, in part, by the discursive co-production of gender and technology and the cultural myths surrounding male and female skills and attributes. A woman feels she is not meant to be technical because she is a woman whilst she cannot be a woman if she presents herself as technical. She cannot really be a woman with social skills if she is also a woman with technical skills since these are (supposedly) mutually exclusive as the former are deemed feminine and the latter masculine. She may have social skills but she worries that these may not be enough to over-ride her primary identity as a 'techie.' The very detail of technical knowledge and practice is gendered in complex, and often contradictory ways. In addition skills attributed to women, whether social or technical are rendered invisible an insufficient; witness the woman who felt her diplomacy skills were never enough. Yet the ease and confidence with which men identify themselves with IT, displaying no such ambivalence about their masculinity runs all the way through accounts of men in the world of IT from accounts of the exclusively male arena of early hacking (Levy 1984), to stories of the race to build new computers (Kidder 1981) to Tierney's (1995) account of the 'lads' networking and negotiating a career in software.

5.3 On the confidence issue

Following on from this, one of key issues that has arisen from our fieldwork thus far is that of confidence, which relates to the above participant's downplaying of her femininity until she gained enough confidence (through extended tenure in her post and through support from other women in a formalised IT network) to 'show herself'. It has been argued that some women suffer 'impostor syndrome' because they feel guilty or unsure about their successes, particularly in the technical sphere (Miller and Jagger 2001). This results in a reluctance to challenge issues such as pay inequality, and leads to the taking on of extra responsibilities without commensurate rewards for fear of appearing too 'pushy' (Kolb 2003).

Throughout the material we have gathered, women in IT report difficulties with confidence, often framing the problem in individualistic terms, as Zoe demonstrates:

'Yeah well part of it's me and my personality so I lack confidence just in general I think. I'm really shy...it's probably stopped myself pushing forward, I'm more self-critical in my work, whereas a guy might do an Excel spreadsheet and think that looks alright, I like to put mine in colours and make it look absolutely perfect.'

Women reported lacking confidence and this they often attributed to personal failings. However it is hardly surprising that confidence was hit when reviewing the amount of fear and loathing faced and intimidation even bordering on threatening and violent harassment. Yvonne:

'I had problems where it was all mainly men and I had one guy in particular who worked for me who was a real problem. He was older than me and he had a real problem with me being a female boss. He was quite intimidating physically, he was 6ft 5ins and I'm 5ft.'

Yvonne discussed later how her experiences had changed the way she dealt with people:

'Yes it certainly has helped me learn to deal with people, you can't discount for handling people screaming and shouting at you.'

Little wonder that confidence takes a hit. Confidence can however be acquired through gaining extra skills and training in order to be able to prove oneself in relation to the skills and achievements of male colleagues, and to be wholly confident in their knowledge before they spoke up in the workplace. This amounts to the well-documented phenomenon in which women feel that they have to be 'much better' that their male counterparts in order to receive equal recognition. A questionnaire respondent reported:

'Men in my job get paid more and have less expectation put on them to perform. They progress to a higher level without having to prove themselves.'

Xena felt that it was a confidence thing that stopped her progressing compared to her male counterparts:

'I think had I been male - it's a confidence thing about selling yourself I never pushed

for it I know some guys who have threatened to leave and got another job and used that as bargaining and I never did that, again there's nothing stopping me doing it but it's more likely for men to do that. And although I came in at a lower level probably because I came in from a non IT background.'

When you then find out that Xena has a PhD in Computational Maths, there is probably more to the story than Xena's individual lack of confidence. Woodfield (2000) notes that a situation is produced whereby the sex of the worker rather than the work they do persists in being of overwhelming importance determining skill ascription and status. This ties in with Wajcman's (1991) and Cockburn's (1985) ascription of technical skills as mutually constitutive of masculinity. With confidence taking a battering on a daily basis, it is hardly surprising that women silence themselves. Tess:

'I have seen a lot of discrimination. I must be careful not to say anymore about that.'

Ursula:

'They were horrible men who went to the pub every dinner time and never asked me and they used to talk about football all the time. Apart from feeling intimidated, scarred and unconfident I just hated them all. They used to talk about there wives, women they had met and that sort of thing and I used to think how dare you talk about them like that. I wouldn't let that go now but then I didn't dare say anything.'

Xena:

'I would never introduce the male female issue because we are in the minority.'

5.4 On masculinity and organisational culture – exclusion from masculine spaces

The positive experiences women in IT recount are marred by the need to 'fit in' with the culture of the IT workplace. We have already suggested that some of the reason for this lies in the ambivalence that women experience against technical skills and also in the way that they are treated by men in relation to technical skills. This leaves some women uncomfortable, as the quotes below demonstrate. Xena:

'I think you've got to 'fit in', you've not got to be too girly, you've got to be quite tough and that's not naturally me.'

Vanessa:

'I'd say it's a tough industry (IT), not many women would have entered into it and the ones that have entered will have shied away by the fact that they are women and they would have to adapt to be just like men.'

The difficulties women face in the IT industry may not however take the form of overt misogyny and discrimination, but instead be a more subtle 'demand' to 'fit in' with male-dominated workplace cultures. Yvonne spoke of how she was able to 'fit in' to the IT industry given her previous 'tomboy' tendencies and drinking abilities, as the following quote indicates:

'Well I used to be a bit of a tomboy when I was a kid but I don't think that I'm one of the lads but when we have sales conferences and things like that, you know you have to do all the drinking and everything, really you have to fit in with the majority of men and not be upset by their banter. You can't let it offend you. You wouldn't last two minutes if you did.'

Again, we see how working in IT is still seen as a deeply masculine sphere, and how the women that do pursue careers in this area often highlight that how they are 'different' to other women who 'would not last two minutes'. Again women are expected to be able to cope with overt sexism (here in the form of 'dirty jokes') but responses to the problem become individualised so that women who are positioned as 'sensitive and delicate' are encouraged to pursue other career paths. The issue then becomes the ability of a woman to 'cope' in an all-male, sometimes, sexist environment, rather than how this environment can be changed to make IT more amenable to all women, however 'sensitive and delicate' they may be.

There is continued existence of male-dominated informal social networks within the IT sector. Following a discussion about a group of male colleagues who regularly go mountain biking together, Xena maintained:

'No they're just mates. I'm sure they don't discuss work. I haven't really heard of that going on, but you always find that on an away day or something the options will be golf or go-carting, there's that sort of thing.'

At a later point in the interview she elaborates:

'But I do know some guys out of the office that do play golf after work but they don't talk about business and make decisions.'

Other forms of exclusion may actually be spatial in nature, in terms of women in the IT workplace being discouraged from using certain technologies, or being excluded from particular 'male' spaces, as Vanessa detailed:

'It took me half a year to gain access to my own training lab, because my guys considered that no girls or females should be allowed in the lab so I asked "Can I just go and see it?" and (they responded) "women are not allowed in the lab, what are you going to do there?" I said "Excuse me there must be a difference as a manager. I must be allowed in even if it is just to look around. I'm allowed in. I'm a manager".'

Vanessa reported her pro-activeness in 'invading' these male spaces, using her job-related status (as manager) to procure entry in the lab, with manager acting as a distinctly 'different' status to that of 'woman'. It is interesting that through appeals to her managerial position, she was able to stake her claim to "'be allowed' (again implying ownership of the lab-space by the men involved), as she simultaneously downplays her wish to enter the lab space by saying 'even if it is just to look around'. Whilst it may be problematic to argue that women are being *actively* excluded from IT posts *per se*, instances and accounts by women in IT such as the above point to a more deeply

293

entrenched negative stance towards women in IT, and towards women using technology. Women who have overcome recruitment obstacles and entered this 'masculine domain' are still being excluded from core organisational activities, resulting in the loss of social and material benefits from informal networking and collaborating, an in turn exacerbating female marginalisation (Woodfield 2000). Women can be quite literally 'put in their place' as in the example of the woman excluded from her own lab. This point is highlighted if we look again at the ways in which different skills and attributes in IT, and in management in particular, are perceived as 'masculine' and 'feminine'. This is reinforced by or interviewees' ambivalence to their mix of technical and social skills and their resulting loss of confidence. Woodfield (2000) states that to understand the relationship between skills and gender we have to explore the value that our culture places on skills. This point is reinforced by Cockburn (1985). Masculine qualities are seen as positive and of high status while women's qualities are generally seen as less positive and of lower status (even if they are the same skill!). Cockburn (1985) argues that masculinity and technical skills are mutually constitutive. Much of what is taken to be masculine is defined in terms of technical skills. Conversely technical skills are defined as those skills which men have. Consequently women entering the workplace often carry a subordinate status with them. This has little or no bearing on qualifications, training or ability required for the job in hand. As Woodfield (2000) notes the same skill may be viewed differently when displayed by a man rather than a woman e.g. 'feminine' listening skills may be prized more highly in a man than in a woman.

6. Conclusion: good intentions are not enough

Commenting on silent voices Law (1991:2) makes this generalisation:

> 'First the dispossessed have no voice at all. Then, when they start to create a voice, they are derided. Then (I'm not sure of the order), they are told that they are wrong, or they are told that this was something that everyone knew all along. Then they are told that they are a danger. Then finally, in a very partial form, it may be that their voices are heard and taken seriously. And it has been a struggle all the way.'

From our experiences through this research we seem to be trapped in a 'no voice-danger' loop and the IT labour market still remains a place of struggle for all the women we've been privileged to talk with. We have argued that cyclical views on skills shortages and women's relationship to them in the IT industry, the relationship between masculinity and technical skill and women's threat to masculinity when they acquire these technical skills, their discomfort in relation to technical skills, and the response of male organisational groups to them all reflect in women's continuing marginalisation in the UK's contemporary IT industry.

In terms of policy making and managing diversity, evidence indicates that the ICT industry is losing more women than it is currently recruiting. The reality is that diversity, work life balance, flexible working are finding their way onto boardroom agendas but fundamentally there is little evidence available offering tangible suggestions about how to change organisational culture. Women in IT have talent, skills, demonstrate attributes that the industry cries out for and overcome tremendous excesses of masculine domination verging on misogyny. There are economic and business arguments for the greater inclusion of women in the IT sector. Employers are being 'sold' diversity as relief to the perceived skills shortage in the industry, and as offering a way to leverage corporate assets. There may indeed be an economic argument for creating a more diverse workforce, not least in terms of reflecting diverse customer bases, yet basing calls for the greater representation of women in IT primarily on the economic and business case leaves women vulnerable to any movement in the market and susceptible to shift in diversity discourses. Creating a more diverse workforce, not least in terms of reflecting diverse customer bases may help facilitate cultural change but for what costs? The demand for an ethical perspective should also have a comparable voice in that individuals should be treated equally and fairly in the workplace because of legal, moral, social and ethical reasons not just because it is financially beneficial. The fear and loathing will not be overcome by polite requests for change in organisational culture or fresh and shiny policies – the time for noise and agitation is surely here. We asked whether anyone would recommend going into IT. Although our interviewees did report positive aspects of jobs in IT, many felt that for a woman to survive, she needed to be able to cope in what is still essentially a man's world. Yvonne's answer sums things up admirably:

'It's the ideal career for women who have grown up with lots of brothers.'

References

Alvesson,M and Deetz, S. (2000) *Doing Critical Management Research* SAGE London

APC (2004) Association for Progressive Communications (2004) *Gender and Information and Communication Technology: Towards an analytical framework (Electronic)*, HYPERLINK "http://www.apcwomen.org/work/research/analytical-framework.html" http://www.apcwomen.org/work/research/analytical-framework.html, (Accessed-January 2004).

Cockburn, C. (1985) *Machinery of Dominance: Women, Men and Technical Know-How*, London: Pluto.

Davies, A and Thomas, R (2000) 'Gedner and Human Resource Management: a critical review' *International Journal of Human Resource Management*, Vol 11:6 pp1125-1136

e-Skills (2003) 'Quarterly review of the ICT labour market', *e-Skills Bulletin, Quarter 2.*

EOC (2004) Equal Opportunities Commission (EOC) (2004b) 'Plugging Britain's skills gap: challenging gender segregation in training and work', *Report of phase one of the EOC's investigation into gender segregation and Modern Apprenticeships*, May 2004.

George, R. (2004) 'Achieving workforce diversity in the e-business on demand era' HYPERLINK "http://www.intellectuk.org/sectors/it/women_it/2003/Achievingworkforcediversity.pdf" http://www.intellectuk.org/sectors/it/women_it/2003/Achievingworkforcediversity.pdf

Grint, K. and Gill, R. (eds.) (1995) *The Gender-Technology Relation: Contemporary Theory and Research*, London: Taylor & Francis.

Henwood, F. (1996) 'WISE Choices? Understanding Occupational Decision-making in a Climate of Equal Opportunities for Women in Science and Engineering', *Gender and Education*, Vol. 8, No.2, pp199-214.

Hoque, K. and Noon, M. (2004) 'Equal Opportunities Policy and Practice in Britain: Evaluating the 'Empty Shell' Hypothesis', *Work, Employment and Society*, Vol. 18, No. 3, pp 481-506.

Institute for Employment Research (IER) and IFF Research Ltd (2004) National Employers Skill Survey 2003, Sheffield: DfES.

Kidder, T. (1981) The Soul of a New Machine, Boston, MA: Little, Brown & Co.

Kolb, D. (2003) *Everyday Negotiation: negotiating the hidden agendas in bargaining*, San Francisco: Jossey-Bass,

Kvasny, L. Greenhill, A. Trauth, E. (2004 forthcoming) 'Creating Space for Feminist Methods in Management Information Systems Research', *International Journal of Technology and Human Interaction*, Volume unknown.

Law, J. (1991) 'Introduction: Monsters, Machines and Sociotechnical Relations', in J. Law (ed.) A Sociology of Monsters: Essays on Power, Technology and Domination, pp. 1–23. London: Routledge .

Levy, S. (1984) Hackers. heroes of the computer revolution. Penguin, Harmondsworth UK.

Liff, S. (1999) 'Diversity and equal opportunities: room for a constructive compromise?', *Human Resource Management Journal*, Vol.9, No.1.

Lohan, M. (2001) 'Men, masculinities and 'mundane' technologies: The domestic telephone', in E. Green and A. Adam (Eds.) *Virtual Gender: Technology, consumption and identity*, London: Routledge.

Morgan, A. J., Quesenberry, J. L. and Trauth, E. M. (2004) 'Exploring the Importance of Social Networks in the IT workforce: Experiences of the 'Boy's Club', Proceedings of the Tenth Americas Conference on Information Systems, New York, August.

Newell, S. (2002) *Creating the Healthy Organisation: Well-being, diversity and ethics at work*, London: Thomson Learning.

Office of National Statistics (2003) *New Earnings Survey*, Labour Market Trends, available at HYPERLINK "http://www.ons.gov.uk/" http://www.statistics.gov.uk/ (accessed August 2004).

Platman, K. and Taylor, R. (2004) *Workforce Ageing in the new Economy: A Comparative Study of Information Technology Employment. A European summary report focusing on the United Kingdom, Germany & the Netherlands*, available at HYPERLINK "http://www.cira.cam.ac.uk/index.html" www.cira.cam.ac.uk/index.html (accessed 04.10.04).

Siann, G. (1997) 'We Can, We Don't Want to: Factors Influencing Women's Participation in Computing' In R. Lander and A. Adam. (Eds) Women in Computing, Intellect. Exeter

Stone, G. (2004) from Aurora Gender Capital Management interviewed by Yvonne Roberts *'Hostages to fortune: has feminism been hijacked by capitalism'* The Guardian newspaper 24.06.04

Tierney, M. (1995) "Negotiating a software Career: Informal Work Practices and 'The Lads'" in a Software Installation' in Grint, K. and Gill, R. (eds.) (1995) *The Gender-Technology Relation: Contemporary Theory and Research*, London: Taylor & Francis, pp 192-209.

Wajcman, J. (1991) *Feminism Confronts Technology*, London: Polity Press.

Woodfield, R. (2000) *Women, Work and Computing*, Cambridge: Cambridge University Press.

Notes

1 WITI – Women In Technology International - WITI's mission is to empower women to achieve unimagined possibilities and transformation through technology, leadership and economic prosperity.

22 Networking and Career Advancement Strategies for Women

A study of the effects of networking and mentoring on ICT careers for women

Frances S. Grodzinsky

Computer Science/Information Technology, Sacred Heart University, Connecticut, USA

Andra Gumbus

Management, Sacred Heart University, Connecticut, USA

Abstract

Career counsellors have long encouraged job seekers to develop a network as a way to identify opportunities for career advancement, to gain entry and facilitate job searches. Many job seekers have heard that 'it's not what you know, but who you know, if you want to get ahead.' In order to ascertain how important networking and mentoring are for women employees in the world of ICT and business, we conducted interviews with eighteen Human Resource recruiters for high technology positions in the ICT, healthcare, telecommunications and pharmaceutical industries. Our survey focused on the hiring for technology positions in these industries. We also surveyed three executive ICT recruiters in private practice. Part One of this paper reports the findings of our survey on the impact of networking on recruitment practices. In Part Two, an analysis reveals that there are issues in networking that may promote or hinder career advancement for women in ICT. Behavioural differences between men and women also affect networking and mentoring relationships.

Introduction

Career counsellors have long encouraged job seekers to develop a network as a way to identify opportunities for career advancement, to gain entry and facilitate job searches. Many job seekers have heard that 'it's not what you know, but who you know, if you want to get ahead.' Recently, in the USA, we have seen evidence of this in the popular television show, The Apprentice, where young men and women vie for a chance to work and be mentored by Donald Trump. Why has this show generated so much interest?

Catching a glimpse of the inner workings of the Trump organisation fascinates not only those in the corporate world, but also others who seek to understand the interaction, relationships and challenges of working in an organisation.

Research suggests that the informal organisation (networking) can be as effective, or perhaps more effective, in getting organisation members to support initiatives in the workplace. A networking approach is based on five principles that are fundamental to the process. According to Baker they are:

> Relationships are a fundamental human need
> People tend to do what is expected of them
> People tend to associate with others like themselves
> Repeated interaction encourages cooperation
> It's a small world (Baker 1994)

All of these beliefs are predicated upon the notion that being on the 'inside' provides an advantage and that whatever we can do to enhance the chance of being 'in the know' or on the 'inside' is good.

Networking is defined as 'the building and nurturing of personal and professional relationships to create a system or chain of information, contacts, and support' (DeJanasz, Dowd & Schneider 2002). This occurs on different levels. For example, in business networking, a person must be able to define business goals clearly and meet people who can help his/her company achieve these goals. Our focus, however, is on employee networking. At the employee level, individuals must be clear, concise and confident in describing past accomplishments and future career aspirations (Klaus 2003) when networking. This requires being proactive in a business and social setting and, therefore, can be difficult for those not outgoing by nature (Misner 2003).

Networking implies helping others and giving advice, industry information, contacts or assistance, but should not be false or manipulative (Fisher 2001). Contacts should be approached on a professional level with respect and not simply used as a means towards an end. Networking results in securing jobs, especially at a managerial level and, therefore, can be a particularly important career enhancing strategy for women seeking a managerial or executive level position in ICT and business. The Bureau of Labor Statistics reports that 72% of executives (earning over $ 100,000 per year) found their current job through a friend, relative or business acquaintance (Fisher 2001).

In tough economic times, networking can increase career opportunities and function as a long-term career management strategy (Gumbus & Lussier 2003). Currently, employees are trading off stability and job security for future employability, as they become multi – skilled to increase marketability. This concept of the 'portfolio worker' is different from the historic 'company or organisation person'. The portfolio worker moves from job to job, compiling skill sets and experience from projects in various organisations, resulting in a career progression. This contrasts with the worker who stays in one organisation to gain skills and progress in a job (Handy 1994). Portfolio workers rely on networking skills as they advance in their careers among numerous companies and industries. Therefore, today, employees have to spend more time on the personal skills of career management in order to be competitive in the ever-shrinking job market and ever-changing field of ICT.

In addition, from the point of view of the company, recruiting through a network saves time and money spent on advertising, interviewing, reference checking and other human resource employment activities. Gaining applicants through a network also reduces the amount of risk inherent in all hiring situations by eliminating or mitigating the element of the unknown. Most economic activity is conducted through networks of known individuals and based on personal acquaintance. Granovetter attributes this to human motives for approval, status and social relations (Granovetter 1992). The organisation not only receives superior talent, but also is referred to individuals known for their accomplishments and past achievements.

In order to ascertain how important networking and mentoring are for women employees in the world of ICT and business, we conducted interviews with eighteen Human Resource recruiters for high technology positions in the ICT, healthcare, telecommunications and pharmaceutical industries. We also surveyed three executive ICT recruiters in private practice. Sixteen human resource managers were women and two male. All three executive ICT recruiters were male. Part One of this paper reports the findings of our survey on the impact of networking on recruitment practices. In Part Two, an analysis reveals that there are issues in networking that may promote or hinder career advancement for women in ICT.

1. The Impact of Networking on Recruitment Practices: findings

In this study, we asked the human resource (HR) managers and recruiters to respond to the following questions in order to assess the impact of networking on recruitment practices as it affects women.

> In your opinion, is networking effective in finding a job?
> Do you think one gender is more comfortable using networking? Why?
> Can you give a specific example of when networking was used successfully by you or another female to get a job?
> Can career opportunity for women be enhanced through networking?

The results of this survey confirm the efficacy of networking as a career advancement strategy for women. The response to networking as an effective job search strategy (question 1) was overwhelmingly positive. Most felt that 90% of their jobs and clients were as a result of networking. A female recruiter in the Tampa Bay area mentioned that 'every temporary on-site assignment I've had (three different assignments ranging from 3 – 6 months) resulted from networking.' Another ICT recruiter contacts well-networked women when she has a job to fill. She consistently starts with the most networked woman she knows with a high tech background who worked at AT&T, Lucent and Octel. She emails her and asks her to forward the email to anyone in ICT that she knows who may provide a lead for candidates. Email and the Internet have provided an efficient and effective vehicle for spreading the word quickly about ICT job opportunities. Most recruiters said that networking is the primary vehicle for how they do their business in placing people in ICT jobs.

Responses regarding whether one gender is more comfortable networking were mixed (question2). Most felt that people of the same gender network easily because they have a common ground with which to begin the dialog. Contrary to the research, anecdotally some recruiters felt that women were 'traditionally better at those sorts of things because they are comfortable expanding their circle to include higher levels, colleagues, and lower level contacts. Men, because of ego, network at their current professional level and may be more embarrassed to admit that they need help in any way, or were laid off or fired.' Another female ICT recruiter said, 'Lately, I find it's equal, probably due to the poor economy, lack of jobs, high unemployment, and fierce competition which forces both men and women to attempt all avenues.' A recruiter at a large pharmaceutical firm felt that men are more comfortable using networking and stated, 'men probably use it more frequently because being pushy isn't as much of a concern of men. Women, in my opinion are more likely to use acquaintances to find jobs, men are more likely to network with strangers.' Dan Winschel, President of DRW Associates exclusively recruits for executive level ICT positions. He claimed that men dominate 90% of the ICT field, so men predominantly network with other men in ICT.

In response to questions 3 and 4, a former female HR Vice President felt that networking was effective, 'I got my last 3 HR jobs through networking at the HR Networking Group here in Cleveland. The group meets twice a month; jobs are posted from all over the country. Everyone supports each other and encourages one another.'

Pam, a 27-year veteran ICT executive, secured several positions through networking when she did not use her recruiter. 'My old boss recognized my name, knew my work, and knew what I could do. That's how I got into my current company. He networked me in the door. I have seen other men get hired based on networking and leads from men in the company. Ironically, I tried to get two prior colleagues (males) into the firm but was unsuccessful as a female.' Pam believes men have the advantage over women in networking through an established male network that has existed for decades. 'Twenty years ago a female network did not exist; we're still trying to get the old girl network going in information technology.'

Another female respondent from a university HR department stated, 'as a staffing and recruiting manager, I have referred people I know to hiring managers and ultimately they did get the position. Since I have knowledge about positions and the culture here, it has been extremely helpful. Personally, the positions I have held I got through networking or knowing someone in the organisation. I think it's a great tool to use in the job search process.' An independent female recruiter replied, 'Life in general is about networking, who you know, not necessarily what you know. Lots of skills can be taught in time, but attitude is more difficult to acquire. So, if a candidate is personally known with a good character reference, he/she will have a better chance of getting the job than a candidate who is not known to the recruiter.'

Recruiters also depend on networks of past placements to provide leads for placing candidates. 'After providing a comprehensive service that was kind, efficient and successful to candidates, these past placements are then willing to provide names of colleagues/friends as referrals. In order to develop networks, recruiters need to have a personality that allows for a professional yet personable relationship with candidates. I constantly tap past candidates for potential leads when working a position. The well-networked ones are the ones who get referred.' All twenty-one survey respondents across industries were able to cite multiple examples of when they successfully used networking to place women candidates in jobs and responded overwhelmingly that career opportunities for women can be enhanced through networking.

2. Networking as a Career Advancement Strategy for Women

In this section of the paper we will examine networking as a career advancement strategy for women in ICT focusing on mentoring, power and equal opportunity issues.

2.1 Networking and women in ICT

Work culture, expectations and the rewards system in organisations all impact on the use of networking as a career advancement strategy for women. Singh et al studied the influence of gender on impression management behaviour and found that women prefer to rely on hard work and high performance rather than networking strategies used by males.

Self – promotion, ingratiation and networking skills form part of the criteria for the rules of the game of acknowledgement, recognition and promotion, which most managerial and professional males seem to understand and comply with, in a more straightforward and less emotional way (Singh et al 2002).

They conclude that women may be at a disadvantage for promotion if males successfully use these ingratiation and self-promotion strategies and they do not.

Women do not always want to play the organisational game by the male-constructed unwritten rules, but prefer to trust good management and systems fairness for just rewards. Younger and junior level women managers often recognize that impression management may be a useful tool but reject its use for themselves However, these same junior-level women felt that networking was critically important in loosely structured organisations like consulting where individual contributions might go unnoticed. There, networking was viewed as a vehicle to develop a profile in the company as a prerequisite for advancement. This profile could then lead to sponsors and other advocates in cultures that used personal recommendations for promotion.

In today's flatter organisational structures that utilize project teams, matrix designs and virtual workplaces, networking was found to be important to career success among directors (Vinnicombe et al 2000).

Gender discrepancies in the conceptualisation of networking are not only due to education and culture, but also to access to the field. A male recruiter observed, 'Due to the nature of engineering and ICT positions, women contact me less often than men. This may be due, however, to a more limited female network structure available to women who are in management positions. This has improved over the years, but fewer women in ICT management positions is still quite evident.' The small number of women in ICT and even fewer numbers of managers pose special problems for women advancing their ICT careers. Insufficient numbers may prevent women from networking as successfully as their male counterparts.

The Chesler study supports this anecdotal evidence.

Female leadership in the upper echelon of the business community is also rare; women comprise only 10% of senior managers and less than 4% of the uppermost ranks (CEO, president, executive vice president and COO) in Fortune 500 companies... (Chesler 2002).

Although women hold half of all management and professional jobs only 8% have achieved executive vice president level and 5% are among the top five earners in each Fortune 500 Company (Fortune 10 January 2005). This lack of female leaders places the burden of mentoring and networking on the few senior women ICT executives. Women in lower level positions have less influence and resources at their disposal and may be perceived as less desirable in the social exchange process. Research of 1,050 adults in the N. California Community Study found a correlation between socioeconomic background and successful networking. Personal and professional resources of family, educational attainment and job stature increase likelihood of reaching hiring managers and decision makers (Campbell, Marsden, Hurlbert 1986). In addition, the fact that women are underrepresented in the field contributes to an uneven economic playing field and raises ethical issues concerning hiring practices especially if they are built around mentoring and/or networking through an 'old-boys network'.

The problem of women and technology as researched by Gorniak-Kocikowska is not new. It has its roots in the history of the relation between women and technology since the industrial revolution. Women have greater professional choices and may have less interest in ICT in competition with other career fields. Lack of early encouragement to pursue science, math, together with statistics of women engineering graduates who do not work in the field reflects this gap. Discrimination exists in the male dominated ICT culture. 'There are still many ways of subtle and not so subtle discrimination against women in the workplace, and the ICT-related institutions and organisations are not completely free from it. The culture of ICT is definitely male-created and male-oriented. A computer science lab might have as much a macho atmosphere as did a 19th century science lab'(Gorniak-Kocikowska & Pakszys 2002). The perception of a male-dominated ICT culture makes it less attractive to goal- oriented women who want equality from the start of their careers in the work place and the possibility of advancement within that career. A strong network at the graduate level of education that begins with mentoring can facilitate entry into the ICT field for junior women.

2.2 Networking behaviour differences: men and women

Alternative networking strategies proven effective by Forret and Dougherty may also advance women in ICT. They include actively seeking and maintaining relationships with contacts, socializing at professional and community based events, participating in professional activities, workshops, association or club meetings and being active in community, civic or religious organisations (Forret & Dougherty 2001). Their research indicates that women perceive greater barriers to networking but these difficulties do not prevent women from networking. Although they found that men are more likely to engage in socializing behaviours than women, Forret and Dougherty question if this is due to less after work time available to women due to child rearing activities. Women with family responsibilities are disadvantaged in both networking and mentoring relationships.

In today's economy, women must not only hone their skills, but also be proactive in demonstrating why they are best for promotion or advancement. Accepting that networking is part of the business culture is the first step in that direction. Actively seeking a mentor or mentoring network, participating in interpersonal skill building training, or pursuing an advanced degree or certification provide visibility that adds depth to a resume and more contacts to the network.

Research indicates that women do not benefit from networking as much as their male counterparts. This may be due to the greater influence structures and dominant power status of men in the workplace and the token status of women. Forret and Dougherty studied the effect of gender on career outcomes and hypothesized that gender will moderate the relationship between networking and career outcomes, being stronger for men than women. Using their networking scale of five types of networking behaviours they found that gender based socializing was related to number of promotions, gender based engagement in professional activities was related to total compensation, and gender difference was significant in internal visibility and career outcomes. Their research showed that engaging in professional activities had a negative impact on compensation for women, but a positive impact on compensation for men. Greater internal visibility was a positive factor for men, but a negative for women (Forret & Dougherty 2004). These disturbing results may be due to the fact that women have low visibility assignments and are structurally at a lower level in the workplace; therefore, this reduces women's ability to develop networks for career advancement.

Networks provide power to the individual through association with determinants of power, i.e., positions in the network and the amount of dependence on the network

(Burt 1992). The problem of women connecting to a network is compounded in a male dominated field such as ICT where men dominate managerial and non-managerial levels. The quality and quantity of the individual's network results in information and referrals that can either help or hinder the opportunity for return on investment. A dependent power relationship exists when those with less power are dependent upon those with power to gain access, information, opportunity for jobs, or favours. The asymmetry of the power relationship is clearly marked by those on the 'inside' who have power by virtue of their position, reputation and relationship with those in the network, and those who are 'outside' and depend on the network to move them forward in their job search. If a well-respected member of the network champions an outsider, his/her odds of being considered for a position increase. The question of how to connect with those inside the network remains a difficult one for those who are 'unconnected': typically, women and minorities.

2.3 Networking and mentoring

Senior managers credit their relationships with other people as key to their corporate success, particularly relationships with mentors and formal networks. Both genders use the following groups to enhance their career options: mentors, informal and formal networks of colleagues, and spouses (Schor 1997). The connection with others and mentoring from others are important planned career development strategies particularly for women and other non-traditional or underrepresented managers. An understanding of the organisation's networking and mentoring systems are an important aspect of a personal development plan (Mathews 1995). Haring-Hidore suggests networking-mentoring as a career enhancement strategy for women (Haring-Hidore 1987).

Are there different mentoring models based on gender? The male dominated model of grooming-mentoring that encourages fast movement up the corporate ladder can be contrasted to the female dominated model introduced by Swoboda and Miller. This model consists of 'more flexible and mutually interdependent patterns of training, information sharing and support.' It is mutually beneficial to both the mentor and mentee enhancing both careers, however it does not move a woman up the corporate ladder as does grooming-mentoring (Swoboda & Millar 1986). It does eliminate the problem of finding senior executive women to develop junior managers, and the authors report fewer problems of favouritism or career setbacks.

> Mentors ... provide both psychosocial functions, such as role modelling, acceptance and affirmation, as well as career functions, such as sponsorship, coaching and networking', say the experts (Schlegel 2000).

Typically first time employees in ICT come out of either an undergraduate or graduate program in technology. Studies done on the expectations of graduate students are instructive in trying to analyze the role of mentoring as viewed by junior level employees. According to Lucia Gilbert, PhD, at the University of Texas at Austin, not only do female graduate students need mentors, they particularly need female mentors who can model the greater diversity in women's lives today. Her research shows that female graduate students, more than male students, rated the same-sex mentor's lifestyle and values as highly important to their own professional development (Schlegel 2000).

Gilbert also stresses that female students working with female mentors may provide an important antidote to some women's socialisation to please and defer to men. Rather than being in a relationship of unequal power, in female mentor-female protégé relationships, students may learn that empowering relationships mobilize the energies, resources and strengths of both people. Carol Williams, now APA's associate executive director for the American Psychological Association of Graduate Students, also did research on mentoring and found that gender does make a difference to female students.

Women can have good and supportive mentoring relationships with men; however, women want mentoring relationships with women as well—and female students want women mentors who are willing to expose more of their personal sides, she explains (Schlegel 2000).

Chesler found that young women typically place a greater priority on interpersonal satisfaction and integration than do men, potentially resulting in different career (and life) priorities (Chesler 2002). What did young women find helpful in mentoring relationships with women mentors? Women mentors were good at teaching how to face challenges within the workplace, when there is a conflict between work and family, and how to prioritize tasks. 'She didn't tell me what to do, she empowered me...to make my own choices, demonstrated that there can be more than one road to success, that family obligations do not mean an end to a career (Schlegel 2002).

2.4 Why women do not mentor or ' womentor' other women

In spite of the desires and expectations of young women that are often fostered in graduate schools, women who would be good mentors are usually those who have no time to do it ——or they see this as a 'stereotypic role that just adds to an already overloaded agenda.' We surveyed Pam, an ICT executive with a 27-year career in various ICT roles from programmer to project leader on three SAP implementations in Fortune 100 companies. She stated, 'Unfortunately, I don't have time to mentor young women. Although I believe mentoring is very important to career advancement, I don't have the time to commit to being a mentor or to being mentored myself – the company requires a formal commitment of 2 hours per month and I don't have the time.' It is interesting that although she acknowledges that mentoring is good for women and organisations, Pam still chooses her other job obligations over mentoring other women, even though the company requires it of both men and women. Implicitly, this suggests that mentoring, in this case a company service, may be perceived as less valued in her mind because she suffers no repercussions by ignoring the mandate. Until the culture changes and mentoring becomes a management value on a par with performance, women may continue to underutilize networking.

Mentoring is a critical career strategy for both men and women, yet women find it more difficult than men to find a mentor because of attitudes such as these. Is there something more profound underlying the hesitancy of senior women to monitor junior women in ICT and business? The term' womentoring' was coined by Hetherington and Barcelo to encourage cross – cultural and cross- gender mentoring (Hetherington & Barcelo 1985). If women are perceived as being less powerful in organisations due to numbers as well as positions, young women may intentionally seek out male mentors who are more powerful. Or if women are underrepresented in top management positions, it may be perceived that they would be unable to help advance the careers of junior women. Senior women may also be devoting considerable time and energy to break through the glass ceiling to advance their own careers. Corporate cultures that foster stereotypes also contribute to the lack of female mentoring (Gumbus & Grodzinsky 2004).

Males mentoring females adds a level of complexity to the mentoring relationship that has been dealt with by Chesler and others and is beyond the scope of this paper. We will focus on senior women mentoring junior women, a relationship that can also be difficult for both parties in ICT and business. This contrasts sharply with the views of graduate students in the Gilbert study.

Women often discover that mentoring relationships with other women are unsatisfying. Senior business women report feeling either discounted or overburdened as mentors; junior women complain that senior women are competitive with or unreceptive to them as potential proteges (Parker 1993).

At the university there is no perceived risk to taking on a graduate student. In fact, mentoring epitomizes the role of teacher. However, the reality of ICT and business is that an up-and-coming star might be the one to replace you, so some senior women are afraid of risking their careers by devoting time to mentoring other women, and some feel unprepared or not skilled to mentor (Ragins & Cotton 1991).. In addition, women may feel vulnerable to the exposure of mentoring an up-and-coming junior female executive due to the high visibility of the success or failure of the 'token' protégé. It can be risky for the senior woman in a male dominated profession like ICT if her coaching fails or if she is perceived as favoring women. (Ragins & Cotton 1991).

In her study of a senior woman mentoring a junior woman, Parker noted that self-disclosure, listening and feedback were absent in the mentoring relationship and attributed this to a possible mother/ daughter dynamic that did not foster positive mentoring. Confusion around expectations of each other and dependencies may distort the mentoring relationship. Parker suggests five strategies for removing obstacles to connections among women: increase self- awareness, make undermining dynamics discussable, challenge untested assumptions, build multiple relationships, and create a supportive culture. She mentions the following assumptions that can prevent alliances.

- Don't assume that she has it all together, that she will disapprove, or that she is

not interested in mentoring.
- Don't assume that being a good role model means never disclosing personal difficulties and challenges encountered at work.
- Don't collude with the dominant culture in undermining women's self-esteem and power base.
- Don't assume a prospective mentor feels qualified to mentor and doesn't need positive feedback.
- Consider the possibility that proteges can provide support to senior women up against the glass ceiling (Parker 1993).

The complexity of the mentoring relationship for women can be defined in part as a boundary issue. If mentoring is largely a work relationship, then how much personal data should be shared? Can one mentor successfully without sharing it? Parker asserts that a positive aspect for junior women is their mentor has experienced similar gender struggles of balancing career, family and the balance of work/life demands. '

This struggle touches on parts of identity that are very important to women: What does it mean to be committed to relationships, to be a primary nurturer in the family, and to achieve in a career? Much is at stake in mentor relationships between women if these central identity issues are shared...(Parker 1993).

Is this a realistic expectation that has been realized in the last decade? We argue that if senior women feel vulnerable about the expectation of intimacy, then this might contribute to their hestitancy to mentor junior women. At the university mentors successfully guide their protoges without a great sharing of personal history. Personal anecdotes to encourge empowerment are inserted when appropriate, but graduate students are usually not a part of their professors' personal lives. If this model were carried over to the ICT and business workplace, perhaps there would be a more positive reaction among senior women around mentoring.

2.5 Multiple mentors

If at first you don't succeed, try again. This old adage pertains to finding a mentor or mentoring network. Chesler suggests that there are alternative mentoring models that include multiple mentors, peer mentors and mentoring teams (Chesler 2002). A positive aspect of having multiple mentors is that they can address the diverse needs that arise in the workplace. In ICT, for example, a mentor in technological problems might not serve the same needs as one who is skilled in interpersonal relationships and team building. Having multiple mentors takes the pressure off of one relationship and increases the network. If women establish multiple mentoring relationships, this 'mentoring culture' provides a broader spectrum of learning opportunities and contacts. Research on mentoring illustrates that different groups (gender, racial and ethnic) benefit from mentoring relationships due to diverse experiences for development (Kram & Bragar 1992). If mentors fall into stereotypical roles of the female mentor for counseling and caring and the male mentor for powerful career contacts then women will not increase their power base. Until the culture changes and women perceive mentoring as a way to increase networking and make inroads into an organisation for women, they may continue to underutilize networking.

How does informal networking deal with the issues of equal opportunities? Networking offers the first step in the door. Once the contact is made, especially in the corporate culture, the applicant is on his/her own. One could argue that giving preference to a reference through a network undermines the concept of equal opportunities because everyone is not treated fairly. If one put on Rawl's blindfold of justice, there would definitely be an advantage for a well-connected employee/applicant vs. one who has no network. The gender issue comes into play because typically, those who are advantaged by networking have been males. If women had this opportunity as well, it would level the playing field for women in a corporate culture that relies heavily on networking for career advancement and strengthens the argument for networking as a strategy for all who want to get ahead in ICT and business today.

3. The Future of Networking: Internetworking and Social – Networking Software

A new generation of software is enabling professional acquaintances to broaden their contacts in order to find jobs, sales leads and close deals. The premise behind this new technology is the ability to access contacts beyond an employee's acquaintances. 'You may know a lot of people from work, college, church, or your neighbourhood, but you probably don't know exactly who their friends are – or their friends' friends. But join an online social network and invite a few acquaintances and the software will begin to reveal previously hidden second or third degree connections that can lead to an interview, business meeting, or tee time with that elusive potential client or employer' (Fitzgerald 2004). Since most face-to-face social networks have a digital component, members use technology to advantage business relationships. Fitzgerald cites 30 social network startups in the past 3 years and he predicts that social networks will become a part of the online experience. 'Harvard University psychologist Stanley Milgram's famous finding that on average we're only six acquaintances away from anyone else on the planet was still almost 30 years ahead of the technology needed to take advantage of it. Broadband connections reach 38% of U.S. Internet users – almost 50 million people, up from virtually zero in 1997: and the spread of programs like Microsoft Outlook means that most home Internet users and office workers already have the names and addresses of their acquaintances in electronic form' (Fitzgerald 2004). As a long-term strategy to manage careers, email or informal chat can be used to maintain contact, or pass along an article or Internet link to a past employer, colleague, search firm or others in the network. Online networking is effective using chat rooms and interest groups in a current or targeted industry. Online networking can be used to notify the network of a new job, added responsibility, or other career enhancements so the network can represent a candidate accurately (Gumbus 2003).

Not everyone will be connected and sceptics cite pitfalls that can cause problems with this new technology. Will people choose to share their best contacts with others and thereby perhaps dilute their own network? Digital divide, equity of access, and computer literacy raise issues about who is connected, and the cost of connecting and training for those without computer skills. Advancement into managerial positions suggests a level of education and computer literacy not equally available to all. Concerns about privacy of personal information often deter women from sharing information online. These are serious ethical issues that go beyond the scope of this paper, but they need to be addressed if online recruitment becomes the de facto modeof hiring.

Conclusion

Promotional opportunities for women to break through the glass ceiling in ICT include networking opportunities with other females, mentoring by senior women, building a team environment with other women, assignments that are visible and of high importance, and being technologically competent. Legislation and affirmative action quotas do not easily mandate ethical and equitable treatment regarding assignments and high profile opportunities. Organisations should ensure that their promotional opportunities are open to all who have the potential to advance, not just to those who are skilled at and comfortable with using networking and other impression management strategies. Corporate climates that promote employee growth, equity, mentoring and career advancement will attract and retain key talent. These progressive companies have an inclusive culture that allows women to advance in ICT.

Future career prospects for women will depend increasingly on their ability to use technology to build their networks. In an era of layoffs and increasing competition, the need for mentors and visibility at high levels is important in career development for women. Networking is of particular importance to women who tend to underutilize influential colleagues and may participate less in mentoring and building a team environment with other women. Networking may also be a critical response to the perception that women are excluded from informal networks and, therefore, hampered in initiatives to advance their careers. Women students in ICT might be encouraged as they seek to define their future careers if networking and mentoring among women become a visibly strong reality that aids career advancement in ICT.

References

Burt, R.S. 1992, *Structural holes: the social structure of competition*, Harvard University Press, Cambridge, MA

Campbell, K. Marsden, P. & Hurlbert, J. 1986, 'Social resources and economic status', *Social Networks* , 8, pp. 97 – 117

Chesler,N. & Chesler, M. 2002, 'Gender-informed mentoring strategies for women engineering scholars: on establishing a caring community', *Journal of Engineering Education*, pp. 49-55

DeJanasz, S., Dowd, K.O. & Schneider, B.Z. 2002, *Interpersonal Skills in Organisations*, New York, NY: McGraw Hill

Etzkowitz, H. Kemelgor,C., Uzzi, B. 1999, *Social Capital and Career Dynamics in Hard Science: Gender, Networks and Advancement*, New York: Cambridge University Press

Fisher, A. 2001, 'Surviving the Downturn', *Fortune*. New York: Time, Inc. 2 April 2001, pp. 98– 106

Fitzgerald, M. 2004,'Internetworking: A new wave of social-networking software is helping people find friends, get work, close deals', *MIT magazine of innovation technology review*. 107 (3)

Forret, M. & Dougherty, T. 2001, 'Correlates of networking behavior for managerial and professional employees'. *Group and organisation management*; 26 (3) pp. 283-311

Forret, M. & Dougherty, T. 2004, 'Networking behaviors and career outcomes: differences for men and women? '*Journal of Organizational Behavior* 25, pp. 419 – 437

Gorniak-Kocikowska, K. & Pakszys, E.B. 2002, 'Women, ICT, values and the future' in *Proceedings of Ethicomp international conference*, Lisbon, Portugal

Granovetter, M. 1992, 'Problems of explanation in economic sociology' in Nohira and Eccles, *Networks and organizations: structure, form and action* (p. 2556), Harvard Business School Press, Boston

Gumbus, A. 2003, 'Networking: A long term management strategy', *Clinical Leadership & Management Review*, May/June 2003

Gumbus, A. & Grodzinsky, F. S. 2004, 'Gender bias in internet employment: a study of career advancement opportunities for women in the field of ICT', *Information, Communication & Ethics in Society* 2 (1) pp. 77 - 86

Gumbus, A & Lussier, R. 2003, 'Career Development: Enhancing your networking skills', *Clinical Leadership & Management Review*, Jan/Feb 2003

Handy, C. 1994, *The empty raincoat*. Hutchinson, London

Haring-Hidore, M. 1987, 'Mentoring as a career enhancement strategy for women', *Journal of Counseling & Development*, Nov 1987 Vol 66 . pp. 147 – 148

Hetherington, C. & Barcelo, R. 1985, 'Womentoring: A Cross-Cultural Perspective', *Journal of NAWDAC*, 48, pp. 12 – 15

Klaus, P. 2003, *Brag! The Art of Tooting Your Own Horn Without Blowing It*, Warner Books New York, NY

Kram, K.E. & Bragar, M.C. 1992, 'Development through mentoring: a strategic Approach' in Montross & Shrinkman, eds, *Career Development: Theory and Practice*. Chicago: Thomas Press, pp. 221- 254

Mathews, Audrey. 1994, 'The Diversity Connections: Mentoring and Networking', *Public Manager*. Potomac: Winter 1994/1995 Vol 23 ,4. P, 23 – 27

Misner, I. 2003, 'Networking like a pro', *Entrepreneur Magazine*, February 24.

Morris, B. 2005, 'How corporate America is betraying women', Fortune Magazine. 10 January 2005, pp. 64 – 74

Parker, V. 2004, *Women mentoring women: Creating conditions for connection* http://www.findarticles.com/p/articles/mi_m1038/is_n2_v36/ai_13815069 [16 December 2004]

Ragins, B.R. & Cotton, J.L. 1991, Gender differences in willingness to mentor, in Wall and Jauch, eds, *Academy of Management Best Papers Proceedings*, p. 57 – 61

Schlegel, M 2000, 'Women mentoring women', *Monitor on Psychology*, Vol 31, 10, http://www.apa.org/monitor/nov00/mentoring.html [16 December 2004]

Schor, S. 1997, 'Separate and unequal: the nature of women's and men's career building relationships', *Business Horizons*. Greenwich: Sept/Oct 1997 Vol 40, 5 pp. 51-58

Singh, V., Kumra, S. & Vinnicombe, S. 2002, 'Gender and impression management: Playing the promotion game', *Journal of Business Ethics*: Dordrecht 37(1) p. 77

Swoboda, M.J. & Millar, S.B. 1986, 'Networking-mentoring: career strategy of women in academic administration', *Journal of NAWDAC*, 49, pp. 8 – 13

Vinnicombe, S., Singh, V. & Sturges, J. 2000, 'Making it to the top in Britain' in Burke and Mattis, *Women on corporate boards of directors: international challenges and Opportunities*, Kluwer, Dordrecht, pp. 57 – 74

Referenced Websites

Center for Women in Technology http://www.umbc.edu/cwitcheri1956@adelphia.net

American Association of University Women http://www.aauw.org/home.html

Women in Technology international http://www.witi.com

23 The Potential of Adaptive Collaborative Work

A proposal for a new working style for Japanese women

Mayumi Hori

Hakuoh University, Oyama City, Japan

Masakazu Ohashi

Chuo University, Tokyo, Japan

Abstract

In this paper, we propose a new model of Telework for public and private sectors as Telework is required to shift its nature to the Adaptive Collaborative Work. Furthermore, we discuss the potential of Adaptive Collaborative Telework for encouraging Japanese female workers to better balance the responsibilities of home and career which would ultimately increase their employment opportunities. Adaptive Collaboration promotes new lateral services that link knowledge and expertise between public and private sectors of different ontological levels. It is different from the Telework Centres which only change the location of work while the quality of work remains the same. Adaptive Collaboration divides and distributes work by its nature and quality such as research and writing papers that can be conducted outside of the conventional office.

1. Introduction

Low birth rate, rapid increase of ageing people, globalisation of the economy and corporate competition, and development of Information and Communication Technology (ICT) — these are mega trends that are forcing Japanese organisations to review and revise some of their traditional employment practices that were once the strengths of Japanese companies during the period of high economic growth. Consequently ICT and these environmental shifts in society and business mentioned above are having a strong impact on the labour environment. Combined with an increased presence of women in the workforce, these trends are forcing organisations to alter their traditional practice that women should play only a supporting role. Many organisations are now seriously exploring the potential of women as integral members of the team.

The progress and popularisation of ICT has placed a major impact on the Japanese working environment. Telework, which is not yet commonly practiced in Japan, has attracted a great deal of attention from Japanese women in recent years for its potential for the enhanced utilisation of the female workforce. Telework has realized a new employment style free from the conventional fixed working time and place. In Japan most women, particularly those in rural areas, still live under the traditional belief that women should stay at home. Fortunately, Telework expects the home to create favourable and flexible working arrangements which will improve the quality of life for Japanese women providing them with more opportunities.

The Adaptive Collaborative Telework we discuss in this paper presents a further networked Telework environment that offers multiple opportunities such as improving the quality of policies of public and private sectors and prompting closer ties between citizens, Non-Profit Organizations (NPO), and corporations. The philosophy of Adaptive Collaboration is not only to computerise all the operations in the public sector such as local government, which intertwine varied needs and relationships with the private sector but also to build a society where diversity is embraced and creativity is appreciated therefore allowing workers to pursue their mission in a coordinated manner. In this paper, we would like to emphasise the important role that Adaptive Collaborative Telework, which pushes back the boundaries of the traditional Telework, may play in realising this harmonised, collaborative society.

2. ICT and Job Opportunities for Women

2.1 Changing women's employment structures and their desire to work

Table 1 shows the trends in female labour force participation rates in the industrialised countries. In all these countries, the rates continuously increased from 1991 to 2001; in1991 the percentage of Japanese female participation was 61.4% and the figure rose to 64.4% in 2001 rivalling those of France and Germany. Factors such as late marriage, higher education, higher priority on work than family, and many other attitudes towards

	Female Participation Rate(a)	
(%)	2001	1991
Canada	70.5	67.9
United States	69.7	68.5
United Kingdom	67.5	66.3
Netherlands	66.3	54.5
Australia	66.1	61.7
Japan	64.4	61.4
Germany	64.4	61.0
France	63.3	58.2
EU	60.7	56.6
Korea	55.0	51.8
Spain	50.8	42.1
Italy	47.8	46.2

Defined as female labour for all ages divided by female population aged 15-65
*Labour Force Statistics 1981-2001, OECD, Paris, 2002

Table 1 Female Employment

work are thought to have contributed to the remarkable changes in the labour market in the industrialised countries especially in Japan. In addition to these factors, the impact of ICTs which has brought far greater flexibility in terms of time and place, has contributed to the expansion of job alternatives for women and the promotion of the employment of women workers. As information processing is thought to solve the vital issues in labour and employment for the 21st Century, more people have become interested in implementing information technology in the Japanese labour market.

Recent trends in the number of Japanese women workers suggest that the changes in the quality of work are a contributing factor in their employment, and we summarise these changes as follows:

First, Japanese women workers are growing older as they extend the length of employment before having children and after finishing childcare. In recent years, the number of women workers aged 35 and over has increased remarkably, accounting for about 60% of the total number of women workers. Second, after childcare, many housewives prefer to be employed as part-time workers because they can work fewer hours and make their jobs compatible with their domestic duties. Third, the number of women workers with higher education has increased remarkably. This implies the emergence of a high quality large labour force with a strong will to exercise their expertise. Fourth, the types of jobs have changed since the mid 1970s as blue-collar occupations decreased while white-collar occupations increased. The number of women managers and officials has also increased appreciably.

Despite the increase in women's participation in the labour force and women's level of education, there are still women who experience sex discrimination in the working place where the traditional concept of gender roles is still persisting. In Japan, it is often said that 'a woman's place is in the home, a man's is at work.' This attitude has long been a central value in male-female relations in Japan and this outdated tradition is still causing enormous stress on Japanese women workers.

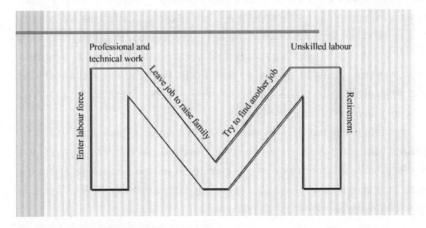

Figure 1 M-shape in Women's Life-cycle

The M-curve (Figure 1) represents the women's participation in the Japanese labour force. The first stage of the 'M' shows that after obtaining education (compulsory education at the age of 15, junior college at the age of 19, and university at the age of 21) women enter the labour force to engage in professional and technical work with job training offered in the company. The next stage shows a drop as women leave their jobs to raise children, and the labour force participation rate reaches its lowest level in the age group 30 to 34. Then again, from the age 34 the curve rises up again as they start trying to find a job and often return to unskilled jobs. From age 50 the curve again drops as they retire.

The M-Curve demonstrates a characteristic feature of the Japanese women's workforce. The prominent aspect of the M-curve indicates that the rate for women labours (the ratio of the female workforce to the national population over 15 years old) hits its lowest point between 30 and 34 years of age. This feature is inconsistent with that of Europe which draws a trapezoid shaped curve.

Looking at the female workforce in Japan by age (Figure 2), there is clearly a stronger tendency for Japanese women, compared to Western women, to drop out during the child-rearing years. The common pattern is to drop out to have children, then re-enter the workforce when the children are raised to some extent. The percentages for women working from 25 to 29 and from 30 to 34 in Japan are 69.7% and 56.7%, respectively (1998). These same figures are 77.3% and 74.9% for the US (1997); 82.1% and 80.6 % for France (1998), 74.4% and 73.5% for Germany (1997), 60.4% and 61.2% for Italy (1996), 76.9% and 81.4% for Sweden (1997) and 73.4% for England (1997, no data for 30-35 year olds).(ILO Year Book of Labour Statistics) Thus, it is clear that the burden of childcare and housework is heavier for Japanese women compared to Western women, especially for those in the 30 to 35 year age range. However, the bottom of this M-curve is inching up, as is the drop-out age. For example, in 1975 the low point for women in the labour force was down in the 25 to 29 age group. By 1998, it was in the 30 to 39 year range. Couples are marrying later, women are getting more education, more women place a higher priority on work than family, and many other attitudes toward work are changing. Consequently, the valley of the M-shaped curve can become shallow (Hori Mayumi 2003, pp. 2-3).

An increase in the number of women in the workplace will inevitably lead to the collapse of rigid role consciousness—the idea of 'woman's place is at home, man's is at work.' Today, with advanced levels of education, more women are seeking positions to exercise their expertise, which would also provide them with independence and allow them to continue working without *dropping out.*

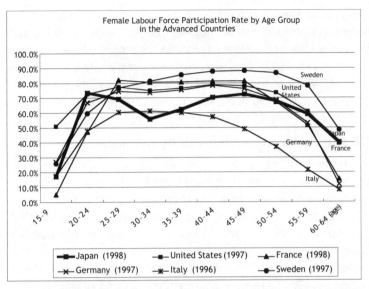

Figure 2: Female labour force participation by age group in the advanced counties

[Source: Japan Institute of Workers' Evaluation, White Papers on female labour 2000]

2.2 The impact of telework on Japanese women

Telework challenges the realities of the M-curve by providing women with the means to continue working at home during the childrearing process. When compared with non-Teleworkers, women in the age range of 30-34 (those traditionally situated at the bottom of the M-Curve) were able to decrease the severity of the curve through Teleworking at home. This change is a 10% increase for those working more than 8 hours per week and an 8% increase for those working less than 8 hours per week.

Women in Japan have traditionally been limited to clerical work and conventional support positions. In today's work environment, factors such as fewer children, more elderly people, and other changes in social structure as well as increasing educational levels and social effectiveness among women are encouraging government agencies and companies to look seriously at ways to actively engage the full talents of women. To put it another way, the factors mentioned above are demanding changes in traditional ideas about 'women's work'. It is no longer simply assumed that women must carry full responsibility for housework and childcare or that the support function is the only appropriate role for women in a company. Furthermore, with ever-higher levels of academic achievement, more women are looking for jobs that make use of their special expertise and allow for long-term employment.

More women are entering the workforce with every intention of continuing to perform housework and raise children. According to the survey on the intentions of women with a spouse, about 60% of those aged 20 to 44 say they want to work. Of these, more than

60% in their peak childbearing years (between 20 to 39 years old) want to work. The most prominent reason married women aged between 20 and 34 do not seek to work was that they are 'too busy with children, housework, or school' (Management and Coordination Agency survey 1997). Comparing the results of the survey in 1992 and 1997, the number of married women with jobs aged between 20 and 34 had declined, and the lack of job-seeking activities among women aged between 25 and 34 indicates the magnitude of the burden women have to bear from childrearing and housework?

2.3 How ICT and Telework are viewed by the Japanese

In addition to the attitudinal changes among women, the ICT revolution, which has brought far greater flexibility in terms of time and place, is expanding job alternatives and promoting employment opportunities for female workers. In fact, ICT is not merely increasing the number of jobs but creating entirely new types of jobs. Utilising ICT, Telework is a 'new work method' with enormous potential for revolutionising conventional work and employment formats.

The chief merits of Telework are 'elimination of fatigue from commuting (61.8%)', 'high job productivity 38.2%)', and 'more time for housework and children (32.4%)' (Japan Telework Association 2001). Thus, Telework holds the promise of increasing job opportunities for working women who still bear the burden of housework and childcare.

For working women, Telework utilising ICT may enable them to 1) exercise their expertise, 2) engage in responsibilities for both home and job, 3) be free from restrictions of time and place (and commuting), and 4) be free from other problems associated with a large workplace. For corporations, Telework means outsourcing tasks to the skilled human resources, thus saving expenses on personnel and office space. Telework and ICT therefore are attracting a great deal of attention as they may solve the vital issues of labour and employment for the 21st Century.

In 2003, 40.4% of all households in Japan owned a personal computer or word processor with access to the Internet: 45.3% of the households with more than two family members and 28.3% of the single-person households (Japan Information Processing Development Corporation 2003, p. 435).

As for the present situation of Telework in Japan, the Telework population was 0.81 million in 1996, 2.46 million in 2000, 4.08 million in 2002, and is expected to be 4.45 million in 2005 (Japan Telework Association 2001). The number will increase 1.8 times—to approximately 4.5 million—in 2005. The total population of Japan is 126.3 million and the total active population is 6.3 million.

Some large corporations have adopted this new work format but it has not yet sufficiently penetrated. Accordingly there are few researches conducted on Telework and women workers. The following are the possible reasons for an insufficient penetration of Telework: first, 'face to face' communication is perceived as a proper working style for the Japanese. Second, Japanese decision making is carried out through group-style management, which is one of the prominent features of Japanese management. Third, Telework has often been considered as 'electronic homework' or unskilled low-paid work. Many female workers have engaged in monotonous work besides being responsible for childcare and the Japanese consider Telework as being a female domain. Consequently, most Teleworkers are employed as outsourcing employees therefore they can not gain an objective and a comprehensive outlook on their work. Such working conditions result in mental stress, lowering their morale and intensifying their depression.

Telework is commonly assumed to maintain good health by being disengaged from stress and contamination of the office and commuting (Steward 1999). On the other hand, it is also reported that Telework may cause stress and social and professional isolation which are the physical and psychological issues resulting from stressful family relations and separation from co-workers. According to the Telework WG of the Japan Multimedia Forum, in their In-home Work Online Survey (2000), one of the disadvantages of telework for women is 'Emotional stress of self-management' (30%). This view seems to result from childbearing, housework and social isolation.

In this paper we challenge the limitations of traditional Telework by introducing Adaptive Collaborative Telework, and demonstrate its potential not only for solving female workforce issues but also for revitalising communities, increasing employment opportunities, alleviating environmental problems, and improving the quality of life.

3. Potentialities of Adaptive Collaborative Work (ACW)

3.1 The concept of Adaptive Collaboration

Conventional business models had built information systems that operated only within the organisation, and interchangeability or interactivity was not necessarily considered. However, the rapid development of ICT has encouraged the creation of a seamless networked environment regardless of an organisation's type and size. It has also encouraged the development of an environment where public institutions such as government and local governments can freely utilise each other's information and collaborate together without the boundaries of time and space.

Today, in order for corporations and government agencies to achieve swift decision-making and innovation, they need to utilise a system that efficiently manages large-scale information and data — both in terms of quantity and quality — existing within and outside of the organisation, and to make these resources sharable. Expansion of the versatility of ICT has facilitated many corporations and administrative agencies to merge and collaborate with each other and enabled them to enter into new business schemes. On the other hand, it has become extremely difficult to maintain the competitive advantage in the present market as the culture of sharing and collaboration prevail. Furthermore, government and local governments have been urged to meet the diverse needs of the people while improving economic efficiency. In accordance with these situations, we would like to propose Adaptive Collaboration (AC) as an essential concept for the new paradigm of

319

knowledge integration and collaboration in the Ubiquitous Society.

Adaptive Collaboration (AC) is defined as a system that efficiently relates, shares, and utilises data, information, and knowledge in the Ubiquitous Society where the amount of information created grows at an accelerated pace. This system would also allow entities of different ontological level to be linked laterally therefore making it easier for people in the organisation to appreciate each other's expertise and know-how, which essentially encourages further development and innovation. Likewise, the system breaks the conventional relationships within and between organisations (Hori Mayumi & Ohashi Masakazu 2005, p. 4).

3.2 Demonstration experiment of Adaptive Collaborative Work

In our proposals for Adaptive Collaborative Telework (ACW), we examined the potential of this new working style. We have been building the Next Generation Collaboration Studies Platform in Tokyo since April 2003 supported by the Ministry of Post and Telecommunications (Ohashi Masakazu 2004, pp. 55-60). In order to examine the effectiveness of collaborative work through Telecommunication, an experiment utilising knowledge management systems and Wavelength Division Multiplexing (WDM) was conducted in cooperation with several universities and research institutes in Japan. This experiment was unique in that we developed a collaborative research system that allows researchers to work on several different projects at same time and also a project management system that manages all the collaborative projects as a whole.

Results from the experiment proved Adaptive Collaborative Telework to be very effective. Beyond merely sharing data though telecommunication, the experiment demonstrated that utilising the knowledge management systems in conjunction with the WDM provides an enhanced communication structure. In essence, the union of the two systems creates a real-time collaborative research environment by allowing users to share the processes and results of researches between the institutions regardless of their location, therefore creating a real-time collaborative research environment.

Thus, this experiment also proved the effectiveness of collaborative work through telecommunications such as Internet, which indicates that Telework has much potential as an alternative working style and yet is capable of efficiently yielding great results through collaboration that are also shared in real-time. As challenges for the future, we would like to involve more organisations in the experiment for further sophistication of the knowledge management systems and to include advanced utilisation of the human resource management system.

4. Proposal for Adaptive Collaborative Telework

4.1 The benefits of utilising AC

Adaptive Collaboration also generates innovative ways to make an effective use of human resources of both in-house and outside staffing with ICT. Better management of human resources may enable in-house Teleworkers to promote and maintain their mental and physical health. Furthermore, for in-house Teleworkers a collaborative, group-work environment may help them maintain favourable working conditions as well as achieve good results in their work.

Additionally, deconstructing the existing structure of an organisation by adopting Telework would permit the viewing of the system and its internal relationships within the organisation. This also encourages the discovery of new connections between different branches of the organisation at the same or different ontological levels. By doing so, they will be able to allocate financial and human resources appropriately and avoid bottlenecks. Furthermore, through efficient coordination and collaboration, organisations will be able to share the know-how and the expertise that each worker possesses.

Adaptive Collaboration requires one to work toward common goals with other members of the group who have perspectives and values other than one's own. It can also assist group members in creating shared new values and understanding. Although collaboration requires harmony, it does not suppress or discard different perspectives and values. Sharing of common goals encourages each member to assume a responsibility and commitment for creating new knowledge that in turn benefits the group as a whole. Therefore, instilling this culture of 'sharing' is critical for the success of Adaptive Collaboration.

To illustrate the dynamics between Teleworkers in the system, four elements are drawn in Figure 3; the vertical axis shows 'interacting' and 'acting' and the horizontal axis shows 'real' and 'virtual.' Utilising the AC allows traditional in-house Teleworkers working as outsource or professional workers in real/acting domain with different expertise or in different fields—those who do not share the same terminology or methodology—to work collaboratively on the same project. Thus, Figure 3 shows the effectiveness of collaborative work through Telecommunications by, not only highlighting the inherent nature of Telework as an alternative working style, but also by suggesting its clear potency for yielding significant results through real-time collaboration.

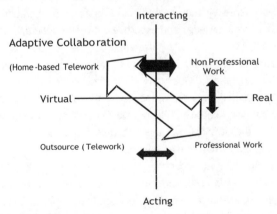

Figure 3: Adaptive Collaborative Work

4.2 Adaptive Collaborative Telework

Adaptive Collaborative Work (ACW) aims to shift the concept of computerisation and information processing from a mere development of ICT to further sophistication of the system of society itself. This underlies a mission coming from the need to rebuild the Japanese society centred on digitalisation. In 21st century society, regional characteristics are valued as well as the concept of globalisation. Today, decentralisation is receiving more interest and more demand for elaborate, finely-tuned services for individuals and innovative measures for promoting their region are increasing. In other words, people are seeking individually tailored services rather than *many-to-many*, ready-made services. In order to swiftly and appropriately satisfy a variety of needs of residents and local organisations, further development and utilisation of ICT and its infrastructure in local regions—especially within the local municipalities—are essential.

Today, municipalities and local organisations are required to seriously consider the implementation of Telework in order to utilise the expertise within and outside of their organisations in a collaborative, networked manner. Additionally, like the private sector, municipalities are expected to increase their productivity and become more output-oriented. For these reasons, Telework has drawn considerable interests in that it would increase an individual's productivity, network human resources and encourage collaboration between different branches in the organisation, and utilise outsourced human resources for advanced knowledge and expertise.

Adaptive Collaborative Telework promotes rationalisation and efficiency by enabling the distribution, sharing, and enhanced use of information through utilising ICT. Hence, it would assist e-Government and e-Local Governments to build a society that is sensitive enough to be aware of the social changes and flexible enough to respond to these changes appropriately while minimising risks.

Adaptive Collaboration would make a significant difference to the nature of the work of public officials as it would change the way they carry out their job at home by aggrandising the definition of Telework. In other words, unlike the conventional unilateral services offered by the government, Adaptive Collaboration promotes new lateral services that link knowledge and expertise between public and private sectors at different ontological levels. It is also different from the Telework Centre which only changes the location of work while the quality of work remains the same. On the other hand, Adaptive Collaboration divides and distributes work which by its nature and quality can be conducted outside of the conventional office. For instance, many software engineers utilise Adaptive Collaborative Telework as a favourable working style since the nature of their work allows them to work independently while high-quality collaboration is enabled by ICT so that they can remotely and continuously check their system's integrity with other engineers.

Although Telework has been considered as a mere means of outsourcing, ICT has expanded its breadth and enables Adaptive Collaborative Telework. Consequently, as the global economy has moved further from a manufacturing base towards a service base, we believe the demand for Adaptive Collaborative Telework would grow, and determining how to divide and distribute the work by its nature and quality is critical. Telework would ultimately create an environment where organisations and individuals bring their expertise and generate innovative ideas, which lead to new business opportunities, expansion of employment opportunities, and the development of ICT-related engineers; hence it would produce the driving force for local revitalisation.

5. Conclusion

Telework in this paper does not mean mere outsourcing or computerisation of administrative operations. Telework enabled by the development of information technology has a potential to diminish traditional boundaries that have long been a burden to Japanese women and to build a more flexible 'small-world' network in which people with different expertise can share their high-quality knowledge and collaborate towards common goals. More women today are better educated than before and thus willing to build their career resulting in a shift in the attitude toward working women in Japan. However, there are still only a few women engaging in high-level decision making processes or utilising their expertise. Consequently, the rapid growth of the female workforce has increased the interests in the potential of Telework as an avenue for Japanese female workers to fully exercise their capabilities. We believe Telework can positively affect policies and decision-making processes through collaboration and knowledge sharing. This is the reason we call it Adaptive Collaborative Telework, which embraces diversity and creativity, thereby allowing workers to pursue their mission in a coordinated manner through sharing. Our agenda for the future is to realise the society we have proposed and discussed in this paper — where people with different expertise collaborate with each other, work concurrently on different projects, and accomplish tasks with consistency and compatibility.

References

Asakura Takahashi 1997, *Working Women and Mental Stress*, Highlights in Japanese Labour Issues, Vol., The Japan Institute of Labour, pp.134-137.

Grundy AF, Köhler D, Oechtering, V & Petersen U (eds) 1997, *Women, Work and Computerization*, Proceedings of the 6th International IFIP-Conference, Bonn, Germany, Springer-Verlag, Berlin & Heidelberg.

Hori Mayumi & Ohashi Masakazu 2005,'Applying Web Services into Health Care Management', *Proceedings of the Thirty-Eighth Annual Hawaii International Conference on System Sciences*, HICSS-38, Hawaii.

Hori Mayumi & Ohashi Masakazu 2005, 'Adaptive Collaboration: The Road Map Leading Telework to a More Advanced and Professional Working Format', *Journal Transaction on Advanced Research*, Vol1, IPSI, Belgrade, Serbia.

Hori Mayumi & Ohashi Masakazu 2004, 'Implementing Adaptive Collaborative Telework in Public Administration', in *eAdoption and the Knowledge Economy: Issues, Applications, Case Studies*, eds Paul Cunningham and Miriam Cunningham, IOS Press.

Hori Mayumi & Ohashi Masakazu 2004, 'Telework Changes Working Style for Japanese Women', *Proceedings of AWEEB2004*, International Workshop on Advanced Web Engineering for E-Business, Frankfurt, Germany.

Hori Mayumi & Masakazu Ohashi 2004, 'Telework and Mental Health-Collaborative Work to Maintain and Manage the Mental Health', *Proceedings of the Thirty-Seventh Annual Hawaii International Conference on System Sciences*, Hawaii.

Hori Mayumi 2003, *Society of Telework and Working for Women*, Publishers of Chuo University, Tokyo, Japan.

Hori Mayumi 2002, 'The present Situation and Perspective of Women's Work: How does IT work?' *Hakuoh Business Review*, vol. 11, no.1, Institute of Business Research, Hakuoh University, Tochigi, Japan.

Hori Mayumi 2001, 'The Development of IT and a New Work Format for Women in Japan', ed. Reima Suomi, *Proceedings of t-world 2001*, Ministry of Labour Finland.

Hori Mayumi & Masakazu Ohashi 2001, 'Information Technology and The Possibility of Women's Work: A New Work Format for Women in Japan', in *The 6th International ITF Workshop and Business Conference 'Working in the New Economy'*, Amsterdam.

Illegems, Viviane & Verbeke, Alain 2004, *Moving Towards the Virtual Workplace: Managerial and Societal Perspectives on Telework*, Edward Elgar Pub.

Japan Information Processing Development Corporation 2003, *Information White Paper*, JIPDEC.

Japan Multimedia Forum 2000, *Research Report on Home-based Teleworkers1999*, pp. 32-35.

Nickson, David & Siddons, Suzy 2003, *Working: Linking people and organizations*, Butterworth Heinemann.

OECD, OECD EMPLOYMENT OUTLOOK, 2002.

OECD 2001, *Health at Glance.*

Ohashi Masakazu & Hori Mayumi 2005 'On the studies of the Adaptive Collaborative Work', *Journal of Policy Studies*, vol. 12, Chuo University, Tokyo, Japan, pp. 83-112.

Ohashi Masakazu Sasaki Kaoru & Hori Mayumi 2004, 'On the Study of Knowledge Structuralization and Adaptive Process Based on Project Based Learning', *Journal of IPCS* vol. 7,Chuo University, Tokyo, Japan

Ohashi Masakazu (ed.) 2004, 'The Report of the Advanced Studies for the Social Capital of e-Society', *The Society of the Basis for the e-Community.*

Ohashi Masakazu (ed.) 2003, 'The Report of Society for the Advance Study on e-Society', *The Society of the Basis for the e-Community.*

Ohashi Masakzu 2003, *Public iDC and c-Society*, Kogaku Tosho, Tokyo, Japan.

Ohashi Masakazu 2003, *Time Business*, NTT Publication, Tokyo, Japan.

Ohashi Masakazu & Sasaki Kaoru 2003, 'On the Study of Knowledge Structuralization, Process Based on Project Based Learning', *Journal of Policy Studies*, vol.10, Chuo University, Tokyo, Japan.

Ohashi Masakazu (ed.) 2003, 'Knowledge-Based Collaborative Work', Report of Supplementary Budget Project of the Ministry of Post and Telecommunication.

Ohashi Masakazu & Nagai Masatoshi 2001, *Internet Data Centre Revolution*, Impress, Tokyo, Japan.

Sasaki Kaoru & Ohashi Masakazu 2002,'Key Issues for the Next Generation Knowledge Management', *Journal of Policy Studies*, vol. 9, Chuo University, Tokyo, Japan.

Steward Barbara 1999, 'Sickness absenteeism in Telework: A sociological study', Proceedings, The Fourth International Telework Workshop Telework *Strategies for the New Workforce*, pp. 61-68.